CASANOVA
LUXURIA

MATT FRACTION
GABRIEL BÁ

colors by Cris Peter
letters by Dustin Harbin

book design

Drew Gill & Gabriel Bá

IMAGE COMICS, INC.

Robert Kirkman – Chief Operating Officer
Erik Larsen – Chief Financial Officer
Todd McFarlane – President
Marc Silvestri – Chief Executive Officer
Jim Valentino – Vice-President

Eric Stephenson – Publisher
Ron Richards – Director of Business Development
Jennifer de Guzman – Director of Trade Book Sales
Kat Salazar – Director of PR & Marketing
Corey Murphy – Director of Retail Sales
Jeremy Sullivan – Director of Digital Sales
Emilio Bautista – Sales Assistant
Branwyn Bigglestone – Senior Accounts Manager
Emily Miller – Accounts Manager
Jessica Ambriz – Administrative Assistant
Tyler Shainline – Events Coordinator
David Brothers – Content Manager
Jonathan Chan – Production Manager
Drew Gill – Art Director
Meredith Wallace – Print Manager
Monica Garcia – Senior Production Artist
Addison Duke – Production Artist
Tricia Ramos – Production Assistant
IMAGECOMICS.COM

CASANOVA, THE COMPLETE EDITION VOLUME 1: LUXURIA. First printing. October 2014. Published by Image Comics, Inc. Office of publication: 2001 Center Street, Sixth Floor, Berkeley, CA 94704. Contains material originally published in magazine form as CASANOVA #1-7 and CASANOVA: LUXURIA #1-4. Printed in Canada. For international rights, contact: foreignlicensing@imagecomics.com. ISBN: 978-1-63215-161-2

Matt Fraction:
For my friend Héctor Sebastián Casanova
who had cancer when I started writing this
and didn't when I stopped.
Life is Grand.

Gabriel Bá:
Dedicated to Laerte Coutinho,
whose images live in my head and have
inspired me throughout this series.

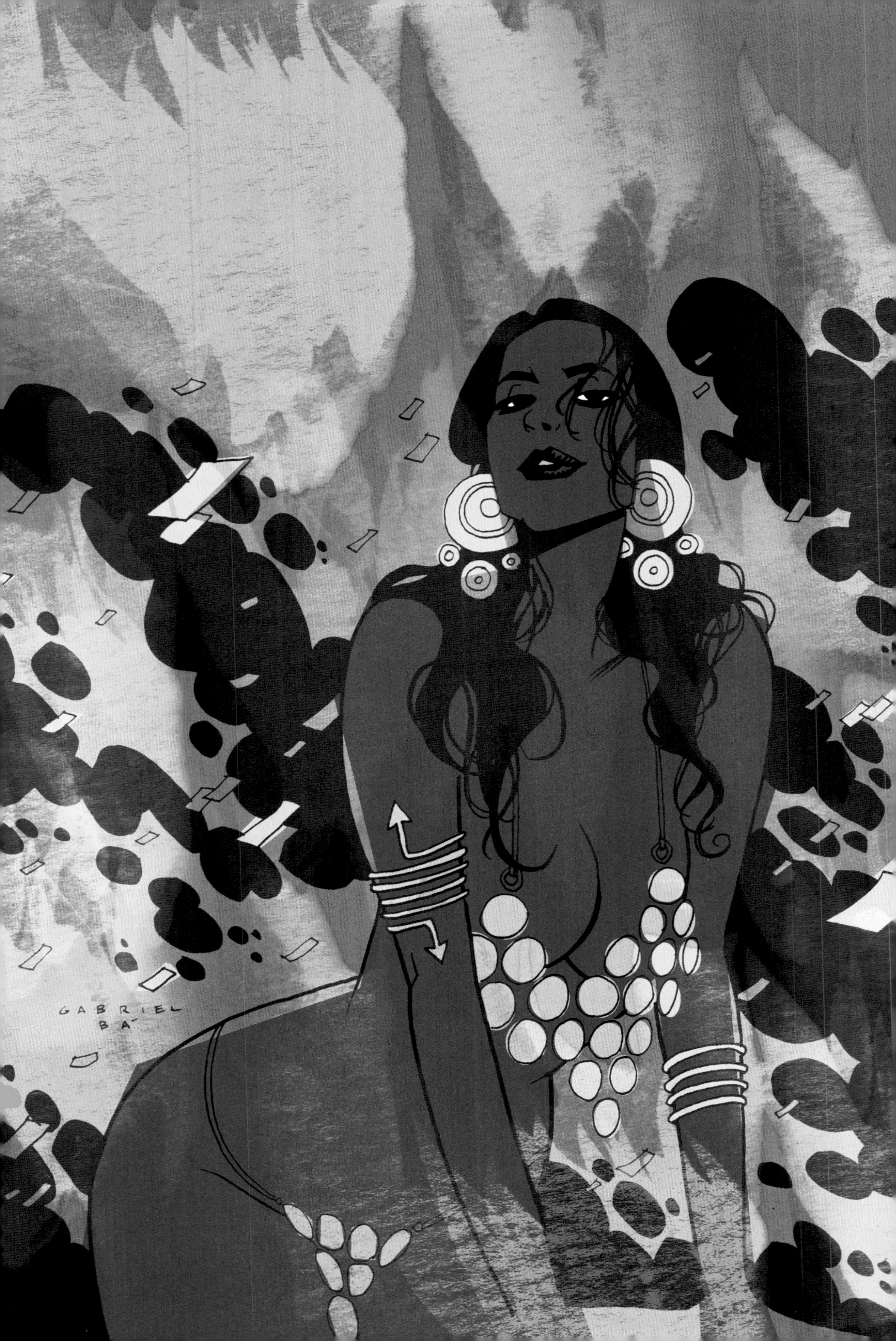
GABRIEL
BÁ

"Quantum mechanics
forbids a single history."

Thomas Hertog

"... My parents... don't worry in the
least about their own insignificance;
they don't give a damn about it...
While I... I feel only
boredom and anger."

Ivan Turgenev
Fathers and Sons (1862)

"Boys, Girls, Men, Women!
The world is on FIRE
Serve the LORD
and You Can Have These Prizes!"

Ad on the back cover of
WEIRD SCIENCE-FANTASY #24
June 1954

EXECUTION DAYS

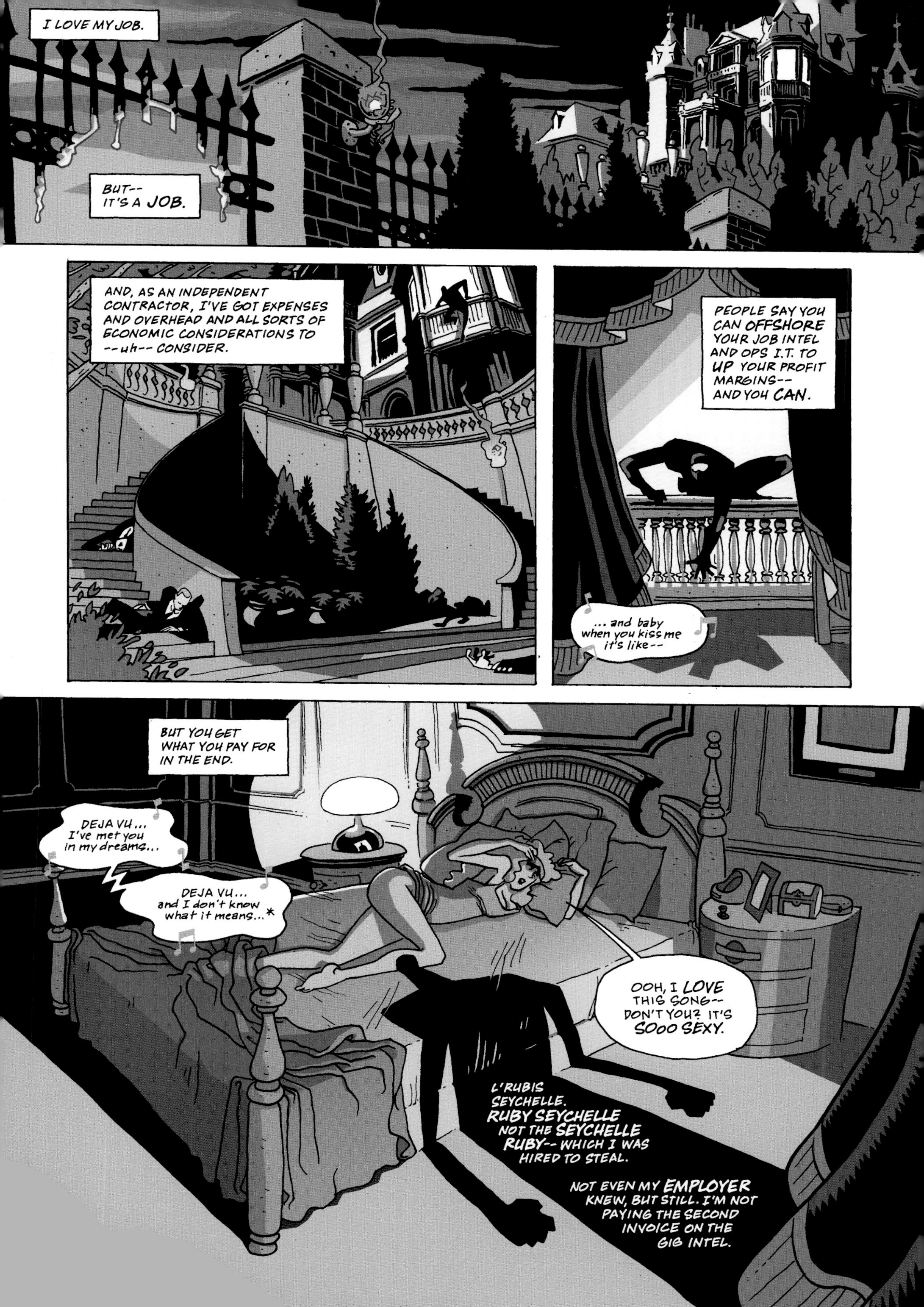

I LOVE MY JOB.
BUT-- IT'S A JOB.
AND, AS AN INDEPENDENT CONTRACTOR, I'VE GOT EXPENSES AND OVERHEAD AND ALL SORTS OF ECONOMIC CONSIDERATIONS TO --uh-- CONSIDER.
PEOPLE SAY YOU CAN OFFSHORE YOUR JOB INTEL AND OPS I.T. TO UP YOUR PROFIT MARGINS-- AND YOU CAN.
... and baby when you kiss me it's like--
BUT YOU GET WHAT YOU PAY FOR IN THE END.
DEJA VU... I've met you in my dreams...
DEJA VU... and I don't know what it means...*
OOH, I LOVE THIS SONG-- DON'T YOU? IT'S SOoo SEXY.
L'RUBIS SEYCHELLE. RUBY SEYCHELLE NOT THE SEYCHELLE RUBY-- WHICH I WAS HIRED TO STEAL.
NOT EVEN MY EMPLOYER KNEW, BUT STILL. I'M NOT PAYING THE SECOND INVOICE ON THE GIG INTEL.

* "DEJA VU," BY TEEN AGE MUSIC INTERNATIONAL, 'I.M.A.T.A.M.I.' SOMA RECORDS.

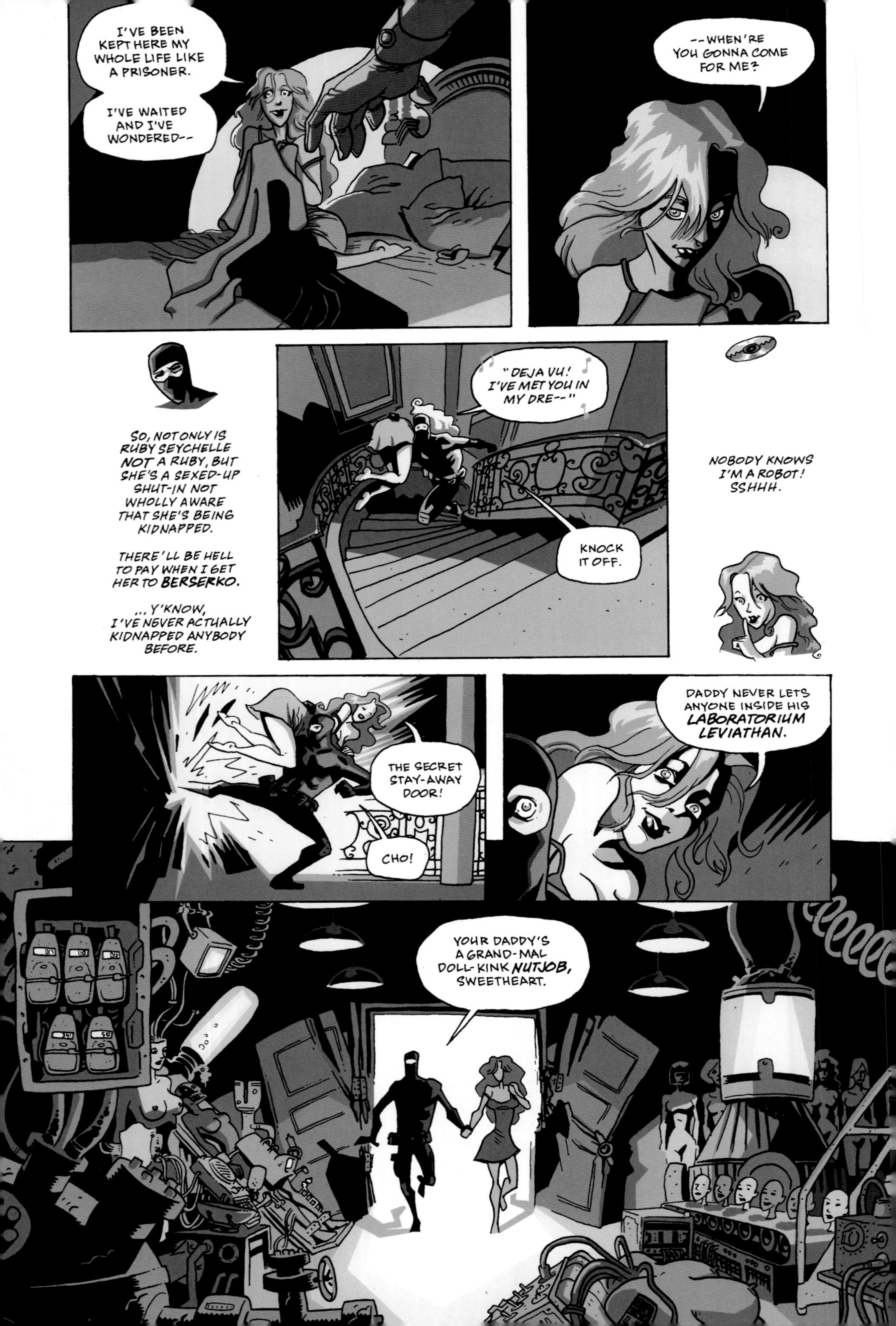
I'VE BEEN KEPT HERE MY WHOLE LIFE LIKE A PRISONER.
I'VE WAITED AND I'VE WONDERED--
--WHEN'RE YOU GONNA COME FOR ME?
SO, NOT ONLY IS RUBY SEYCHELLE NOT A RUBY, BUT SHE'S A SEXED-UP SHUT-IN NOT WHOLLY AWARE THAT SHE'S BEING KIDNAPPED.
THERE'LL BE HELL TO PAY WHEN I GET HER TO BERSERKO.
..., Y'KNOW, I'VE NEVER ACTUALLY KIDNAPPED ANYBODY BEFORE.
"DEJA VU! I'VE MET YOU IN MY DRE--"
KNOCK IT OFF.
NOBODY KNOWS I'M A ROBOT! SSHHH.
THE SECRET STAY-AWAY DOOR!
CHO!
DADDY NEVER LETS ANYONE INSIDE HIS LABORATORIUM LEVIATHAN.
YOUR DADDY'S A GRAND-MAL DOLL-KINK NUTJOB, SWEETHEART.

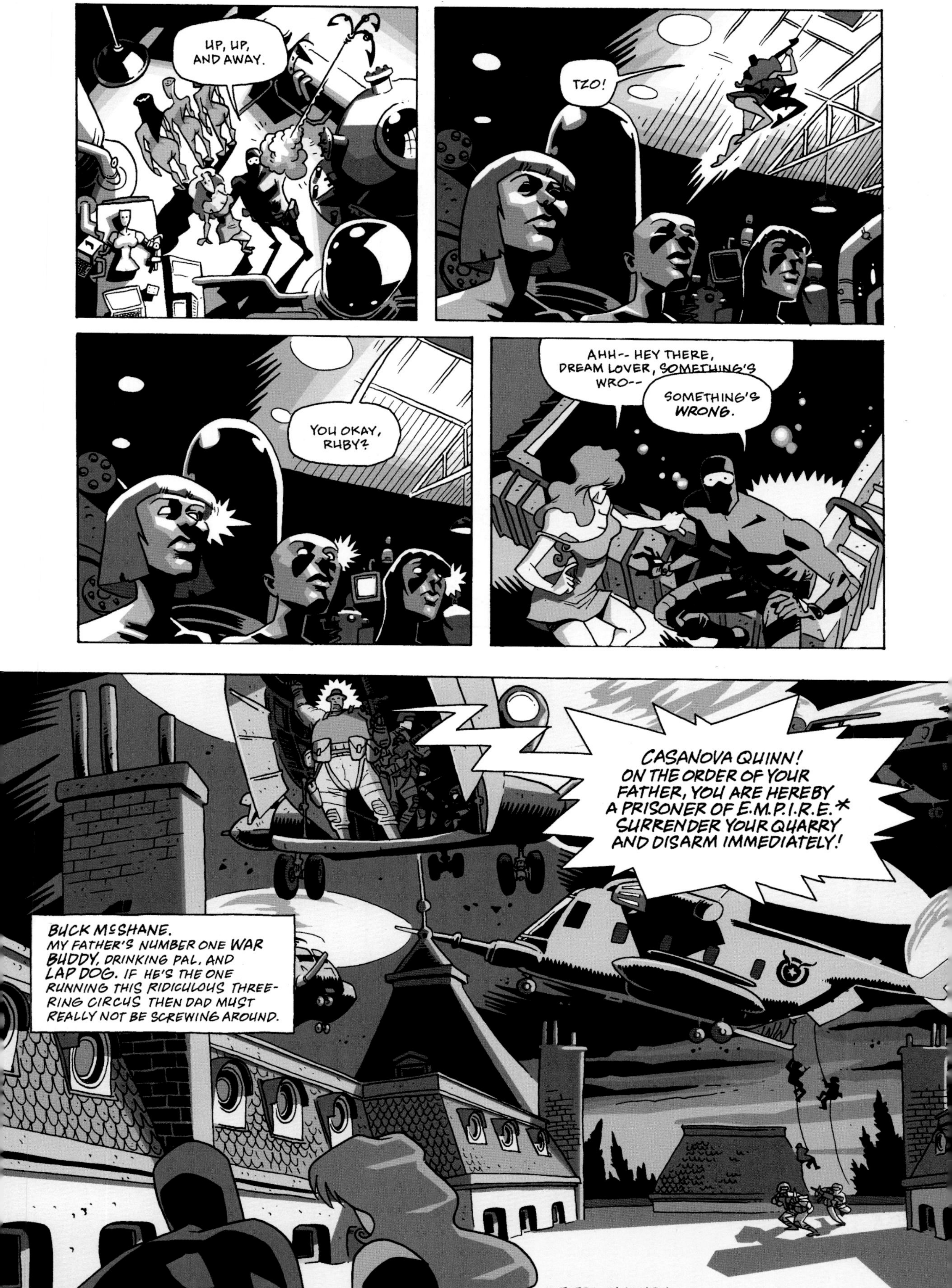
UP, UP, AND AWAY.
TZO!
YOU OKAY, RUBY?
AHH-- HEY THERE, DREAM LOVER, SOMETHING'S WRO--
SOMETHING'S WRONG.
CASANOVA QUINN! ON THE ORDER OF YOUR FATHER, YOU ARE HEREBY A PRISONER OF E.M.P.I.R.E.* SURRENDER YOUR QUARRY AND DISARM IMMEDIATELY!
BUCK McSHANE. MY FATHER'S NUMBER ONE WAR BUDDY, DRINKING PAL, AND LAP DOG. IF HE'S THE ONE RUNNING THIS RIDICULOUS THREE-RING CIRCUS THEN DAD MUST REALLY NOT BE SCREWING AROUND.
*EXTRA-MILITARY POLICE, INTELLIGENCE, RESCUE, AND ESPIONAGE!

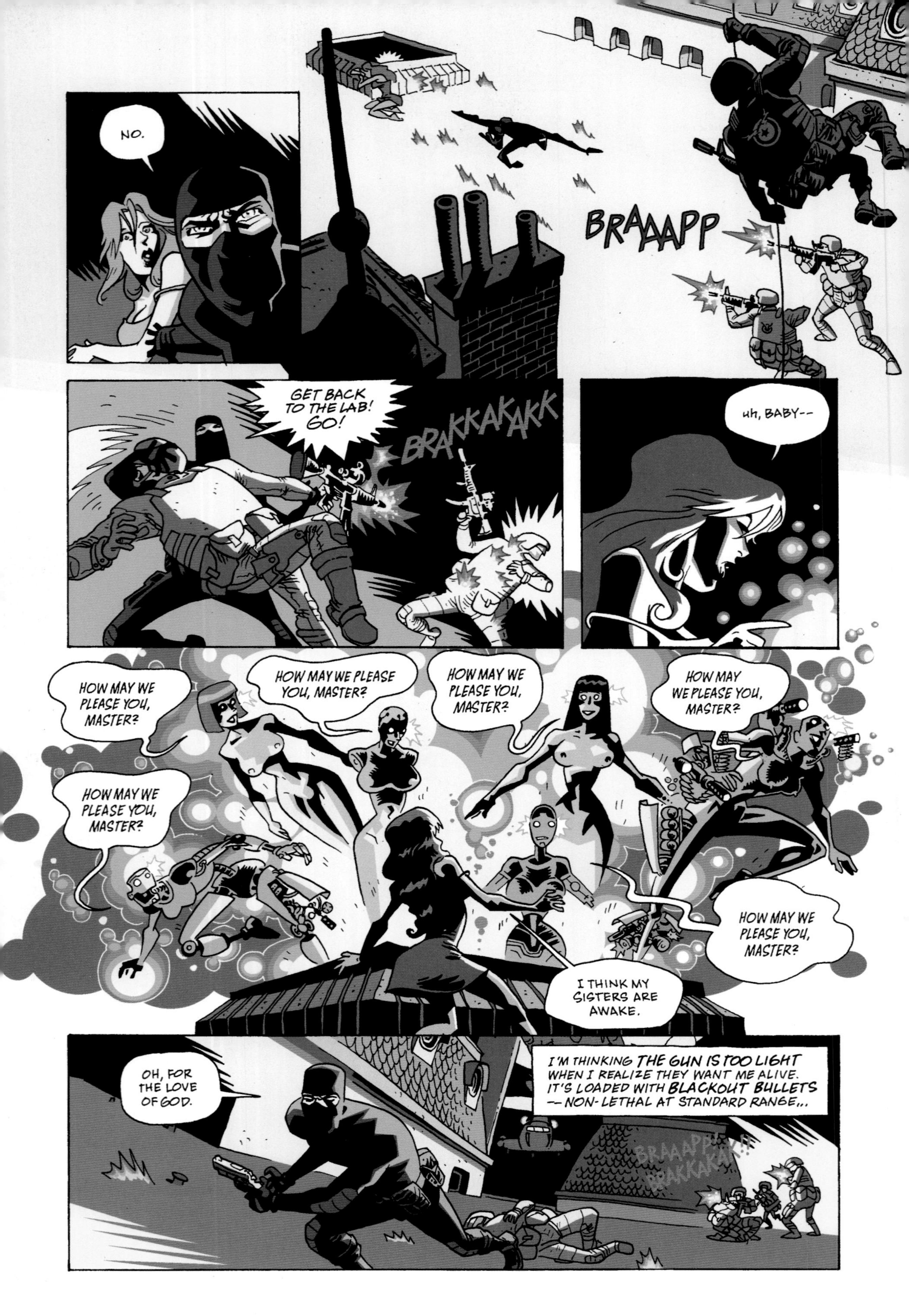
NO.
BRAAAPP
GET BACK TO THE LAB! GO!
BRAKKAKAKK
uh, BABY--
HOW MAY WE PLEASE YOU, MASTER?
HOW MAY WE PLEASE YOU, MASTER?
HOW MAY WE PLEASE YOU, MASTER?
HOW MAY WE PLEASE YOU, MASTER?
HOW MAY WE PLEASE YOU, MASTER?
HOW MAY WE PLEASE YOU, MASTER?
I THINK MY SISTERS ARE AWAKE.
OH, FOR THE LOVE OF GOD.
I'M THINKING THE GUN IS TOO LIGHT WHEN I REALIZE THEY WANT ME ALIVE. IT'S LOADED WITH BLACKOUT BULLETS -- NON-LETHAL AT STANDARD RANGE...
BRAAAPP
BRAKKAKAK!!

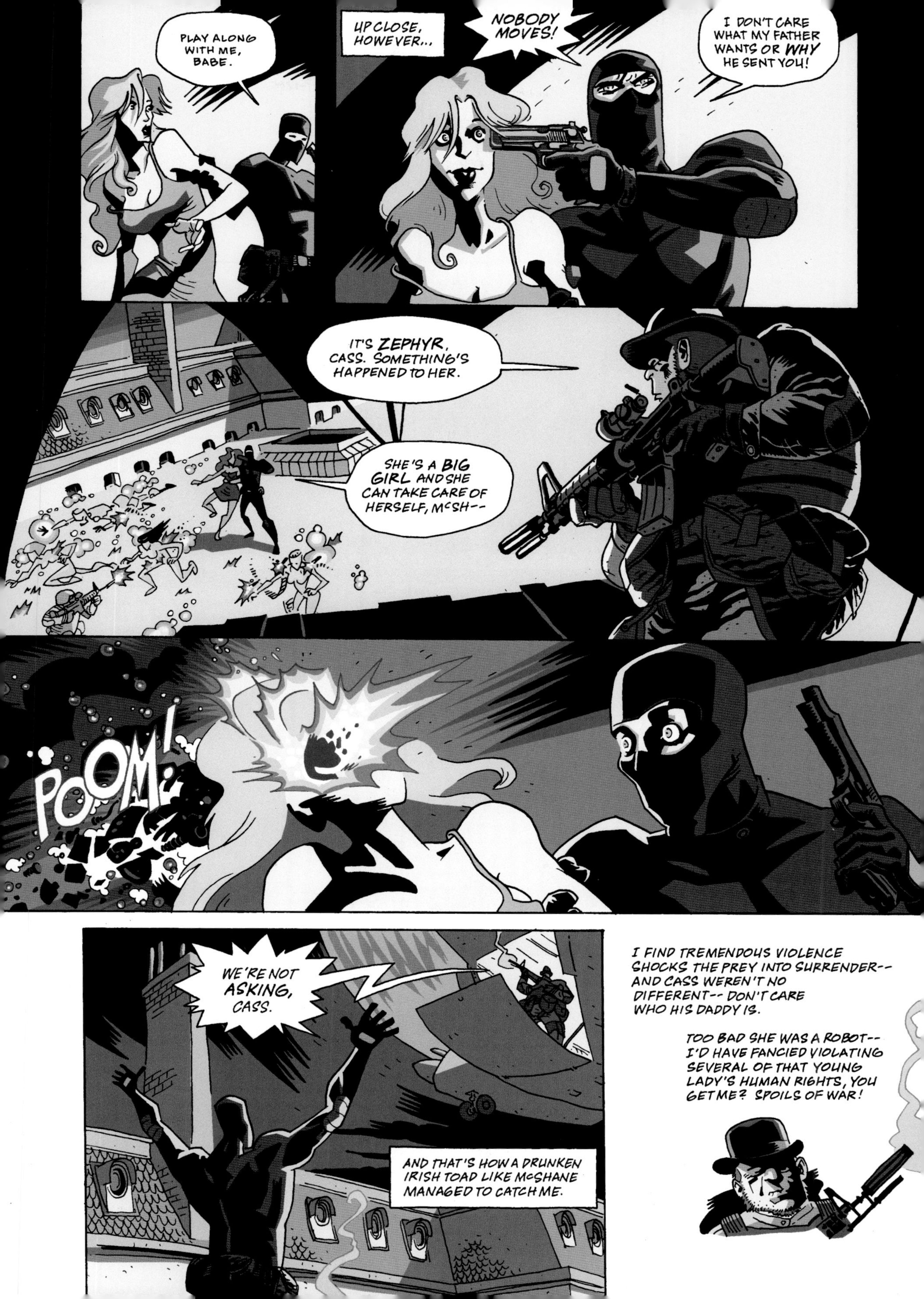
PLAY ALONG WITH ME, BABE.
UP CLOSE, HOWEVER...
NOBODY MOVES!
I DON'T CARE WHAT MY FATHER WANTS OR WHY HE SENT YOU!
IT'S ZEPHYR, CASS. SOMETHING'S HAPPENED TO HER.
SHE'S A BIG GIRL AND SHE CAN TAKE CARE OF HERSELF, McSH--
POOM!
WE'RE NOT ASKING, CASS.
AND THAT'S HOW A DRUNKEN IRISH TOAD LIKE McSHANE MANAGED TO CATCH ME.
I FIND TREMENDOUS VIOLENCE SHOCKS THE PREY INTO SURRENDER-- AND CASS WEREN'T NO DIFFERENT-- DON'T CARE WHO HIS DADDY IS.
TOO BAD SHE WAS A ROBOT-- I'D HAVE FANCIED VIOLATING SEVERAL OF THAT YOUNG LADY'S HUMAN RIGHTS, YOU GET ME? SPOILS OF WAR!

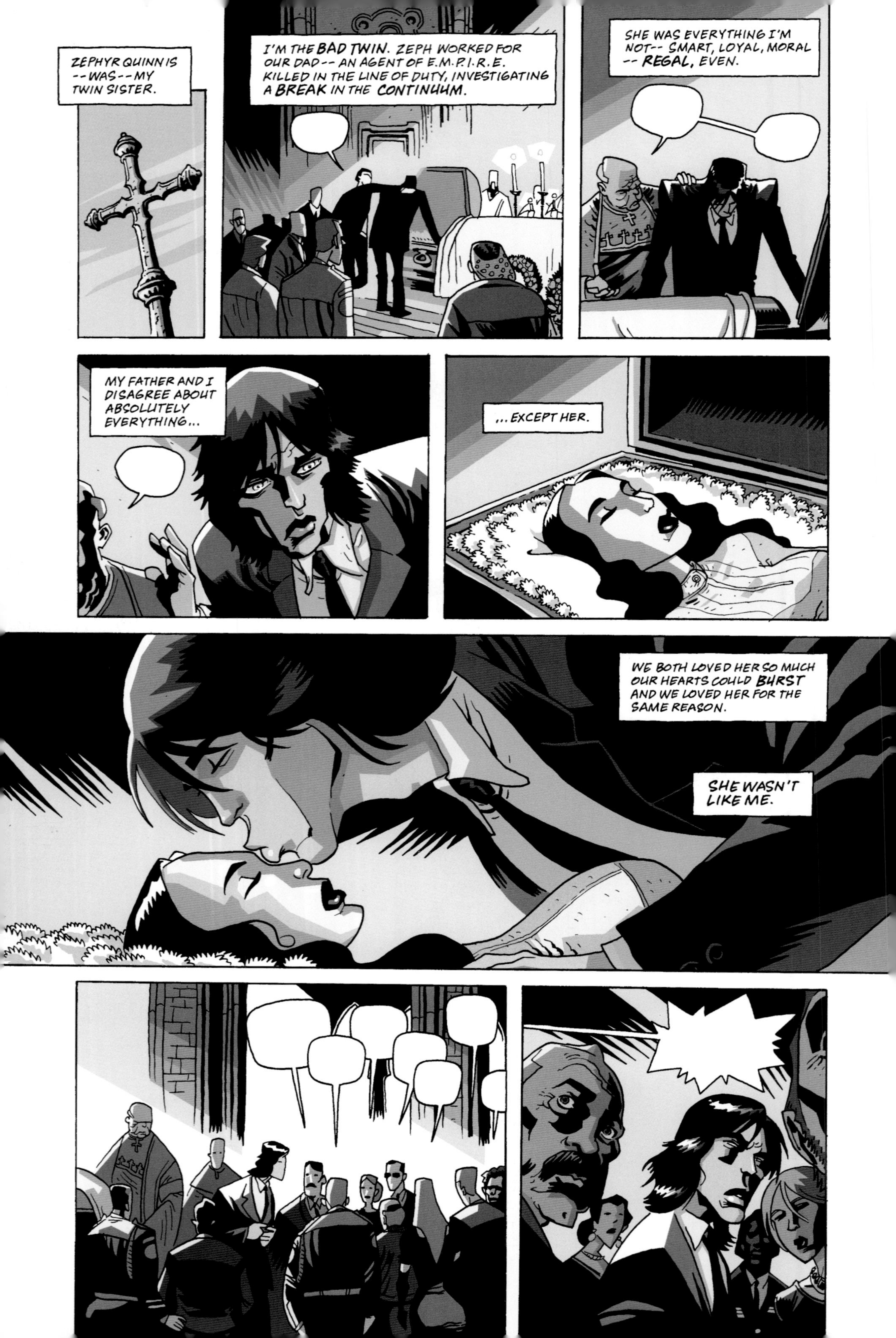
ZEPHYR QUINN IS --WAS--MY TWIN SISTER.
I'M THE BAD TWIN. ZEPH WORKED FOR OUR DAD-- AN AGENT OF E.M.P.I.R.E. KILLED IN THE LINE OF DUTY, INVESTIGATING A BREAK IN THE CONTINUUM.
SHE WAS EVERYTHING I'M NOT-- SMART, LOYAL, MORAL -- REGAL, EVEN.
MY FATHER AND I DISAGREE ABOUT ABSOLUTELY EVERYTHING...
...EXCEPT HER.
WE BOTH LOVED HER SO MUCH OUR HEARTS COULD BURST AND WE LOVED HER FOR THE SAME REASON.
SHE WASN'T LIKE ME.

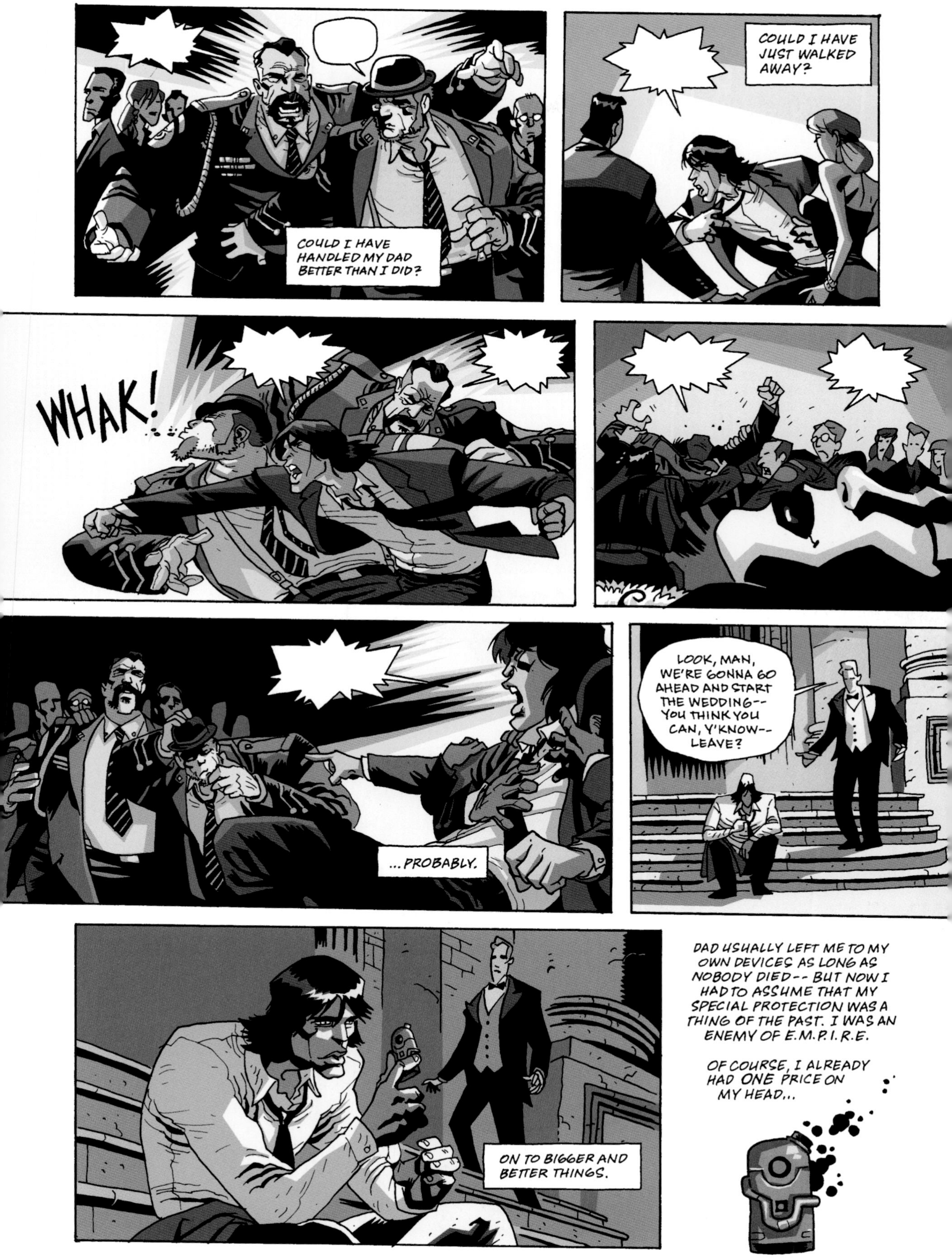
COULD I HAVE HANDLED MY DAD BETTER THAN I DID?
COULD I HAVE JUST WALKED AWAY?
WHAK!
...PROBABLY.
LOOK, MAN, WE'RE GONNA GO AHEAD AND START THE WEDDING-- YOU THINK YOU CAN, Y'KNOW-- LEAVE?
ON TO BIGGER AND BETTER THINGS.
DAD USUALLY LEFT ME TO MY OWN DEVICES AS LONG AS NOBODY DIED-- BUT NOW I HAD TO ASSUME THAT MY SPECIAL PROTECTION WAS A THING OF THE PAST. I WAS AN ENEMY OF E.M.P.I.R.E.
OF COURSE, I ALREADY HAD ONE PRICE ON MY HEAD...

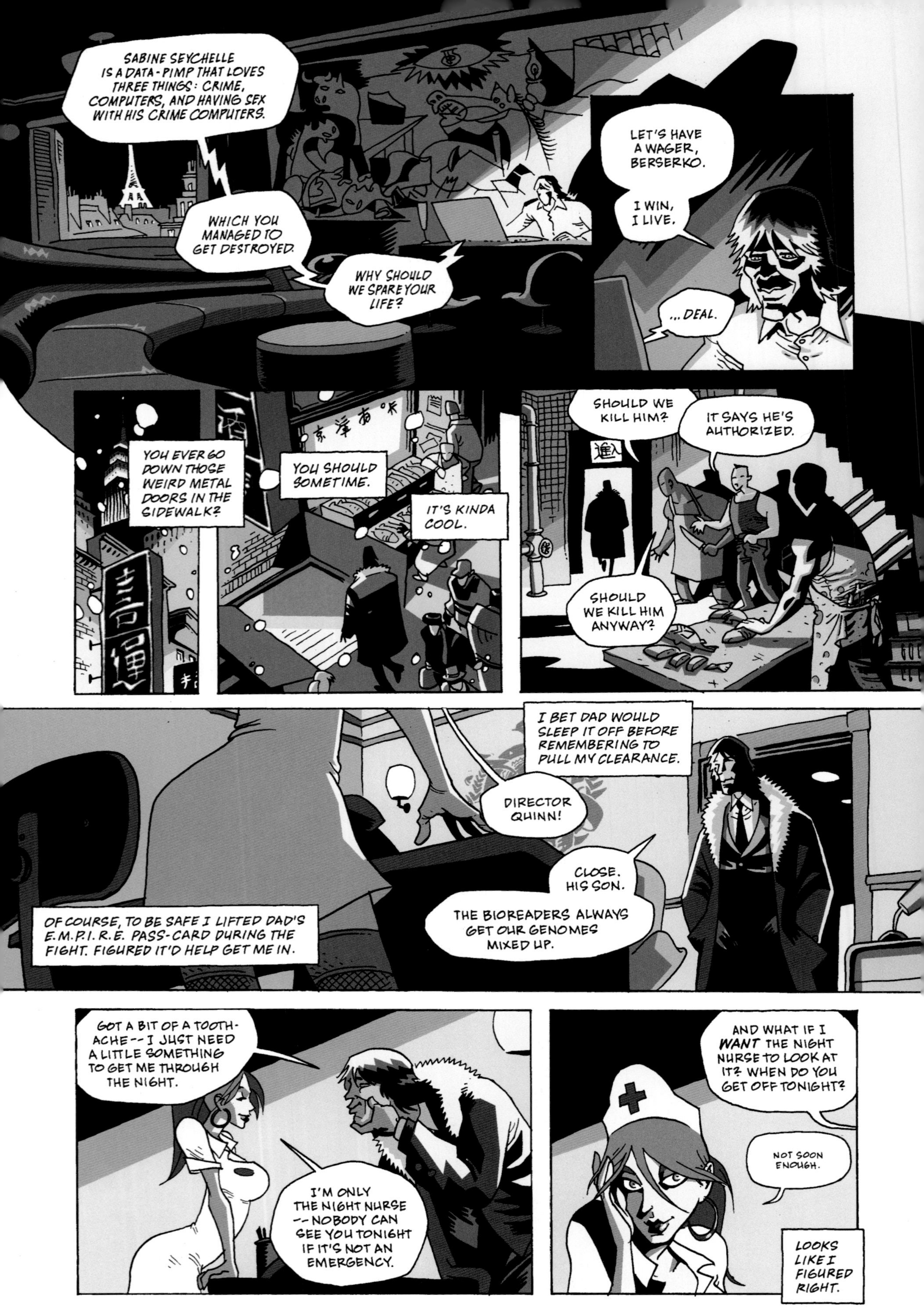
SABINE SEYCHELLE IS A DATA-PIMP THAT LOVES THREE THINGS: CRIME, COMPUTERS, AND HAVING SEX WITH HIS CRIME COMPUTERS.
WHICH YOU MANAGED TO GET DESTROYED.
WHY SHOULD WE SPARE YOUR LIFE?
LET'S HAVE A WAGER, BERSERKO.
I WIN, I LIVE.
...DEAL.
YOU EVER GO DOWN THOSE WEIRD METAL DOORS IN THE SIDEWALK?
YOU SHOULD SOMETIME.
IT'S KINDA COOL.
SHOULD WE KILL HIM?
IT SAYS HE'S AUTHORIZED.
SHOULD WE KILL HIM ANYWAY?
I BET DAD WOULD SLEEP IT OFF BEFORE REMEMBERING TO PULL MY CLEARANCE.
DIRECTOR QUINN!
CLOSE. HIS SON.
THE BIOREADERS ALWAYS GET OUR GENOMES MIXED UP.
OF COURSE, TO BE SAFE I LIFTED DAD'S E.M.P.I.R.E. PASS-CARD DURING THE FIGHT. FIGURED IT'D HELP GET ME IN.
GOT A BIT OF A TOOTH-ACHE-- I JUST NEED A LITTLE SOMETHING TO GET ME THROUGH THE NIGHT.
I'M ONLY THE NIGHT NURSE -- NOBODY CAN SEE YOU TONIGHT IF IT'S NOT AN EMERGENCY.
AND WHAT IF I *WANT* THE NIGHT NURSE TO LOOK AT IT? WHEN DO YOU GET OFF TONIGHT?
NOT SOON ENOUGH.
LOOKS LIKE I FIGURED RIGHT.

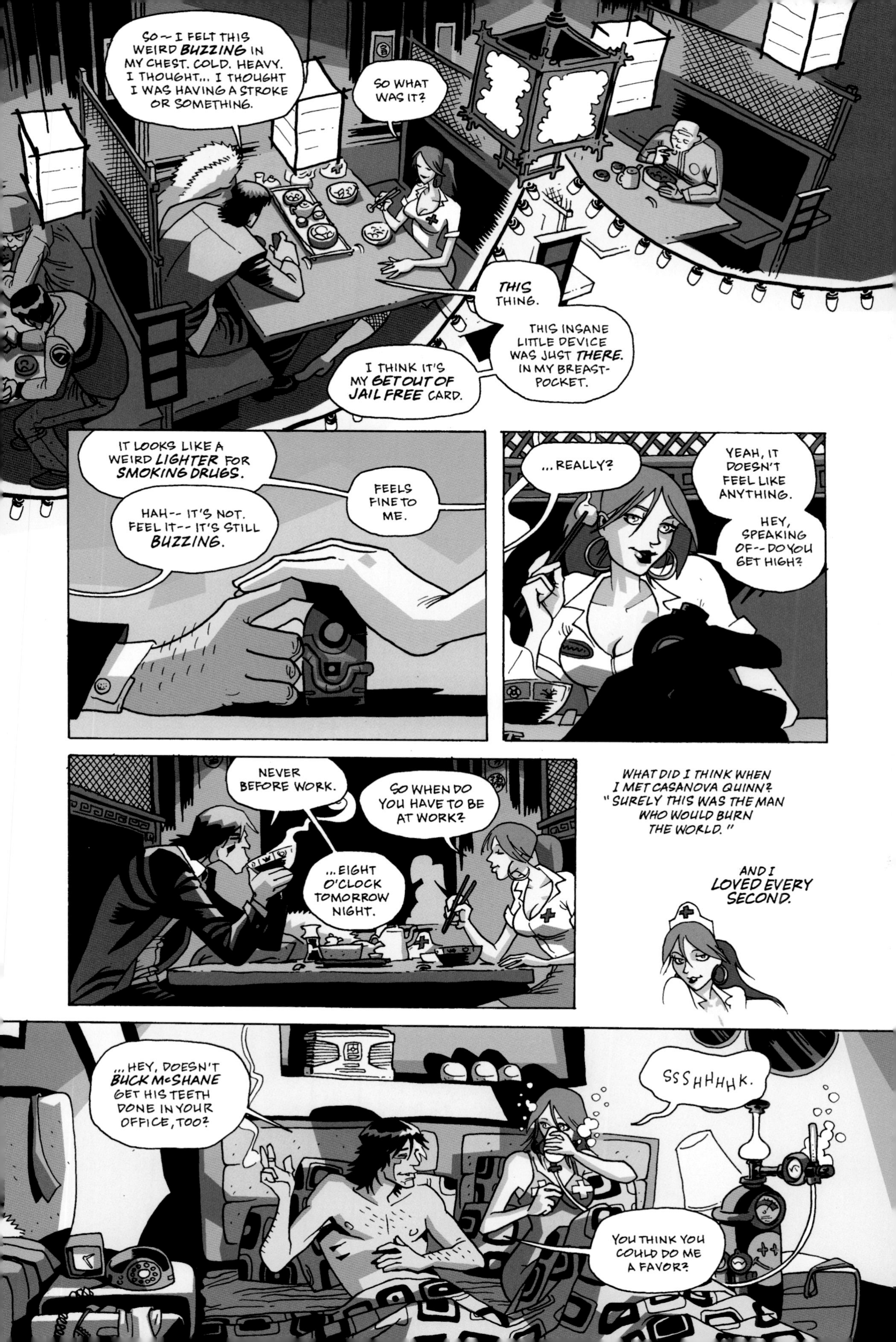
SO-- I FELT THIS WEIRD BUZZING IN MY CHEST. COLD. HEAVY. I THOUGHT... I THOUGHT I WAS HAVING A STROKE OR SOMETHING.
SO WHAT WAS IT?
THIS THING.
THIS INSANE LITTLE DEVICE WAS JUST THERE. IN MY BREAST-POCKET.
I THINK IT'S MY GET OUT OF JAIL FREE CARD.
IT LOOKS LIKE A WEIRD LIGHTER FOR SMOKING DRUGS.
HAH-- IT'S NOT. FEEL IT-- IT'S STILL BUZZING.
FEELS FINE TO ME.
...REALLY?
YEAH, IT DOESN'T FEEL LIKE ANYTHING.
HEY, SPEAKING OF--DO YOU GET HIGH?
NEVER BEFORE WORK.
SO WHEN DO YOU HAVE TO BE AT WORK?
...EIGHT O'CLOCK TOMORROW NIGHT.
WHAT DID I THINK WHEN I MET CASANOVA QUINN? "SURELY THIS WAS THE MAN WHO WOULD BURN THE WORLD."
AND I LOVED EVERY SECOND.
...HEY, DOESN'T BUCK McSHANE GET HIS TEETH DONE IN YOUR OFFICE, TOO?
SSSHHHHK.
YOU THINK YOU COULD DO ME A FAVOR?

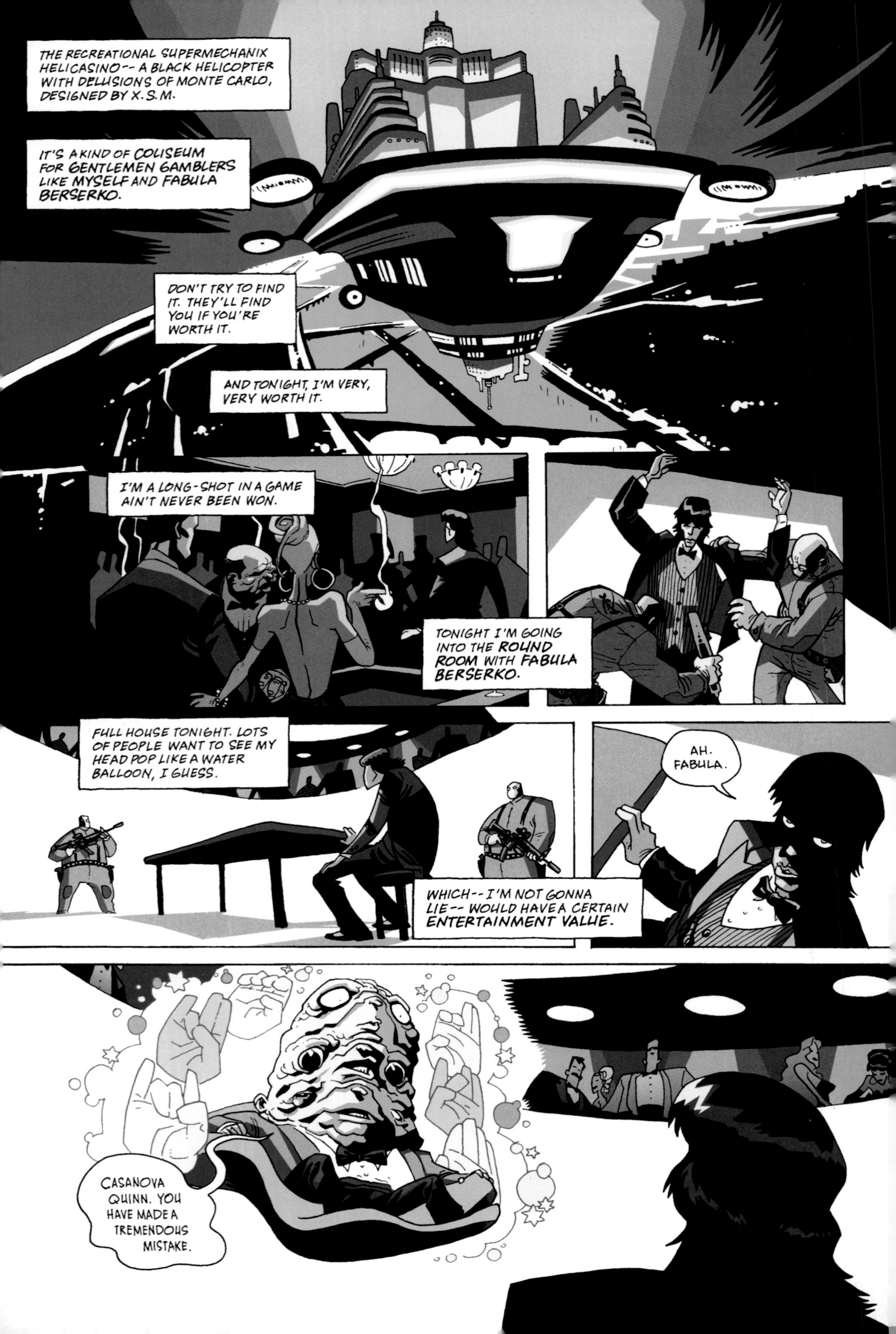
THE RECREATIONAL SUPERMECHANIX HELICASINO-- A BLACK HELICOPTER WITH DELUSIONS OF MONTE CARLO, DESIGNED BY X.S.M.
IT'S A KIND OF COLISEUM FOR GENTLEMEN GAMBLERS LIKE MYSELF AND FABULA BERSERKO.
DON'T TRY TO FIND IT. THEY'LL FIND YOU IF YOU'RE WORTH IT.
AND TONIGHT, I'M VERY, VERY WORTH IT.
I'M A LONG-SHOT IN A GAME AIN'T NEVER BEEN WON.
TONIGHT I'M GOING INTO THE ROUND ROOM WITH FABULA BERSERKO.
FULL HOUSE TONIGHT. LOTS OF PEOPLE WANT TO SEE MY HEAD POP LIKE A WATER BALLOON, I GUESS.
WHICH-- I'M NOT GONNA LIE-- WOULD HAVE A CERTAIN ENTERTAINMENT VALUE.
AH. FABULA.
CASANOVA QUINN. YOU HAVE MADE A TREMENDOUS MISTAKE.

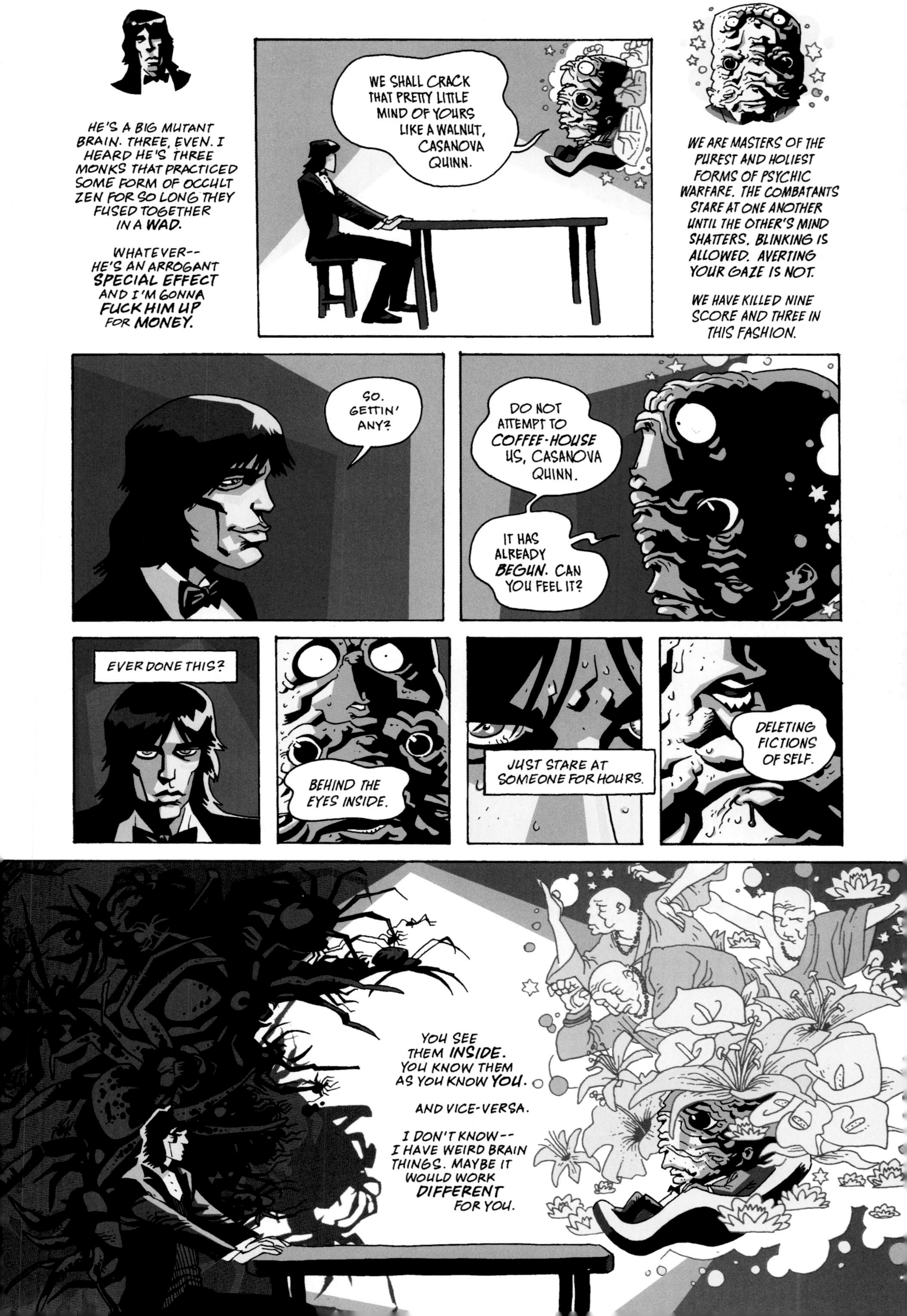
HE'S A BIG MUTANT BRAIN. THREE, EVEN. I HEARD HE'S THREE MONKS THAT PRACTICED SOME FORM OF OCCULT ZEN FOR SO LONG THEY FUSED TOGETHER IN A WAD.
WHATEVER-- HE'S AN ARROGANT SPECIAL EFFECT AND I'M GONNA FUCK HIM UP FOR MONEY.
WE SHALL CRACK THAT PRETTY LITTLE MIND OF YOURS LIKE A WALNUT, CASANOVA QUINN.
WE ARE MASTERS OF THE PUREST AND HOLIEST FORMS OF PSYCHIC WARFARE. THE COMBATANTS STARE AT ONE ANOTHER UNTIL THE OTHER'S MIND SHATTERS. BLINKING IS ALLOWED. AVERTING YOUR GAZE IS NOT.
WE HAVE KILLED NINE SCORE AND THREE IN THIS FASHION.
SO. GETTIN' ANY?
DO NOT ATTEMPT TO COFFEE-HOUSE US, CASANOVA QUINN.
IT HAS ALREADY BEGUN. CAN YOU FEEL IT?
EVER DONE THIS?
BEHIND THE EYES INSIDE.
JUST STARE AT SOMEONE FOR HOURS.
DELETING FICTIONS OF SELF.
YOU SEE THEM INSIDE. YOU KNOW THEM AS YOU KNOW YOU.
AND VICE-VERSA.
I DON'T KNOW-- I HAVE WEIRD BRAIN THINGS. MAYBE IT WOULD WORK DIFFERENT FOR YOU.

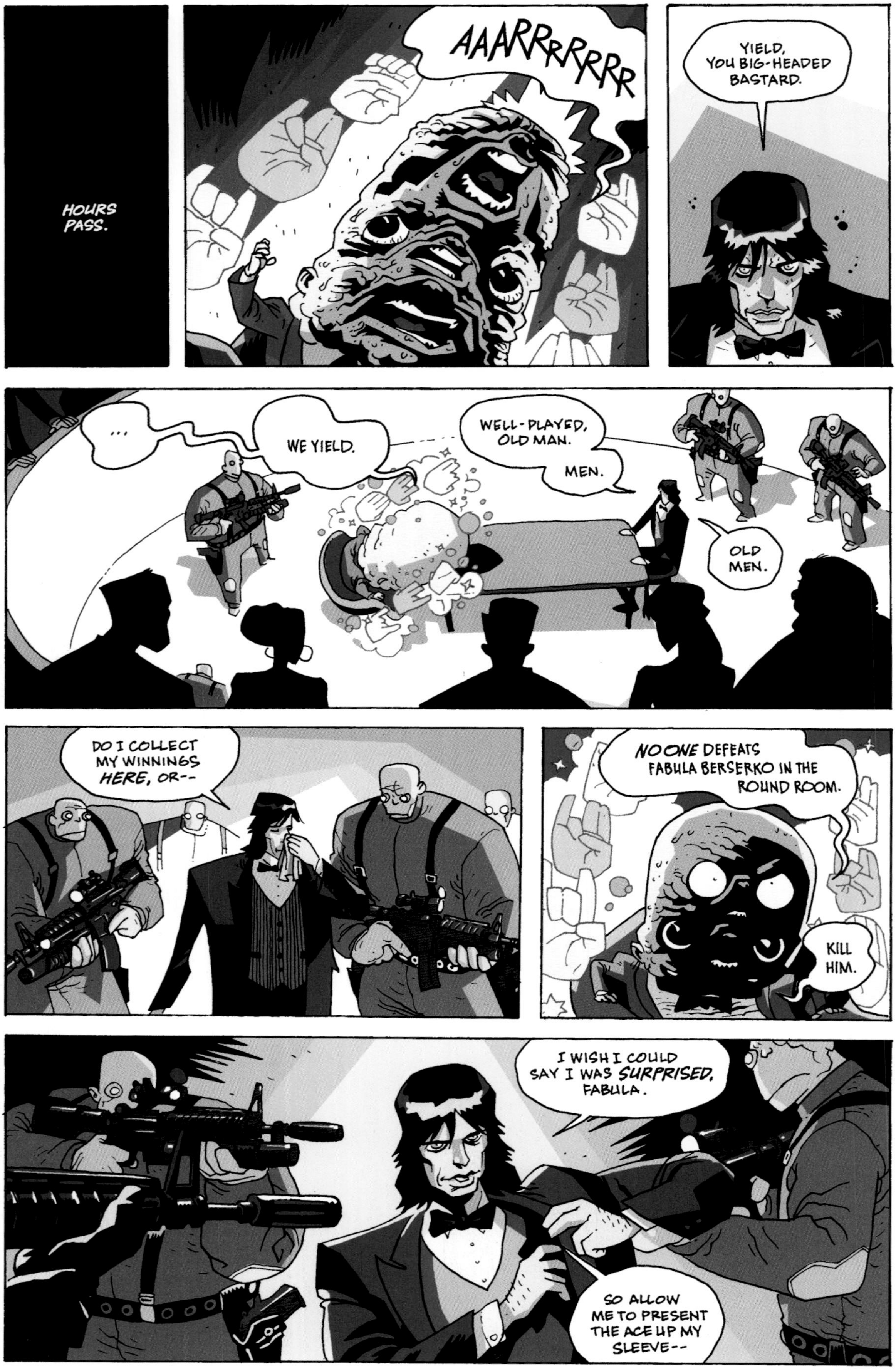
HOURS PASS.
AAARRRRRRRR
YIELD, YOU BIG-HEADED BASTARD.
...
WE YIELD.
WELL-PLAYED, OLD MAN.
MEN.
OLD MEN.
DO I COLLECT MY WINNINGS HERE, OR--
NO ONE DEFEATS FABULA BERSERKO IN THE ROUND ROOM.
KILL HIM.
I WISH I COULD SAY I WAS SURPRISED, FABULA.
SO ALLOW ME TO PRESENT THE ACE UP MY SLEEVE--

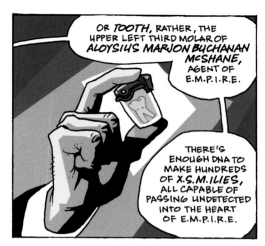

OR *TOOTH*, RATHER, THE UPPER LEFT THIRD MOLAR OF *ALOYSIUS MARJON BUCHANAN McSHANE*, AGENT OF E.M.P.I.R.E.

THERE'S ENOUGH DNA TO MAKE HUNDREDS OF X.S.M.ILIES, ALL CAPABLE OF PASSING UNDETECTED INTO THE HEART OF E.M.P.I.R.E.

HOW DID YOU ACQUIRE THIS... *TREASURE*?

HE DID *WHAT*?

THAT'S AN N-STATE PROBABILITY CAP IT'S SEALED WITH, FABS.

BEING OPENED WITHOUT DETONATION DEPENDS ON *ME* BEING ALIVE AND *TWENTY KLICKS AWAY* WHEN THE CAP COMES OFF.

THEN I'LL HAVE THE PILOTS ELEVATE US TO *THIRTY* TO MAKE SURE YOU'VE GOT ENOUGH TIME.

LOVE THE JUMPSUIT, GUY.

WE'LL BE CERTAIN TO GIVE OUR REGARDS TO YO

OOOuuuuuuuRRRRRRRR

RR FFFA

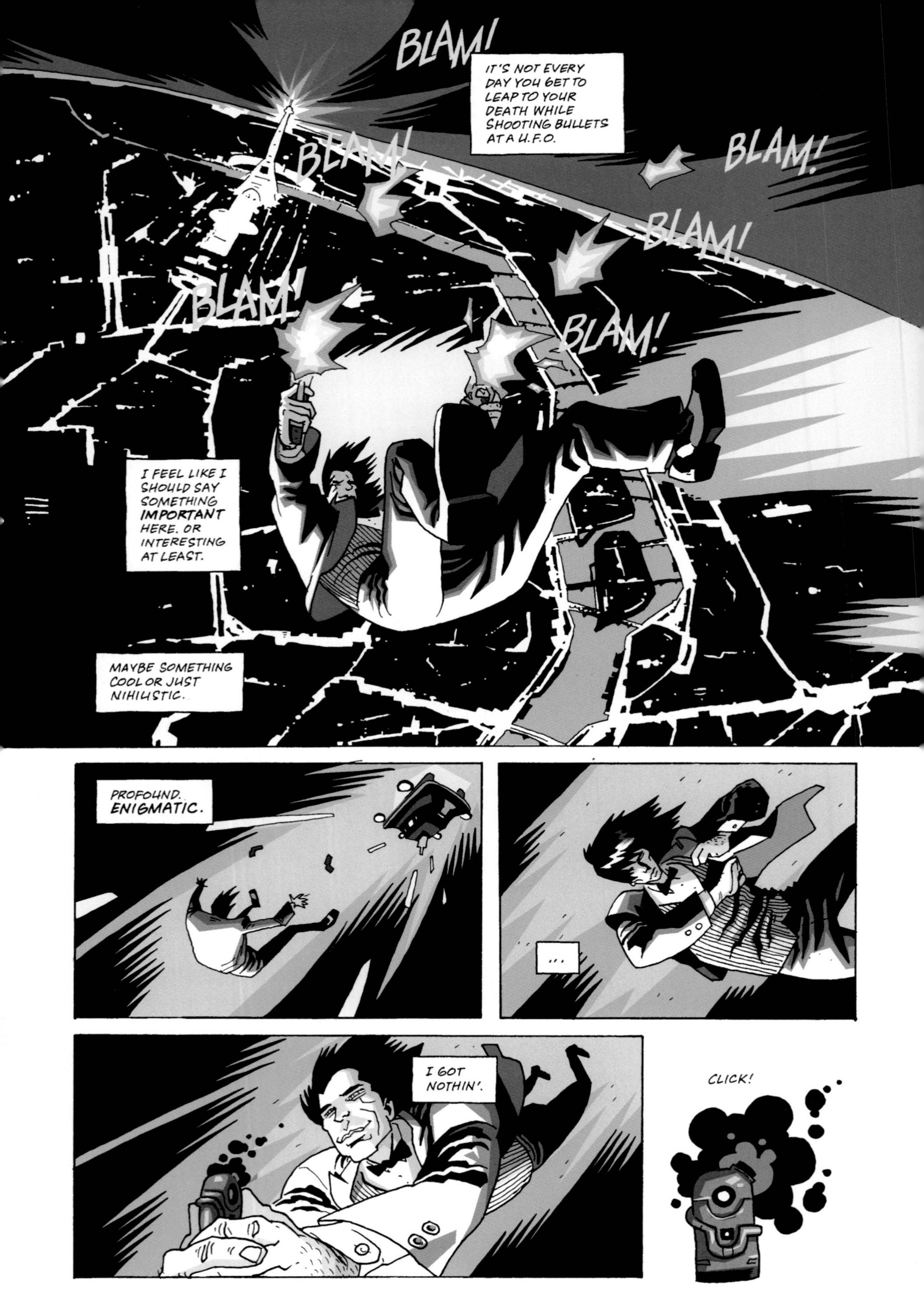
BLAM!
IT'S NOT EVERY DAY YOU GET TO LEAP TO YOUR DEATH WHILE SHOOTING BULLETS AT A U.F.O.
BLAM!
BLAM!
BLAM!
BLAM!
BLAM!
I FEEL LIKE I SHOULD SAY SOMETHING IMPORTANT HERE. OR INTERESTING AT LEAST.
MAYBE SOMETHING COOL OR JUST NIHILISTIC.
PROFOUND. ENIGMATIC.
...
I GOT NOTHIN'.
CLICK!

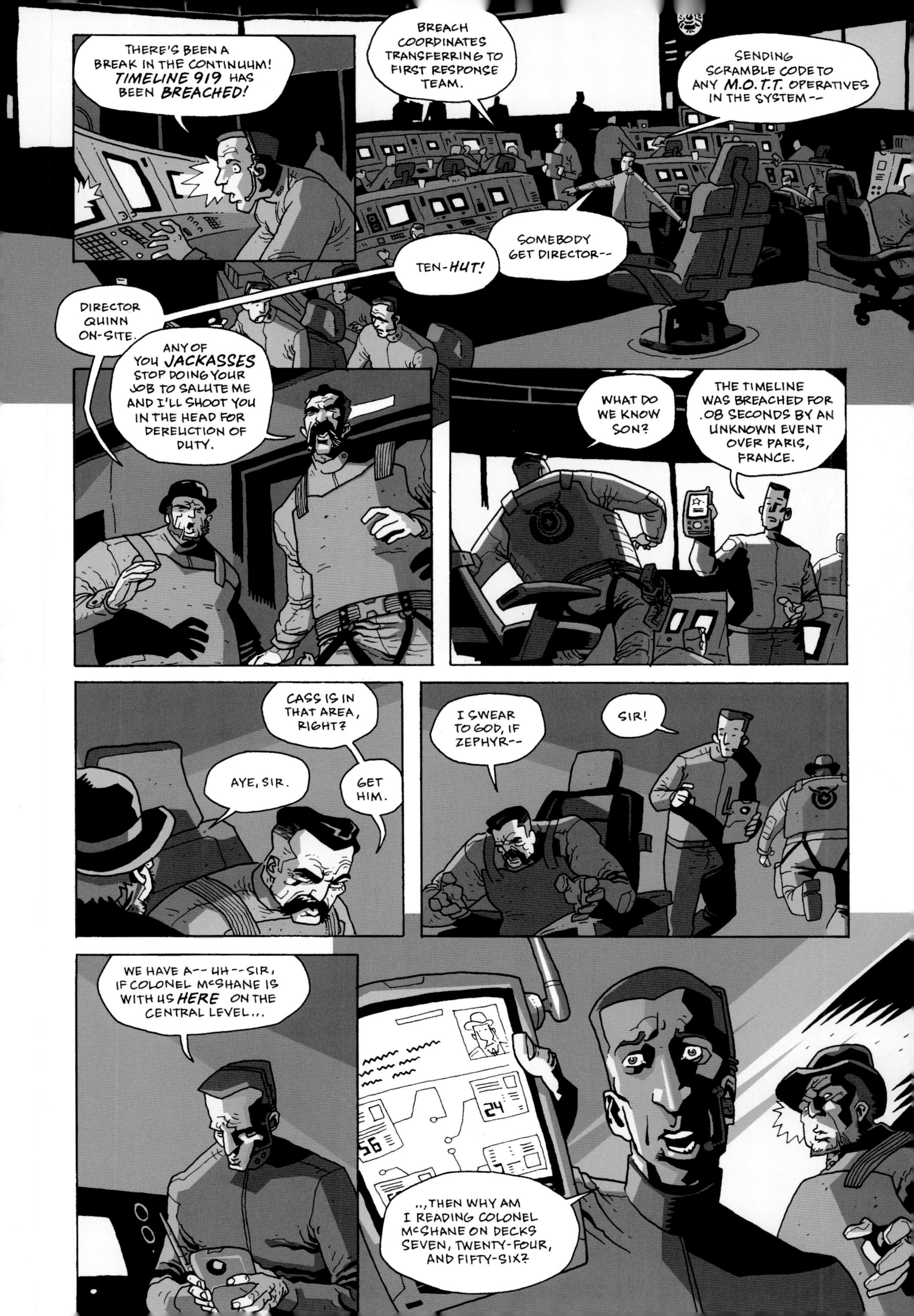
THERE'S BEEN A BREAK IN THE CONTINUUM! TIMELINE 919 HAS BEEN BREACHED!
BREACH COORDINATES TRANSFERRING TO FIRST RESPONSE TEAM.
SENDING SCRAMBLE CODE TO ANY M.O.T.T. OPERATIVES IN THE SYSTEM--
SOMEBODY GET DIRECTOR--
TEN-HUT!
DIRECTOR QUINN ON-SITE.
ANY OF YOU JACKASSES STOP DOING YOUR JOB TO SALUTE ME AND I'LL SHOOT YOU IN THE HEAD FOR DERELICTION OF DUTY.
WHAT DO WE KNOW SON?
THE TIMELINE WAS BREACHED FOR .08 SECONDS BY AN UNKNOWN EVENT OVER PARIS, FRANCE.
CASS IS IN THAT AREA, RIGHT?
AYE, SIR.
GET HIM.
I SWEAR TO GOD, IF ZEPHYR--
SIR!
WE HAVE A-- UH-- SIR, IF COLONEL McSHANE IS WITH US HERE ON THE CENTRAL LEVEL...
...THEN WHY AM I READING COLONEL McSHANE ON DECKS SEVEN, TWENTY-FOUR, AND FIFTY-SIX?

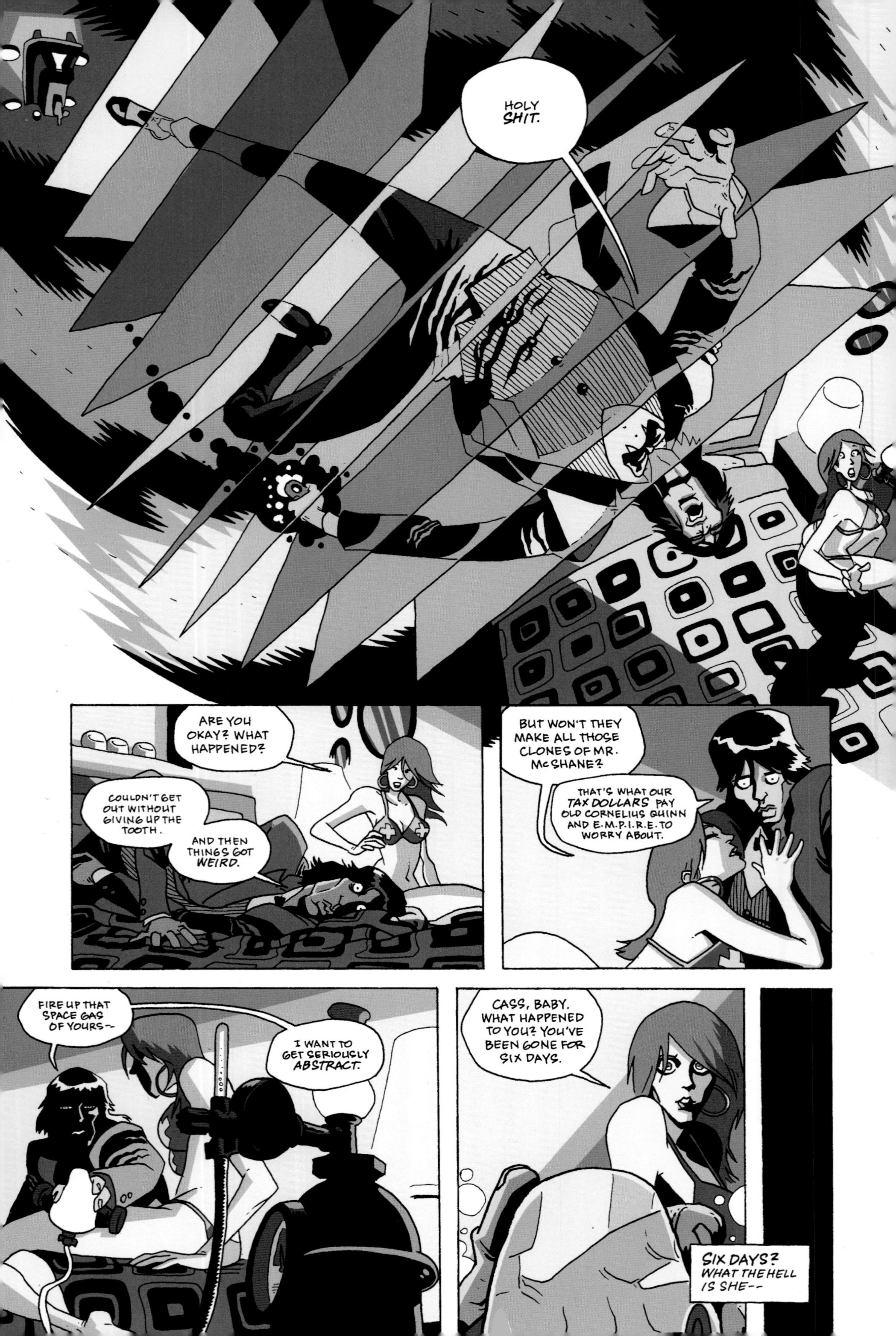
HOLY SHIT.
ARE YOU OKAY? WHAT HAPPENED?
COULDN'T GET OUT WITHOUT GIVING UP THE TOOTH.
AND THEN THINGS GOT WEIRD.
BUT WON'T THEY MAKE ALL THOSE CLONES OF MR. McSHANE?
THAT'S WHAT OUR TAX DOLLARS PAY OLD CORNELIUS QUINN AND E.M.P.I.R.E. TO WORRY ABOUT.
FIRE UP THAT SPACE GAS OF YOURS--
I WANT TO GET SERIOUSLY ABSTRACT.
CASS, BABY. WHAT HAPPENED TO YOU? YOU'VE BEEN GONE FOR SIX DAYS.
SIX DAYS? WHAT THE HELL IS SHE--

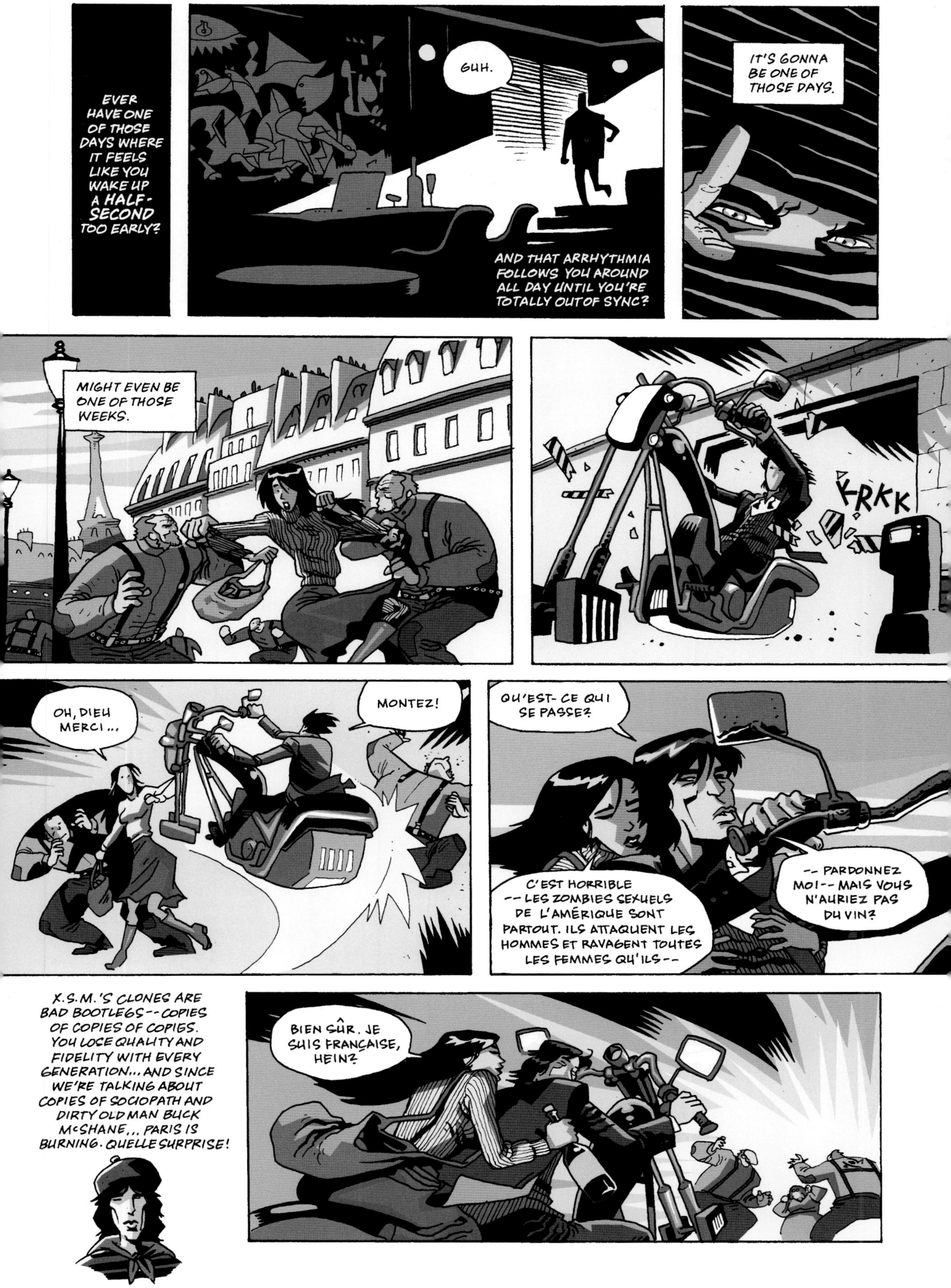
EVER HAVE ONE OF THOSE DAYS WHERE IT FEELS LIKE YOU WAKE UP A HALF-SECOND TOO EARLY?
GUH.
AND THAT ARRHYTHMIA FOLLOWS YOU AROUND ALL DAY UNTIL YOU'RE TOTALLY OUT OF SYNC?
IT'S GONNA BE ONE OF THOSE DAYS.
MIGHT EVEN BE ONE OF THOSE WEEKS.
KRKK
OH, DIEU MERCI...
MONTEZ!
QU'EST-CE QUI SE PASSE?
C'EST HORRIBLE --LES ZOMBIES SEXUELS DE L'AMÉRIQUE SONT PARTOUT. ILS ATTAQUENT LES HOMMES ET RAVAGENT TOUTES LES FEMMES QU'ILS--
--PARDONNEZ MOI--MAIS VOUS N'AURIEZ PAS DU VIN?
X.S.M.'S CLONES ARE BAD BOOTLEGS--COPIES OF COPIES OF COPIES. YOU LOSE QUALITY AND FIDELITY WITH EVERY GENERATION... AND SINCE WE'RE TALKING ABOUT COPIES OF SOCIOPATH AND DIRTY OLD MAN BUCK McSHANE... PARIS IS BURNING. QUELLE SURPRISE!
BIEN SÛR. JE SUIS FRANÇAISE, HEIN?

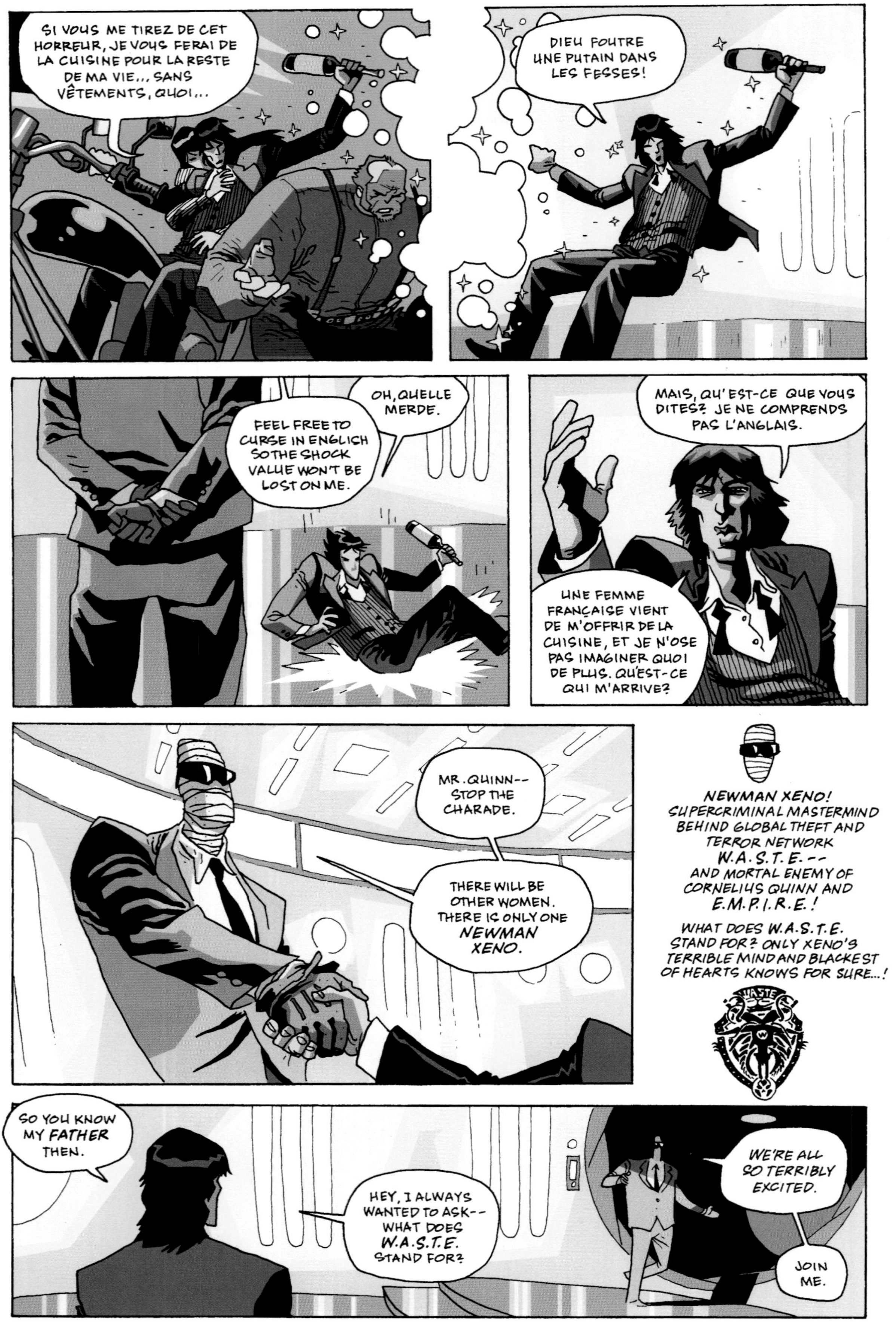
SI VOUS ME TIREZ DE CET HORREUR, JE VOUS FERAI DE LA CUISINE POUR LA RESTE DE MA VIE... SANS VÊTEMENTS, QUOI...
DIEU FOUTRE UNE PUTAIN DANS LES FESSES!
FEEL FREE TO CURSE IN ENGLISH SO THE SHOCK VALUE WON'T BE LOST ON ME.
OH, QUELLE MERDE.
MAIS, QU'EST-CE QUE VOUS DITES? JE NE COMPRENDS PAS L'ANGLAIS.
UNE FEMME FRANÇAISE VIENT DE M'OFFRIR DE LA CUISINE, ET JE N'OSE PAS IMAGINER QUOI DE PLUS. QU'EST-CE QUI M'ARRIVE?
MR. QUINN-- STOP THE CHARADE.
THERE WILL BE OTHER WOMEN. THERE IS ONLY ONE NEWMAN XENO.
NEWMAN XENO! SUPERCRIMINAL MASTERMIND BEHIND GLOBAL THEFT AND TERROR NETWORK W.A.S.T.E.-- AND MORTAL ENEMY OF CORNELIUS QUINN AND E.M.P.I.R.E.!
WHAT DOES W.A.S.T.E. STAND FOR? ONLY XENO'S TERRIBLE MIND AND BLACKEST OF HEARTS KNOWS FOR SURE...!
SO YOU KNOW MY FATHER THEN.
HEY, I ALWAYS WANTED TO ASK-- WHAT DOES W.A.S.T.E. STAND FOR?
WE'RE ALL SO TERRIBLY EXCITED.
JOIN ME.

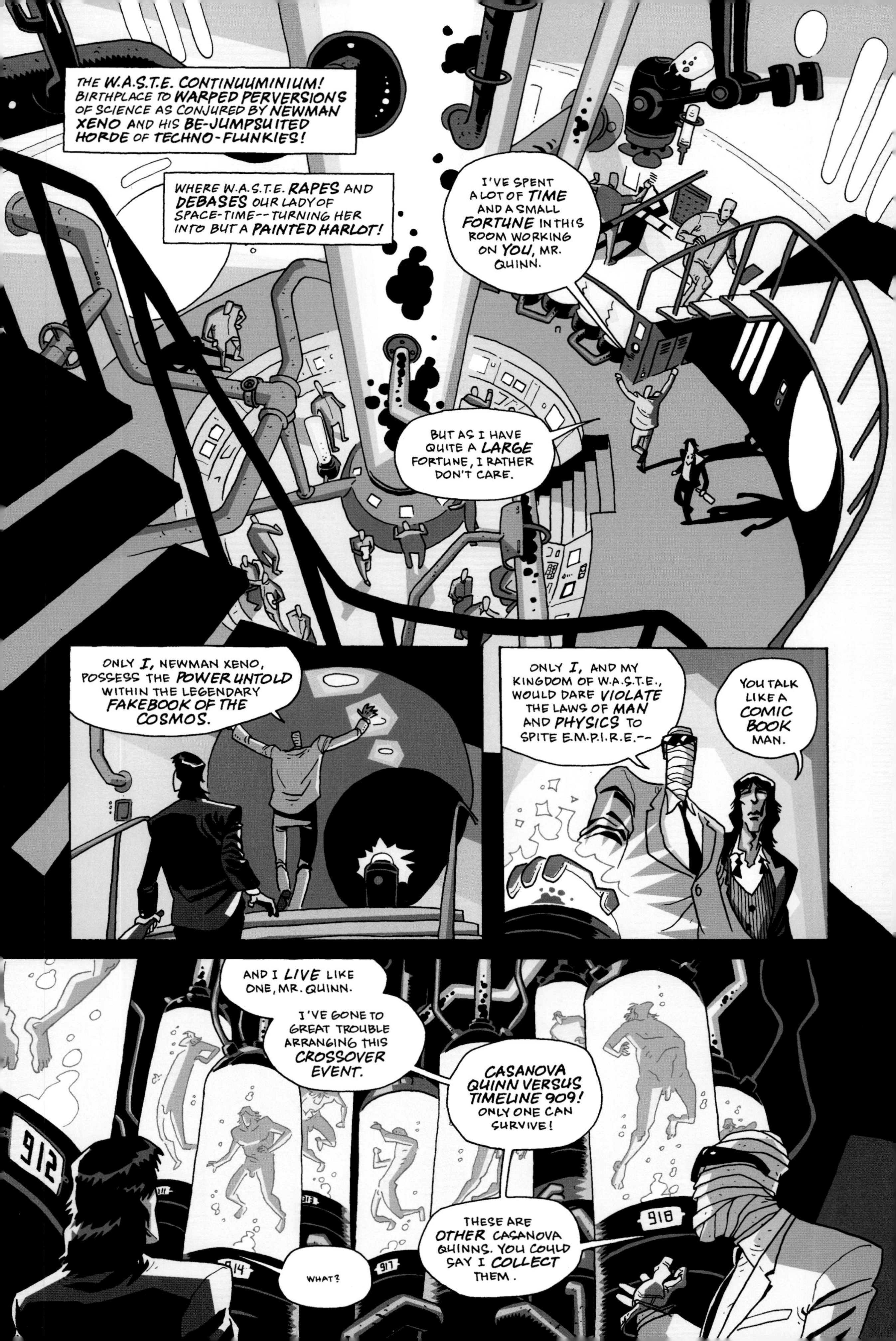
THE W.A.S.T.E. CONTINUUMINIUM! BIRTHPLACE TO WARPED PERVERSIONS OF SCIENCE AS CONJURED BY NEWMAN XENO AND HIS BE-JUMPSUITED HORDE OF TECHNO-FLUNKIES!
WHERE W.A.S.T.E. RAPES AND DEBASES OUR LADY OF SPACE-TIME--TURNING HER INTO BUT A PAINTED HARLOT!
I'VE SPENT A LOT OF TIME AND A SMALL FORTUNE IN THIS ROOM WORKING ON YOU, MR. QUINN.
BUT AS I HAVE QUITE A LARGE FORTUNE, I RATHER DON'T CARE.
ONLY I, NEWMAN XENO, POSSESS THE POWER UNTOLD WITHIN THE LEGENDARY FAKEBOOK OF THE COSMOS.
ONLY I, AND MY KINGDOM OF W.A.S.T.E., WOULD DARE VIOLATE THE LAWS OF MAN AND PHYSICS TO SPITE E.M.P.I.R.E.--
YOU TALK LIKE A COMIC BOOK MAN.
AND I LIVE LIKE ONE, MR. QUINN.
I'VE GONE TO GREAT TROUBLE ARRANGING THIS CROSSOVER EVENT.
CASANOVA QUINN VERSUS TIMELINE 909! ONLY ONE CAN SURVIVE!
912
THESE ARE OTHER CASANOVA QUINNS. YOU COULD SAY I COLLECT THEM.
WHAT?

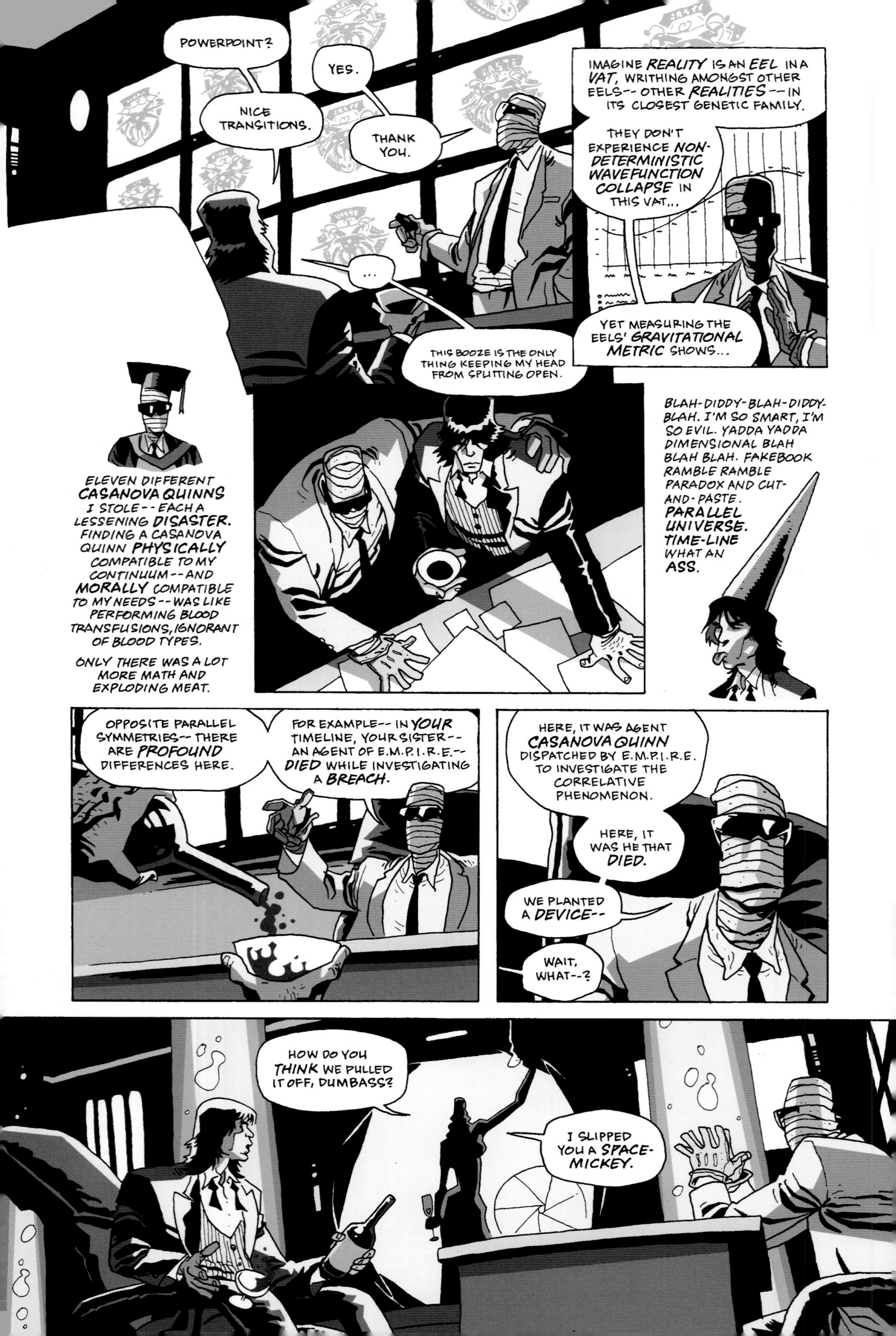

POWERPOINT?
YES.
NICE TRANSITIONS.
THANK YOU.
...
THIS BOOZE IS THE ONLY THING KEEPING MY HEAD FROM SPLITTING OPEN.
IMAGINE REALITY IS AN EEL IN A VAT, WRITHING AMONGST OTHER EELS-- OTHER REALITIES -- IN ITS CLOSEST GENETIC FAMILY.
THEY DON'T EXPERIENCE NON-DETERMINISTIC WAVEFUNCTION COLLAPSE IN THIS VAT...
YET MEASURING THE EELS' GRAVITATIONAL METRIC SHOWS...
ELEVEN DIFFERENT CASANOVA QUINNS I STOLE--EACH A LESSENING DISASTER. FINDING A CASANOVA QUINN PHYSICALLY COMPATIBLE TO MY CONTINUUM--AND MORALLY COMPATIBLE TO MY NEEDS--WAS LIKE PERFORMING BLOOD TRANSFUSIONS, IGNORANT OF BLOOD TYPES.
ONLY THERE WAS A LOT MORE MATH AND EXPLODING MEAT.
BLAH-DIDDY-BLAH-DIDDY-BLAH. I'M SO SMART, I'M SO EVIL. YADDA YADDA DIMENSIONAL BLAH BLAH BLAH. FAKEBOOK RAMBLE RAMBLE PARADOX AND CUT-AND-PASTE. PARALLEL UNIVERSE. TIME-LINE WHAT AN ASS.
OPPOSITE PARALLEL SYMMETRIES-- THERE ARE PROFOUND DIFFERENCES HERE.
FOR EXAMPLE-- IN YOUR TIMELINE, YOUR SISTER-- AN AGENT OF E.M.P.I.R.E.-- DIED WHILE INVESTIGATING A BREACH.
HERE, IT WAS AGENT CASANOVA QUINN DISPATCHED BY E.M.P.I.R.E. TO INVESTIGATE THE CORRELATIVE PHENOMENON.
HERE, IT WAS HE THAT DIED.
WE PLANTED A DEVICE--
WAIT, WHAT--?
HOW DO YOU THINK WE PULLED IT OFF, DUMBASS?
I SLIPPED YOU A SPACE-MICKEY.

XENO DID THE **CONTINUUM MAMBO** WITH THE FAKEBOOK AND I WENT INTO 909 TO RETRIEVE YOU.

E.M.P.I.R.E. **CONSTANTLY** WATCHES FOR BREACHES-- THEY WERE ON TO YOU IMMEDIATELY.

MR. "I'M A **GAJILLIONAIRE**" HERE **OFFSHORED** THE **JOB INTEL** AND **OPS** I.T. TO LOWER HIS OVERHEAD.

I WAS JUST TELLING SOMEONE THE SAME--

-- WERE YOU WAITING IN THAT LITTLE ROOM THE WHOLE TIME?

AND WAIT-- IF YOU WENT AFTER ME IN 909...

"EXACTLY...

"THEY SENT THEIR BEST AGENT TO INVESTIGATE THE BREACH...

"ZEPHYR QUINN!"

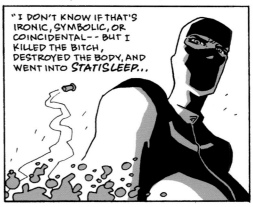

"I DON'T KNOW IF THAT'S IRONIC, SYMBOLIC, OR COINCIDENTAL-- BUT I KILLED THE BITCH, DESTROYED THE BODY, AND WENT INTO **STATISLEEP**...

"AND AT MY OWN **FUNERAL** I SLIPPED YOU THE **BEACON**.

"WE KNEW THE REST WOULD TAKE CARE OF ITSELF..."

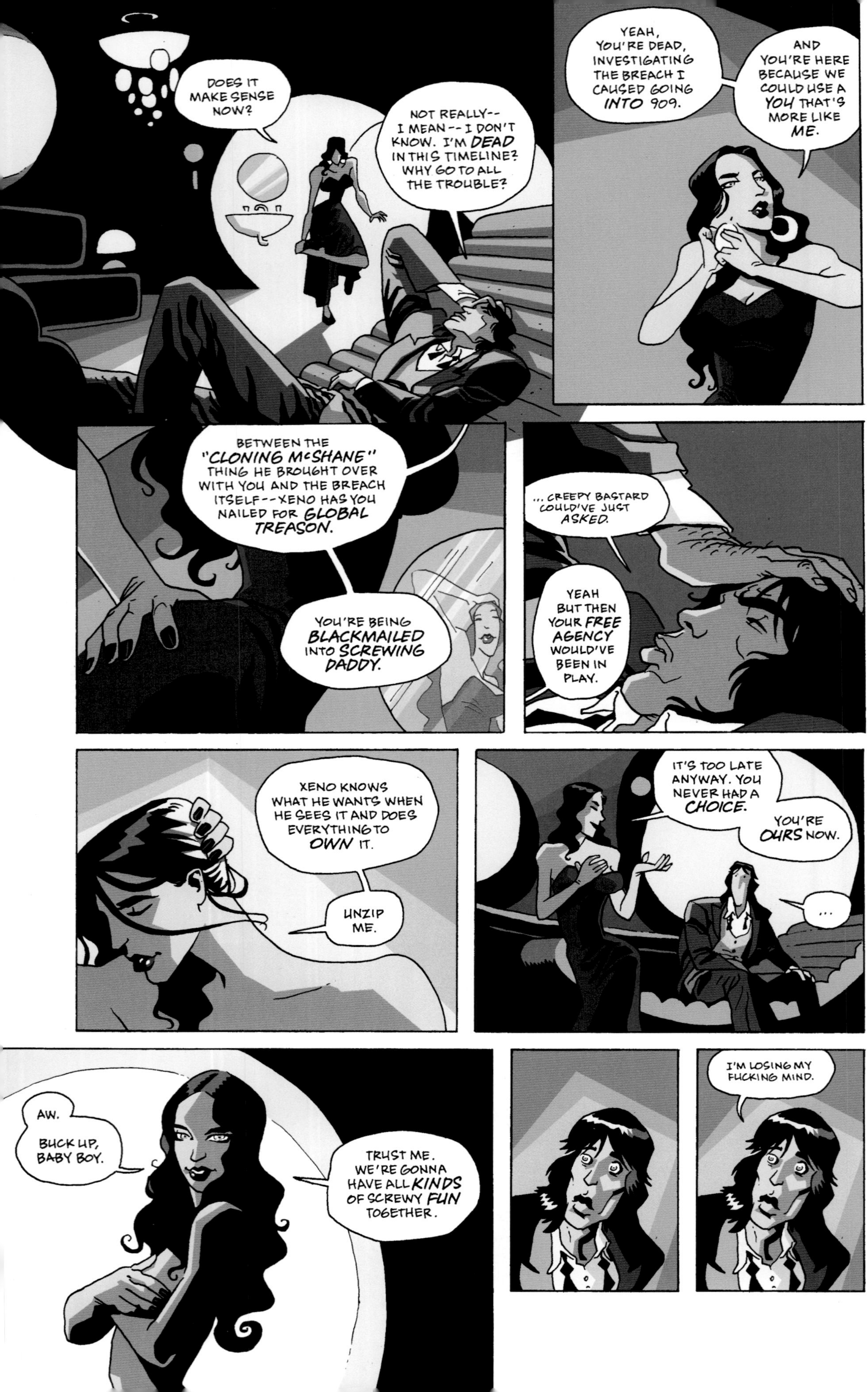

DOES IT MAKE SENSE NOW?
NOT REALLY-- I MEAN-- I DON'T KNOW. I'M DEAD IN THIS TIMELINE? WHY GO TO ALL THE TROUBLE?
YEAH, YOU'RE DEAD, INVESTIGATING THE BREACH I CAUSED GOING INTO 909.
AND YOU'RE HERE BECAUSE WE COULD USE A YOU THAT'S MORE LIKE ME.
BETWEEN THE "CLONING McSHANE" THING HE BROUGHT OVER WITH YOU AND THE BREACH ITSELF--XENO HAS YOU NAILED FOR GLOBAL TREASON.
YOU'RE BEING BLACKMAILED INTO SCREWING DADDY.
...CREEPY BASTARD COULD'VE JUST ASKED.
YEAH BUT THEN YOUR FREE AGENCY WOULD'VE BEEN IN PLAY.
XENO KNOWS WHAT HE WANTS WHEN HE SEES IT AND DOES EVERYTHING TO OWN IT.
UNZIP ME.
IT'S TOO LATE ANYWAY. YOU NEVER HAD A CHOICE.
YOU'RE OURS NOW.
...
AW.
BUCK UP, BABY BOY.
TRUST ME. WE'RE GONNA HAVE ALL KINDS OF SCREWY FUN TOGETHER.
I'M LOSING MY FUCKING MIND.

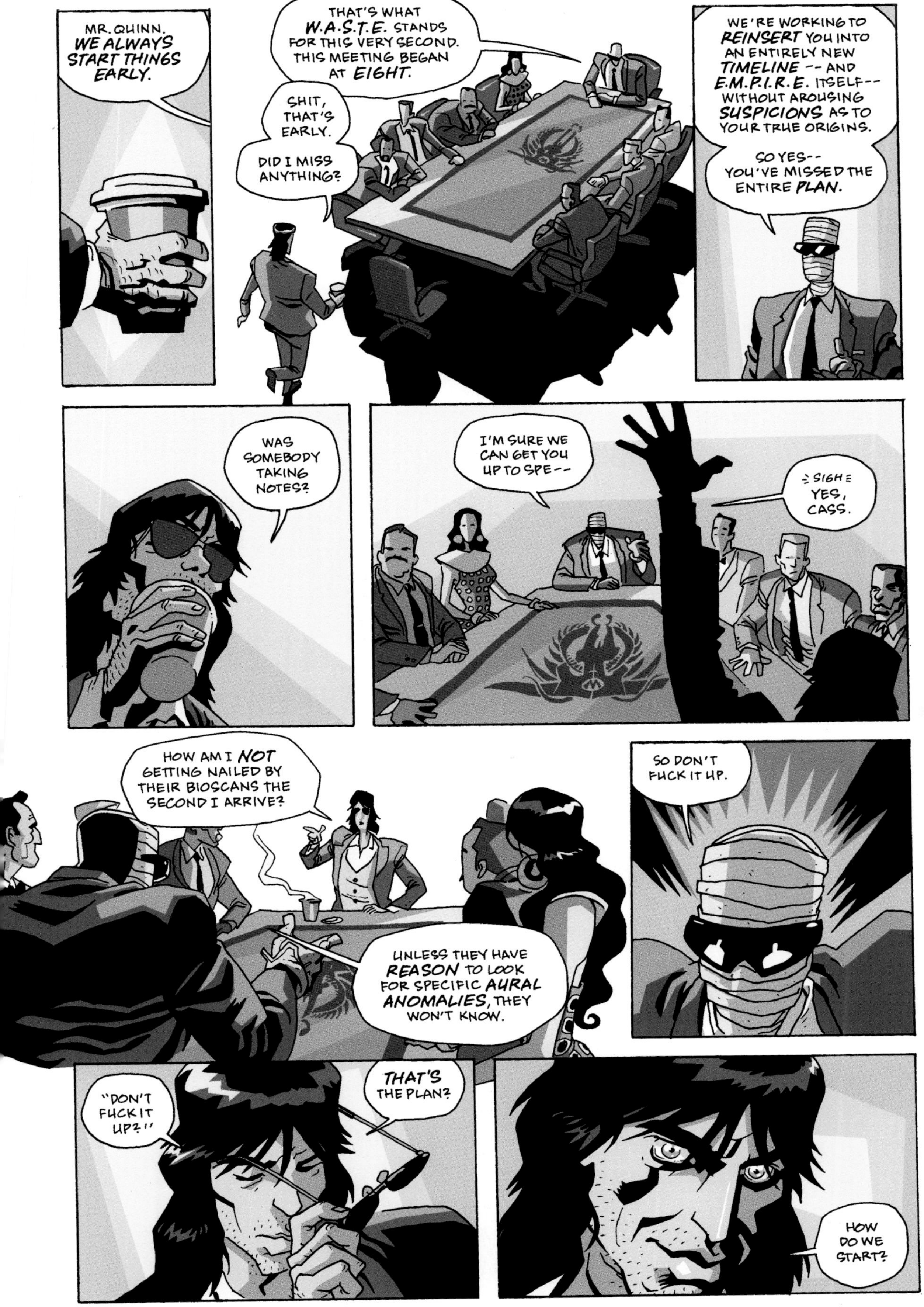
MR. QUINN. WE ALWAYS START THINGS EARLY.
THAT'S WHAT W.A.S.T.E. STANDS FOR THIS VERY SECOND. THIS MEETING BEGAN AT EIGHT.
SHIT, THAT'S EARLY.
DID I MISS ANYTHING?
WE'RE WORKING TO REINSERT YOU INTO AN ENTIRELY NEW TIMELINE -- AND E.M.P.I.R.E. ITSELF -- WITHOUT AROUSING SUSPICIONS AS TO YOUR TRUE ORIGINS.
SO YES -- YOU'VE MISSED THE ENTIRE PLAN.
WAS SOMEBODY TAKING NOTES?
I'M SURE WE CAN GET YOU UP TO SPE--
SIGH
YES, CASS.
HOW AM I NOT GETTING NAILED BY THEIR BIOSCANS THE SECOND I ARRIVE?
UNLESS THEY HAVE REASON TO LOOK FOR SPECIFIC AURAL ANOMALIES, THEY WON'T KNOW.
SO DON'T FUCK IT UP.
"DON'T FUCK IT UP?"
THAT'S THE PLAN?
HOW DO WE START?

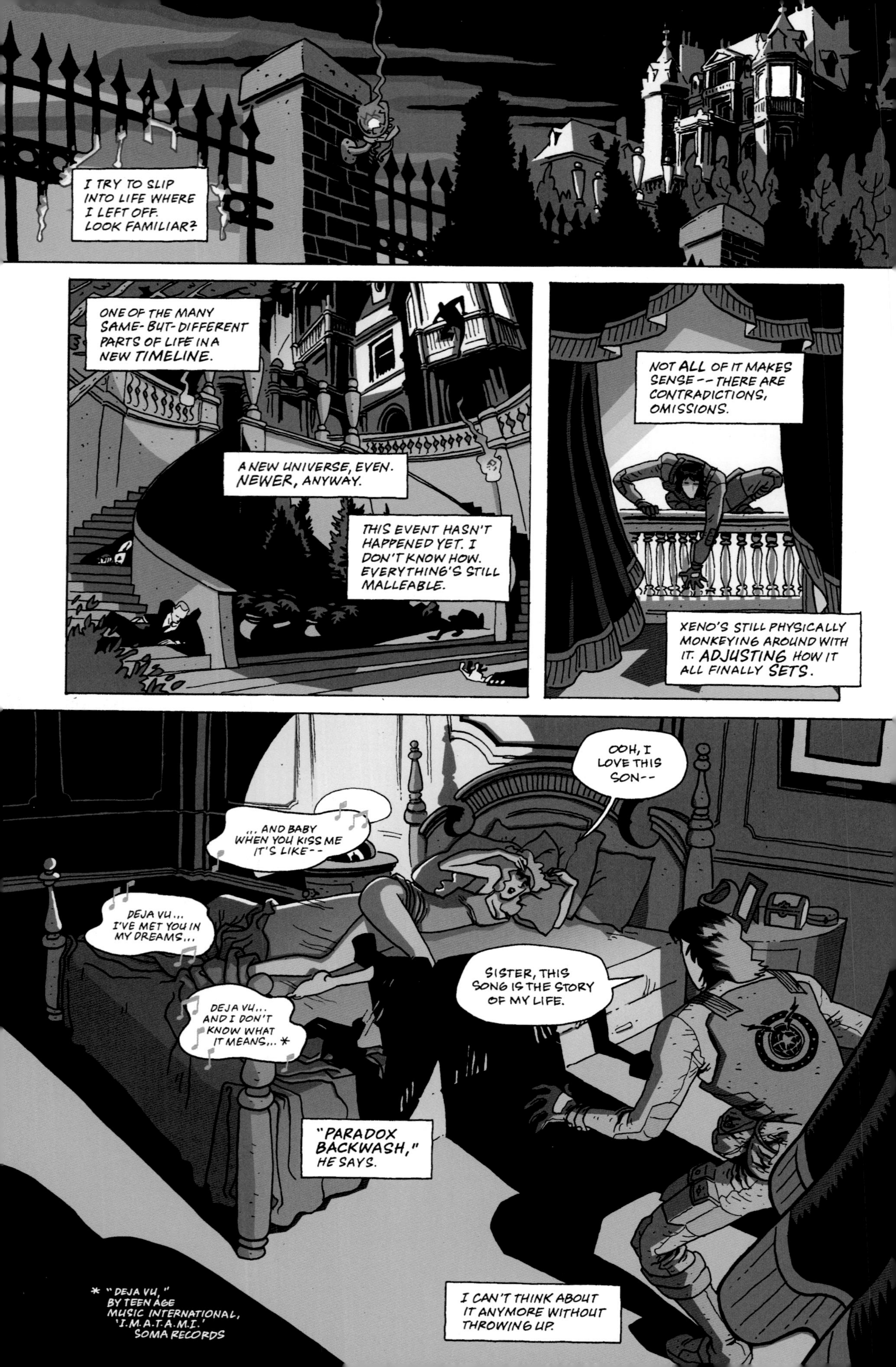
I TRY TO SLIP INTO LIFE WHERE I LEFT OFF. LOOK FAMILIAR?
ONE OF THE MANY SAME-BUT-DIFFERENT PARTS OF LIFE IN A NEW TIMELINE.
A NEW UNIVERSE, EVEN. NEWER, ANYWAY.
THIS EVENT HASN'T HAPPENED YET. I DON'T KNOW HOW. EVERYTHING'S STILL MALLEABLE.
NOT ALL OF IT MAKES SENSE--THERE ARE CONTRADICTIONS, OMISSIONS.
XENO'S STILL PHYSICALLY MONKEYING AROUND WITH IT. ADJUSTING HOW IT ALL FINALLY SETS.
...AND BABY WHEN YOU KISS ME IT'S LIKE--
OOH, I LOVE THIS SON--
DEJA VU... I'VE MET YOU IN MY DREAMS...
DEJA VU... AND I DON'T KNOW WHAT IT MEANS... *
SISTER, THIS SONG IS THE STORY OF MY LIFE.
"PARADOX BACKWASH," HE SAYS.
* "DEJA VU," BY TEEN AGE MUSIC INTERNATIONAL, 'I.M.A.T.A.M.I.' SOMA RECORDS
I CAN'T THINK ABOUT IT ANYMORE WITHOUT THROWING UP.

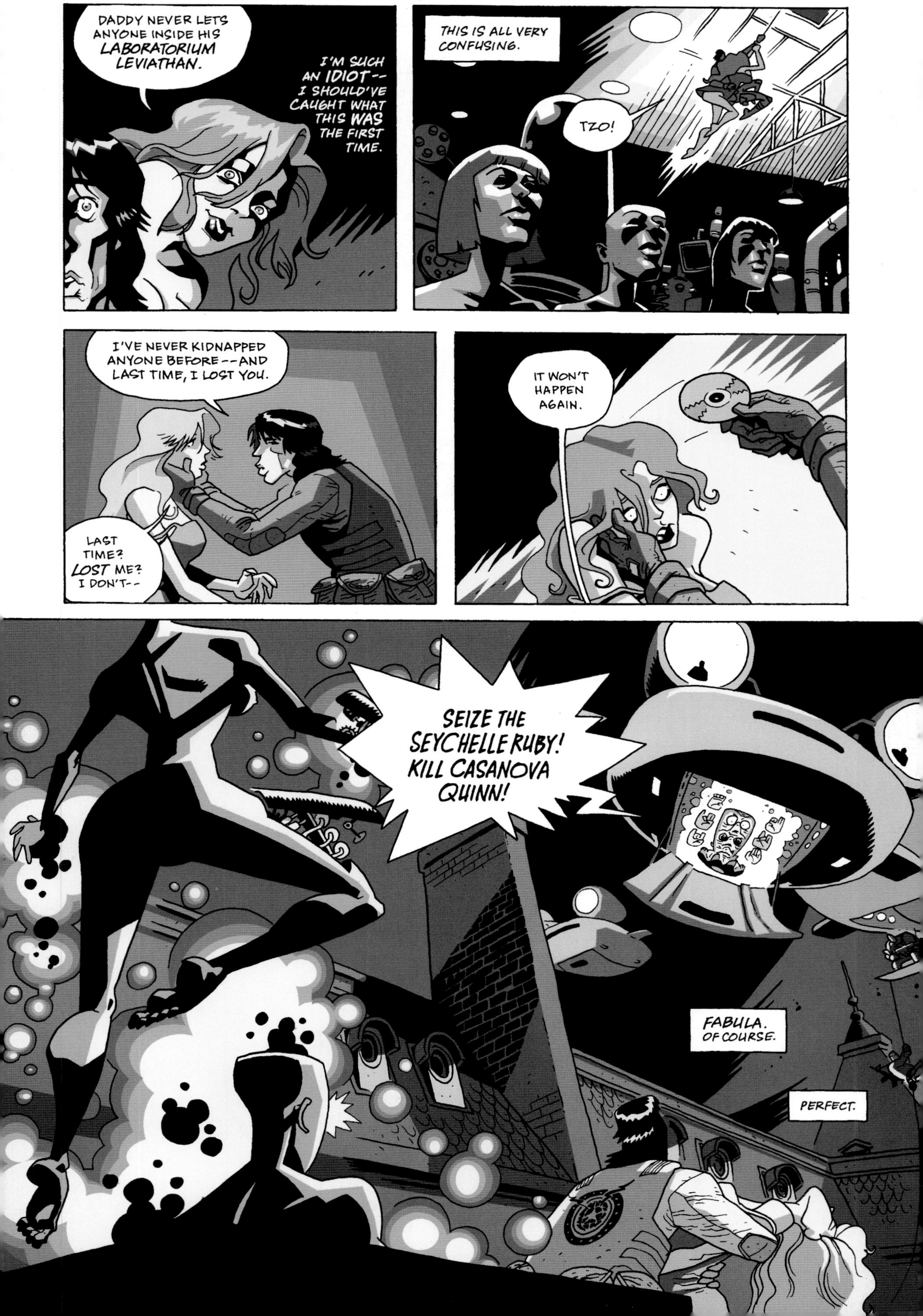
DADDY NEVER LETS ANYONE INSIDE HIS LABORATORIUM LEVIATHAN.
I'M SUCH AN IDIOT-- I SHOULD'VE CAUGHT WHAT THIS WAS THE FIRST TIME.
THIS IS ALL VERY CONFUSING.
TZO!
I'VE NEVER KIDNAPPED ANYONE BEFORE--AND LAST TIME, I LOST YOU.
LAST TIME? LOST ME? I DON'T--
IT WON'T HAPPEN AGAIN.
SEIZE THE SEYCHELLE RUBY! KILL CASANOVA QUINN!
FABULA. OF COURSE.
PERFECT.

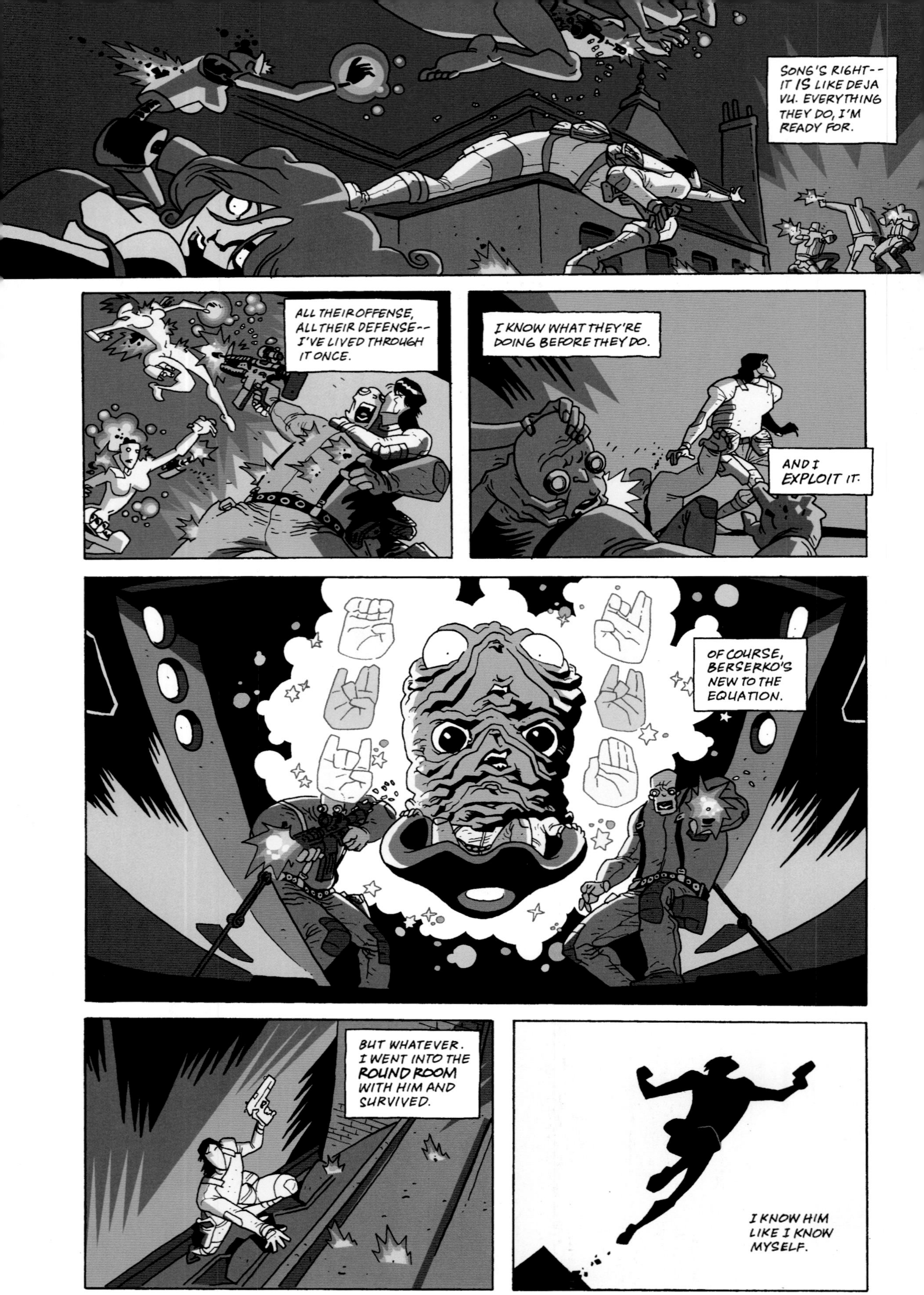
SONG'S RIGHT--
IT IS LIKE DEJA VU. EVERYTHING THEY DO, I'M READY FOR.
ALL THEIR OFFENSE, ALL THEIR DEFENSE--
I'VE LIVED THROUGH IT ONCE.
I KNOW WHAT THEY'RE DOING BEFORE THEY DO.
AND I EXPLOIT IT.
OF COURSE, BERSERKO'S NEW TO THE EQUATION.
BUT WHATEVER.
I WENT INTO THE ROUND ROOM WITH HIM AND SURVIVED.
I KNOW HIM LIKE I KNOW MYSELF.

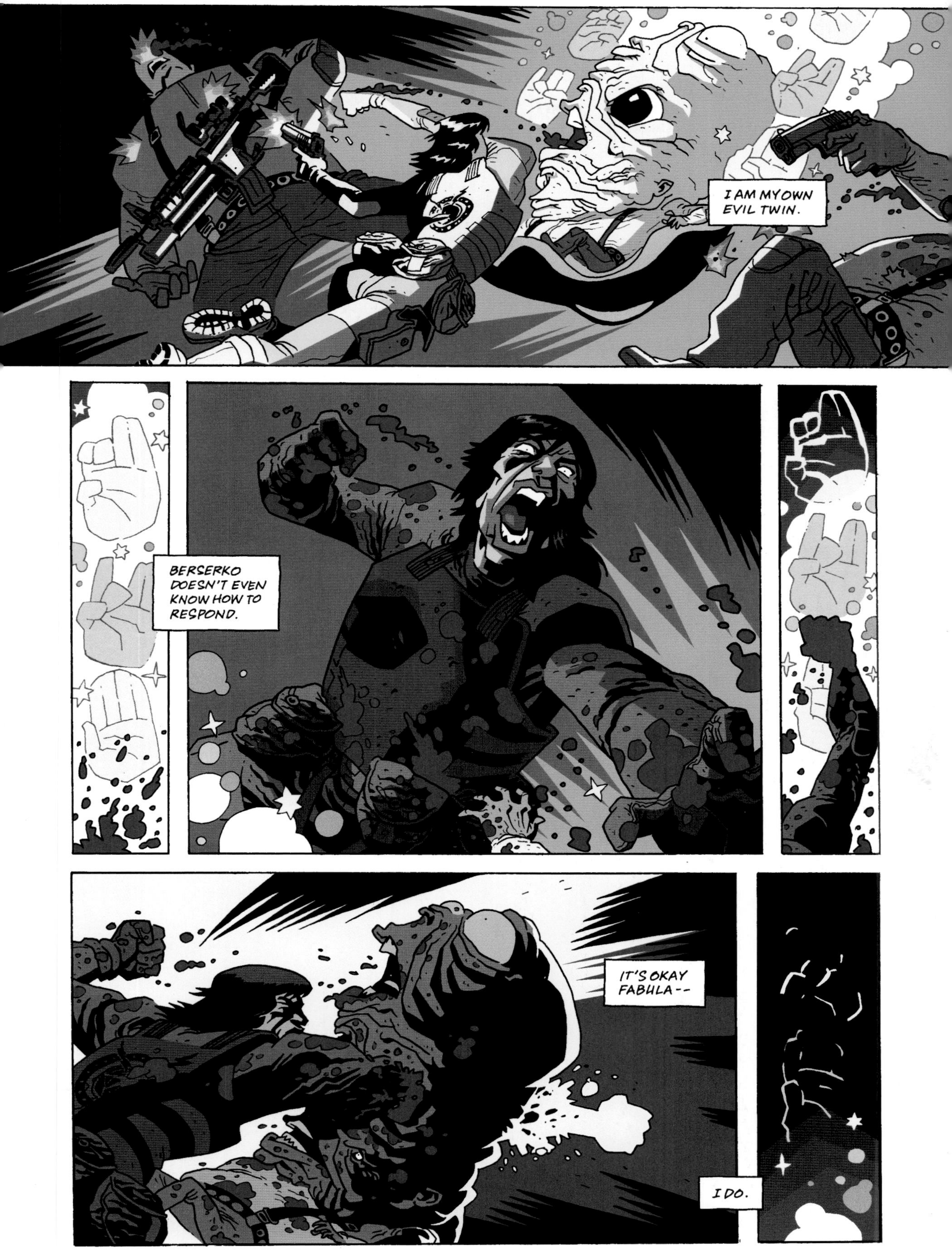
I AM MY OWN EVIL TWIN.
BERSERKO DOESN'T EVEN KNOW HOW TO RESPOND.
IT'S OKAY FABULA--
I DO.

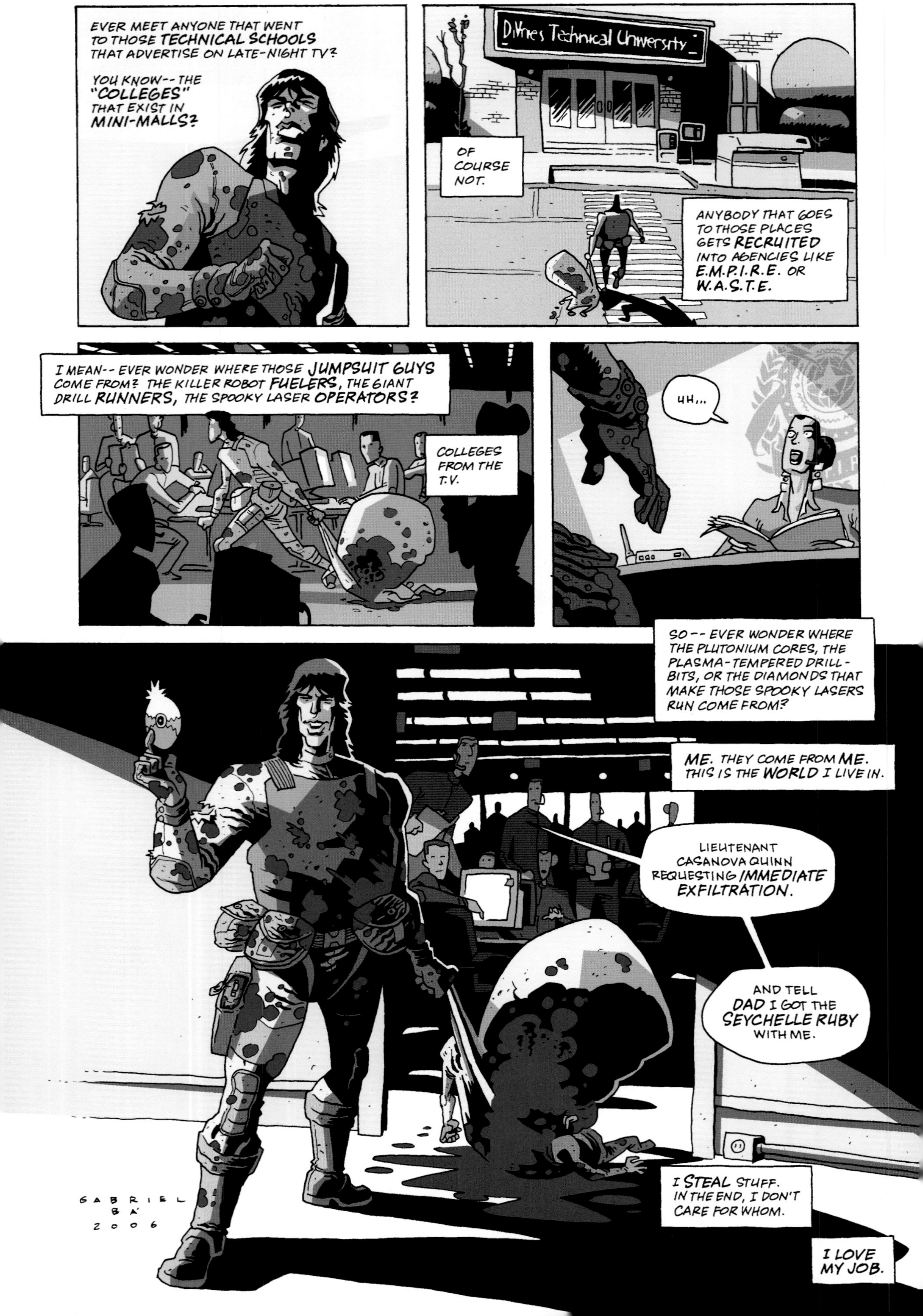
EVER MEET ANYONE THAT WENT TO THOSE TECHNICAL SCHOOLS THAT ADVERTISE ON LATE-NIGHT TV?
YOU KNOW-- THE "COLLEGES" THAT EXIST IN MINI-MALLS?
DiVries Technical University
OF COURSE NOT.
ANYBODY THAT GOES TO THOSE PLACES GETS RECRUITED INTO AGENCIES LIKE E.M.P.I.R.E. OR W.A.S.T.E.
I MEAN-- EVER WONDER WHERE THOSE JUMPSUIT GUYS COME FROM? THE KILLER ROBOT FUELERS, THE GIANT DRILL RUNNERS, THE SPOOKY LASER OPERATORS?
COLLEGES FROM THE T.V.
UH...
SO-- EVER WONDER WHERE THE PLUTONIUM CORES, THE PLASMA-TEMPERED DRILL-BITS, OR THE DIAMONDS THAT MAKE THOSE SPOOKY LASERS RUN COME FROM?
ME. THEY COME FROM ME. THIS IS THE WORLD I LIVE IN.
LIEUTENANT CASANOVA QUINN REQUESTING IMMEDIATE EXFILTRATION.
AND TELL DAD I GOT THE SEYCHELLE RUBY WITH ME.
GABRIEL BÁ 2006
I STEAL STUFF. IN THE END, I DON'T CARE FOR WHOM.
I LOVE MY JOB.

EXECUTION DAYS

PRETTY LITTLE POLICEMAN

MISSION TO YERBA MUERTA

DÉTOURNEMENT

COLDHEART

WOMEN AND MEN (PART ONE)

WOMEN AND MEN (PART TWO)

I THINK I ALMOST LOVED HIM

IS THIS IT? (REDUX)

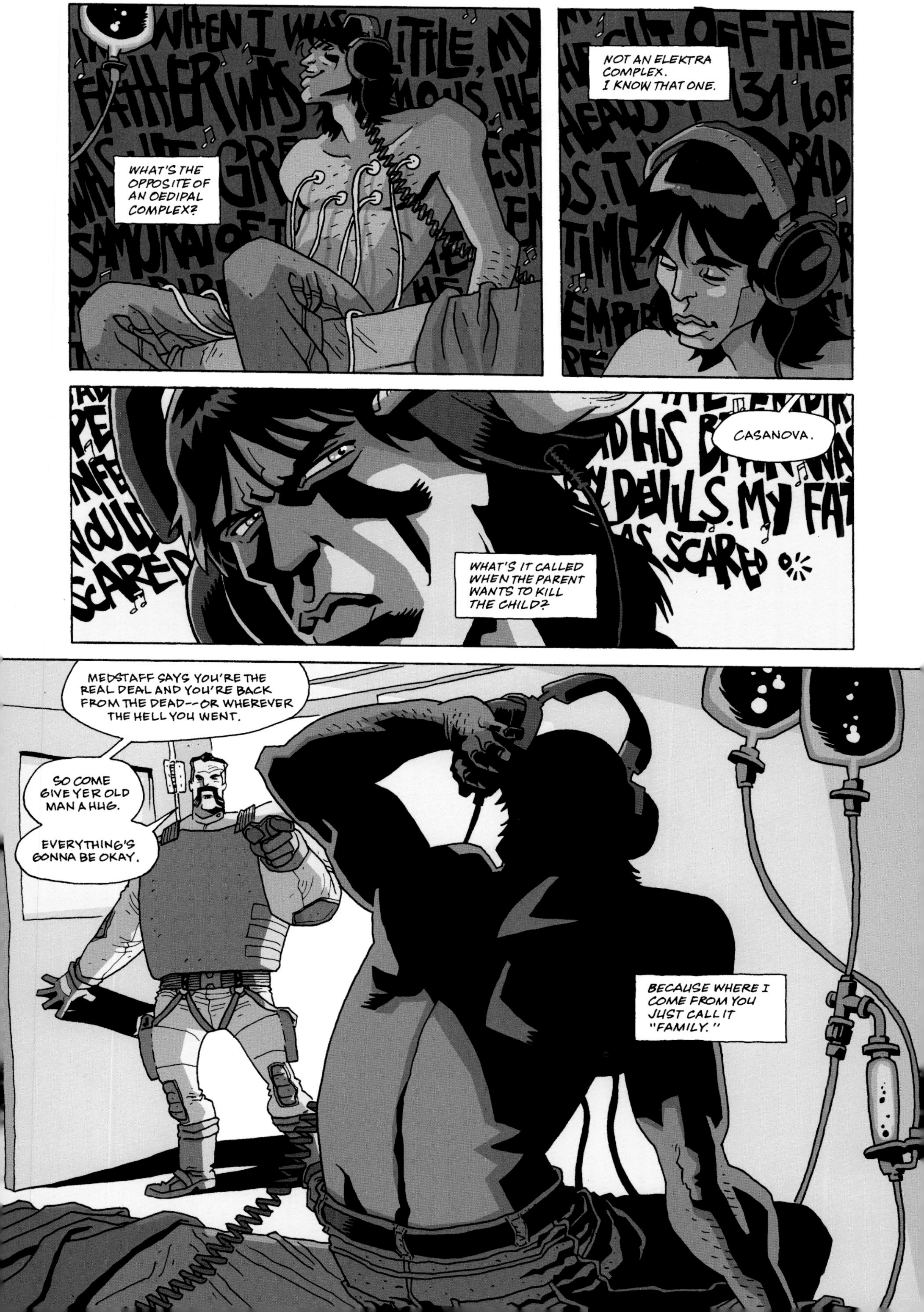
WHAT'S THE OPPOSITE OF AN OEDIPAL COMPLEX?
NOT AN ELEKTRA COMPLEX. I KNOW THAT ONE.
CASANOVA.
WHAT'S IT CALLED WHEN THE PARENT WANTS TO KILL THE CHILD?
MEDSTAFF SAYS YOU'RE THE REAL DEAL AND YOU'RE BACK FROM THE DEAD--OR WHEREVER THE HELL YOU WENT.
SO COME GIVE YER OLD MAN A HUG.
EVERYTHING'S GONNA BE OKAY.
BECAUSE WHERE I COME FROM YOU JUST CALL IT "FAMILY."

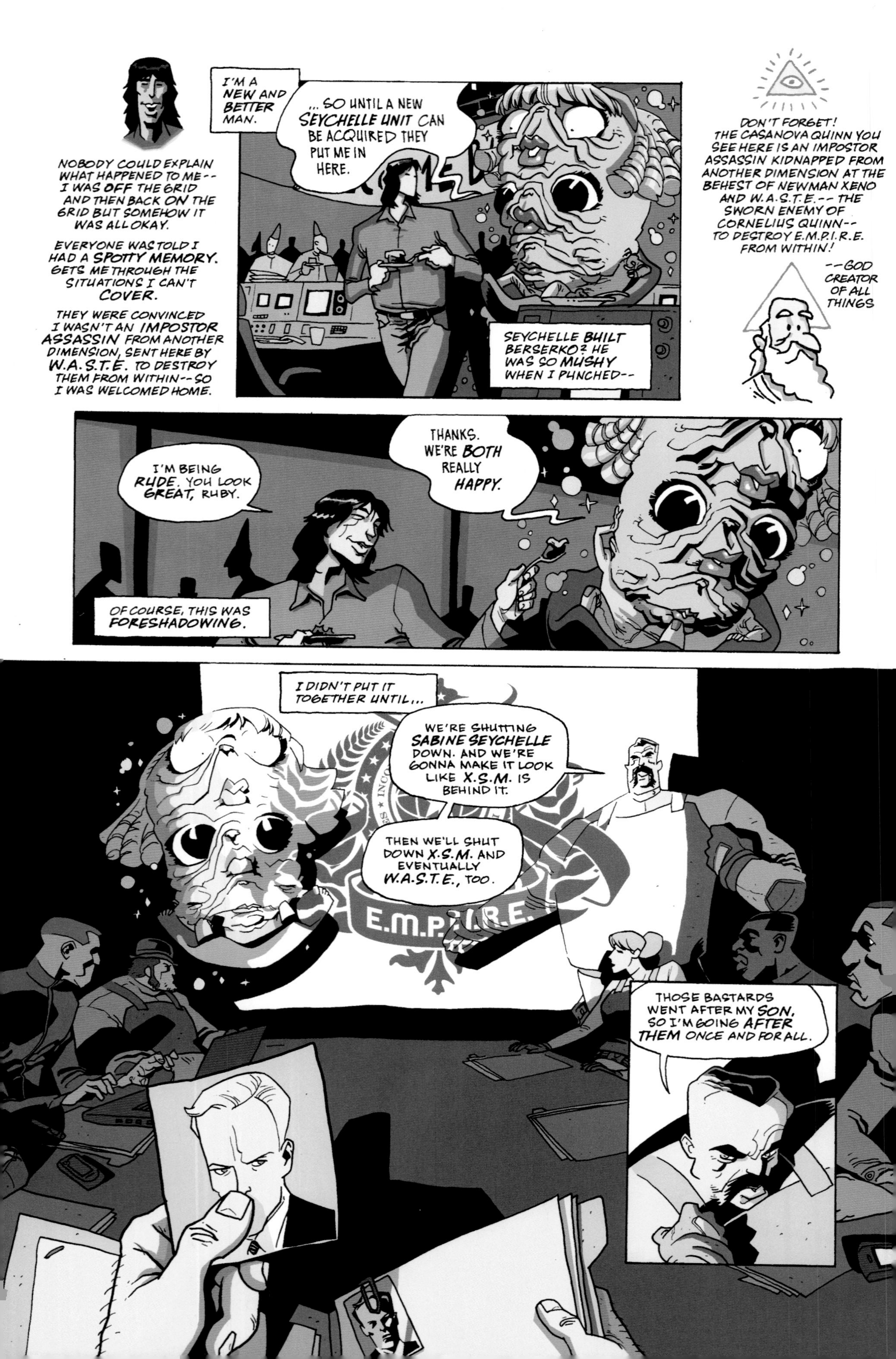
NOBODY COULD EXPLAIN WHAT HAPPENED TO ME-- I WAS OFF THE GRID AND THEN BACK ON THE GRID BUT SOMEHOW IT WAS ALL OKAY.
EVERYONE WAS TOLD I HAD A SPOTTY MEMORY. GETS ME THROUGH THE SITUATIONS I CAN'T COVER.
THEY WERE CONVINCED I WASN'T AN IMPOSTOR ASSASSIN FROM ANOTHER DIMENSION, SENT HERE BY W.A.S.T.E. TO DESTROY THEM FROM WITHIN--SO I WAS WELCOMED HOME.
I'M A NEW AND BETTER MAN.
...SO UNTIL A NEW SEYCHELLE UNIT CAN BE ACQUIRED THEY PUT ME IN HERE.
SEYCHELLE BUILT BERSERKO? HE WAS SO MUSHY WHEN I PUNCHED--
DON'T FORGET! THE CASANOVA QUINN YOU SEE HERE IS AN IMPOSTOR ASSASSIN KIDNAPPED FROM ANOTHER DIMENSION AT THE BEHEST OF NEWMAN XENO AND W.A.S.T.E.-- THE SWORN ENEMY OF CORNELIUS QUINN-- TO DESTROY E.M.P.I.R.E. FROM WITHIN!
--GOD CREATOR OF ALL THINGS
I'M BEING RUDE. YOU LOOK GREAT, RUBY.
THANKS. WE'RE BOTH REALLY HAPPY.
OF COURSE, THIS WAS FORESHADOWING.
I DIDN'T PUT IT TOGETHER UNTIL...
WE'RE SHUTTING SABINE SEYCHELLE DOWN. AND WE'RE GONNA MAKE IT LOOK LIKE X.S.M. IS BEHIND IT.
THEN WE'LL SHUT DOWN X.S.M. AND EVENTUALLY W.A.S.T.E., TOO.
E.M.P.I.R.E.
THOSE BASTARDS WENT AFTER MY SON, SO I'M GOING AFTER THEM ONCE AND FOR ALL.

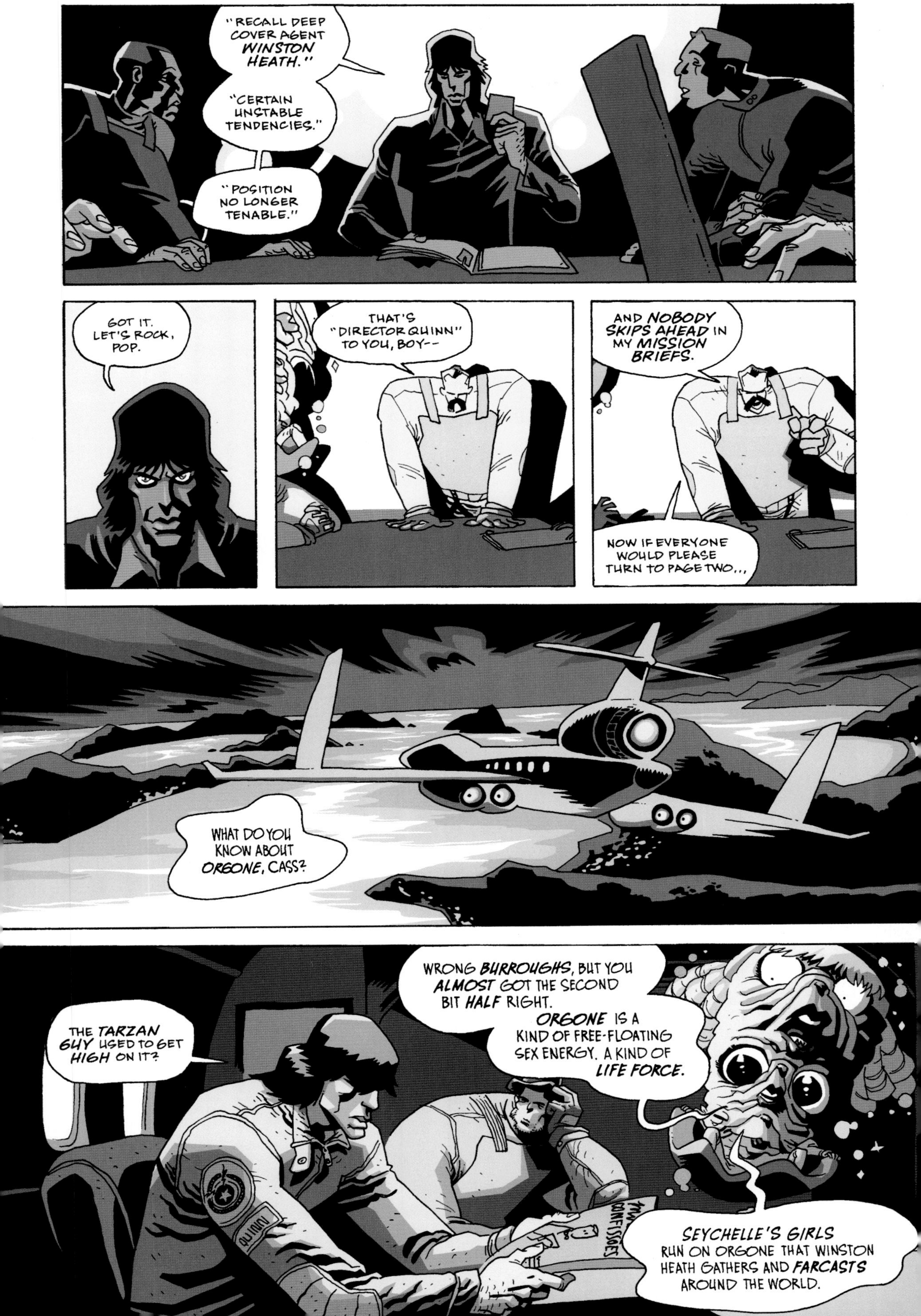
"RECALL DEEP COVER AGENT WINSTON HEATH."
"CERTAIN UNSTABLE TENDENCIES."
"POSITION NO LONGER TENABLE."
GOT IT. LET'S ROCK, POP.
THAT'S "DIRECTOR QUINN" TO YOU, BOY--
AND NOBODY SKIPS AHEAD IN MY MISSION BRIEFS.
NOW IF EVERYONE WOULD PLEASE TURN TO PAGE TWO...
WHAT DO YOU KNOW ABOUT ORGONE, CASS?
THE TARZAN GUY USED TO GET HIGH ON IT?
WRONG BURROUGHS, BUT YOU ALMOST GOT THE SECOND BIT HALF RIGHT.
ORGONE IS A KIND OF FREE-FLOATING SEX ENERGY. A KIND OF LIFE FORCE.
SEYCHELLE'S GIRLS RUN ON ORGONE THAT WINSTON HEATH GATHERS AND FARCASTS AROUND THE WORLD.

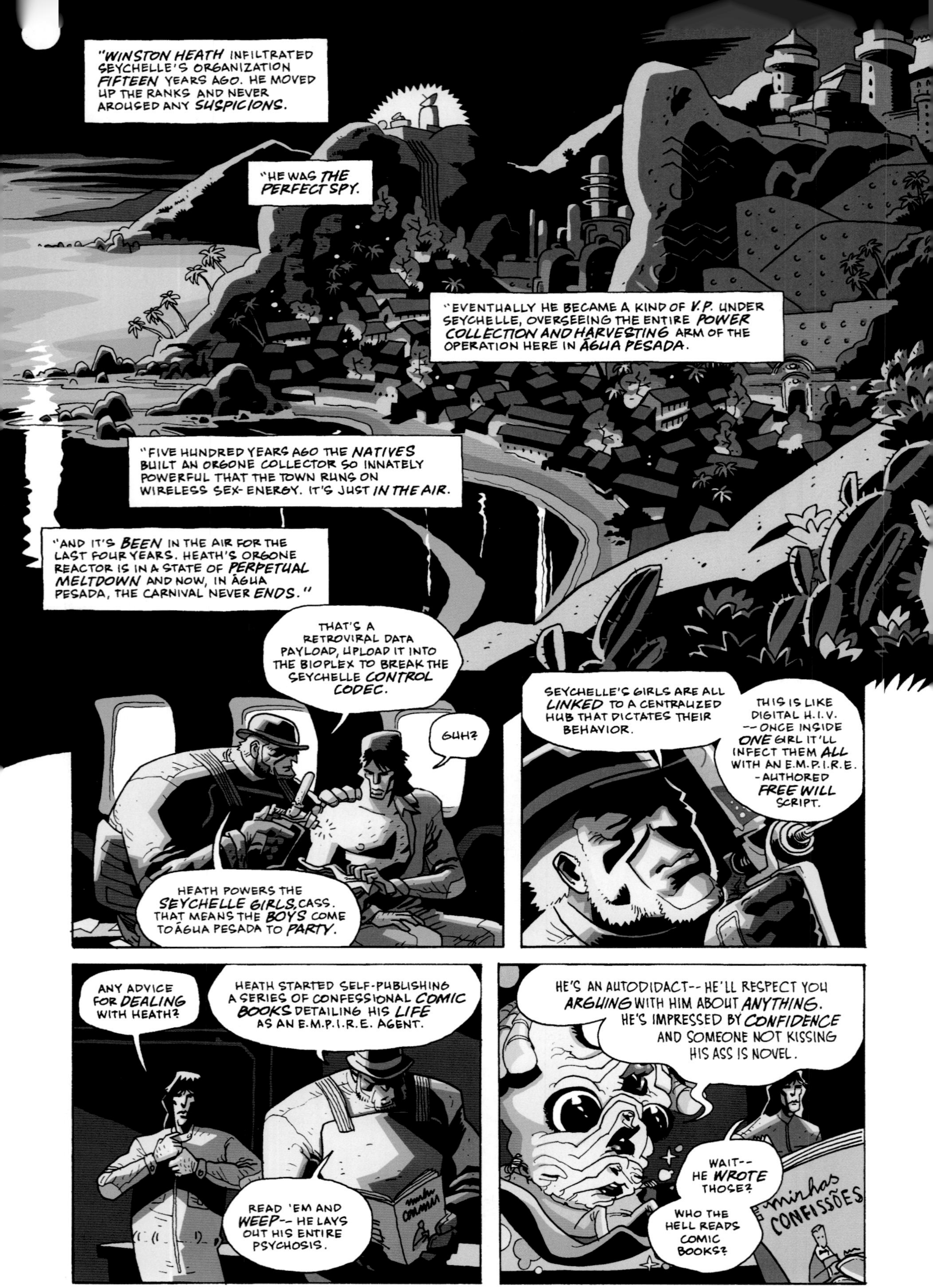
"WINSTON HEATH INFILTRATED SEYCHELLE'S ORGANIZATION FIFTEEN YEARS AGO. HE MOVED UP THE RANKS AND NEVER AROUSED ANY SUSPICIONS.
"HE WAS THE PERFECT SPY.
"EVENTUALLY HE BECAME A KIND OF V.P. UNDER SEYCHELLE, OVERSEEING THE ENTIRE POWER COLLECTION AND HARVESTING ARM OF THE OPERATION HERE IN ÁGUA PESADA.
"FIVE HUNDRED YEARS AGO THE NATIVES BUILT AN ORGONE COLLECTOR SO INNATELY POWERFUL THAT THE TOWN RUNS ON WIRELESS SEX-ENERGY. IT'S JUST IN THE AIR.
"AND IT'S BEEN IN THE AIR FOR THE LAST FOUR YEARS. HEATH'S ORGONE REACTOR IS IN A STATE OF PERPETUAL MELTDOWN AND NOW, IN ÁGUA PESADA, THE CARNIVAL NEVER ENDS."
THAT'S A RETROVIRAL DATA PAYLOAD, UPLOAD IT INTO THE BIOPLEX TO BREAK THE SEYCHELLE CONTROL CODEC.
GUH?
HEATH POWERS THE SEYCHELLE GIRLS, CASS. THAT MEANS THE BOYS COME TO ÁGUA PESADA TO PARTY.
SEYCHELLE'S GIRLS ARE ALL LINKED TO A CENTRALIZED HUB THAT DICTATES THEIR BEHAVIOR.
THIS IS LIKE DIGITAL H.I.V. --ONCE INSIDE ONE GIRL IT'LL INFECT THEM ALL WITH AN E.M.P.I.R.E. -AUTHORED FREE WILL SCRIPT.
ANY ADVICE FOR DEALING WITH HEATH?
HEATH STARTED SELF-PUBLISHING A SERIES OF CONFESSIONAL COMIC BOOKS DETAILING HIS LIFE AS AN E.M.P.I.R.E. AGENT.
READ 'EM AND WEEP-- HE LAYS OUT HIS ENTIRE PSYCHOSIS.
HE'S AN AUTODIDACT-- HE'LL RESPECT YOU ARGUING WITH HIM ABOUT ANYTHING. HE'S IMPRESSED BY CONFIDENCE AND SOMEONE NOT KISSING HIS ASS IS NOVEL.
WAIT-- HE WROTE THOSE?
WHO THE HELL READS COMIC BOOKS?
minhas CONFISSÕES

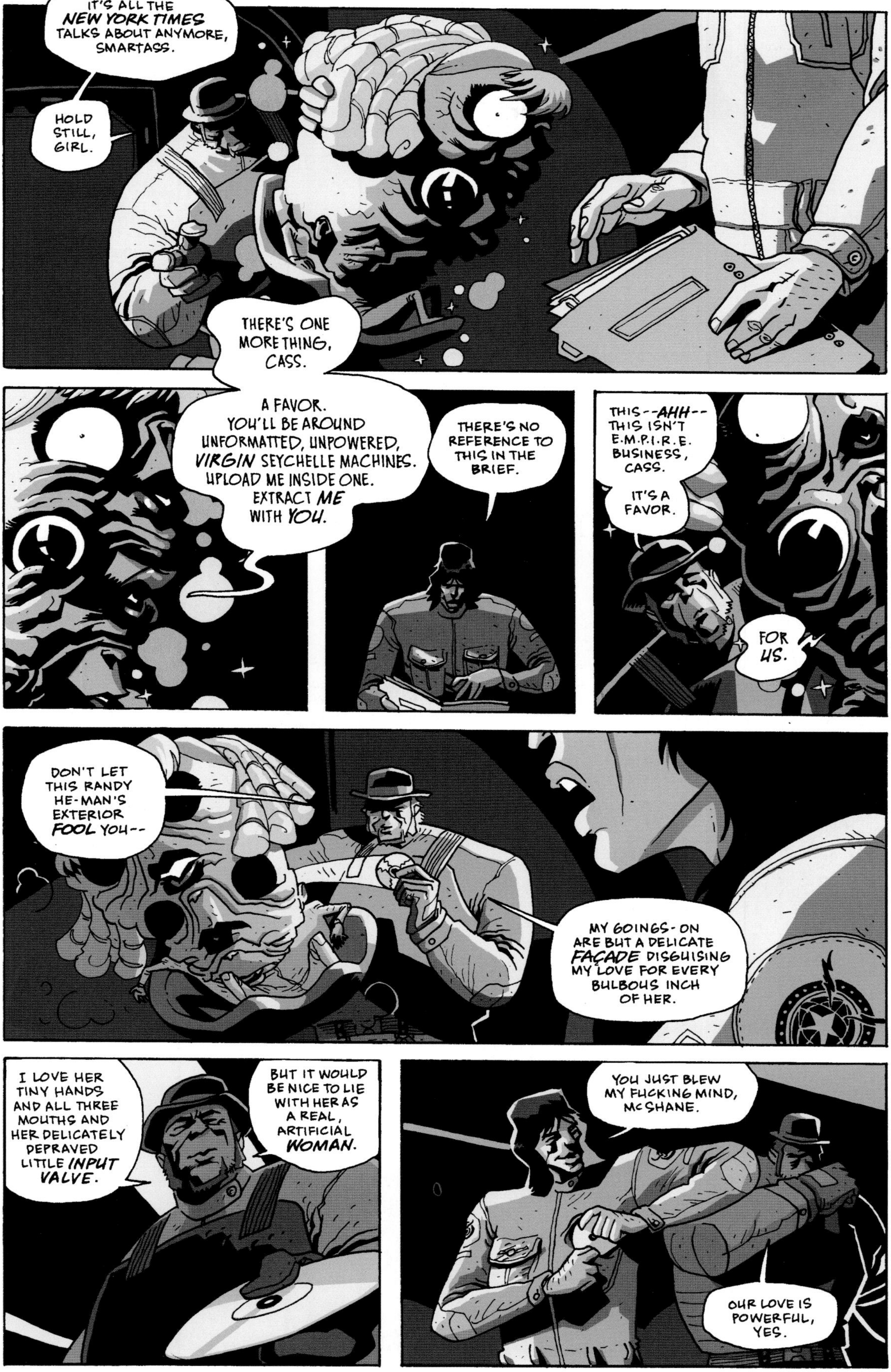
IT'S ALL THE NEW YORK TIMES TALKS ABOUT ANYMORE, SMARTASS.
HOLD STILL, GIRL.
THERE'S ONE MORE THING, CASS.
A FAVOR. YOU'LL BE AROUND UNFORMATTED, UNPOWERED, VIRGIN SEYCHELLE MACHINES. UPLOAD ME INSIDE ONE. EXTRACT ME WITH YOU.
THERE'S NO REFERENCE TO THIS IN THE BRIEF.
THIS--AHH--THIS ISN'T E.M.P.I.R.E. BUSINESS, CASS.
IT'S A FAVOR.
FOR US.
DON'T LET THIS RANDY HE-MAN'S EXTERIOR FOOL YOU--
MY GOINGS-ON ARE BUT A DELICATE FAÇADE DISGUISING MY LOVE FOR EVERY BULBOUS INCH OF HER.
I LOVE HER TINY HANDS AND ALL THREE MOUTHS AND HER DELICATELY DEPRAVED LITTLE INPUT VALVE.
BUT IT WOULD BE NICE TO LIE WITH HER AS A REAL, ARTIFICIAL WOMAN.
YOU JUST BLEW MY FUCKING MIND, McSHANE.
OUR LOVE IS POWERFUL, YES.

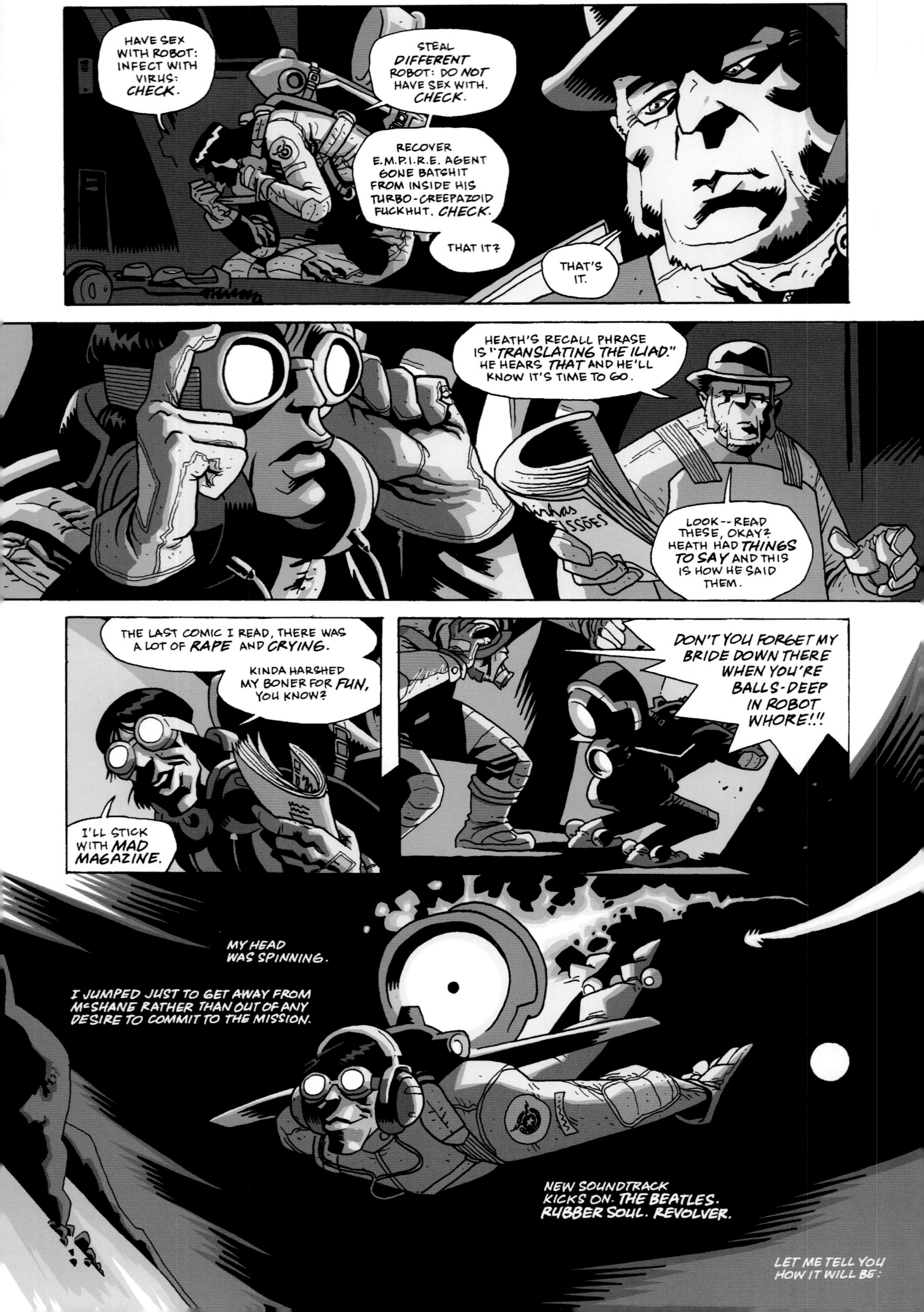
HAVE SEX WITH ROBOT: INFECT WITH VIRUS: CHECK.
STEAL DIFFERENT ROBOT: DO NOT HAVE SEX WITH. CHECK.
RECOVER E.M.P.I.R.E. AGENT GONE BATSHIT FROM INSIDE HIS TURBO-CREEPAZOID FUCKHUT. CHECK.
THAT IT?
THAT'S IT.
HEATH'S RECALL PHRASE IS "TRANSLATING THE ILIAD." HE HEARS THAT AND HE'LL KNOW IT'S TIME TO GO.
LOOK--READ THESE, OKAY? HEATH HAD THINGS TO SAY AND THIS IS HOW HE SAID THEM.
THE LAST COMIC I READ, THERE WAS A LOT OF RAPE AND CRYING.
KINDA HARSHED MY BONER FOR FUN, YOU KNOW?
I'LL STICK WITH MAD MAGAZINE.
DON'T YOU FORGET MY BRIDE DOWN THERE WHEN YOU'RE BALLS-DEEP IN ROBOT WHORE!!!
MY HEAD WAS SPINNING.
I JUMPED JUST TO GET AWAY FROM McSHANE RATHER THAN OUT OF ANY DESIRE TO COMMIT TO THE MISSION.
NEW SOUNDTRACK KICKS ON. THE BEATLES. RUBBER SOUL. REVOLVER.
LET ME TELL YOU HOW IT WILL BE:

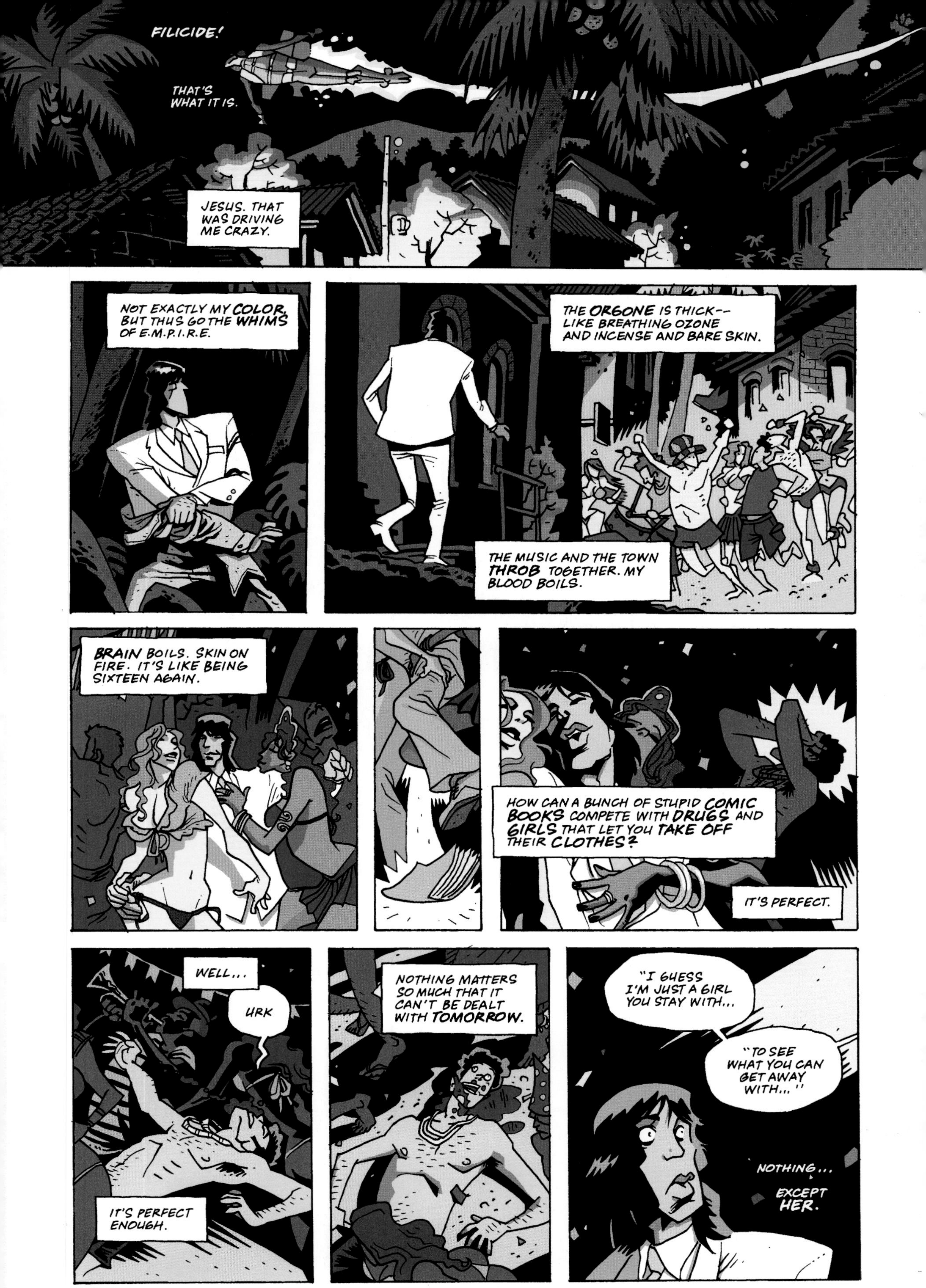
FILICIDE!
THAT'S WHAT IT IS.
JESUS. THAT WAS DRIVING ME CRAZY.
NOT EXACTLY MY COLOR, BUT THUS GO THE WHIMS OF E.M.P.I.R.E.
THE ORGONE IS THICK-- LIKE BREATHING OZONE AND INCENSE AND BARE SKIN.
THE MUSIC AND THE TOWN THROB TOGETHER. MY BLOOD BOILS.
BRAIN BOILS. SKIN ON FIRE. IT'S LIKE BEING SIXTEEN AGAIN.
HOW CAN A BUNCH OF STUPID COMIC BOOKS COMPETE WITH DRUGS AND GIRLS THAT LET YOU TAKE OFF THEIR CLOTHES?
IT'S PERFECT.
WELL...
URK
IT'S PERFECT ENOUGH.
NOTHING MATTERS SO MUCH THAT IT CAN'T BE DEALT WITH TOMORROW.
"I GUESS I'M JUST A GIRL YOU STAY WITH...
"TO SEE WHAT YOU CAN GET AWAY WITH..."
NOTHING...
EXCEPT HER.

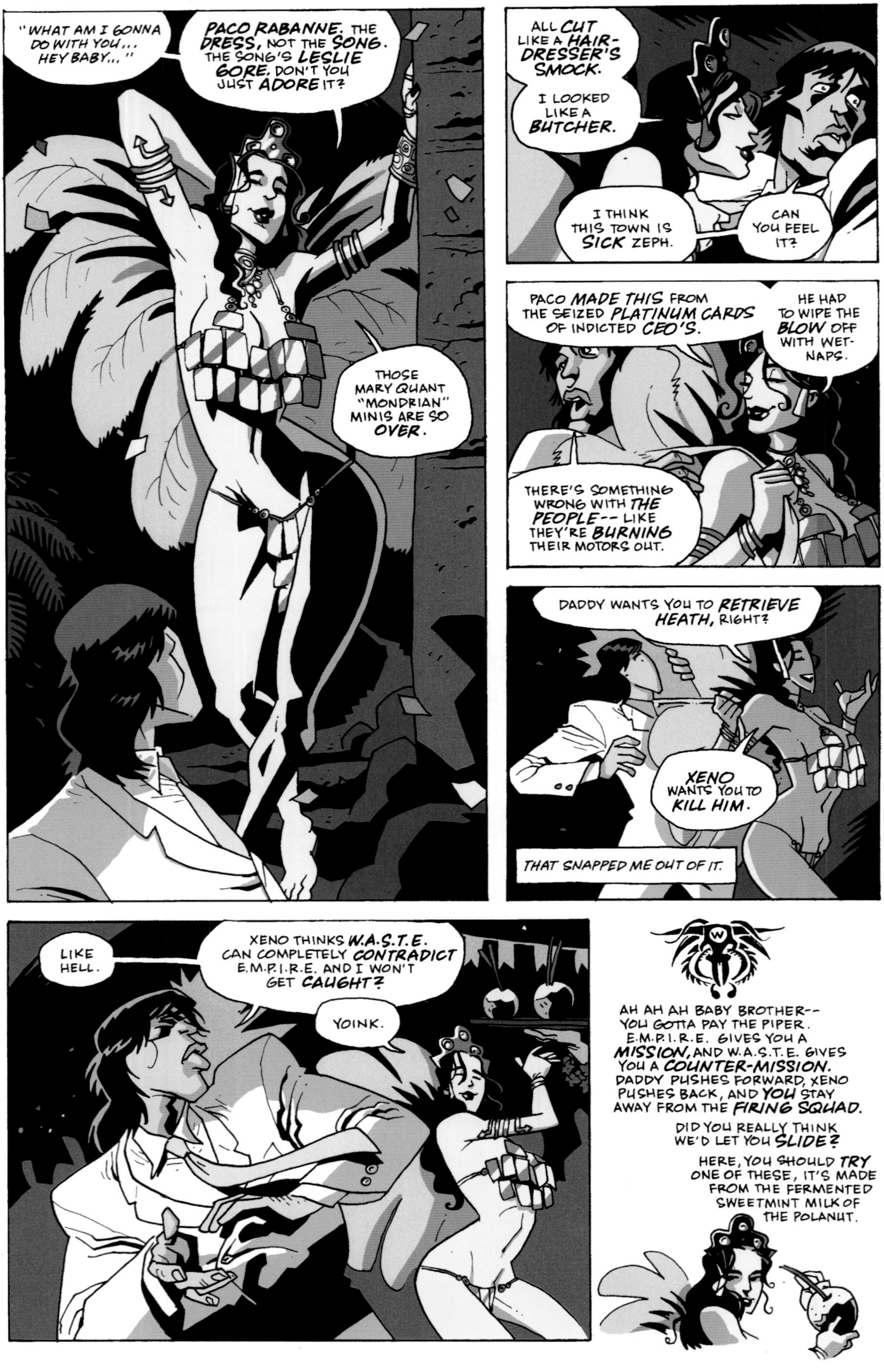
"WHAT AM I GONNA DO WITH YOU... HEY BABY..."
PACO RABANNE. THE DRESS, NOT THE SONG. THE SONG'S LESLIE GORE. DON'T YOU JUST ADORE IT?
THOSE MARY QUANT "MONDRIAN" MINIS ARE SO OVER.
ALL CUT LIKE A HAIR-DRESSER'S SMOCK.
I LOOKED LIKE A BUTCHER.
I THINK THIS TOWN IS SICK ZEPH.
CAN YOU FEEL IT?
PACO MADE THIS FROM THE SEIZED PLATINUM CARDS OF INDICTED CEO'S.
HE HAD TO WIPE THE BLOW OFF WITH WET-NAPS.
THERE'S SOMETHING WRONG WITH THE PEOPLE-- LIKE THEY'RE BURNING THEIR MOTORS OUT.
DADDY WANTS YOU TO RETRIEVE HEATH, RIGHT?
XENO WANTS YOU TO KILL HIM.
THAT SNAPPED ME OUT OF IT.
LIKE HELL.
XENO THINKS W.A.S.T.E. CAN COMPLETELY CONTRADICT E.M.P.I.R.E. AND I WON'T GET CAUGHT?
YOINK.
AH AH AH BABY BROTHER-- YOU GOTTA PAY THE PIPER. E.M.P.I.R.E. GIVES YOU A MISSION, AND W.A.S.T.E. GIVES YOU A COUNTER-MISSION. DADDY PUSHES FORWARD, XENO PUSHES BACK, AND YOU STAY AWAY FROM THE FIRING SQUAD.
DID YOU REALLY THINK WE'D LET YOU SLIDE?
HERE, YOU SHOULD TRY ONE OF THESE, IT'S MADE FROM THE FERMENTED SWEETMINT MILK OF THE POLANUT.

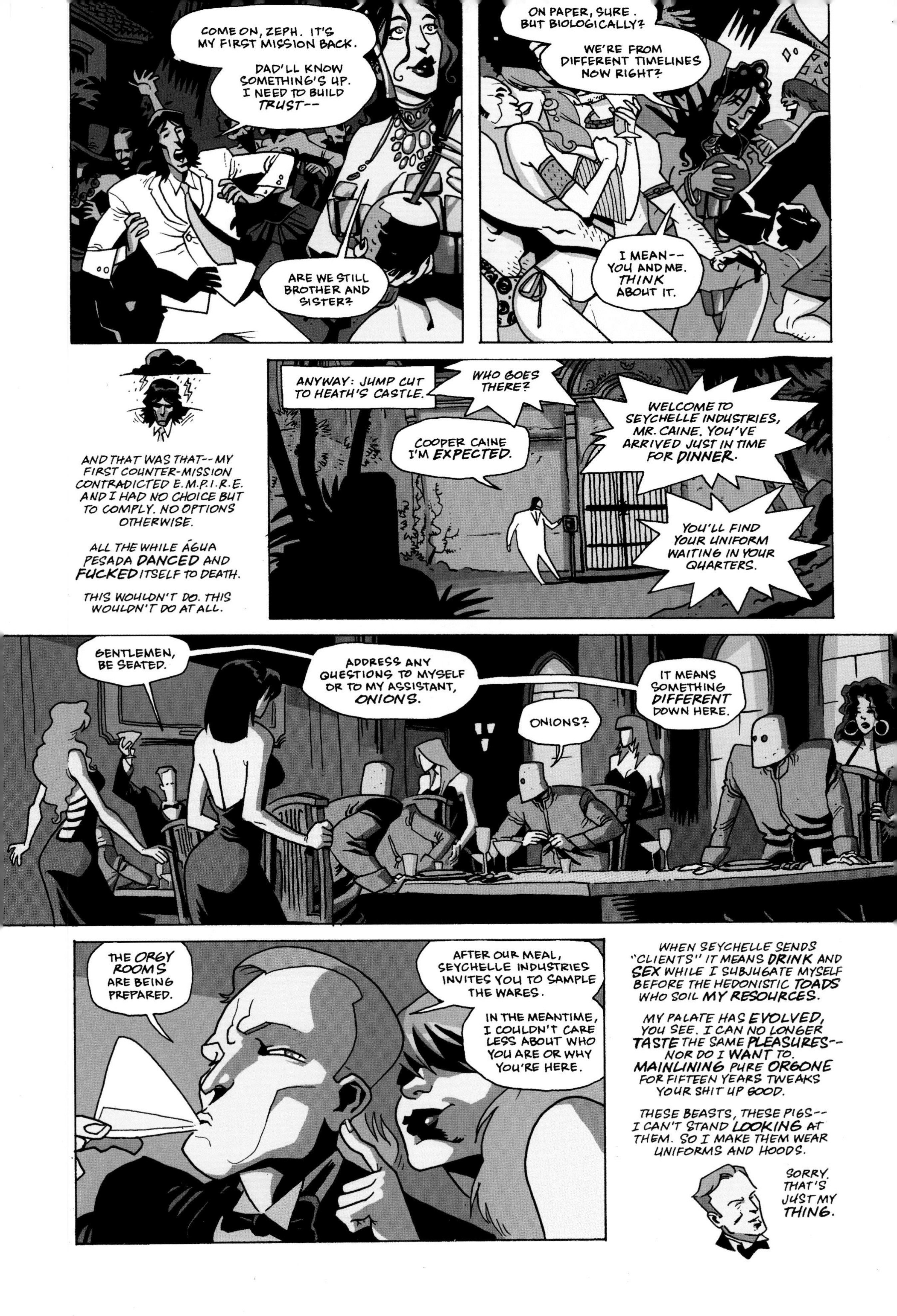
COME ON, ZEPH. IT'S MY FIRST MISSION BACK.
DAD'LL KNOW SOMETHING'S UP. I NEED TO BUILD TRUST--
ARE WE STILL BROTHER AND SISTER?
ON PAPER, SURE. BUT BIOLOGICALLY?
WE'RE FROM DIFFERENT TIMELINES NOW RIGHT?
I MEAN-- YOU AND ME. THINK ABOUT IT.
AND THAT WAS THAT-- MY FIRST COUNTER-MISSION CONTRADICTED E.M.P.I.R.E. AND I HAD NO CHOICE BUT TO COMPLY. NO OPTIONS OTHERWISE.
ALL THE WHILE ÁGUA PESADA DANCED AND FUCKED ITSELF TO DEATH.
THIS WOULDN'T DO. THIS WOULDN'T DO AT ALL.
ANYWAY: JUMP CUT TO HEATH'S CASTLE.
WHO GOES THERE?
COOPER CAINE I'M EXPECTED.
WELCOME TO SEYCHELLE INDUSTRIES, MR. CAINE. YOU'VE ARRIVED JUST IN TIME FOR DINNER.
YOU'LL FIND YOUR UNIFORM WAITING IN YOUR QUARTERS.
GENTLEMEN, BE SEATED.
ADDRESS ANY QUESTIONS TO MYSELF OR TO MY ASSISTANT, ONIONS.
ONIONS?
IT MEANS SOMETHING DIFFERENT DOWN HERE.
THE ORGY ROOMS ARE BEING PREPARED.
AFTER OUR MEAL, SEYCHELLE INDUSTRIES INVITES YOU TO SAMPLE THE WARES.
IN THE MEANTIME, I COULDN'T CARE LESS ABOUT WHO YOU ARE OR WHY YOU'RE HERE.
WHEN SEYCHELLE SENDS "CLIENTS" IT MEANS DRINK AND SEX WHILE I SUBJUGATE MYSELF BEFORE THE HEDONISTIC TOADS WHO SOIL MY RESOURCES.
MY PALATE HAS EVOLVED, YOU SEE. I CAN NO LONGER TASTE THE SAME PLEASURES-- NOR DO I WANT TO. MAINLINING PURE ORGONE FOR FIFTEEN YEARS TWEAKS YOUR SHIT UP GOOD.
THESE BEASTS, THESE PIGS-- I CAN'T STAND LOOKING AT THEM. SO I MAKE THEM WEAR UNIFORMS AND HOODS.
SORRY. THAT'S JUST MY THING.

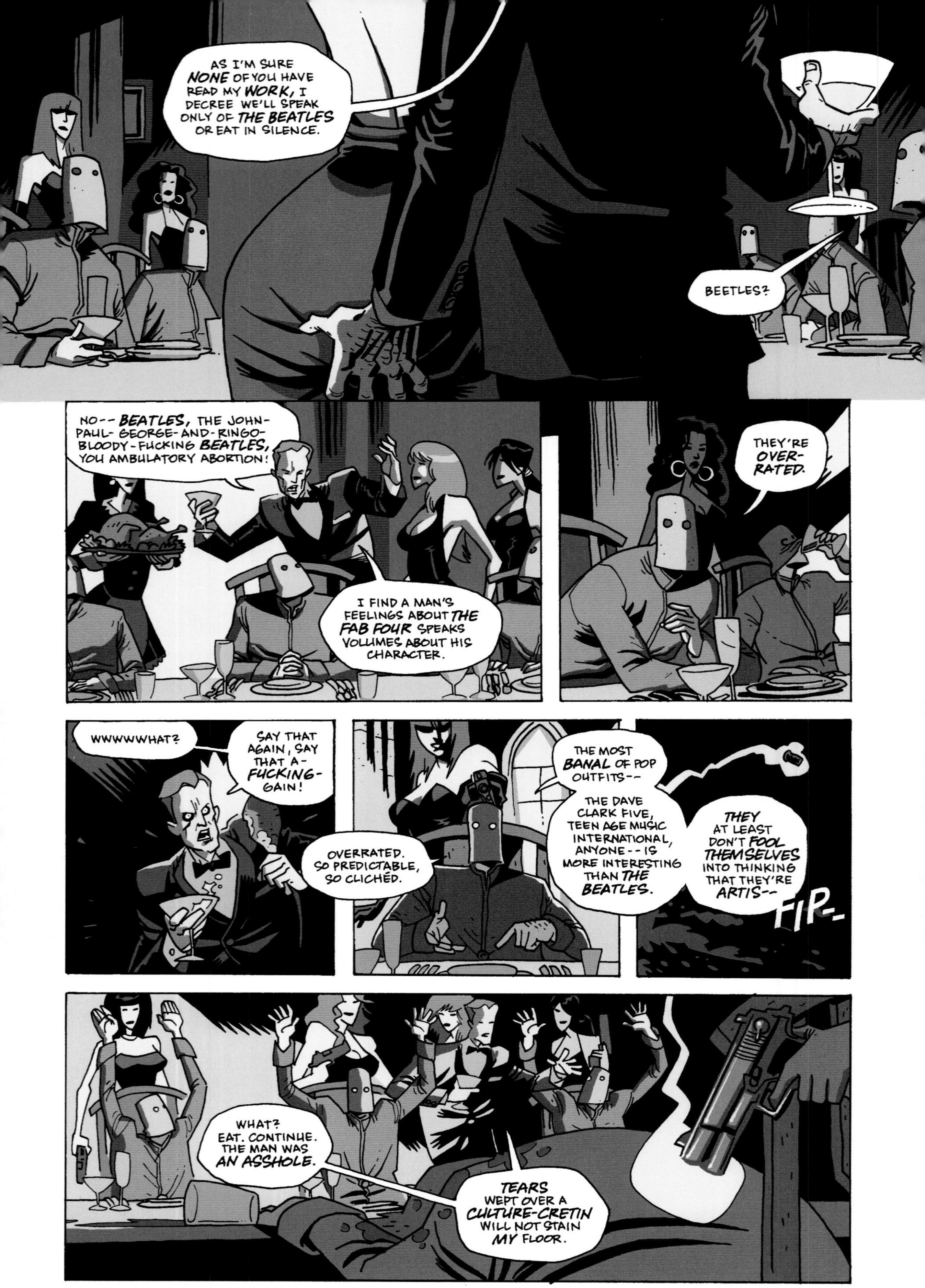
AS I'M SURE NONE OF YOU HAVE READ MY WORK, I DECREE WE'LL SPEAK ONLY OF THE BEATLES OR EAT IN SILENCE.
BEETLES?
NO-- BEATLES, THE JOHN-PAUL-GEORGE-AND-RINGO-BLOODY-FUCKING BEATLES, YOU AMBULATORY ABORTION!
I FIND A MAN'S FEELINGS ABOUT THE FAB FOUR SPEAKS VOLUMES ABOUT HIS CHARACTER.
THEY'RE OVER-RATED.
WWWWWHAT?
SAY THAT AGAIN, SAY THAT A-FUCKING-GAIN!
OVERRATED. SO PREDICTABLE, SO CLICHÉD.
THE MOST BANAL OF POP OUTFITS--
THE DAVE CLARK FIVE, TEEN AGE MUSIC INTERNATIONAL, ANYONE--IS MORE INTERESTING THAN THE BEATLES.
THEY AT LEAST DON'T FOOL THEMSELVES INTO THINKING THAT THEY'RE ARTIS--
FIP-
WHAT? EAT. CONTINUE. THE MAN WAS AN ASSHOLE.
TEARS WEPT OVER A CULTURE-CRETIN WILL NOT STAIN MY FLOOR.

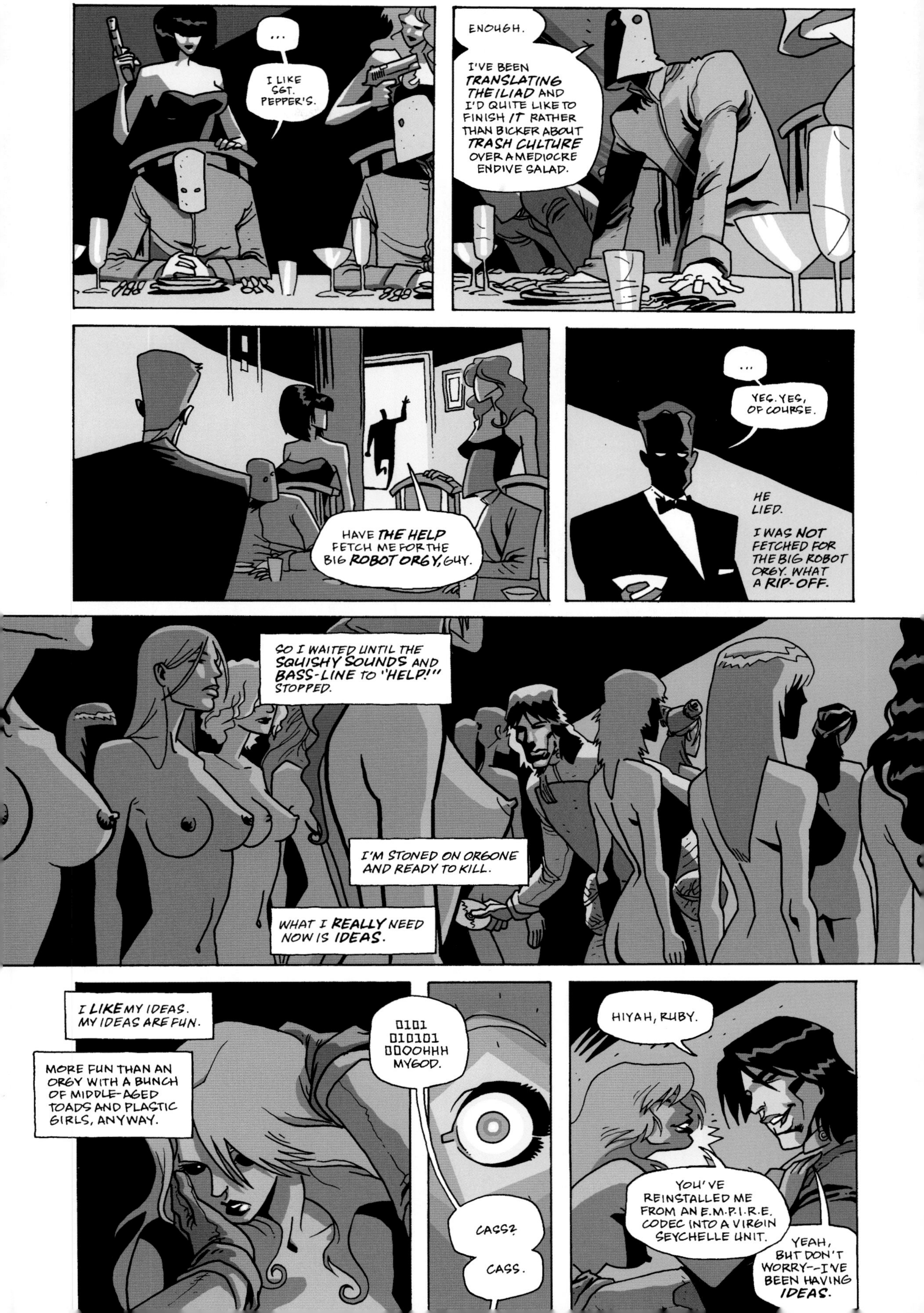
...
I LIKE SGT. PEPPER'S.
ENOUGH.
I'VE BEEN TRANSLATING THE ILIAD AND I'D QUITE LIKE TO FINISH IT RATHER THAN BICKER ABOUT TRASH CULTURE OVER A MEDIOCRE ENDIVE SALAD.
HAVE THE HELP FETCH ME FOR THE BIG ROBOT ORGY, GUY.
...
YES. YES, OF COURSE.
HE LIED.
I WAS NOT FETCHED FOR THE BIG ROBOT ORGY. WHAT A RIP-OFF.
SO I WAITED UNTIL THE SQUISHY SOUNDS AND BASS-LINE TO "HELP!" STOPPED.
I'M STONED ON ORGONE AND READY TO KILL.
WHAT I REALLY NEED NOW IS IDEAS.
I LIKE MY IDEAS. MY IDEAS ARE FUN.
MORE FUN THAN AN ORGY WITH A BUNCH OF MIDDLE-AGED TOADS AND PLASTIC GIRLS, ANYWAY.
0101 010101 OOOOHHH MYGOD.
CASS?
CASS.
HIYAH, RUBY.
YOU'VE REINSTALLED ME FROM AN E.M.P.I.R.E. CODEC INTO A VIRGIN SEYCHELLE UNIT.
YEAH, BUT DON'T WORRY--I'VE BEEN HAVING IDEAS.

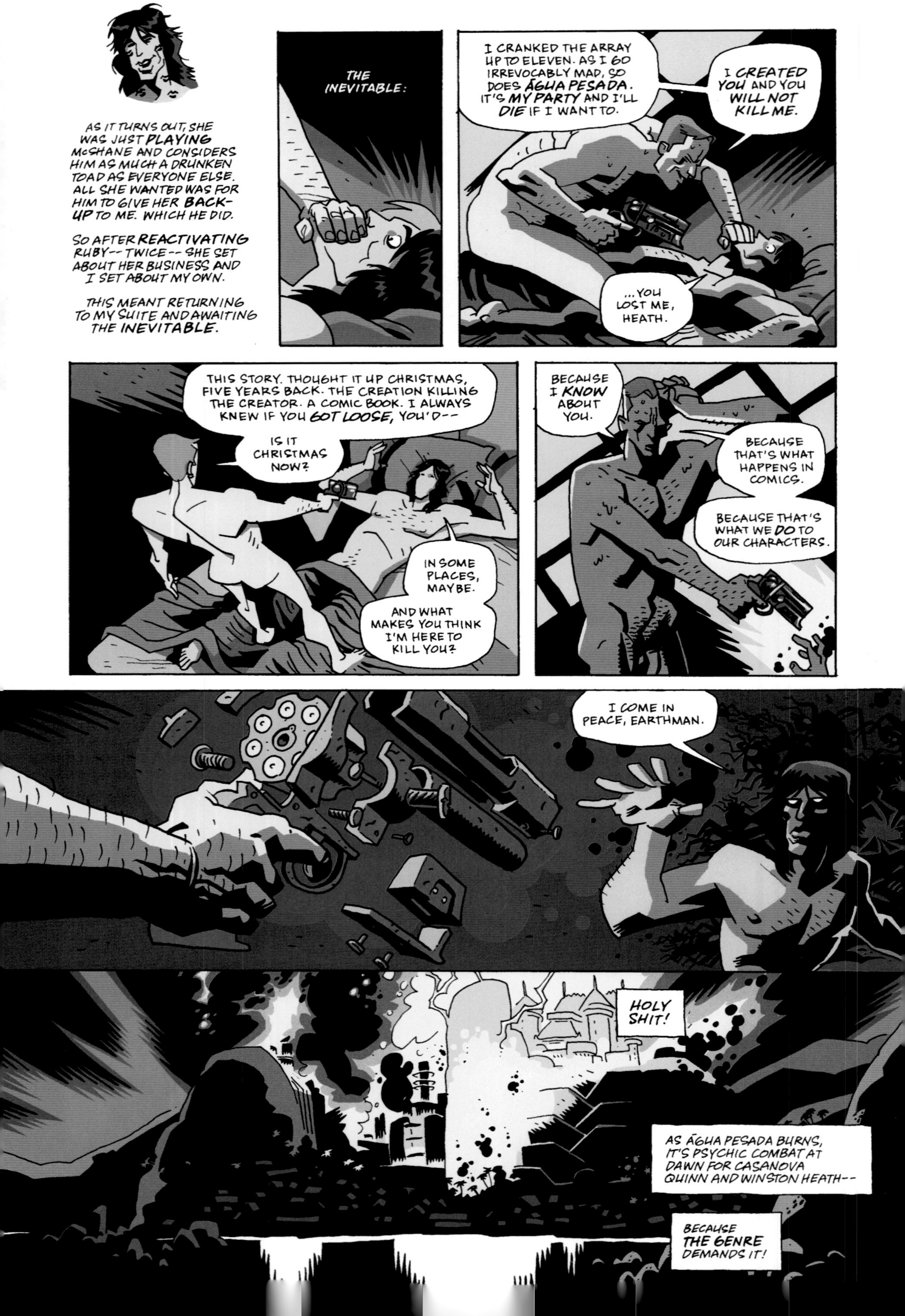
AS IT TURNS OUT, SHE WAS JUST PLAYING McSHANE AND CONSIDERS HIM AS MUCH A DRUNKEN TOAD AS EVERYONE ELSE. ALL SHE WANTED WAS FOR HIM TO GIVE HER BACK-UP TO ME. WHICH HE DID.
SO AFTER REACTIVATING RUBY-- TWICE-- SHE SET ABOUT HER BUSINESS AND I SET ABOUT MY OWN.
THIS MEANT RETURNING TO MY SUITE AND AWAITING THE INEVITABLE.
THE INEVITABLE:
I CRANKED THE ARRAY UP TO ELEVEN. AS I GO IRREVOCABLY MAD, SO DOES ÁGUA PESADA. IT'S MY PARTY AND I'LL DIE IF I WANT TO.
I CREATED YOU AND YOU WILL NOT KILL ME.
...YOU LOST ME, HEATH.
THIS STORY. THOUGHT IT UP CHRISTMAS, FIVE YEARS BACK. THE CREATION KILLING THE CREATOR. A COMIC BOOK. I ALWAYS KNEW IF YOU GOT LOOSE, YOU'D--
IS IT CHRISTMAS NOW?
IN SOME PLACES, MAYBE.
AND WHAT MAKES YOU THINK I'M HERE TO KILL YOU?
BECAUSE I KNOW ABOUT YOU.
BECAUSE THAT'S WHAT HAPPENS IN COMICS.
BECAUSE THAT'S WHAT WE DO TO OUR CHARACTERS.
I COME IN PEACE, EARTHMAN.
HOLY SHIT!
AS ÁGUA PESADA BURNS, IT'S PSYCHIC COMBAT AT DAWN FOR CASANOVA QUINN AND WINSTON HEATH--
BECAUSE THE GENRE DEMANDS IT!

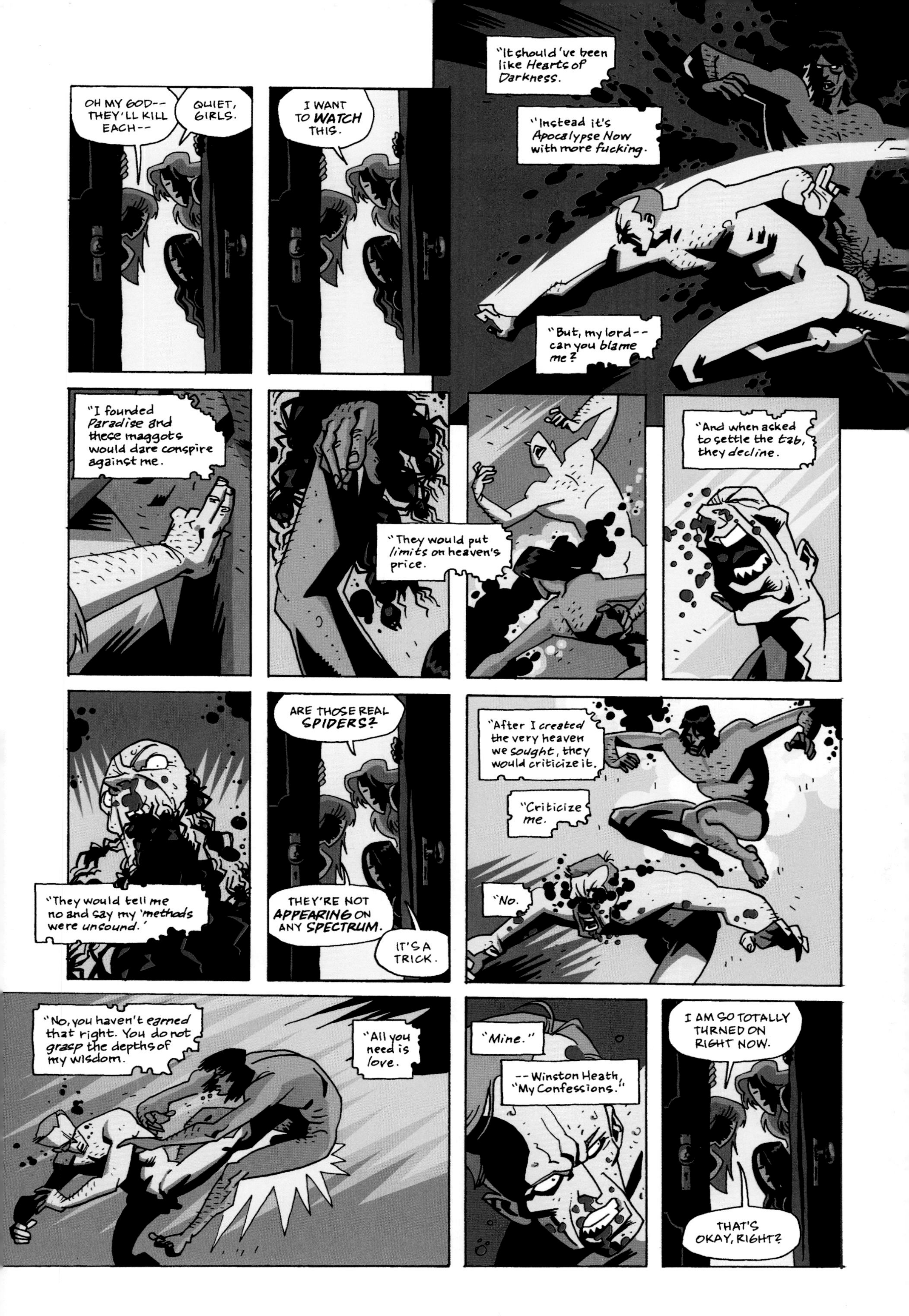
OH MY GOD-- THEY'LL KILL EACH--
QUIET, GIRLS.
I WANT TO WATCH THIS.
"It should've been like Hearts of Darkness.
"Instead it's Apocalypse Now with more fucking.
"But, my lord-- can you blame me?
"I founded Paradise and these maggots would dare conspire against me.
"They would put limits on heaven's price.
"And when asked to settle the tab, they decline.
"They would tell me no and say my 'methods were unsound.'
ARE THOSE REAL SPIDERS?
THEY'RE NOT APPEARING ON ANY SPECTRUM.
IT'S A TRICK.
"After I created the very heaven we sought, they would criticize it.
"Criticize me.
"No.
"No, you haven't earned that right. You do not grasp the depths of my wisdom.
"All you need is love.
"Mine."
--Winston Heath, "My Confessions."
I AM SO TOTALLY TURNED ON RIGHT NOW.
THAT'S OKAY, RIGHT?

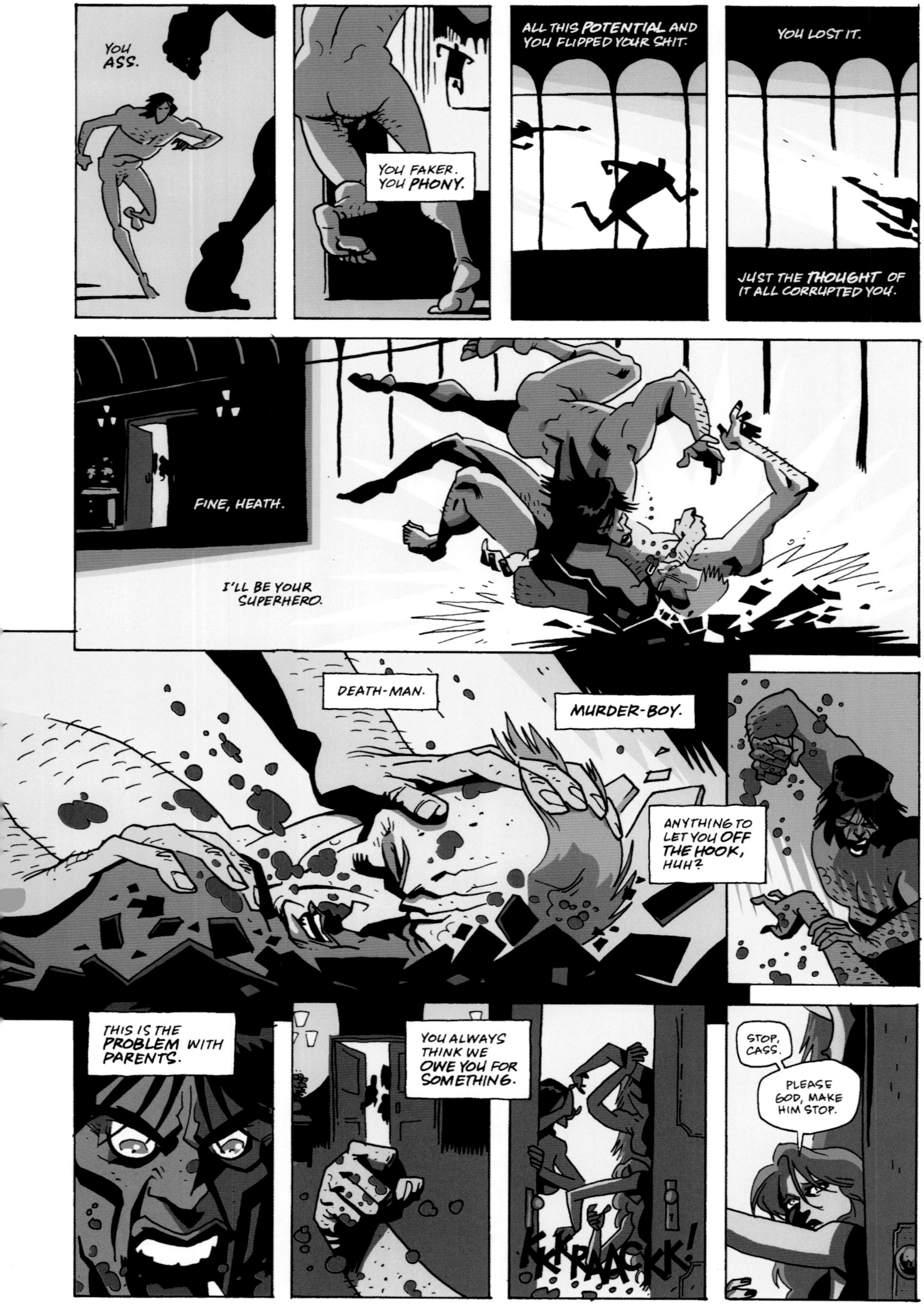
YOU ASS.
YOU FAKER. YOU PHONY.
ALL THIS POTENTIAL AND YOU FLIPPED YOUR SHIT.
YOU LOST IT.
JUST THE THOUGHT OF IT ALL CORRUPTED YOU.
FINE, HEATH.
I'LL BE YOUR SUPERHERO.
DEATH-MAN.
MURDER-BOY.
ANYTHING TO LET YOU OFF THE HOOK, HUH?
THIS IS THE PROBLEM WITH PARENTS.
YOU ALWAYS THINK WE OWE YOU FOR SOMETHING.
KKKRAACKK!
STOP, CASS.
PLEASE GOD, MAKE HIM STOP.

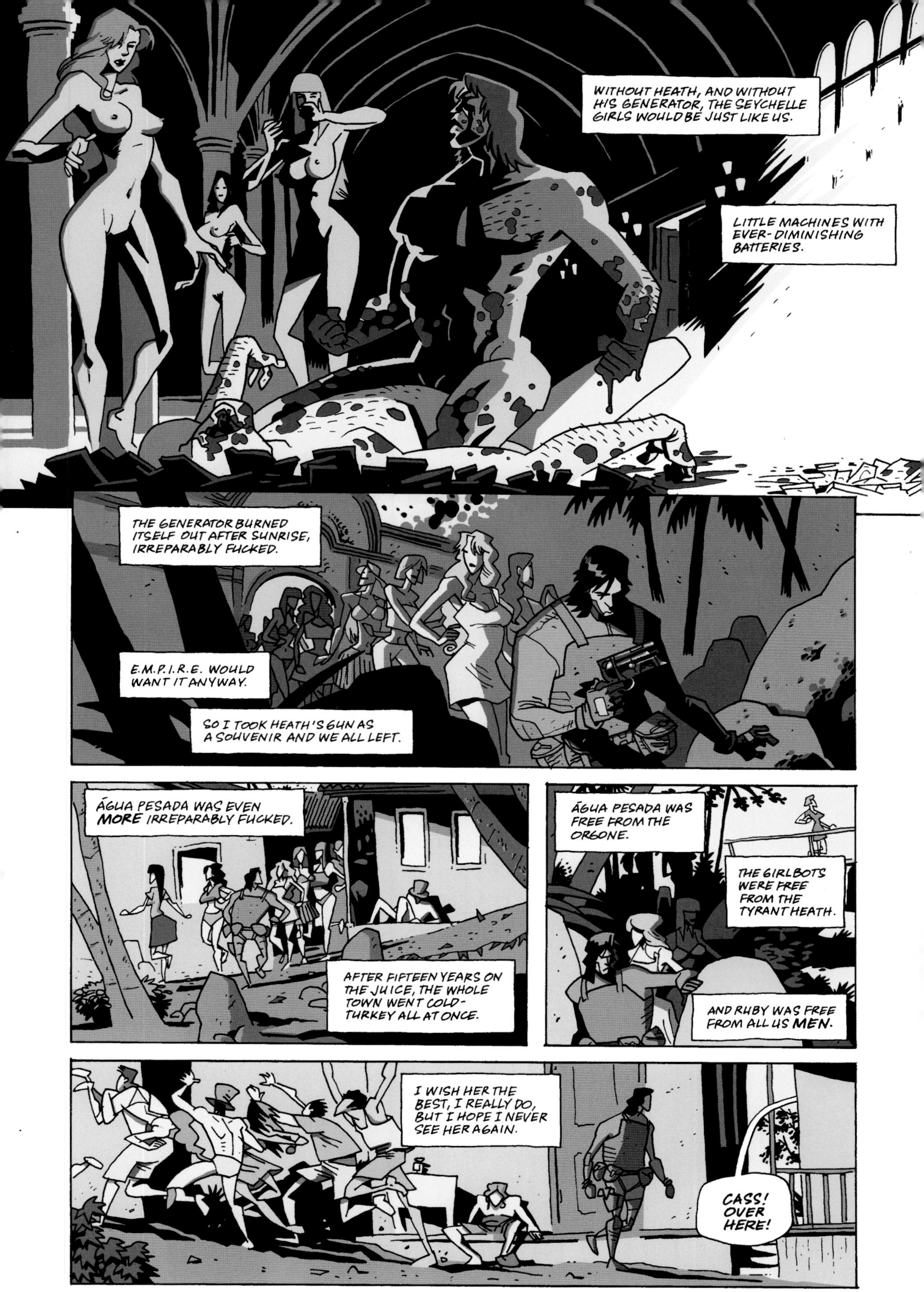
WITHOUT HEATH, AND WITHOUT HIS GENERATOR, THE SEYCHELLE GIRLS WOULD BE JUST LIKE US.
LITTLE MACHINES WITH EVER-DIMINISHING BATTERIES.
THE GENERATOR BURNED ITSELF OUT AFTER SUNRISE, IRREPARABLY FUCKED.
E.M.P.I.R.E. WOULD WANT IT ANYWAY.
SO I TOOK HEATH'S GUN AS A SOUVENIR AND WE ALL LEFT.
ÁGUA PESADA WAS EVEN MORE IRREPARABLY FUCKED.
AFTER FIFTEEN YEARS ON THE JUICE, THE WHOLE TOWN WENT COLD-TURKEY ALL AT ONCE.
ÁGUA PESADA WAS FREE FROM THE ORGONE.
THE GIRLBOTS WERE FREE FROM THE TYRANT HEATH.
AND RUBY WAS FREE FROM ALL US MEN.
I WISH HER THE BEST, I REALLY DO, BUT I HOPE I NEVER SEE HER AGAIN.
CASS! OVER HERE!

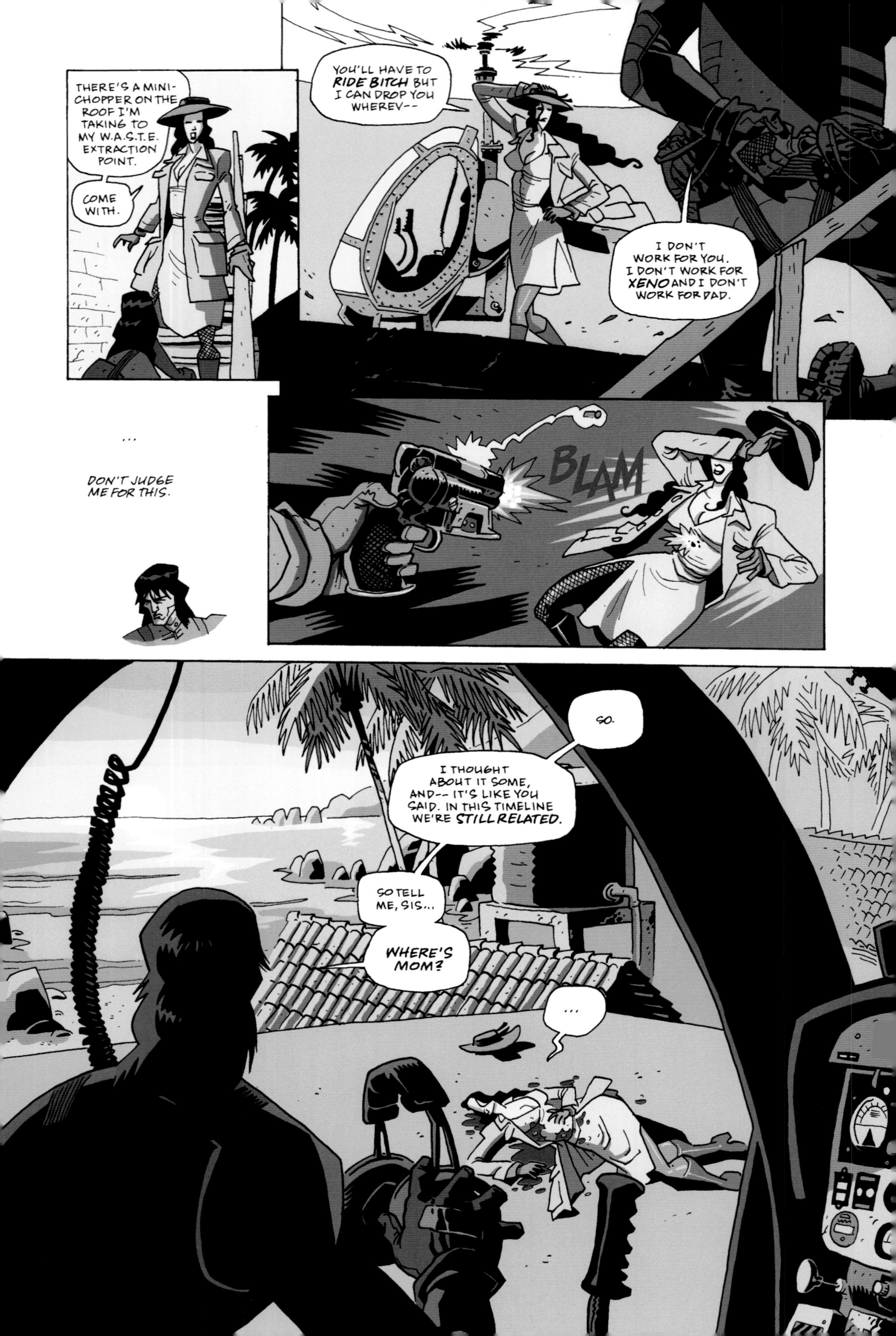
THERE'S A MINI-CHOPPER ON THE ROOF I'M TAKING TO MY W.A.S.T.E. EXTRACTION POINT.
COME WITH.
YOU'LL HAVE TO RIDE BITCH BUT I CAN DROP YOU WHEREV--
I DON'T WORK FOR YOU. I DON'T WORK FOR XENO AND I DON'T WORK FOR DAD.
...
DON'T JUDGE ME FOR THIS.
BLAM
SO.
I THOUGHT ABOUT IT SOME, AND-- IT'S LIKE YOU SAID. IN THIS TIMELINE WE'RE STILL RELATED.
SO TELL ME, SIS...
WHERE'S MOM?
...

EXECUTION DAYS

PRETTY LITTLE POLICEMAN

MISSION TO YERBA MUERTA

DÉTOURNEMENT

COLDHEART

WOMEN AND MEN (PART ONE)

WOMEN AND MEN (PART TWO)

I THINK I ALMOST LOVED HIM

IS THIS IT? (REDUX)

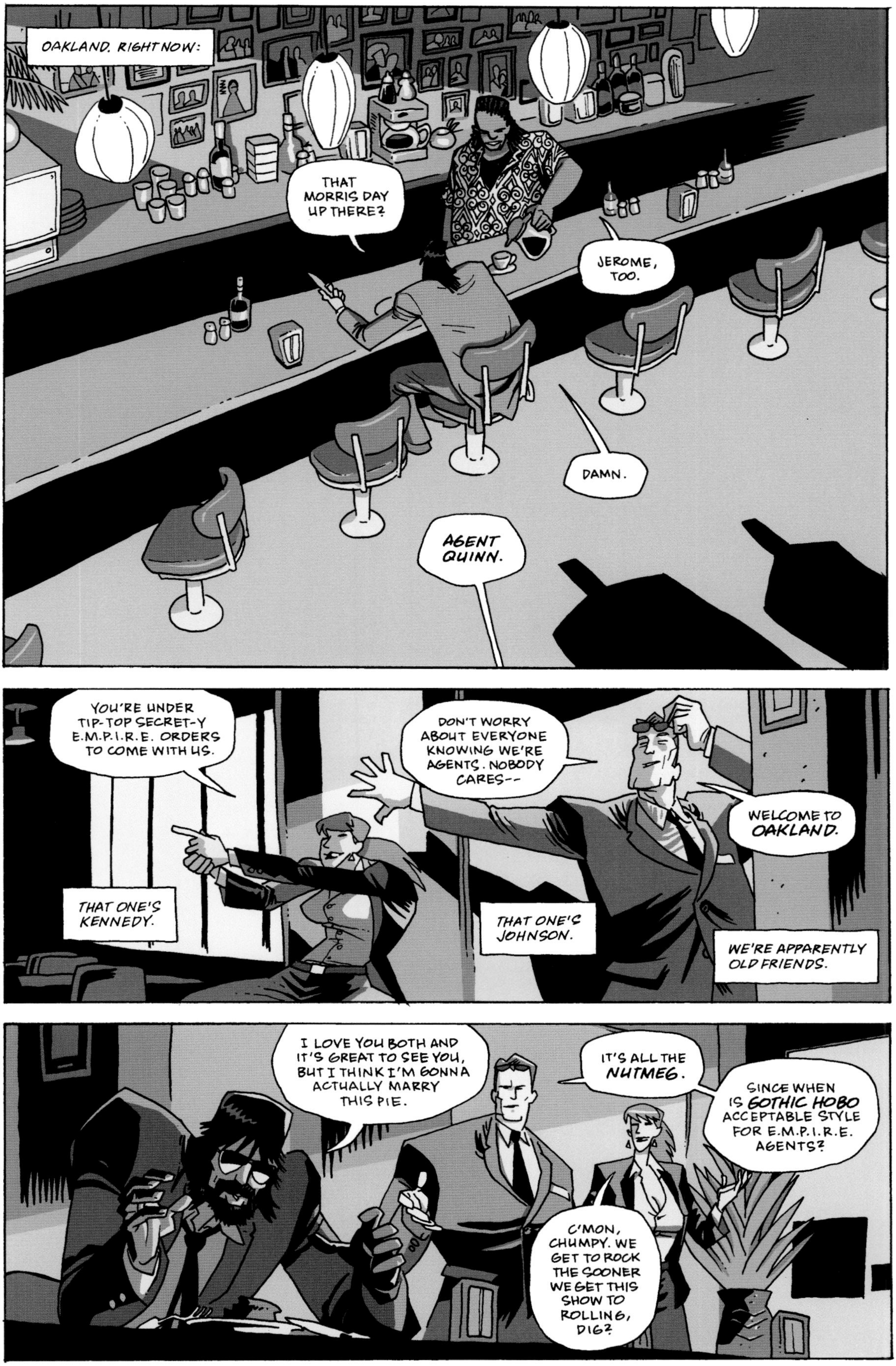
OAKLAND. RIGHT NOW:
THAT MORRIS DAY UP THERE?
JEROME, TOO.
DAMN.
AGENT QUINN.
YOU'RE UNDER TIP-TOP SECRET-Y E.M.P.I.R.E. ORDERS TO COME WITH US.
THAT ONE'S KENNEDY.
DON'T WORRY ABOUT EVERYONE KNOWING WE'RE AGENTS. NOBODY CARES--
THAT ONE'S JOHNSON.
WELCOME TO OAKLAND.
WE'RE APPARENTLY OLD FRIENDS.
I LOVE YOU BOTH AND IT'S GREAT TO SEE YOU, BUT I THINK I'M GONNA ACTUALLY MARRY THIS PIE.
IT'S ALL THE NUTMEG.
SINCE WHEN IS GOTHIC HOBO ACCEPTABLE STYLE FOR E.M.P.I.R.E. AGENTS?
C'MON, CHUMPY. WE GET TO ROCK THE SOONER WE GET THIS SHOW TO ROLLING, DIG?

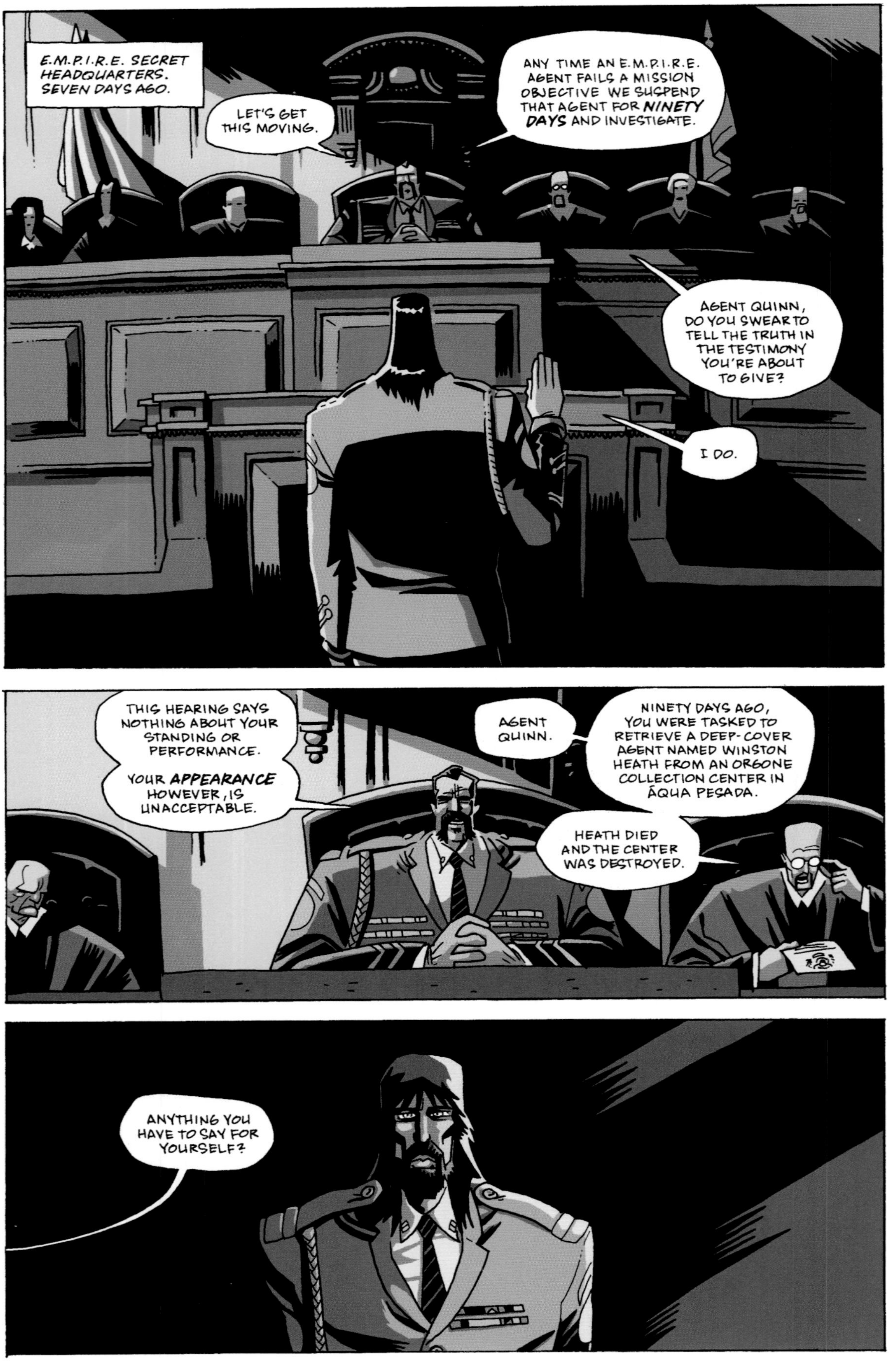
E.M.P.I.R.E. SECRET HEADQUARTERS. SEVEN DAYS AGO.
LET'S GET THIS MOVING.
ANY TIME AN E.M.P.I.R.E. AGENT FAILS A MISSION OBJECTIVE WE SUSPEND THAT AGENT FOR NINETY DAYS AND INVESTIGATE.
AGENT QUINN, DO YOU SWEAR TO TELL THE TRUTH IN THE TESTIMONY YOU'RE ABOUT TO GIVE?
I DO.
THIS HEARING SAYS NOTHING ABOUT YOUR STANDING OR PERFORMANCE.
YOUR APPEARANCE HOWEVER, IS UNACCEPTABLE.
AGENT QUINN.
NINETY DAYS AGO, YOU WERE TASKED TO RETRIEVE A DEEP-COVER AGENT NAMED WINSTON HEATH FROM AN ORGONE COLLECTION CENTER IN ÁQUA PESADA.
HEATH DIED AND THE CENTER WAS DESTROYED.
ANYTHING YOU HAVE TO SAY FOR YOURSELF?

W.A.S.T.E. OPIUM LOUNGE. NINETY-SEVEN DAYS AGO:

WHAT ON EARTH CAN YOU POSSIBLY SAY TO ME TO EXPLAIN HOW YOUR ÁGUA PESADA MISSION WAS SUCH A PARTICULAR CLUSTER-FUCK?

E.M.P.I.R.E. HAS PUT YOU ON *ICE* FOR *NINETY DAYS*, CORRECT? AS PER PROCEDURE YOU'VE BEEN BENCHED, YES?

YES.

THEY'RE DOING AFTER-ACTION FORENSICS WORK. THERE WILL BE A HEARING AND YOU'LL HAVE A LOT TO *ANSWER* FOR.

AND TO *ME*-- WHILE YOU MANAGED TO *KILL HEATH* YOU ALSO MANAGED TO ALMOST KILL YOUR SISTER.

SO NO DRUGS FOR YOU.

NO ACTION. NO ADVENTURE. JUST QUIET *CONTEMPLATION.*

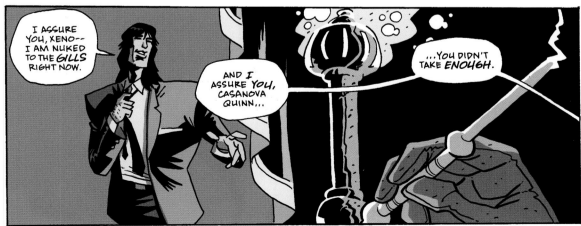

I ASSURE YOU, XENO-- I AM NUKED TO THE *GILLS* RIGHT NOW.

AND *I* ASSURE *YOU*, CASANOVA QUINN...

...YOU DIDN'T TAKE *ENOUGH.*

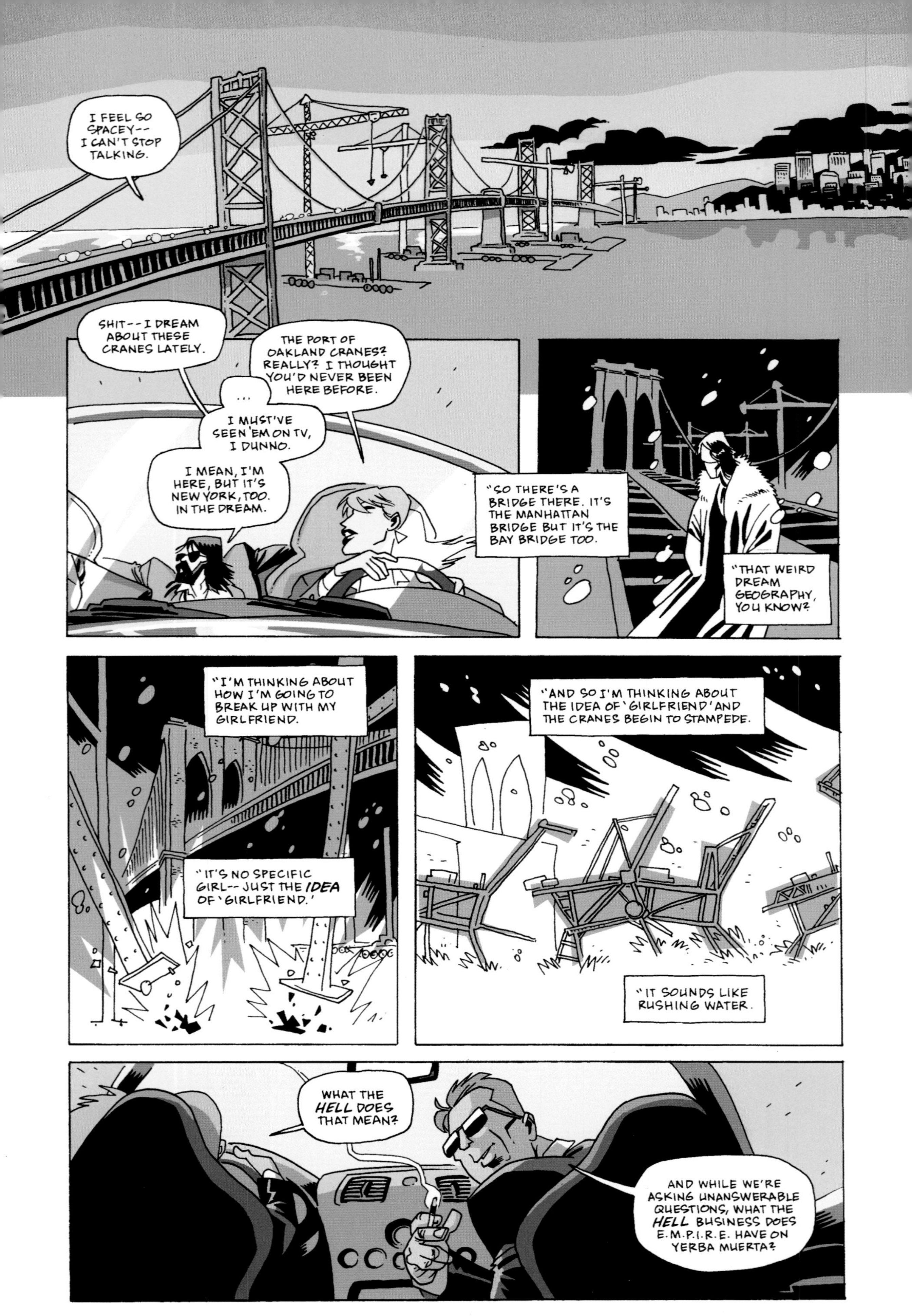
I FEEL SO SPACEY-- I CAN'T STOP TALKING.
SHIT--I DREAM ABOUT THESE CRANES LATELY.
THE PORT OF OAKLAND CRANES? REALLY? I THOUGHT YOU'D NEVER BEEN HERE BEFORE.
...
I MUST'VE SEEN 'EM ON TV, I DUNNO.
I MEAN, I'M HERE, BUT IT'S NEW YORK, TOO. IN THE DREAM.
"SO THERE'S A BRIDGE THERE. IT'S THE MANHATTAN BRIDGE BUT IT'S THE BAY BRIDGE TOO.
"THAT WEIRD DREAM GEOGRAPHY, YOU KNOW?
"I'M THINKING ABOUT HOW I'M GOING TO BREAK UP WITH MY GIRLFRIEND.
"IT'S NO SPECIFIC GIRL-- JUST THE *IDEA* OF 'GIRLFRIEND.'
"AND SO I'M THINKING ABOUT THE IDEA OF 'GIRLFRIEND' AND THE CRANES BEGIN TO STAMPEDE.
"IT SOUNDS LIKE RUSHING WATER.
WHAT THE *HELL* DOES THAT MEAN?
AND WHILE WE'RE ASKING UNANSWERABLE QUESTIONS, WHAT THE *HELL* BUSINESS DOES E.M.P.I.R.E. HAVE ON YERBA MUERTA?

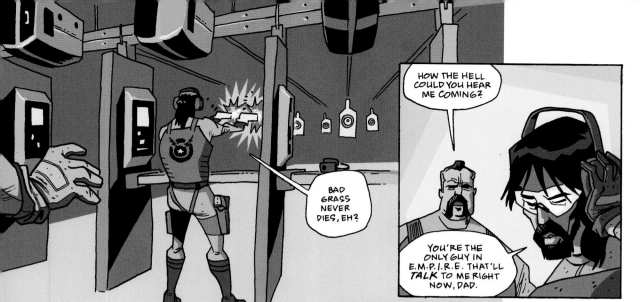

BAD GRASS NEVER DIES, EH?

HOW THE HELL COULD YOU HEAR ME COMING?

YOU'RE THE ONLY GUY IN E.M.P.I.R.E. THAT'LL *TALK* TO ME RIGHT NOW, DAD.

E.M.P.I.R.E.'S MADE UP OF A LOT OF HIGH PRESSURE LITTLE ACHIEVERS.

AND-- RIGHT OR WRONG -- YOU BLEW A MISSION. PEOPLE ARE GONNA AVOID YOU FOR A SPELL, SON. YOU'RE BAD LUCK.

DID YOU HAVE TO BREAK MY BALLS OVER THE BEARD THING, TOO?

GODDAMN RIGHT I DID. THIS IS A MILITARY ORGANIZATION.

MY BOY DOESN'T GET IT ANY EASIER THAN ANYONE ELSE.

LOOK, SON-- WHY DON'T YOU COME TO THE HOUSE FOR A NIGHT BEFORE WE SEND YOU BACK OUT INTO THE WORLD?

BACK--?

WE'VE AGREED ON A SLOW TACTICAL ENTRY.

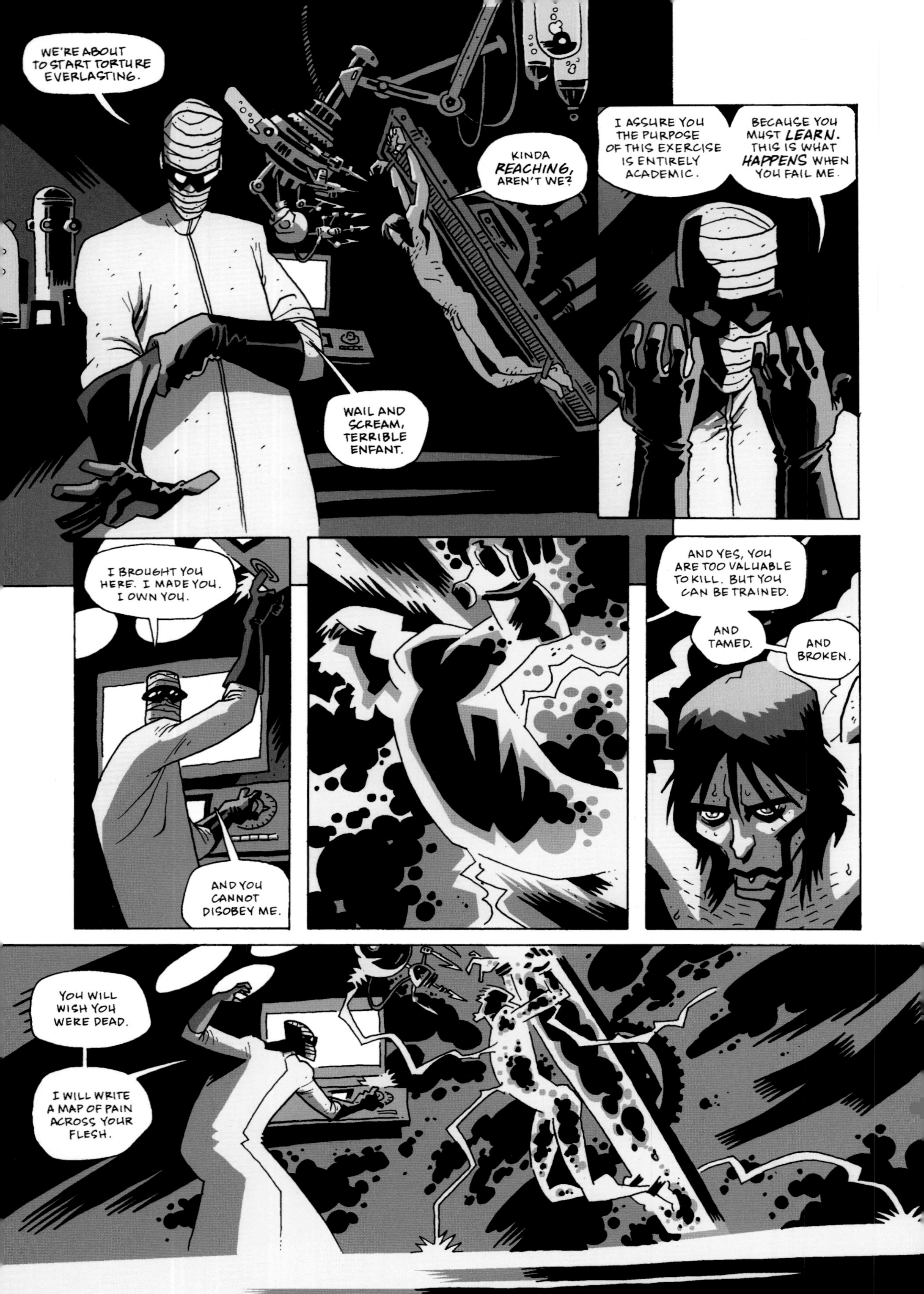
WE'RE ABOUT TO START TORTURE EVERLASTING.
KINDA REACHING, AREN'T WE?
WAIL AND SCREAM, TERRIBLE ENFANT.
I ASSURE YOU THE PURPOSE OF THIS EXERCISE IS ENTIRELY ACADEMIC.
BECAUSE YOU MUST LEARN. THIS IS WHAT HAPPENS WHEN YOU FAIL ME.
I BROUGHT YOU HERE. I MADE YOU. I OWN YOU.
AND YOU CANNOT DISOBEY ME.
AND YES, YOU ARE TOO VALUABLE TO KILL. BUT YOU CAN BE TRAINED.
AND TAMED.
AND BROKEN.
YOU WILL WISH YOU WERE DEAD.
I WILL WRITE A MAP OF PAIN ACROSS YOUR FLESH.

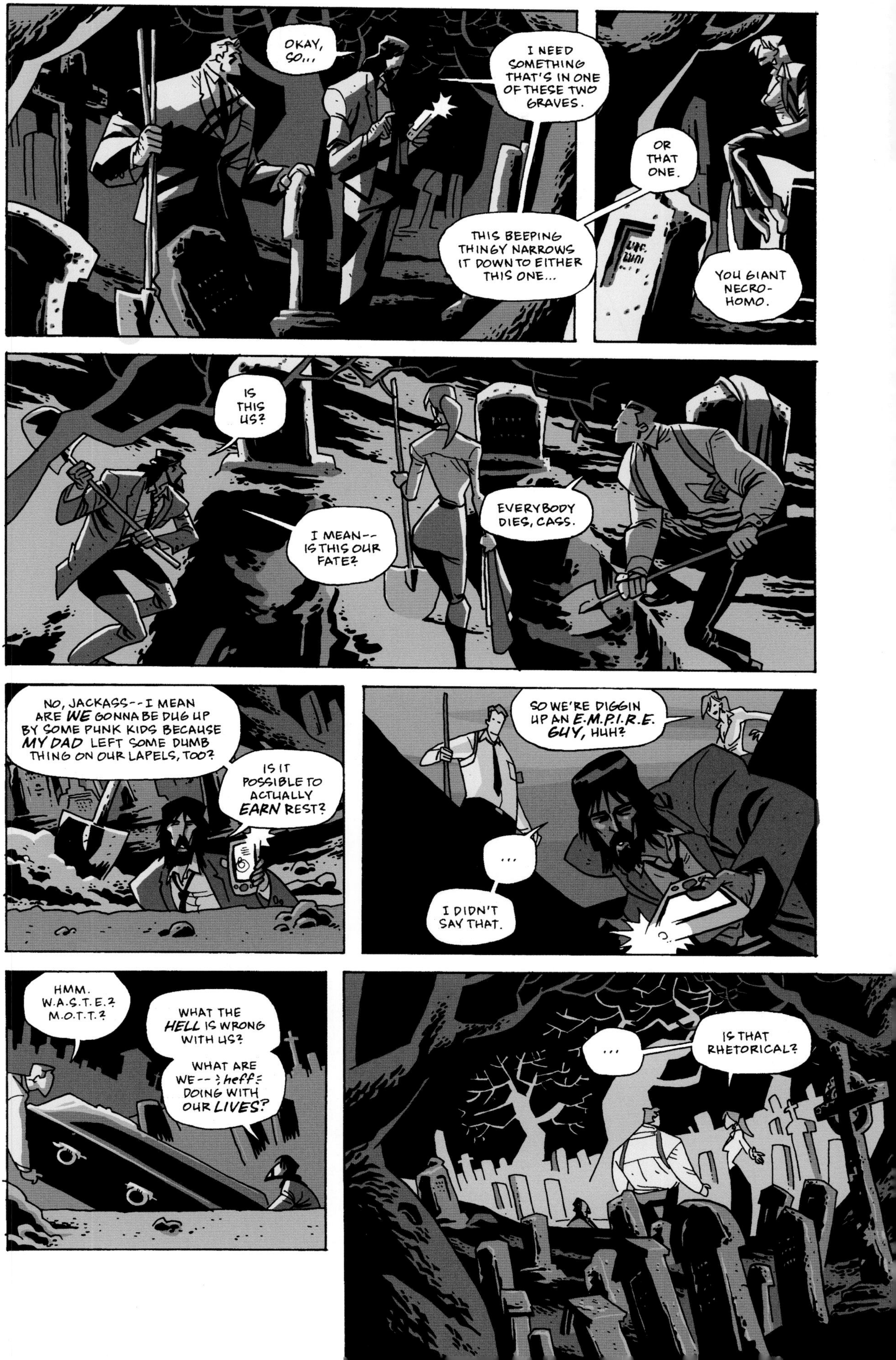
OKAY, SO...
I NEED SOMETHING THAT'S IN ONE OF THESE TWO GRAVES.
THIS BEEPING THINGY NARROWS IT DOWN TO EITHER THIS ONE...
OR THAT ONE.
YOU GIANT NECRO-HOMO.
IS THIS US?
I MEAN-- IS THIS OUR FATE?
EVERYBODY DIES, CASS.
NO, JACKASS--I MEAN ARE WE GONNA BE DUG UP BY SOME PUNK KIDS BECAUSE MY DAD LEFT SOME DUMB THING ON OUR LAPELS, TOO?
IS IT POSSIBLE TO ACTUALLY EARN REST?
SO WE'RE DIGGIN UP AN E.M.P.I.R.E. GUY, HUH?
...
I DIDN'T SAY THAT.
HMM. W.A.S.T.E.? M.O.T.T.?
WHAT THE HELL IS WRONG WITH US?
WHAT ARE WE-- *heff* DOING WITH OUR LIVES?
...
IS THAT RHETORICAL?

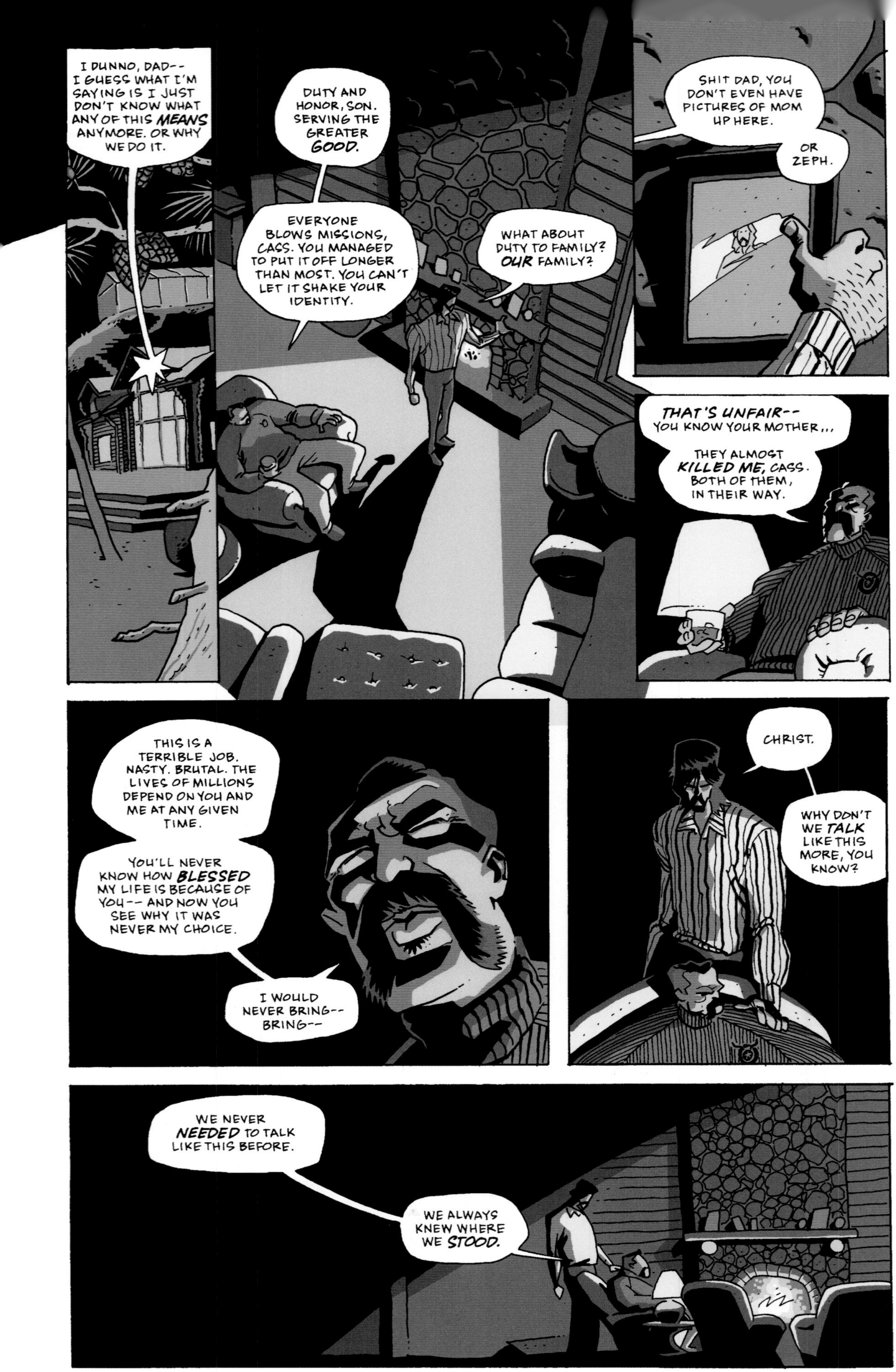
I DUNNO, DAD-- I GUESS WHAT I'M SAYING IS I JUST DON'T KNOW WHAT ANY OF THIS MEANS ANYMORE. OR WHY WE DO IT.
DUTY AND HONOR, SON. SERVING THE GREATER GOOD.
EVERYONE BLOWS MISSIONS, CASS. YOU MANAGED TO PUT IT OFF LONGER THAN MOST. YOU CAN'T LET IT SHAKE YOUR IDENTITY.
WHAT ABOUT DUTY TO FAMILY? OUR FAMILY?
SHIT DAD, YOU DON'T EVEN HAVE PICTURES OF MOM UP HERE.
OR ZEPH.
THAT'S UNFAIR-- YOU KNOW YOUR MOTHER...
THEY ALMOST KILLED ME, CASS. BOTH OF THEM, IN THEIR WAY.
THIS IS A TERRIBLE JOB. NASTY. BRUTAL. THE LIVES OF MILLIONS DEPEND ON YOU AND ME AT ANY GIVEN TIME.
YOU'LL NEVER KNOW HOW BLESSED MY LIFE IS BECAUSE OF YOU-- AND NOW YOU SEE WHY IT WAS NEVER MY CHOICE.
I WOULD NEVER BRING-- BRING--
CHRIST.
WHY DON'T WE TALK LIKE THIS MORE, YOU KNOW?
WE NEVER NEEDED TO TALK LIKE THIS BEFORE.
WE ALWAYS KNEW WHERE WE STOOD.

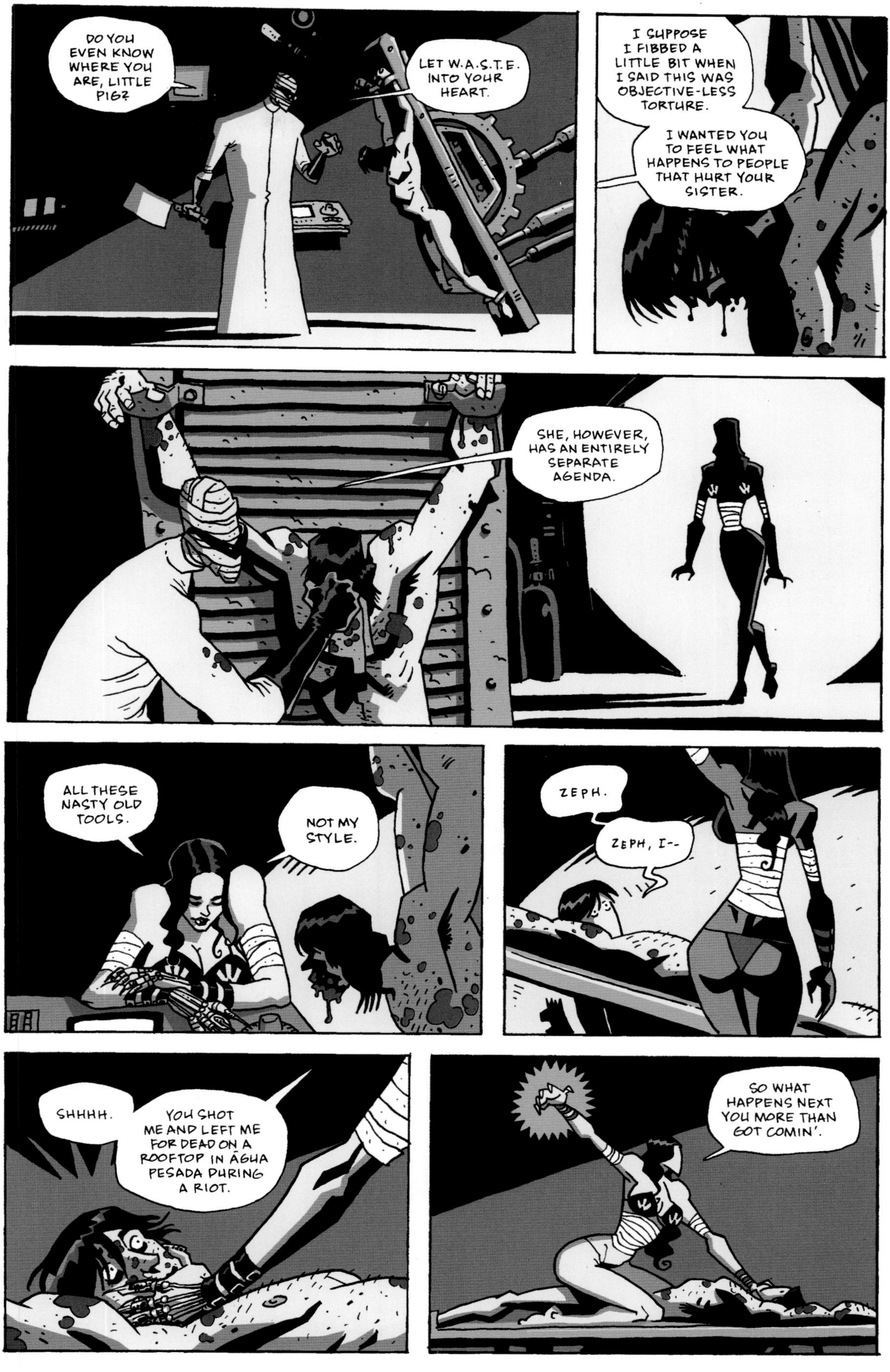
DO YOU EVEN KNOW WHERE YOU ARE, LITTLE PIG?
LET W.A.S.T.E. INTO YOUR HEART.
I SUPPOSE I FIBBED A LITTLE BIT WHEN I SAID THIS WAS OBJECTIVE-LESS TORTURE.
I WANTED YOU TO FEEL WHAT HAPPENS TO PEOPLE THAT HURT YOUR SISTER.
SHE, HOWEVER, HAS AN ENTIRELY SEPARATE AGENDA.
ALL THESE NASTY OLD TOOLS.
NOT MY STYLE.
ZEPH.
ZEPH, I--
SHHHH.
YOU SHOT ME AND LEFT ME FOR DEAD ON A ROOFTOP IN ÁGUA PESADA DURING A RIOT.
SO WHAT HAPPENS NEXT YOU MORE THAN GOT COMIN'.

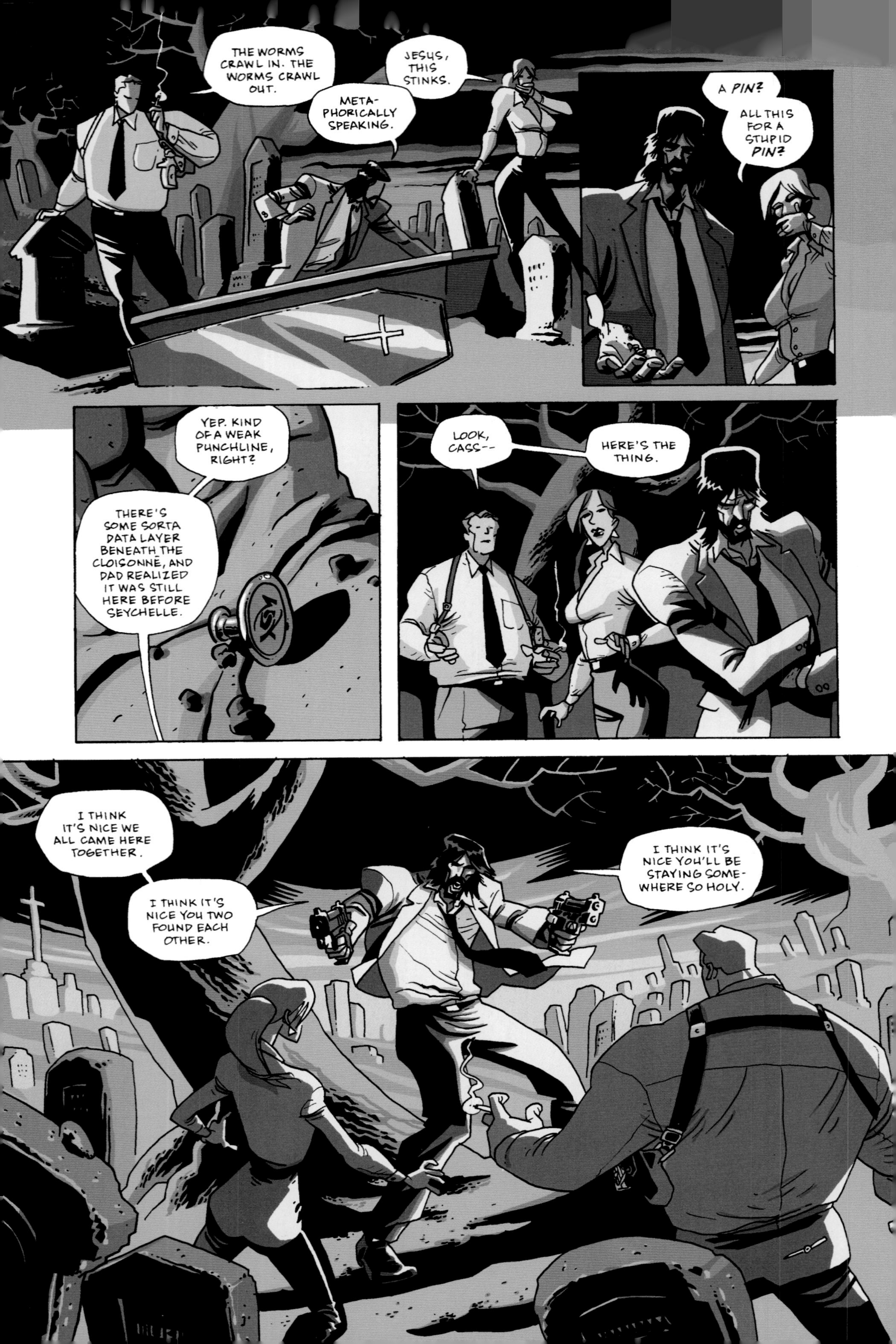
THE WORMS CRAWL IN. THE WORMS CRAWL OUT.
JESUS, THIS STINKS.
META-PHORICALLY SPEAKING.
A PIN?
ALL THIS FOR A STUPID PIN?
YEP. KIND OF A WEAK PUNCHLINE, RIGHT?
THERE'S SOME SORTA DATA LAYER BENEATH THE CLOISONNÉ, AND DAD REALIZED IT WAS STILL HERE BEFORE SEYCHELLE.
LOOK, CASS--
HERE'S THE THING.
I THINK IT'S NICE WE ALL CAME HERE TOGETHER.
I THINK IT'S NICE YOU TWO FOUND EACH OTHER.
I THINK IT'S NICE YOU'LL BE STAYING SOME-WHERE SO HOLY.

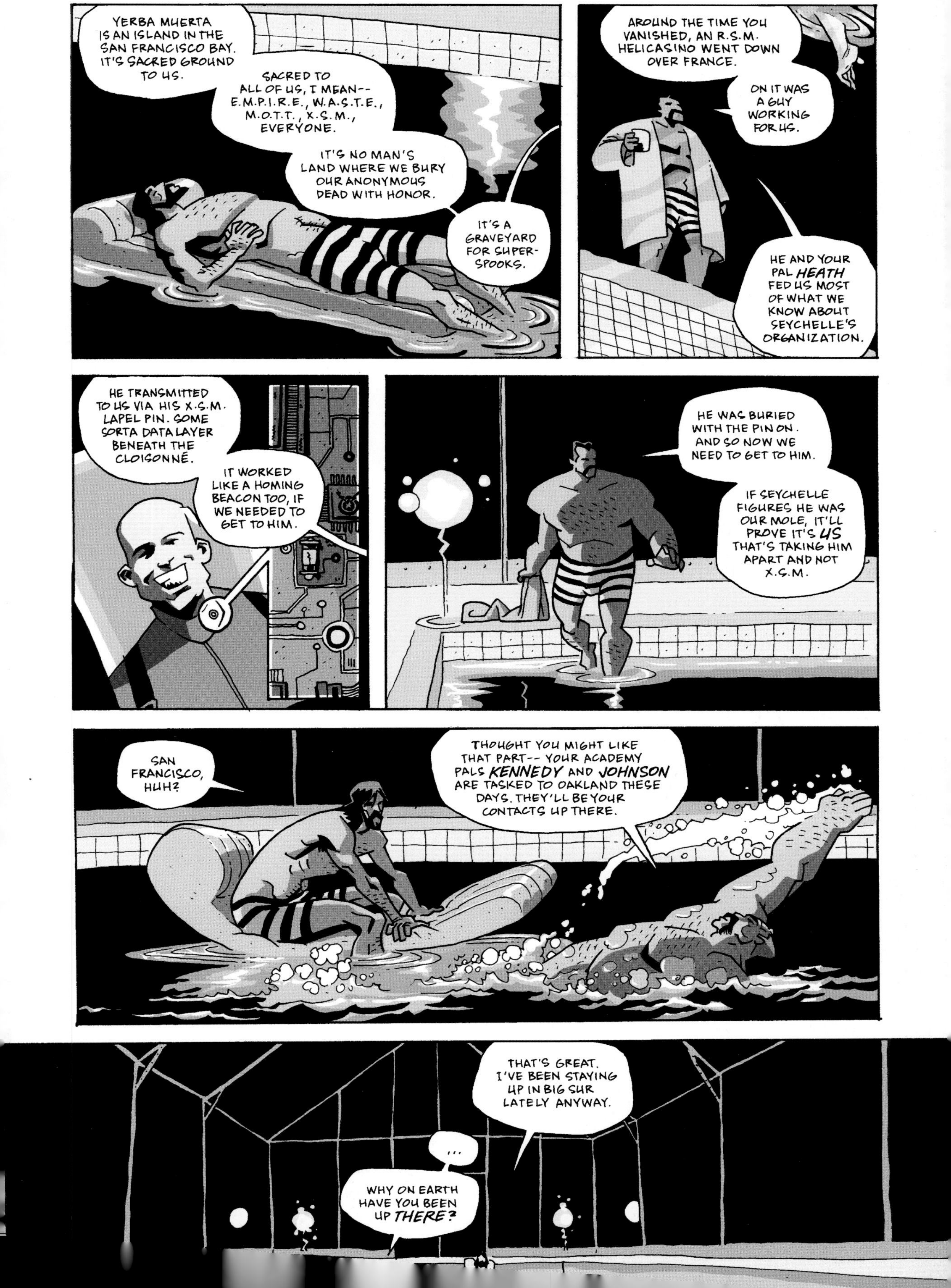
YERBA MUERTA IS AN ISLAND IN THE SAN FRANCISCO BAY. IT'S SACRED GROUND TO US.
SACRED TO ALL OF US, I MEAN-- E.M.P.I.R.E., W.A.S.T.E., M.O.T.T., X.S.M., EVERYONE.
IT'S NO MAN'S LAND WHERE WE BURY OUR ANONYMOUS DEAD WITH HONOR.
IT'S A GRAVEYARD FOR SUPER-SPOOKS.
AROUND THE TIME YOU VANISHED, AN R.S.M. HELICASINO WENT DOWN OVER FRANCE.
ON IT WAS A GUY WORKING FOR US.
HE AND YOUR PAL HEATH FED US MOST OF WHAT WE KNOW ABOUT SEYCHELLE'S ORGANIZATION.
HE TRANSMITTED TO US VIA HIS X.S.M. LAPEL PIN. SOME SORTA DATA LAYER BENEATH THE CLOISONNÉ.
IT WORKED LIKE A HOMING BEACON TOO, IF WE NEEDED TO GET TO HIM.
HE WAS BURIED WITH THE PIN ON. AND SO NOW WE NEED TO GET TO HIM.
IF SEYCHELLE FIGURES HE WAS OUR MOLE, IT'LL PROVE IT'S US THAT'S TAKING HIM APART AND NOT X.S.M.
SAN FRANCISCO, HUH?
THOUGHT YOU MIGHT LIKE THAT PART-- YOUR ACADEMY PALS KENNEDY AND JOHNSON ARE TASKED TO OAKLAND THESE DAYS. THEY'LL BE YOUR CONTACTS UP THERE.
THAT'S GREAT. I'VE BEEN STAYING UP IN BIG SUR LATELY ANYWAY.
...
WHY ON EARTH HAVE YOU BEEN UP THERE?

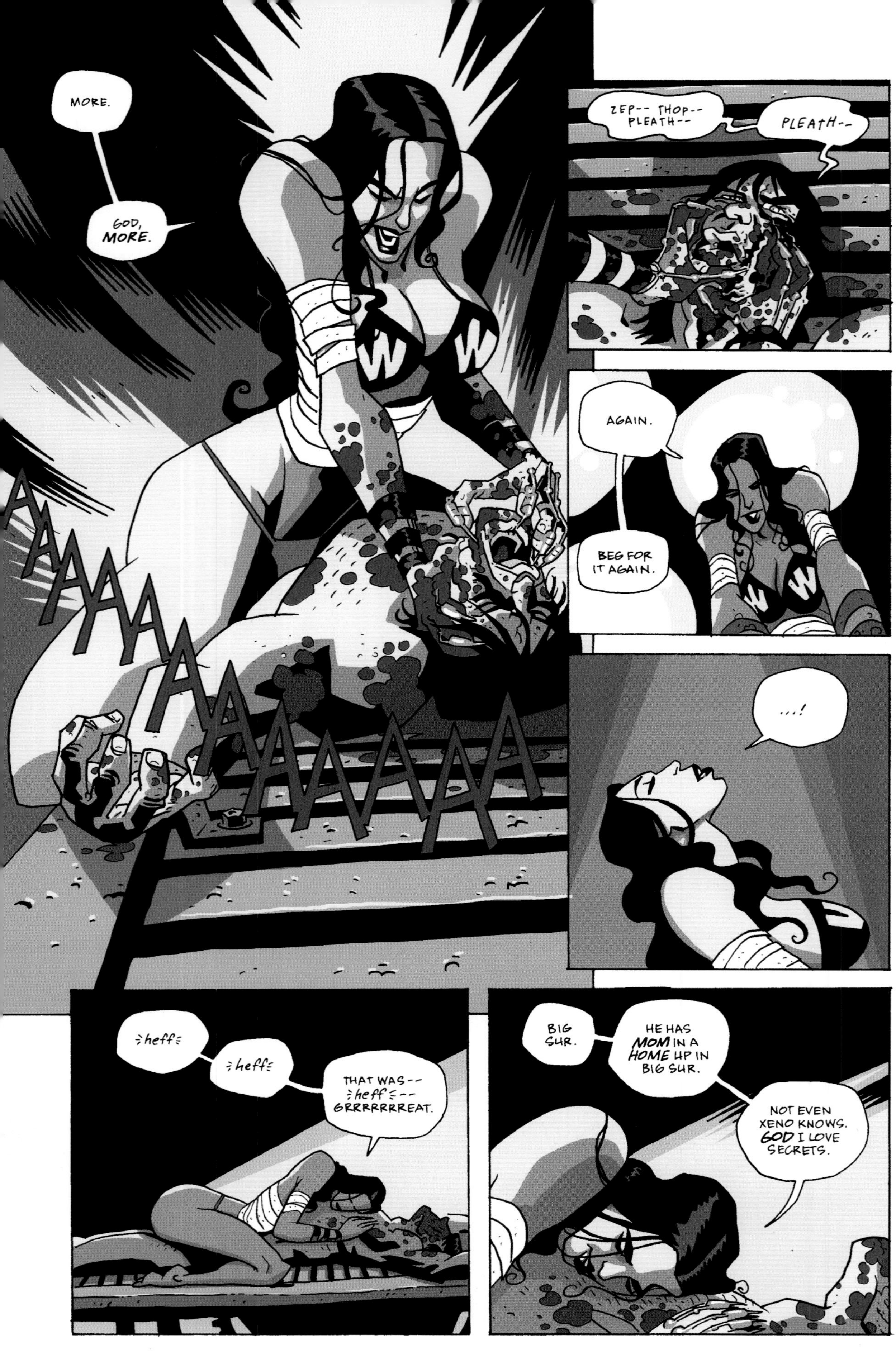

MORE.
GOD, MORE.
AAAAAAAAAAAAAAAAA
ZEP-- THOP-- PLEATH--
PLEATH--
AGAIN.
BEG FOR IT AGAIN.
...!
:heff:
:heff:
THAT WAS-- :heff: -- GRRRRRRREAT.
BIG SUR.
HE HAS MOM IN A HOME UP IN BIG SUR.
NOT EVEN XENO KNOWS. GOD I LOVE SECRETS.

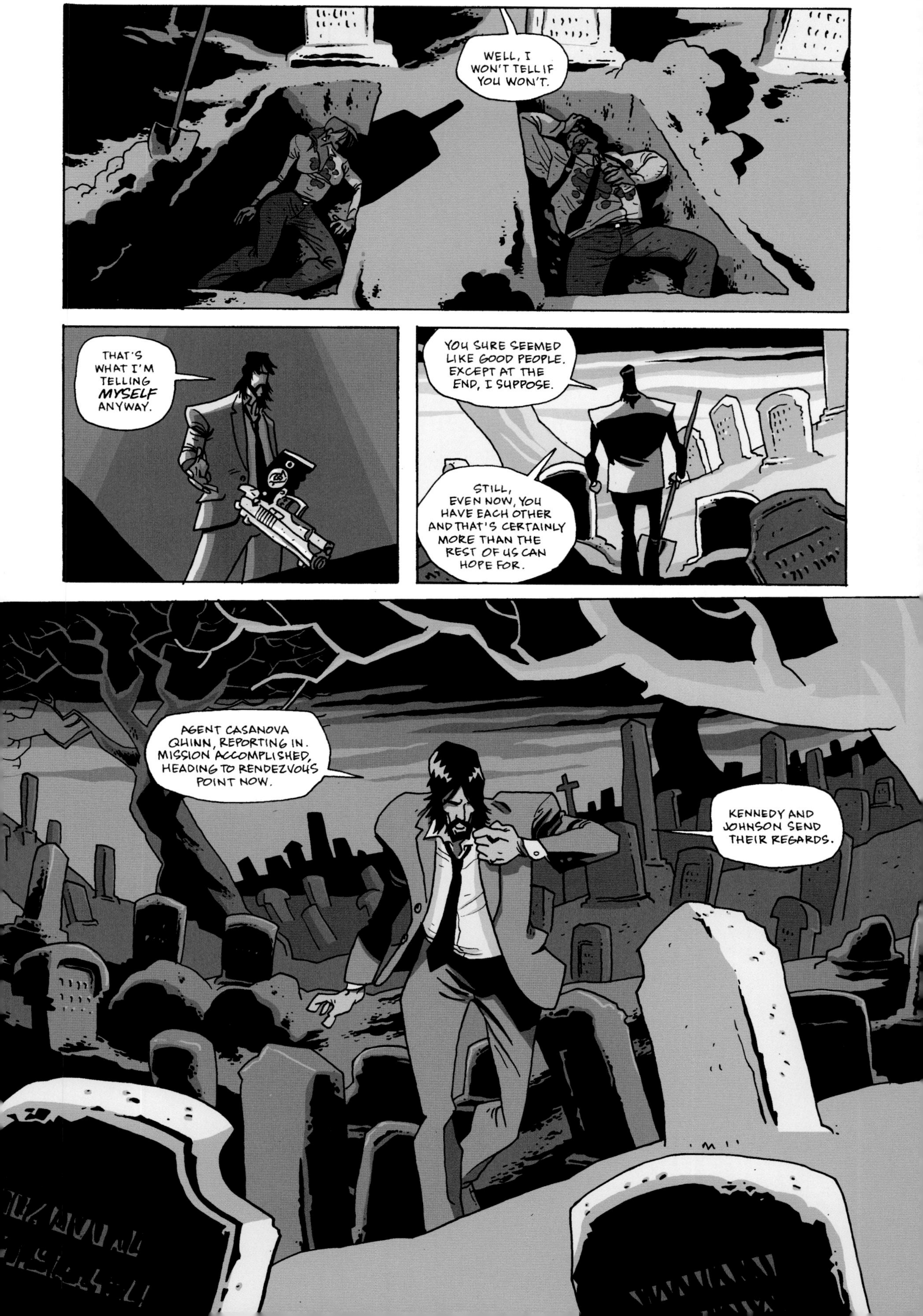
WELL, I WON'T TELL IF YOU WON'T.
THAT'S WHAT I'M TELLING *MYSELF* ANYWAY.
YOU SURE SEEMED LIKE GOOD PEOPLE. EXCEPT AT THE END, I SUPPOSE.
STILL, EVEN NOW, YOU HAVE EACH OTHER AND THAT'S CERTAINLY MORE THAN THE REST OF US CAN HOPE FOR.
AGENT CASANOVA QUINN, REPORTING IN. MISSION ACCOMPLISHED, HEADING TO RENDEZVOUS POINT NOW.
KENNEDY AND JOHNSON SEND THEIR REGARDS.

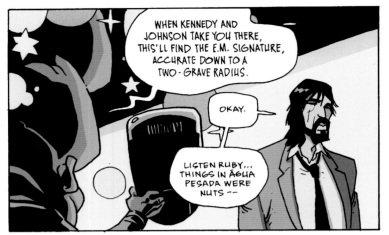

WHEN KENNEDY AND JOHNSON TAKE YOU THERE, THIS'LL FIND THE E.M. SIGNATURE, ACCURATE DOWN TO A TWO-GRAVE RADIUS.

OKAY.

LISTEN RUBY... THINGS IN ÁGUA PESADA WERE NUTS --

NO, IT'S OKAY. THEY JUST *RE-INSTALLED* ME FROM BACK-UP.

I DIDN'T EVEN NOTICE THE TIME I WAS OUT.

OH, NO THANKS, SWEETHEART, I'LL BRING MY OWN GUNS.

GUNS? PLURAL?

YOU CAN NEVER BE TOO SURE THESE DAYS.

LOTS OF *DANGEROUS PEOPLE* IN THE WORLD TO WATCH OUT FOR.

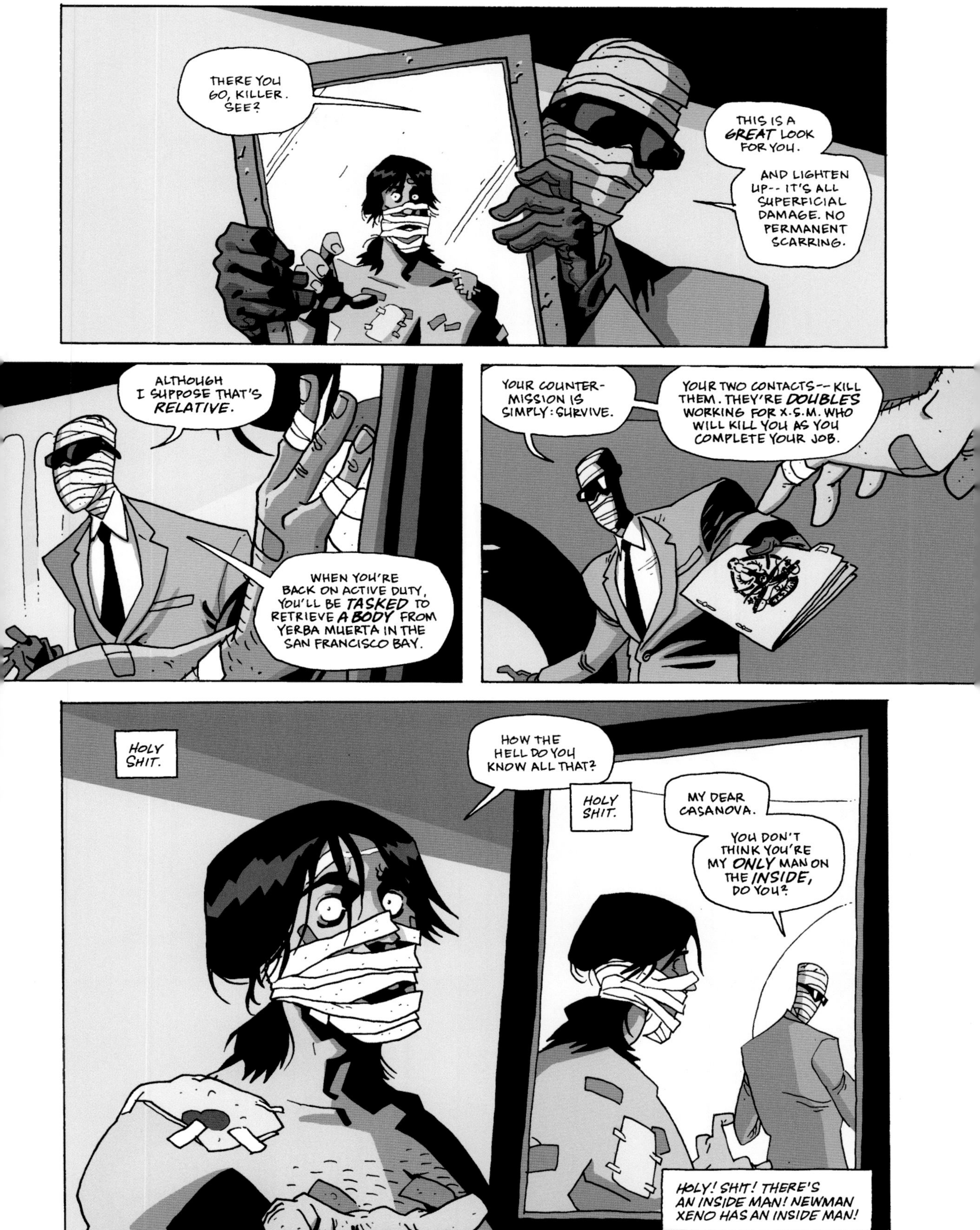
THERE YOU GO, KILLER. SEE?
THIS IS A *GREAT* LOOK FOR YOU.
AND LIGHTEN UP-- IT'S ALL SUPERFICIAL DAMAGE. NO PERMANENT SCARRING.
ALTHOUGH I SUPPOSE THAT'S *RELATIVE.*
WHEN YOU'RE BACK ON ACTIVE DUTY, YOU'LL BE *TASKED* TO RETRIEVE *A BODY* FROM YERBA MUERTA IN THE SAN FRANCISCO BAY.
YOUR COUNTER-MISSION IS SIMPLY: SURVIVE.
YOUR TWO CONTACTS-- KILL THEM. THEY'RE *DOUBLES* WORKING FOR X.S.M. WHO WILL KILL YOU AS YOU COMPLETE YOUR JOB.
HOLY SHIT.
HOW THE HELL DO YOU KNOW ALL THAT?
HOLY SHIT.
MY DEAR CASANOVA.
YOU DON'T THINK YOU'RE MY *ONLY* MAN ON THE *INSIDE,* DO YOU?
HOLY! SHIT! THERE'S AN INSIDE MAN! NEWMAN XENO HAS AN INSIDE MAN!

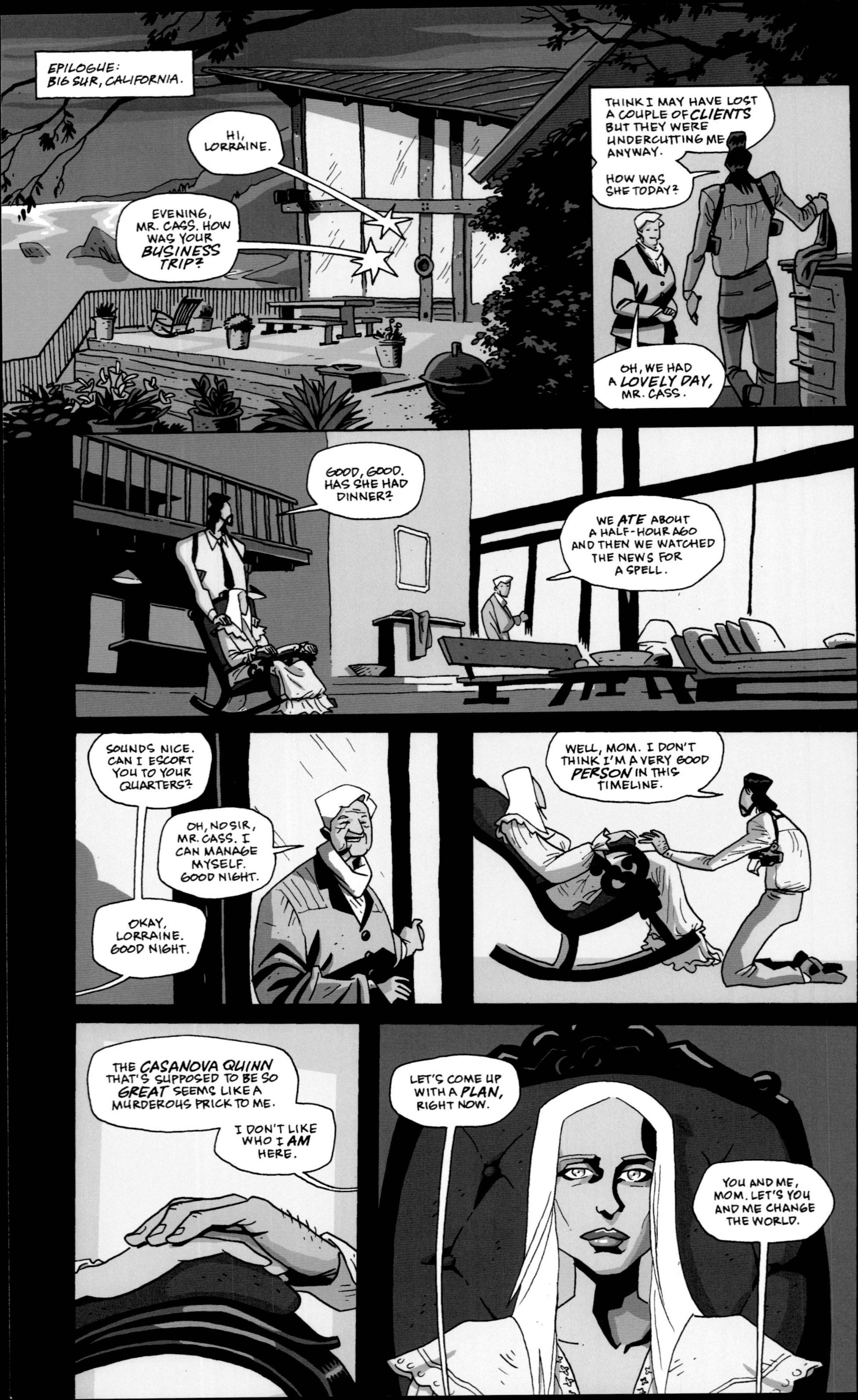
EPILOGUE:
BIG SUR, CALIFORNIA.
HI, LORRAINE.
EVENING, MR. CASS. HOW WAS YOUR BUSINESS TRIP?
THINK I MAY HAVE LOST A COUPLE OF CLIENTS BUT THEY WERE UNDERCUTTING ME ANYWAY.
HOW WAS SHE TODAY?
OH, WE HAD A LOVELY DAY, MR. CASS.
GOOD, GOOD. HAS SHE HAD DINNER?
WE ATE ABOUT A HALF-HOUR AGO AND THEN WE WATCHED THE NEWS FOR A SPELL.
SOUNDS NICE. CAN I ESCORT YOU TO YOUR QUARTERS?
OH, NO SIR, MR. CASS. I CAN MANAGE MYSELF. GOOD NIGHT.
OKAY, LORRAINE. GOOD NIGHT.
WELL, MOM. I DON'T THINK I'M A VERY GOOD PERSON IN THIS TIMELINE.
THE CASANOVA QUINN THAT'S SUPPOSED TO BE SO GREAT SEEMS LIKE A MURDEROUS PRICK TO ME.
I DON'T LIKE WHO I AM HERE.
LET'S COME UP WITH A PLAN, RIGHT NOW.
YOU AND ME, MOM. LET'S YOU AND ME CHANGE THE WORLD.

EXECUTION DAYS

PRETTY LITTLE POLICEMAN

MISSION TO YERBA MUERTA

DÉTOURNEMENT

COLDHEART

WOMEN AND MEN (PART ONE)

WOMEN AND MEN (PART TWO)

I THINK I ALMOST LOVED HIM

IS THIS IT? (REDUX)

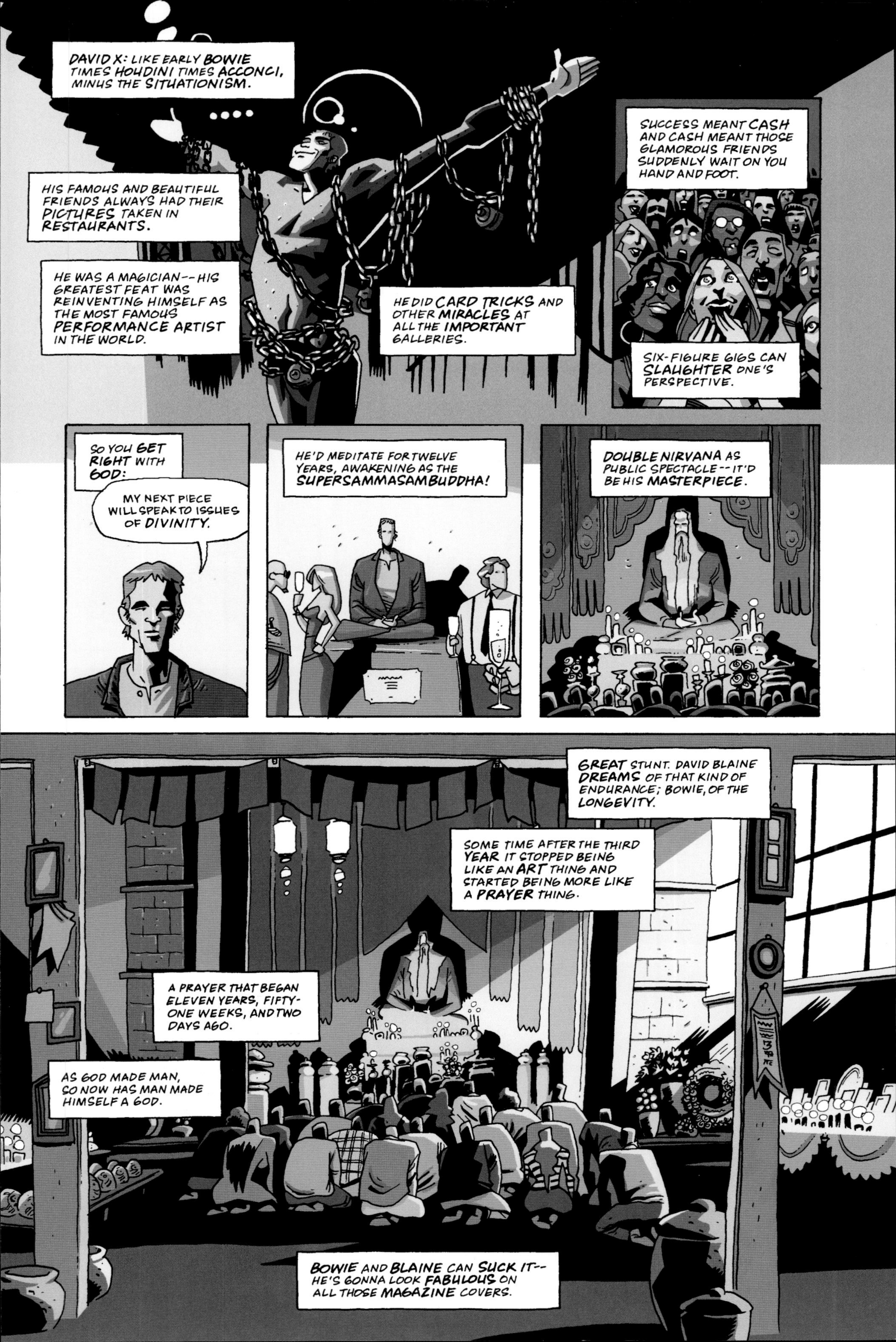
DAVID X: LIKE EARLY BOWIE TIMES HOUDINI TIMES ACCONCI, MINUS THE SITUATIONISM.
HIS FAMOUS AND BEAUTIFUL FRIENDS ALWAYS HAD THEIR PICTURES TAKEN IN RESTAURANTS.
HE WAS A MAGICIAN-- HIS GREATEST FEAT WAS REINVENTING HIMSELF AS THE MOST FAMOUS PERFORMANCE ARTIST IN THE WORLD.
HE DID CARD TRICKS AND OTHER MIRACLES AT ALL THE IMPORTANT GALLERIES.
SUCCESS MEANT CASH AND CASH MEANT THOSE GLAMOROUS FRIENDS SUDDENLY WAIT ON YOU HAND AND FOOT.
SIX-FIGURE GIGS CAN SLAUGHTER ONE'S PERSPECTIVE.
SO YOU GET RIGHT WITH GOD:
MY NEXT PIECE WILL SPEAK TO ISSUES OF DIVINITY.
HE'D MEDITATE FOR TWELVE YEARS, AWAKENING AS THE SUPERSAMMASAMBUDDHA!
DOUBLE NIRVANA AS PUBLIC SPECTACLE-- IT'D BE HIS MASTERPIECE.
GREAT STUNT. DAVID BLAINE DREAMS OF THAT KIND OF ENDURANCE; BOWIE, OF THE LONGEVITY.
SOME TIME AFTER THE THIRD YEAR IT STOPPED BEING LIKE AN ART THING AND STARTED BEING MORE LIKE A PRAYER THING.
A PRAYER THAT BEGAN ELEVEN YEARS, FIFTY-ONE WEEKS, AND TWO DAYS AGO.
AS GOD MADE MAN, SO NOW HAS MAN MADE HIMSELF A GOD.
BOWIE AND BLAINE CAN SUCK IT-- HE'S GONNA LOOK FABULOUS ON ALL THOSE MAGAZINE COVERS.

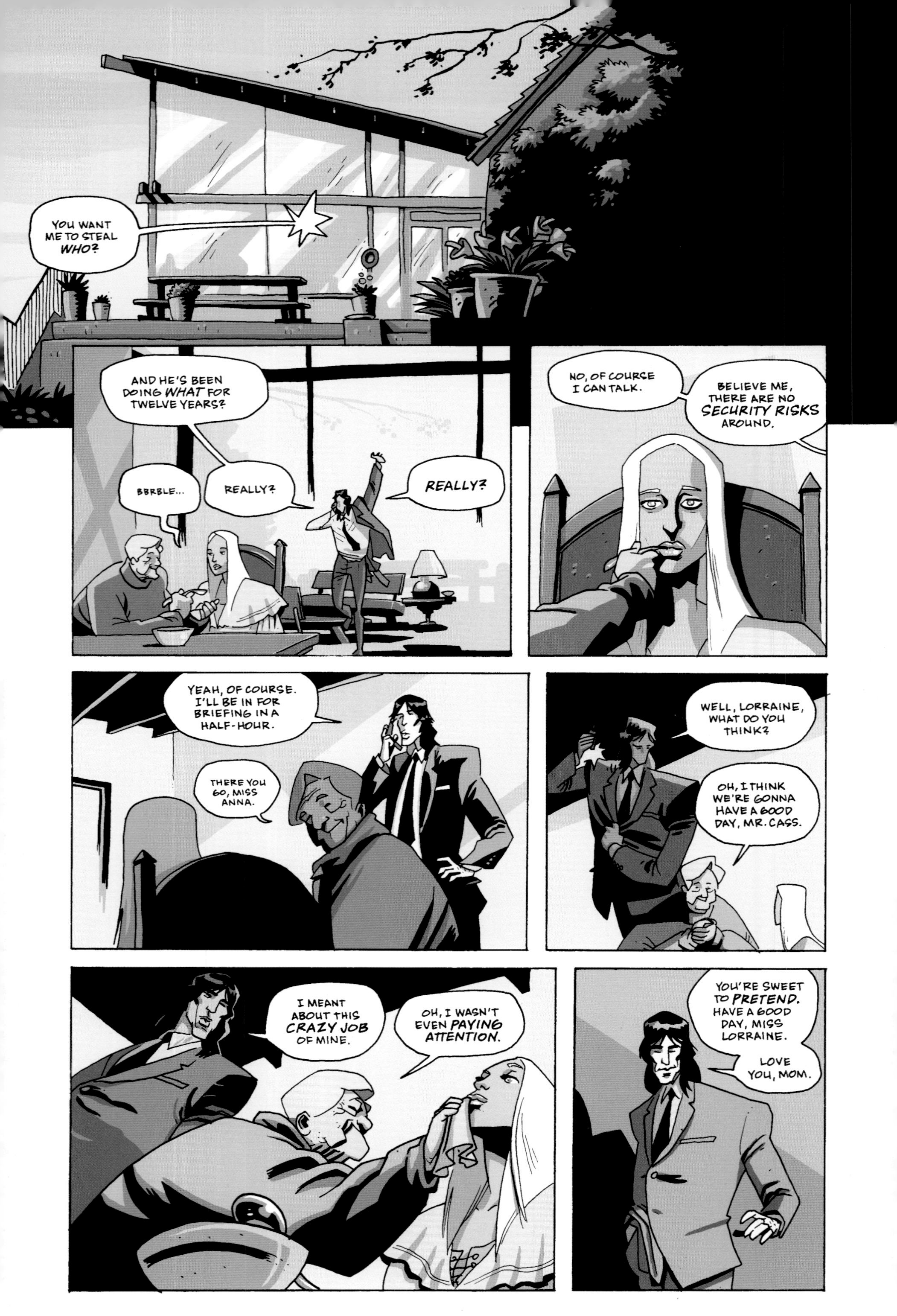
YOU WANT ME TO STEAL WHO?
AND HE'S BEEN DOING WHAT FOR TWELVE YEARS?
BBRBLE...
REALLY?
REALLY?
NO, OF COURSE I CAN TALK.
BELIEVE ME, THERE ARE NO SECURITY RISKS AROUND.
YEAH, OF COURSE. I'LL BE IN FOR BRIEFING IN A HALF-HOUR.
THERE YOU GO, MISS ANNA.
WELL, LORRAINE, WHAT DO YOU THINK?
OH, I THINK WE'RE GONNA HAVE A GOOD DAY, MR. CASS.
I MEANT ABOUT THIS CRAZY JOB OF MINE.
OH, I WASN'T EVEN PAYING ATTENTION.
YOU'RE SWEET TO PRETEND. HAVE A GOOD DAY, MISS LORRAINE.
LOVE YOU, MOM.

GEOPOLITICAL DESTABILIZATION!

GODDAMN, I LOVE THIS JOB!

GOOD TO SEE YOU TOO, DAD.

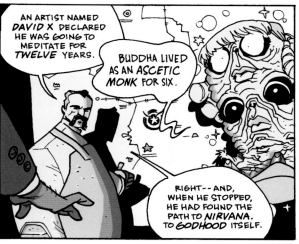

AN ARTIST NAMED DAVID X DECLARED HE WAS GOING TO MEDITATE FOR TWELVE YEARS.

BUDDHA LIVED AS AN ASCETIC MONK FOR SIX.

RIGHT-- AND, WHEN HE STOPPED, HE HAD FOUND THE PATH TO NIRVANA. TO GODHOOD ITSELF.

BELIEVE IT OR NOT, IN LESS THAN 70 HOURS, THE LITTLE JAGOFF'S GONNA DO IT.

E.M.P.I.R.E. ANALYSIS SUGGESTS IF X AWAKENS, BUDDHISTS AROUND THE WORLD WILL COME TO A KIND OF CRITICAL POINT.

LIKE IN, SAY, TIBET.

IT'S IN THE INTEREST OF E.M.P.I.R.E. TO KEEP SOME OF THESE REGIONS WAR-Y AND DESTABILIZED.

AND THE BEST WAY TO ACCOMPLISH THAT IS TO SUBVERT THE NATIVITY.

SUIT UP, SON--

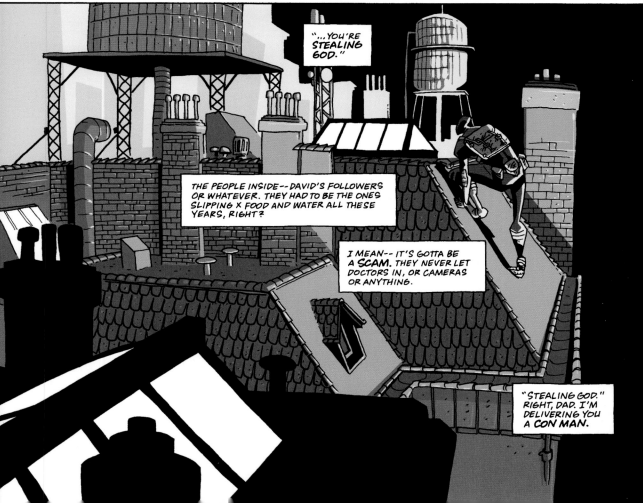

"...YOU'RE STEALING GOD."

THE PEOPLE INSIDE-- DAVID'S FOLLOWERS OR WHATEVER. THEY HAD TO BE THE ONES SLIPPING X FOOD AND WATER ALL THESE YEARS, RIGHT?

I MEAN-- IT'S GOTTA BE A SCAM. THEY NEVER LET DOCTORS IN, OR CAMERAS OR ANYTHING.

"STEALING GOD." RIGHT, DAD. I'M DELIVERING YOU A CON MAN.

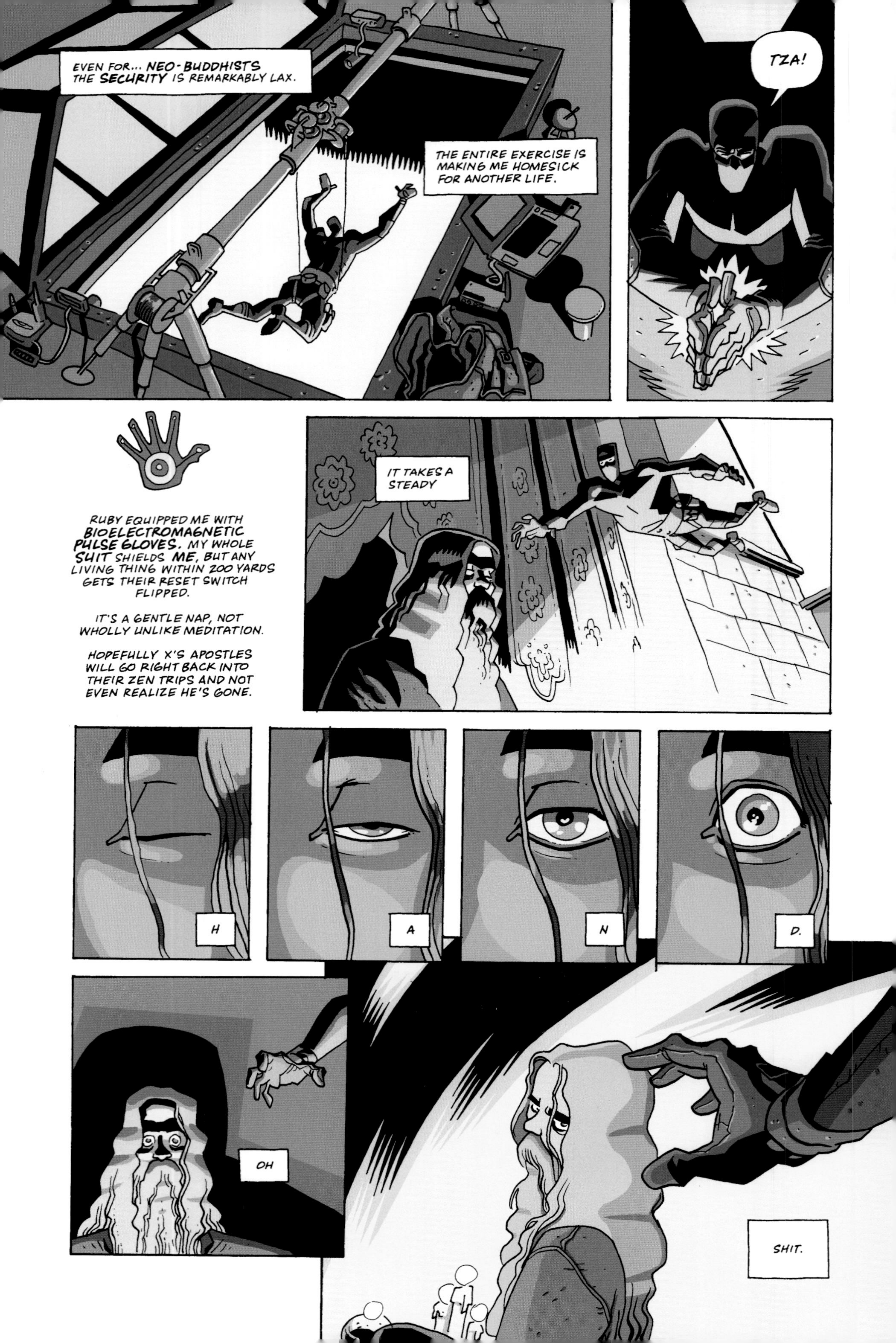
EVEN FOR... NEO-BUDDHISTS THE SECURITY IS REMARKABLY LAX.
THE ENTIRE EXERCISE IS MAKING ME HOMESICK FOR ANOTHER LIFE.
TZA!
RUBY EQUIPPED ME WITH BIOELECTROMAGNETIC PULSE GLOVES. MY WHOLE SUIT SHIELDS ME, BUT ANY LIVING THING WITHIN 200 YARDS GETS THEIR RESET SWITCH FLIPPED.
IT'S A GENTLE NAP, NOT WHOLLY UNLIKE MEDITATION.
HOPEFULLY X'S APOSTLES WILL GO RIGHT BACK INTO THEIR ZEN TRIPS AND NOT EVEN REALIZE HE'S GONE.
IT TAKES A STEADY
H
A
N
D.
OH
SHIT.

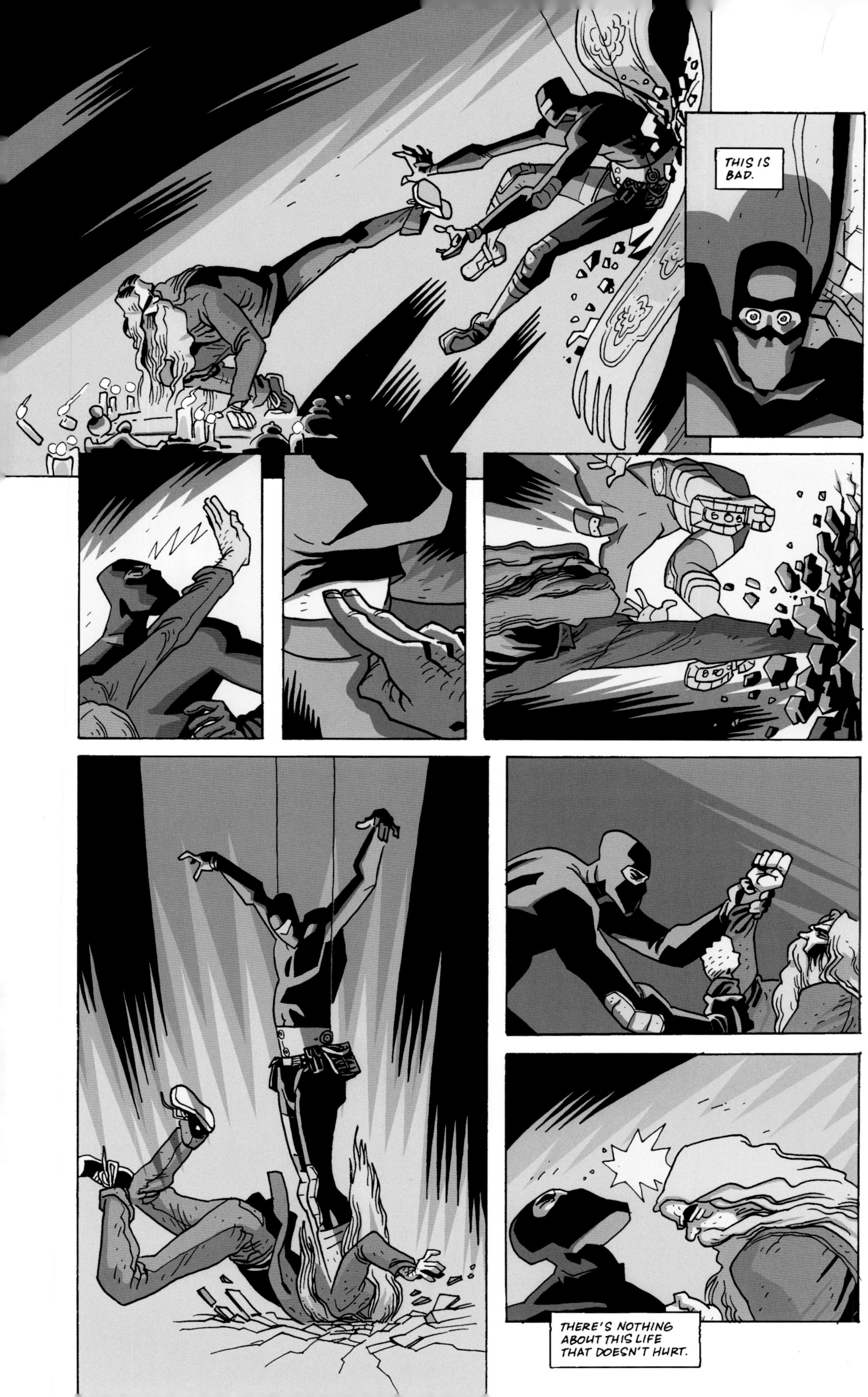
THIS IS BAD.
THERE'S NOTHING ABOUT THIS LIFE THAT DOESN'T HURT.

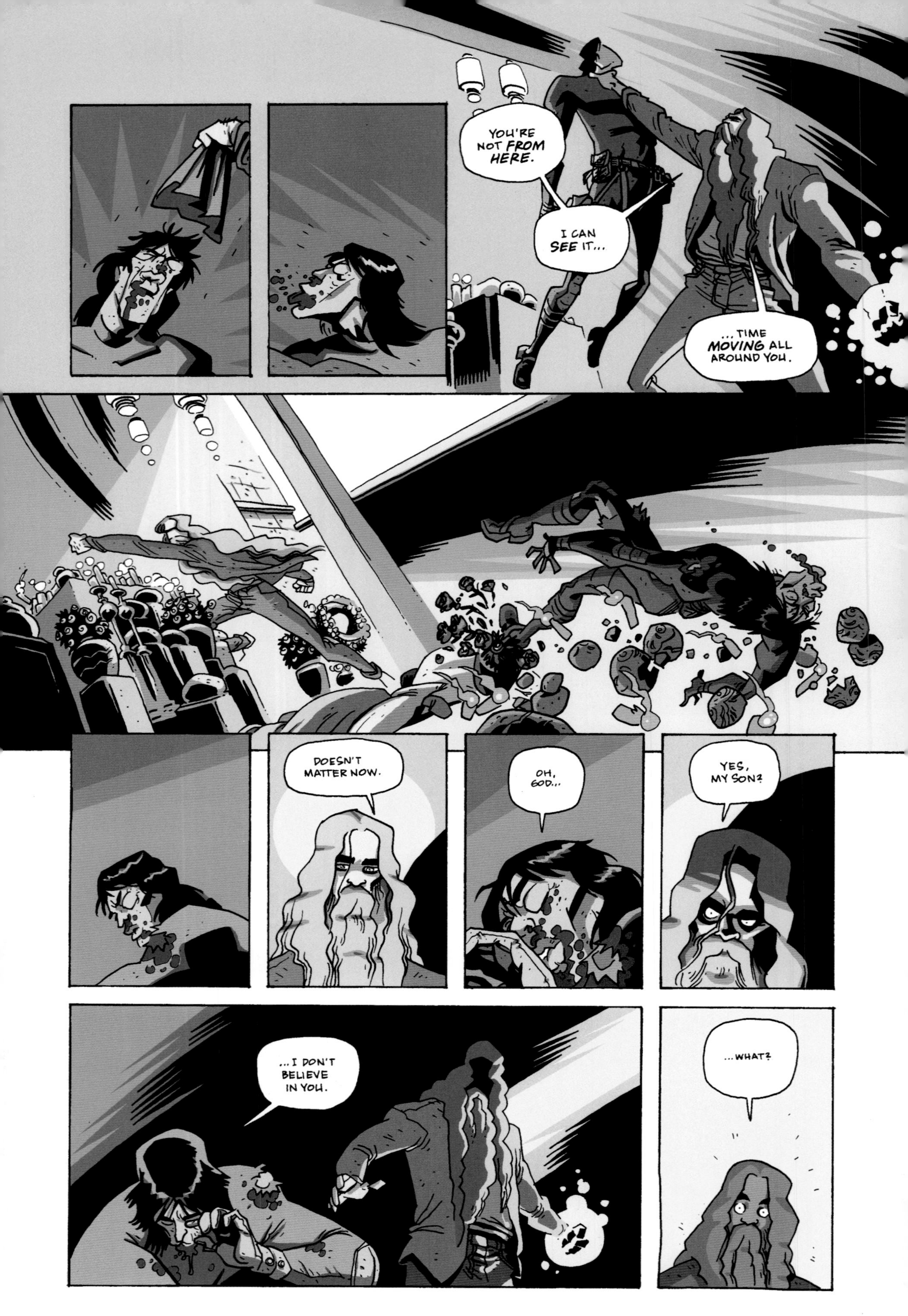
YOU'RE NOT FROM HERE.
I CAN SEE IT...
...TIME MOVING ALL AROUND YOU.
DOESN'T MATTER NOW.
OH, GOD...
YES, MY SON?
...I DON'T BELIEVE IN YOU.
...WHAT?

I....

... I DON'T UNDERSTAND.

YOU'RE A SCAM.

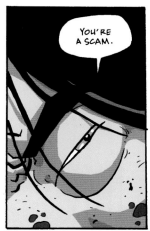

YOUR PEOPLE SNUCK YOU FOOD AND WATER. NO MEDICAL STAFF WAS EVER ALLOWED TO EXAMINE YOU.

THERE WERE TIMES WHEN THE PUBLIC WEREN'T ALLOWED IN THE FACILITY.

...

AND *I CALL BULLSHIT.*

AFTER PUNCHING GOD IN THE BRAIN, I SMUGGLED THE VICIOUS LITTLE BASTARD BACK TO E.M.P.I.R.E.

I HAVE NO IDEA WHAT THEY'LL *DO* WITH A *HOSTAGE GOD*, BUT THE MIND REELS, AND I HOPE IT HURTS.

SO WITH ONE *MASTER* APPEASED AND MY BUZZ VERY THOROUGHLY ON, I WENT TO APPEASE MY *OTHER* MASTER...

THERE WAS NO *TIME*, XENO. IT CAME UP AND AN HOUR LATER I WAS ON A PLANE.

NO NO NO! THIS WILL NEVER DO.

I RATHER *LIKE* THE IDEA OF A LITTLE *ZEN CHAOS.* YOU'LL JUST HAVE TO *REPLACE* HIM IN TIME FOR HIM TO *WAKE UP.*

THERE'S *NO WAY* I'D BE ABLE TO GET HIM OUT OF WHEREVER E.M.P.I.R.E. HAS HIM.

"THEN I SUGGEST *YOU TWO* FIND A *RINGER.* FAST."

SABINE SEYCHELLE.

WE NEED A MAN OF YOUR *UNIQUE TALENTS* AND *RESOURCES* TO SYNTHESIZE A HUMAN MALE IN THE NEXT TWELVE HOURS.

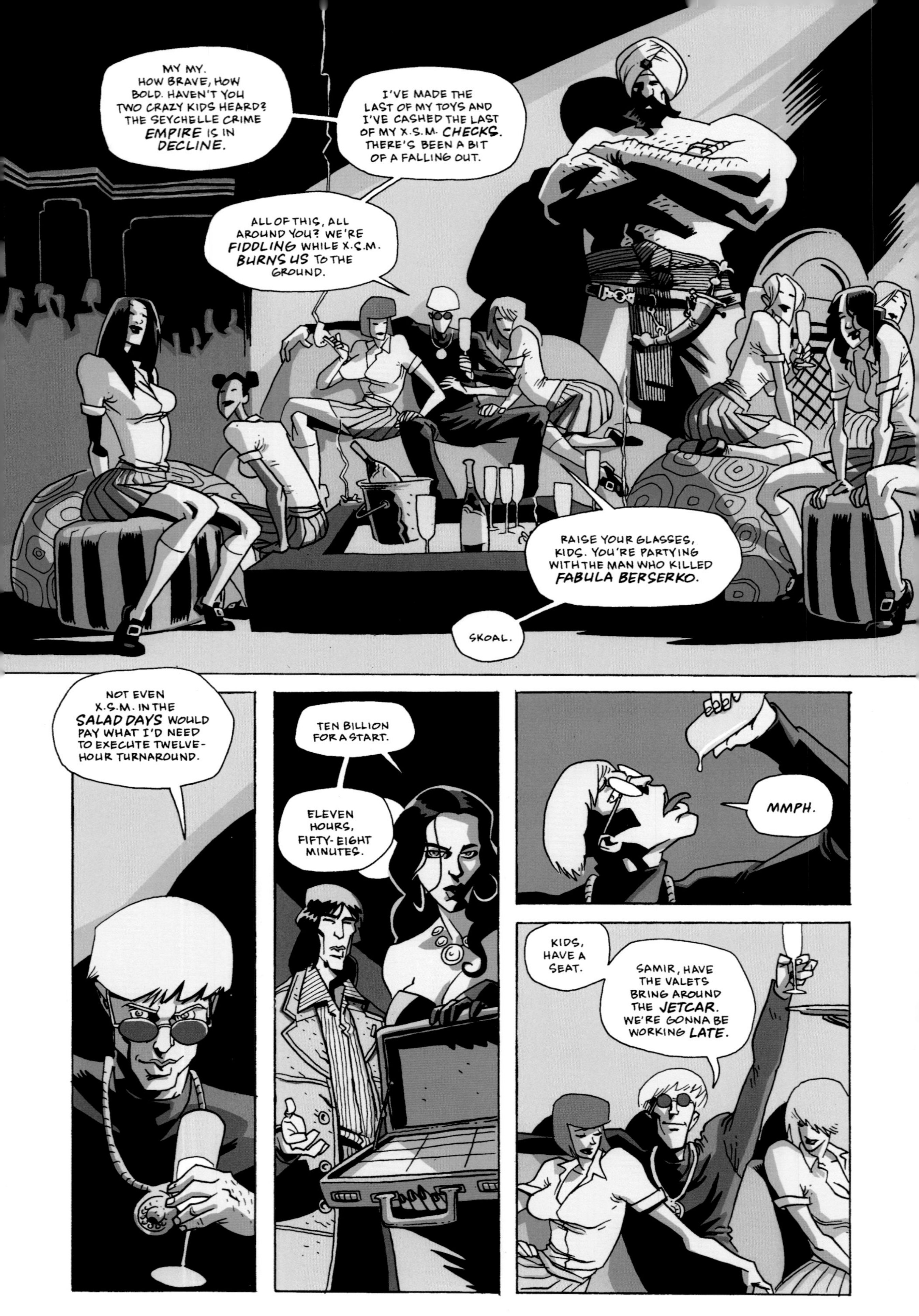
MY MY. HOW BRAVE, HOW BOLD. HAVEN'T YOU TWO CRAZY KIDS HEARD? THE SEYCHELLE CRIME EMPIRE IS IN DECLINE.
I'VE MADE THE LAST OF MY TOYS AND I'VE CASHED THE LAST OF MY X.S.M. CHECKS. THERE'S BEEN A BIT OF A FALLING OUT.
ALL OF THIS, ALL AROUND YOU? WE'RE FIDDLING WHILE X.S.M. BURNS US TO THE GROUND.
RAISE YOUR GLASSES, KIDS. YOU'RE PARTYING WITH THE MAN WHO KILLED FABULA BERSERKO.
SKOAL.
NOT EVEN X.S.M. IN THE SALAD DAYS WOULD PAY WHAT I'D NEED TO EXECUTE TWELVE-HOUR TURNAROUND.
TEN BILLION FOR A START.
ELEVEN HOURS, FIFTY-EIGHT MINUTES.
MMPH.
KIDS, HAVE A SEAT.
SAMIR, HAVE THE VALETS BRING AROUND THE JETCAR. WE'RE GONNA BE WORKING LATE.

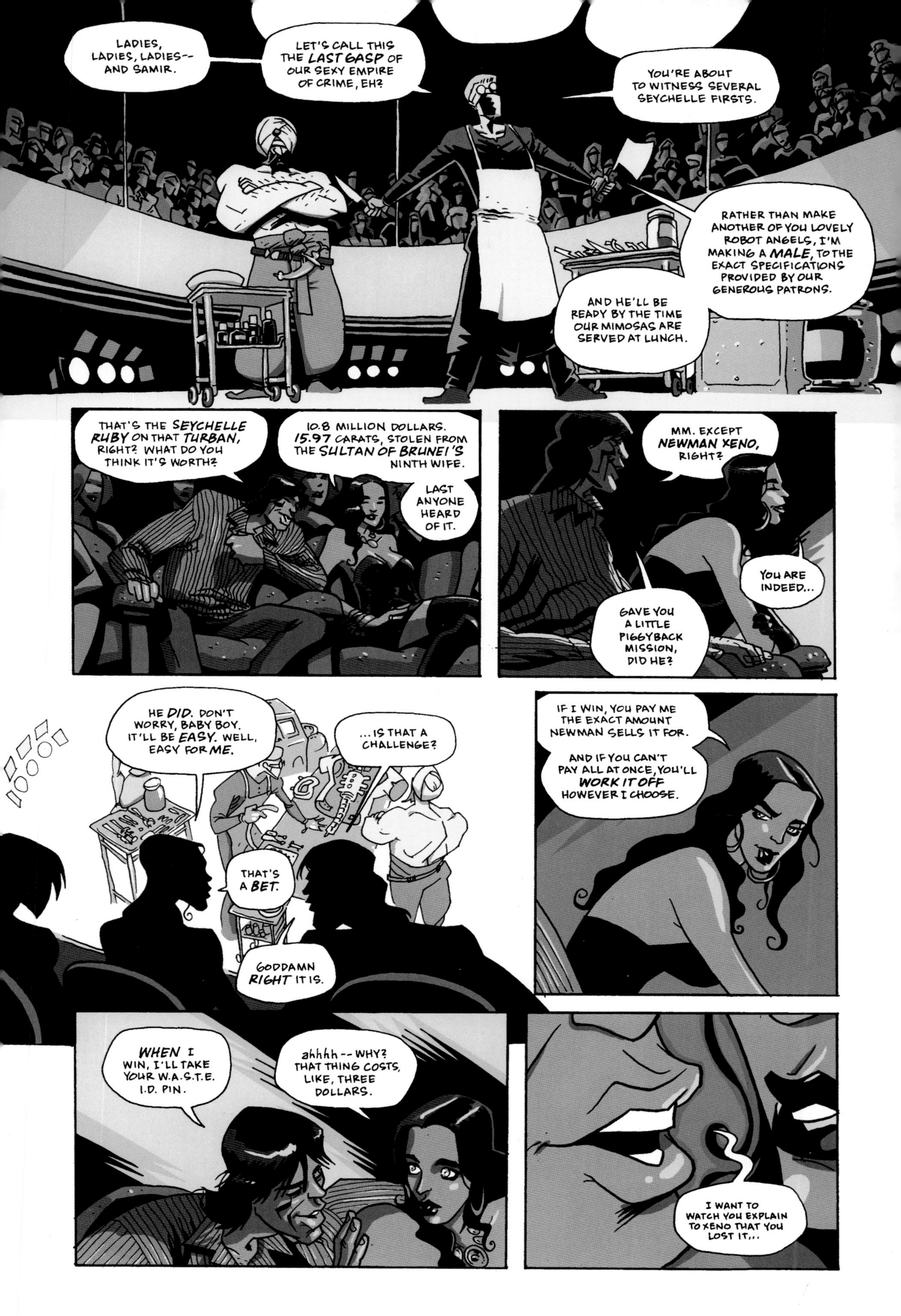
LADIES, LADIES, LADIES-- AND SAMIR.
LET'S CALL THIS THE LAST GASP OF OUR SEXY EMPIRE OF CRIME, EH?
YOU'RE ABOUT TO WITNESS SEVERAL SEYCHELLE FIRSTS.
RATHER THAN MAKE ANOTHER OF YOU LOVELY ROBOT ANGELS, I'M MAKING A MALE, TO THE EXACT SPECIFICATIONS PROVIDED BY OUR GENEROUS PATRONS.
AND HE'LL BE READY BY THE TIME OUR MIMOSAS ARE SERVED AT LUNCH.
THAT'S THE SEYCHELLE RUBY ON THAT TURBAN, RIGHT? WHAT DO YOU THINK IT'S WORTH?
10.8 MILLION DOLLARS. 15.97 CARATS, STOLEN FROM THE SULTAN OF BRUNEI'S NINTH WIFE.
LAST ANYONE HEARD OF IT.
MM. EXCEPT NEWMAN XENO, RIGHT?
YOU ARE INDEED...
GAVE YOU A LITTLE PIGGYBACK MISSION, DID HE?
HE DID. DON'T WORRY, BABY BOY. IT'LL BE EASY. WELL, EASY FOR ME.
...IS THAT A CHALLENGE?
THAT'S A BET.
GODDAMN RIGHT IT IS.
IF I WIN, YOU PAY ME THE EXACT AMOUNT NEWMAN SELLS IT FOR.
AND IF YOU CAN'T PAY ALL AT ONCE, YOU'LL WORK IT OFF HOWEVER I CHOOSE.
WHEN I WIN, I'LL TAKE YOUR W.A.S.T.E. I.D. PIN.
ahhhh -- WHY? THAT THING COSTS, LIKE, THREE DOLLARS.
I WANT TO WATCH YOU EXPLAIN TO XENO THAT YOU LOST IT...

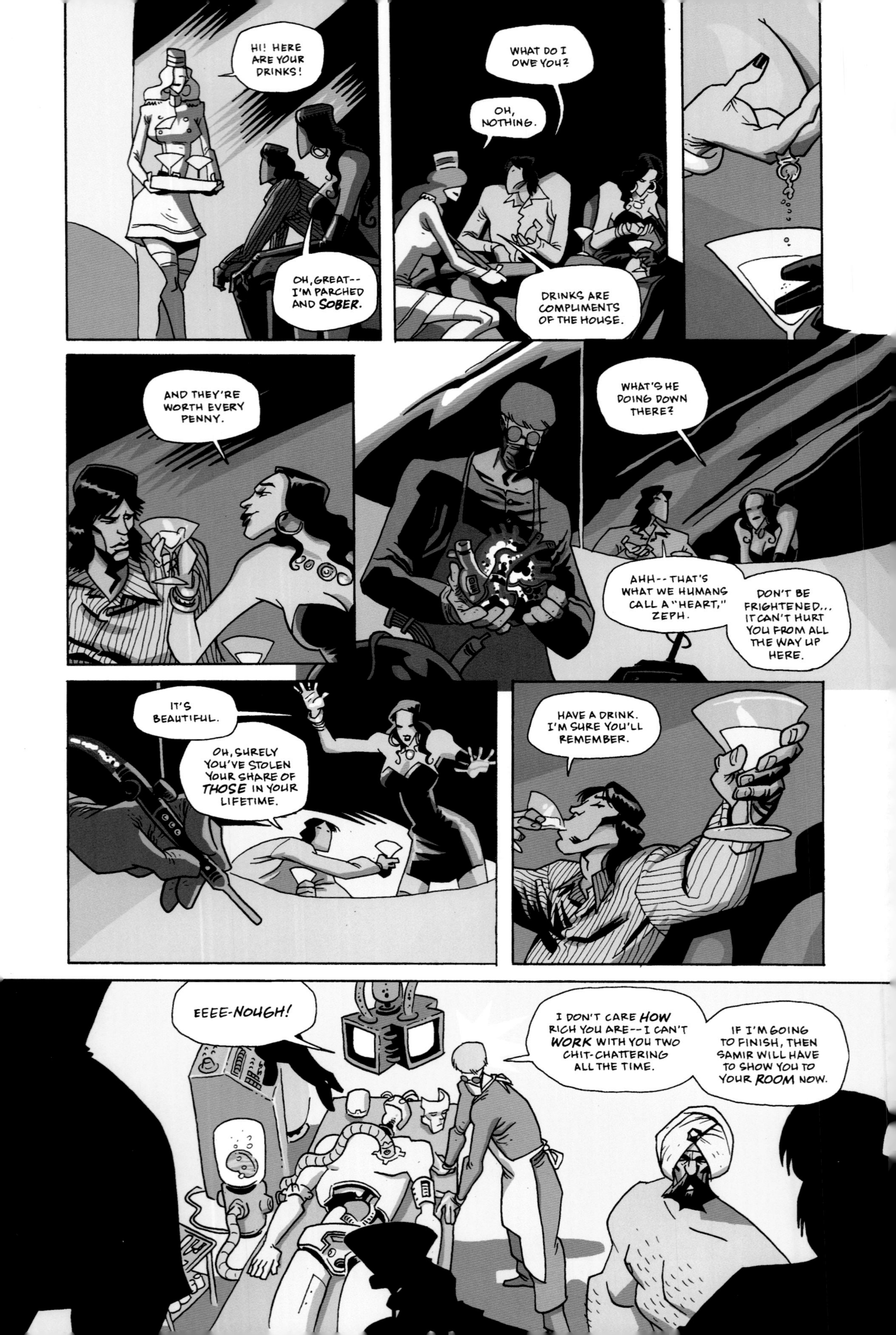
HI! HERE ARE YOUR DRINKS!
OH, GREAT-- I'M PARCHED AND SOBER.
WHAT DO I OWE YOU?
OH, NOTHING.
DRINKS ARE COMPLIMENTS OF THE HOUSE.
AND THEY'RE WORTH EVERY PENNY.
WHAT'S HE DOING DOWN THERE?
AHH-- THAT'S WHAT WE HUMANS CALL A "HEART," ZEPH.
DON'T BE FRIGHTENED... IT CAN'T HURT YOU FROM ALL THE WAY UP HERE.
IT'S BEAUTIFUL.
OH, SURELY YOU'VE STOLEN YOUR SHARE OF THOSE IN YOUR LIFETIME.
HAVE A DRINK. I'M SURE YOU'LL REMEMBER.
EEEE-NOUGH!
I DON'T CARE HOW RICH YOU ARE-- I CAN'T WORK WITH YOU TWO CHIT-CHATTERING ALL THE TIME.
IF I'M GOING TO FINISH, THEN SAMIR WILL HAVE TO SHOW YOU TO YOUR ROOM NOW.

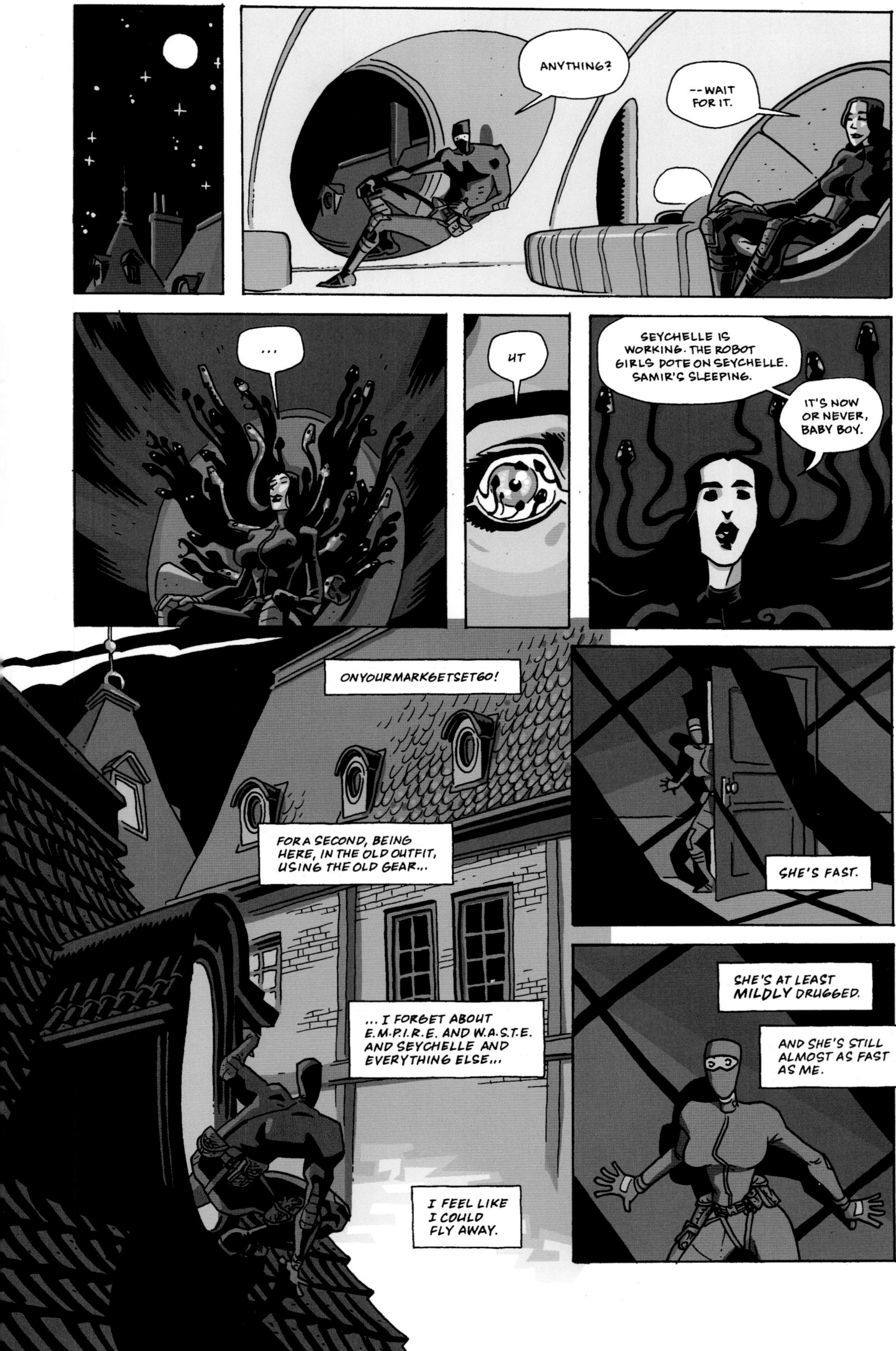
ANYTHING?
--WAIT FOR IT.
...
UT
SEYCHELLE IS WORKING. THE ROBOT GIRLS DOTE ON SEYCHELLE. SAMIR'S SLEEPING.
IT'S NOW OR NEVER, BABY BOY.
ONYOURMARKGETSETGO!
FOR A SECOND, BEING HERE, IN THE OLD OUTFIT, USING THE OLD GEAR...
...I FORGET ABOUT E.M.P.I.R.E. AND W.A.S.T.E. AND SEYCHELLE AND EVERYTHING ELSE...
I FEEL LIKE I COULD FLY AWAY.
SHE'S FAST.
SHE'S AT LEAST MILDLY DRUGGED.
AND SHE'S STILL ALMOST AS FAST AS ME.

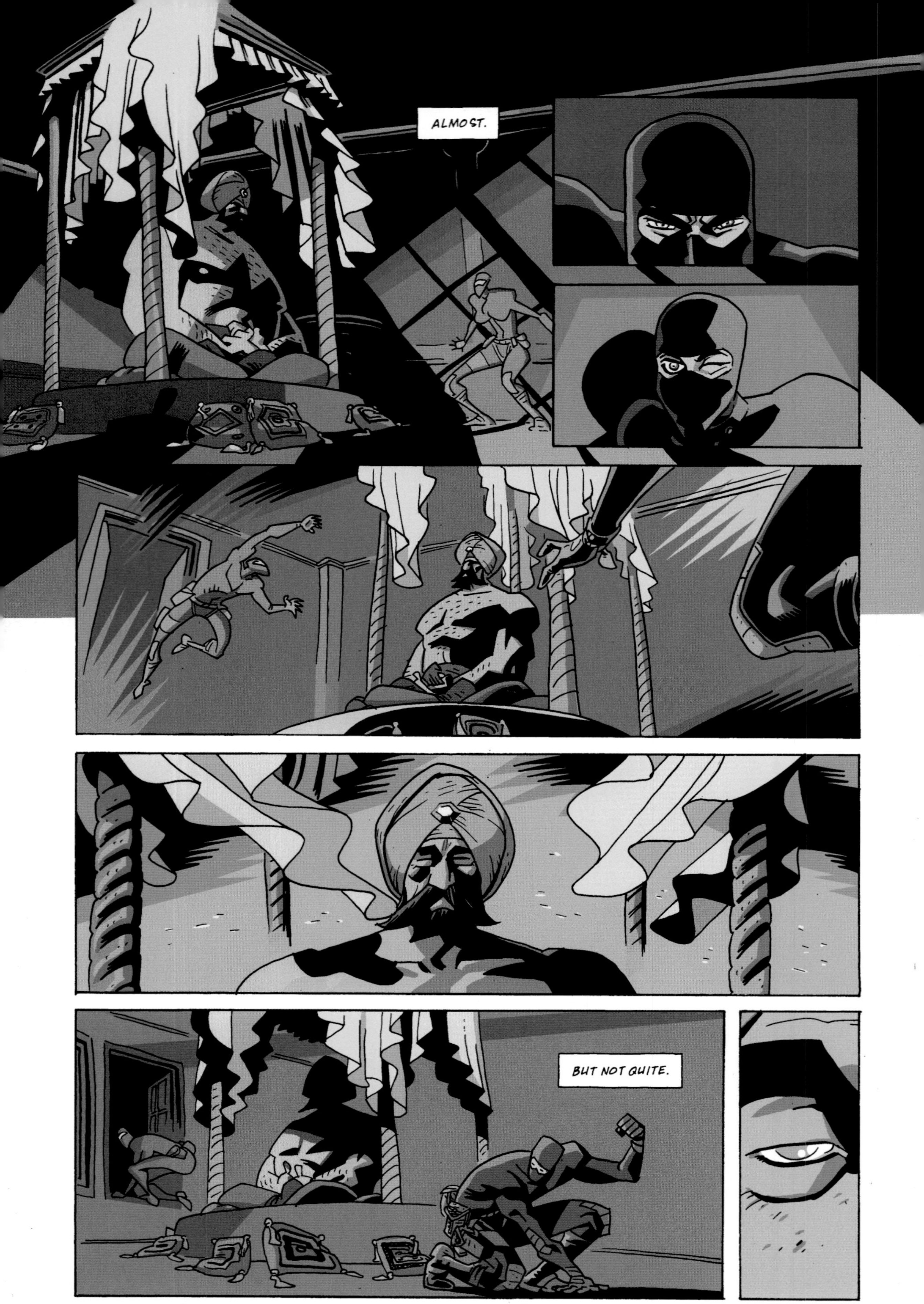
ALMOST.
BUT NOT QUITE.

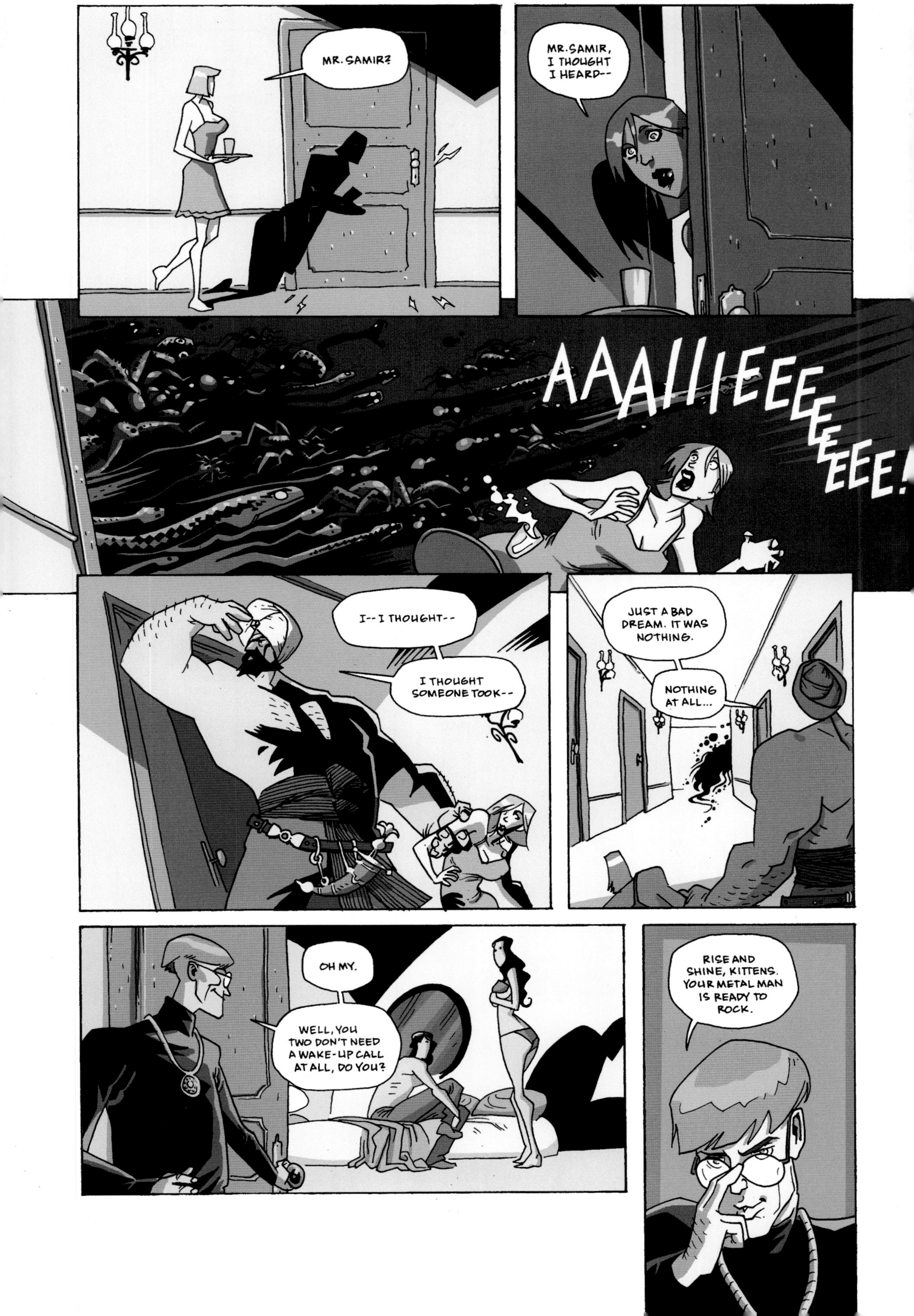
MR. SAMIR?
MR. SAMIR, I THOUGHT I HEARD--
AAAIIIIEEEEEEEE!
I-- I THOUGHT--
I THOUGHT SOMEONE TOOK--
JUST A BAD DREAM. IT WAS NOTHING.
NOTHING AT ALL...
OH MY.
WELL, YOU TWO DON'T NEED A WAKE-UP CALL AT ALL, DO YOU?
RISE AND SHINE, KITTENS. YOUR METAL MAN IS READY TO ROCK.

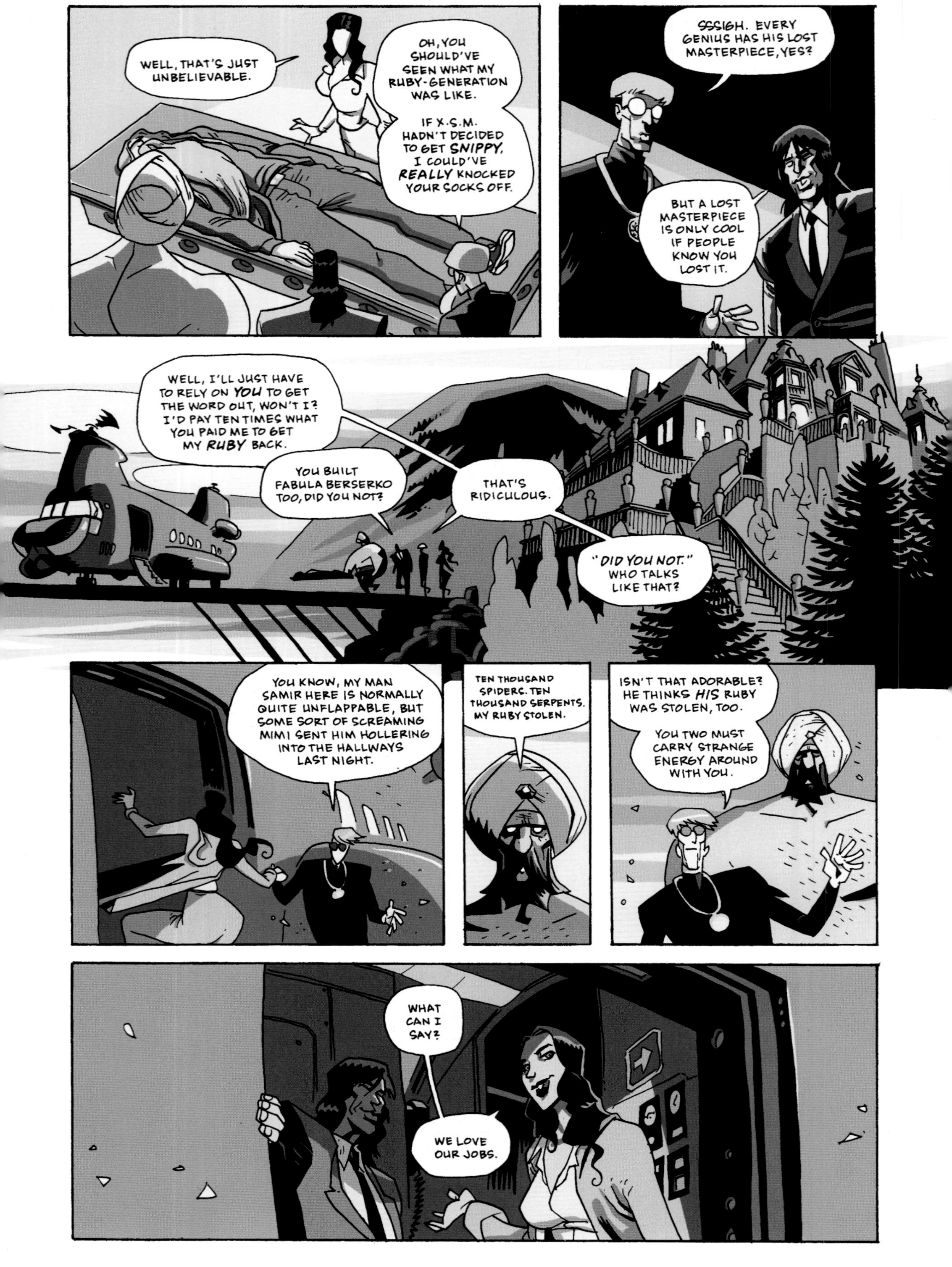

WELL, THAT'S JUST UNBELIEVABLE.
OH, YOU SHOULD'VE SEEN WHAT MY RUBY-GENERATION WAS LIKE.
IF X.S.M. HADN'T DECIDED TO GET SNIPPY, I COULD'VE REALLY KNOCKED YOUR SOCKS OFF.
SSSIGH. EVERY GENIUS HAS HIS LOST MASTERPIECE, YES?
BUT A LOST MASTERPIECE IS ONLY COOL IF PEOPLE KNOW YOU LOST IT.
WELL, I'LL JUST HAVE TO RELY ON YOU TO GET THE WORD OUT, WON'T I? I'D PAY TEN TIMES WHAT YOU PAID ME TO GET MY RUBY BACK.
YOU BUILT FABULA BERSERKO TOO, DID YOU NOT?
THAT'S RIDICULOUS.
"DID YOU NOT." WHO TALKS LIKE THAT?
YOU KNOW, MY MAN SAMIR HERE IS NORMALLY QUITE UNFLAPPABLE, BUT SOME SORT OF SCREAMING MIMI SENT HIM HOLLERING INTO THE HALLWAYS LAST NIGHT.
TEN THOUSAND SPIDERS. TEN THOUSAND SERPENTS. MY RUBY STOLEN.
ISN'T THAT ADORABLE? HE THINKS HIS RUBY WAS STOLEN, TOO.
YOU TWO MUST CARRY STRANGE ENERGY AROUND WITH YOU.
WHAT CAN I SAY?
WE LOVE OUR JOBS.

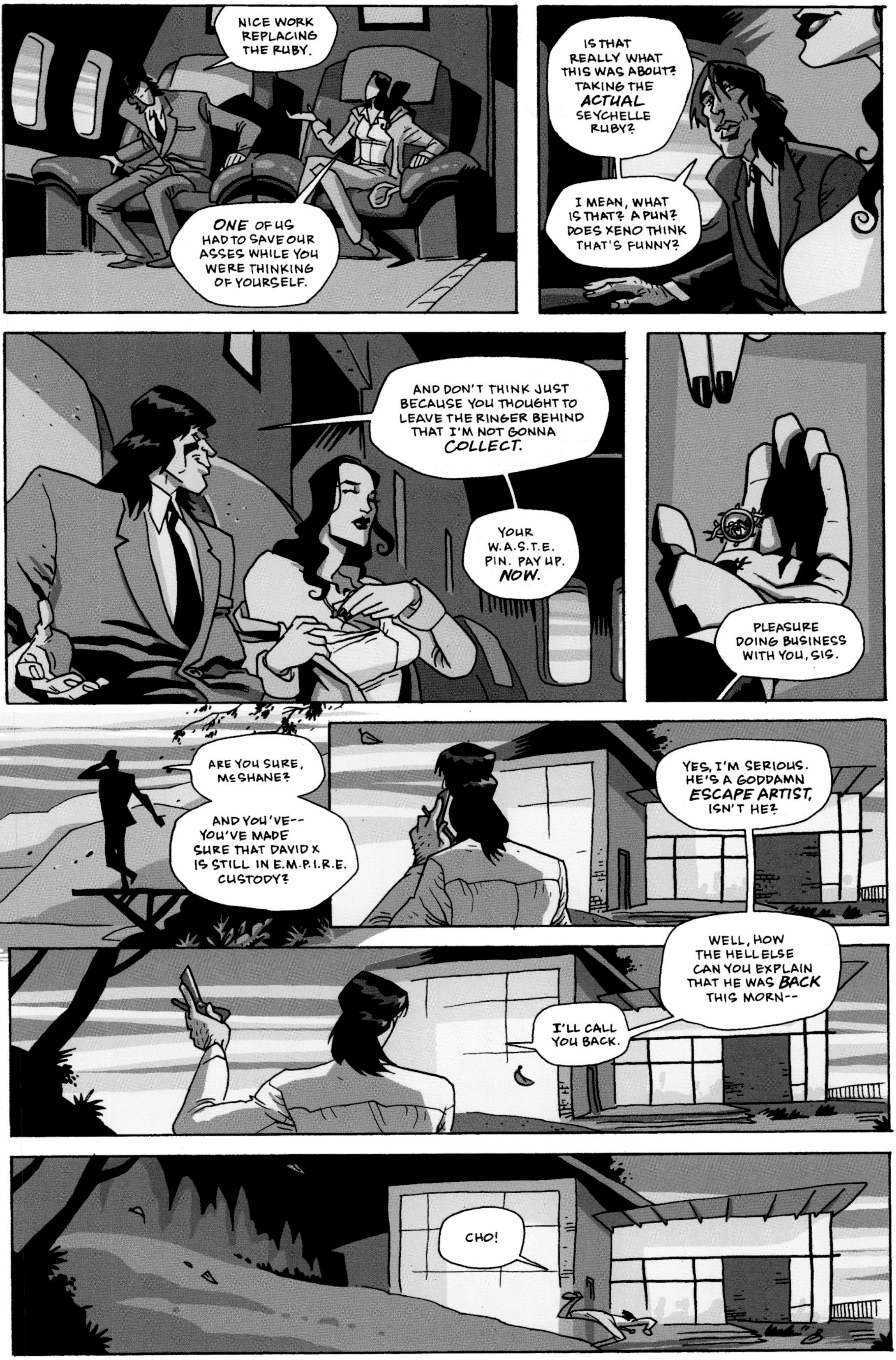
NICE WORK REPLACING THE RUBY.
ONE OF US HAD TO SAVE OUR ASSES WHILE YOU WERE THINKING OF YOURSELF.
IS THAT REALLY WHAT THIS WAS ABOUT? TAKING THE ACTUAL SEYCHELLE RUBY?
I MEAN, WHAT IS THAT? A PUN? DOES XENO THINK THAT'S FUNNY?
AND DON'T THINK JUST BECAUSE YOU THOUGHT TO LEAVE THE RINGER BEHIND THAT I'M NOT GONNA COLLECT.
YOUR W.A.S.T.E. PIN. PAY UP. NOW.
PLEASURE DOING BUSINESS WITH YOU, SIS.
ARE YOU SURE, McSHANE?
AND YOU'VE-- YOU'VE MADE SURE THAT DAVID X IS STILL IN E.M.P.I.R.E. CUSTODY?
YES, I'M SERIOUS. HE'S A GODDAMN ESCAPE ARTIST, ISN'T HE?
WELL, HOW THE HELL ELSE CAN YOU EXPLAIN THAT HE WAS BACK THIS MORN--
I'LL CALL YOU BACK.
CHO!

ZU!

MR. CASS!

I CAN'T TELL WHERE THEY'RE AT!

WHAT'S SCARY IS I CAN'T EITHER--

THEY'RE LIKE BLIND SPOTS. THEY LOOK LIKE... LACK.

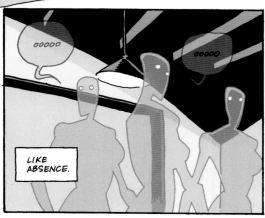

OOOOO

OOOOO

LIKE ABSENCE.

JESUS CHRIST!

MR. CASS! WHO ON EARTH WOULD DO SOMETHING LIKE THIS?

MAYBE **DAD** KNOWS I KNOW WHERE HE HID MOM. MAYBE **XENO** WANTS ME EDGY. MAYBE **ZEPH** IS PISSED OFF ABOUT LOSING OUR **BET.** MAYBE **SEYCHELLE** KNOWS SOMETHING. MAYBE **RUBY** REMEMBERED SOMETHING. MAYBE M^cSHANE KNOWS THERE'S **ANOTHER RUBY** IN ÁGUA PESADA. MAYBE X.S.M. KNOWS IT'S **ME** WHO KILLED **BERSERKO.**

OR MAYBE...

IT'S NOT SAFE FOR **MOM** TO BE HERE ANYMORE.

WE HAVE TO **HIDE** HER...

EXECUTION DAYS

PRETTY LITTLE POLICEMAN

MISSION TO YERBA MUERTA

DÉTOURNEMENT

COLDHEART

WOMEN AND MEN (PART ONE)

WOMEN AND MEN (PART TWO)

I THINK I ALMOST LOVED HIM

IS THIS IT? (REDUX)

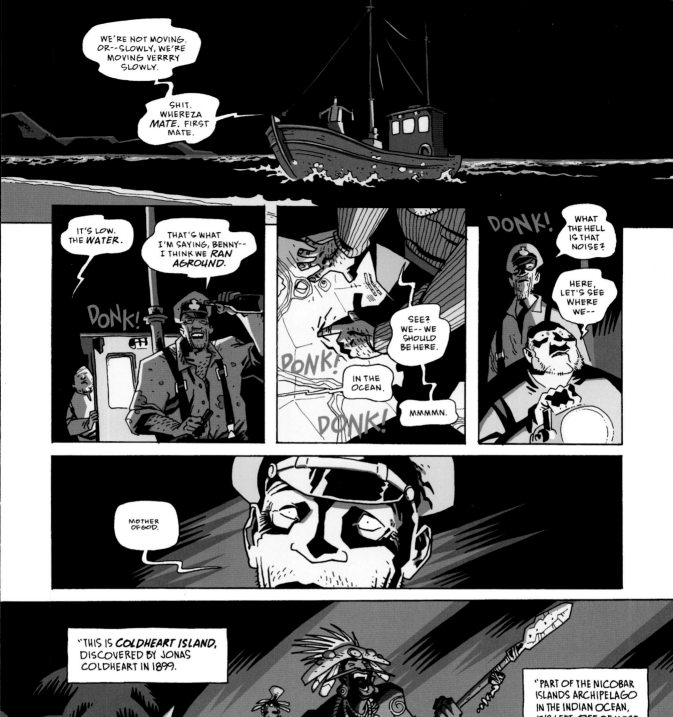

WE'RE NOT MOVING. OR--SLOWLY, WE'RE MOVING VERRRY SLOWLY.

SHIT. WHEREZA *MATE*. FIRST MATE.

IT'S LOW. THE *WATER*.

THAT'S WHAT I'M SAYING, BENNY-- I THINK WE *RAN AGROUND*.

DONK!

SEE? WE-- WE SHOULD BE HERE.

IN THE OCEAN.

MMMMN.

DONK!

DONK!

DONK!

WHAT THE HELL IS THAT NOISE?

HERE, LET'S SEE WHERE WE--

DONK!

MOTHER OF GOD.

"THIS IS *COLDHEART ISLAND,* DISCOVERED BY JONAS COLDHEART IN 1899.

"PART OF THE NICOBAR ISLANDS ARCHIPELAGO IN THE INDIAN OCEAN, IT'S LEFT *OFF* OF MOST COMMERCIAL FISHING AND NAUTICAL MAPS.

"THIS IS BECAUSE, LIVING THERE UNMOLESTED, IS THE *LAST TRIBE* OF *PRE-NEOLITHIC* MAN ON THE PLANET."

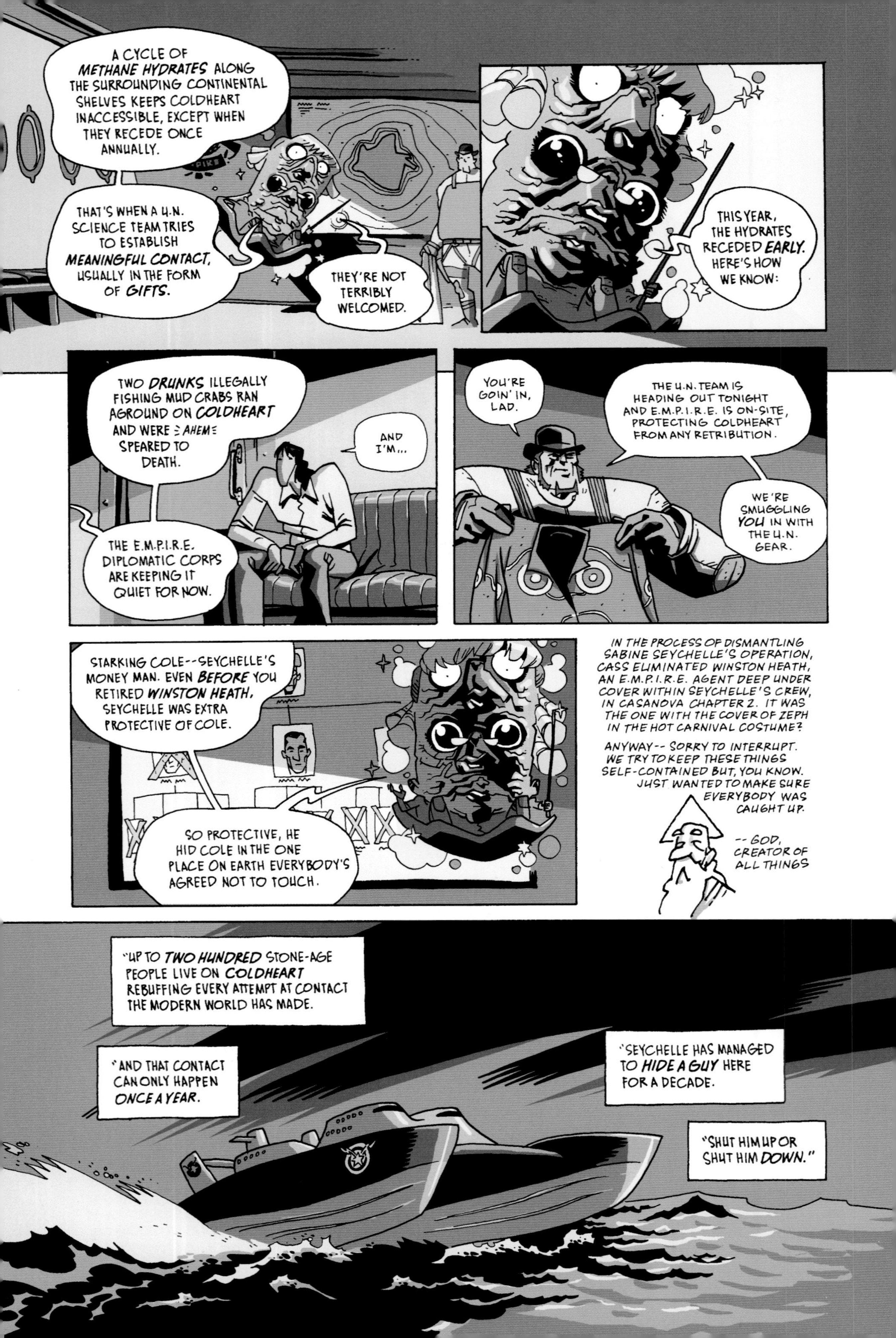

A CYCLE OF METHANE HYDRATES ALONG THE SURROUNDING CONTINENTAL SHELVES KEEPS COLDHEART INACCESSIBLE, EXCEPT WHEN THEY RECEDE ONCE ANNUALLY.
THAT'S WHEN A U.N. SCIENCE TEAM TRIES TO ESTABLISH MEANINGFUL CONTACT, USUALLY IN THE FORM OF GIFTS.
THEY'RE NOT TERRIBLY WELCOMED.
THIS YEAR, THE HYDRATES RECEDED EARLY. HERE'S HOW WE KNOW:
TWO DRUNKS ILLEGALLY FISHING MUD CRABS RAN AGROUND ON COLDHEART AND WERE ≥AHEM≤ SPEARED TO DEATH.
AND I'M...
THE E.M.P.I.R.E. DIPLOMATIC CORPS ARE KEEPING IT QUIET FOR NOW.
YOU'RE GOIN' IN, LAD.
THE U.N. TEAM IS HEADING OUT TONIGHT AND E.M.P.I.R.E. IS ON-SITE, PROTECTING COLDHEART FROM ANY RETRIBUTION.
WE'RE SMUGGLING YOU IN WITH THE U.N. GEAR.
STARKING COLE--SEYCHELLE'S MONEY MAN. EVEN BEFORE YOU RETIRED WINSTON HEATH, SEYCHELLE WAS EXTRA PROTECTIVE OF COLE.
SO PROTECTIVE, HE HID COLE IN THE ONE PLACE ON EARTH EVERYBODY'S AGREED NOT TO TOUCH.
IN THE PROCESS OF DISMANTLING SABINE SEYCHELLE'S OPERATION, CASS ELIMINATED WINSTON HEATH, AN E.M.P.I.R.E. AGENT DEEP UNDER COVER WITHIN SEYCHELLE'S CREW, IN CASANOVA CHAPTER 2. IT WAS THE ONE WITH THE COVER OF ZEPH IN THE HOT CARNIVAL COSTUME?
ANYWAY-- SORRY TO INTERRUPT. WE TRY TO KEEP THESE THINGS SELF-CONTAINED BUT, YOU KNOW. JUST WANTED TO MAKE SURE EVERYBODY WAS CAUGHT UP.
-- GOD, CREATOR OF ALL THINGS
"UP TO TWO HUNDRED STONE-AGE PEOPLE LIVE ON COLDHEART REBUFFING EVERY ATTEMPT AT CONTACT THE MODERN WORLD HAS MADE.
"AND THAT CONTACT CAN ONLY HAPPEN ONCE A YEAR.
"SEYCHELLE HAS MANAGED TO HIDE A GUY HERE FOR A DECADE.
"SHUT HIM UP OR SHUT HIM DOWN."

WHAT ABOUT *W.A.S.T.E.*, McSHANE?

WHAT ABOUT "WHAT ABOUT *W.A.S.T.E.?*"

I DUNNO—WHAT ARE WE DOING ABOUT *W.A.S.T.E.?* SEYCHELLE ISN'T EVEN *X.S.M.* CLASS AND WE'RE FOCUSING ON HIM AND *THEN* THEM WHILE THE *BIG FISH*—

YOU *DON'T QUESTION* THE WISDOM OF *E.M.P.I.R.E.*, CASS, AND YOU DON'T *CHINTZ* ON THE *LONG VIEW.*

I'VE BEEN WORKING WITH YOUR OLD MAN SINCE THE *WAR* AND I STILL DON'T KNOW HOW TO GET THE *BIG MAN'S* ATTENTION.

QUANTUM STRATEGY ENGINES CALCULATE AND RECALCULATE THE RAMIFICATIONS THAT FARTING GNATS IN ARGENTINA HAVE ON THESE MISSIONS.

AND SINCE WHEN DO *YOU* CARE? YOU'VE NEVER BEEN MUCH OF A *BIG PICTURE* GUY.

I DUNNO, McSHANE.

I GUESS WHEN I REALIZED THE *BIG PICTURE* WAS HUNG SO *CROOKED.*

I HOPE TO CHRIST YOU DON'T WANT ME TO EXPLAIN HOW THIS WORKS, BECAUSE I CAN'T. EVEN RUBY CAN'T.

EVER SEEN ANYTHING LIKE IT?

YEAH, ONCE.

SO WHY ISN'T RUBY IN ON THE BRIEFING?

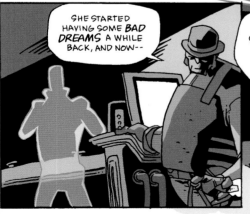

SHE STARTED HAVING SOME *BAD DREAMS* A WHILE BACK, AND NOW—

WELL, I THINK SHE REMEMBERED SOMETHING FROM BEFORE HER TIME AT *E.M.P.I.R.E.* AND WE'RE NO LONGER A GOING CONCERN.

LET'S GET YOU UP-DECK. WE'RE COMING UP ON THE U.N. SHIP NOW.

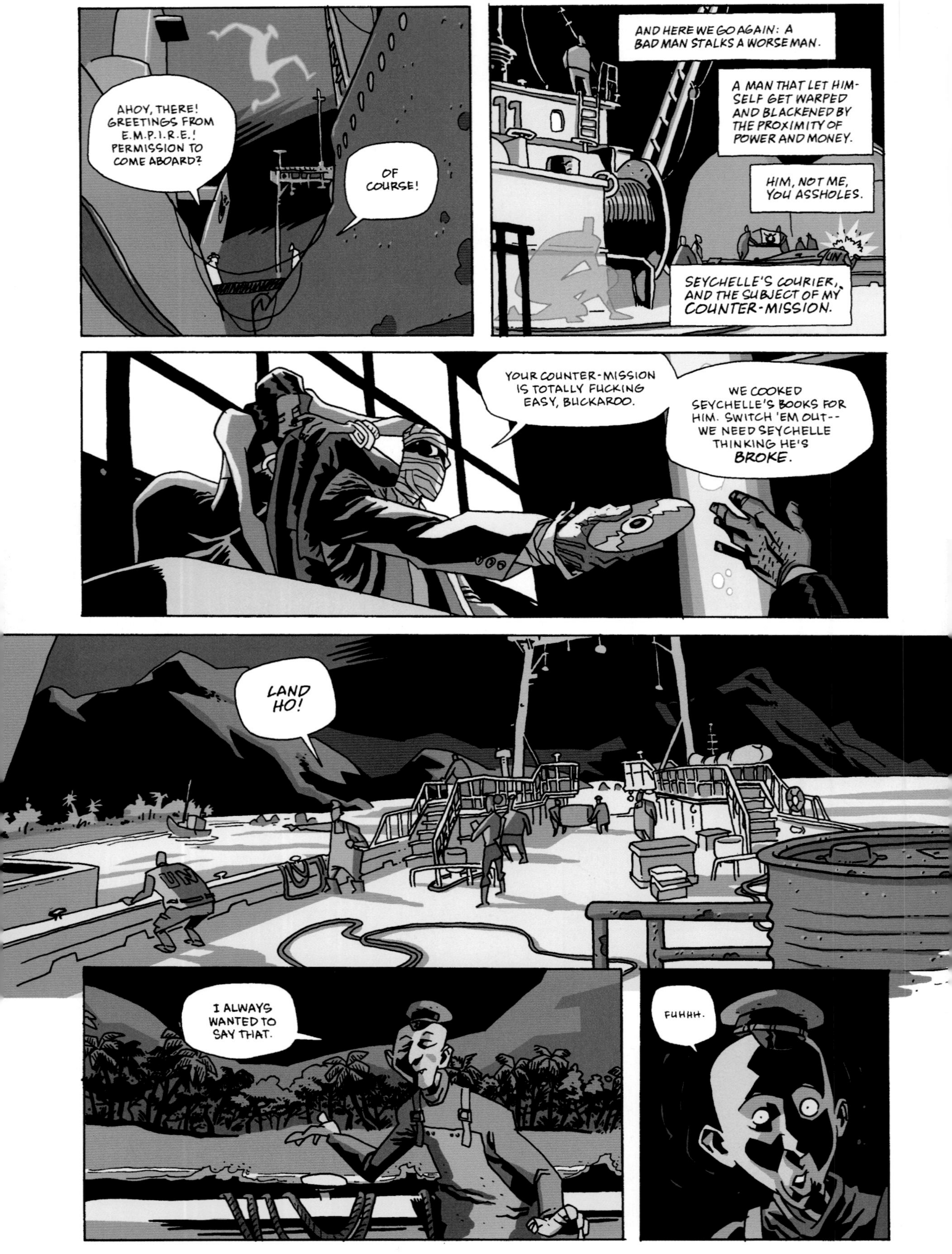
AHOY, THERE! GREETINGS FROM E.M.P.I.R.E.! PERMISSION TO COME ABOARD?
OF COURSE!
AND HERE WE GO AGAIN: A BAD MAN STALKS A WORSE MAN.
A MAN THAT LET HIMSELF GET WARPED AND BLACKENED BY THE PROXIMITY OF POWER AND MONEY.
HIM, NOT ME, YOU ASSHOLES.
UN
SEYCHELLE'S COURIER, AND THE SUBJECT OF MY COUNTER-MISSION.
YOUR COUNTER-MISSION IS TOTALLY FUCKING EASY, BUCKAROO.
WE COOKED SEYCHELLE'S BOOKS FOR HIM. SWITCH 'EM OUT-- WE NEED SEYCHELLE THINKING HE'S BROKE.
LAND HO!
UN
I ALWAYS WANTED TO SAY THAT.
FUHHH.

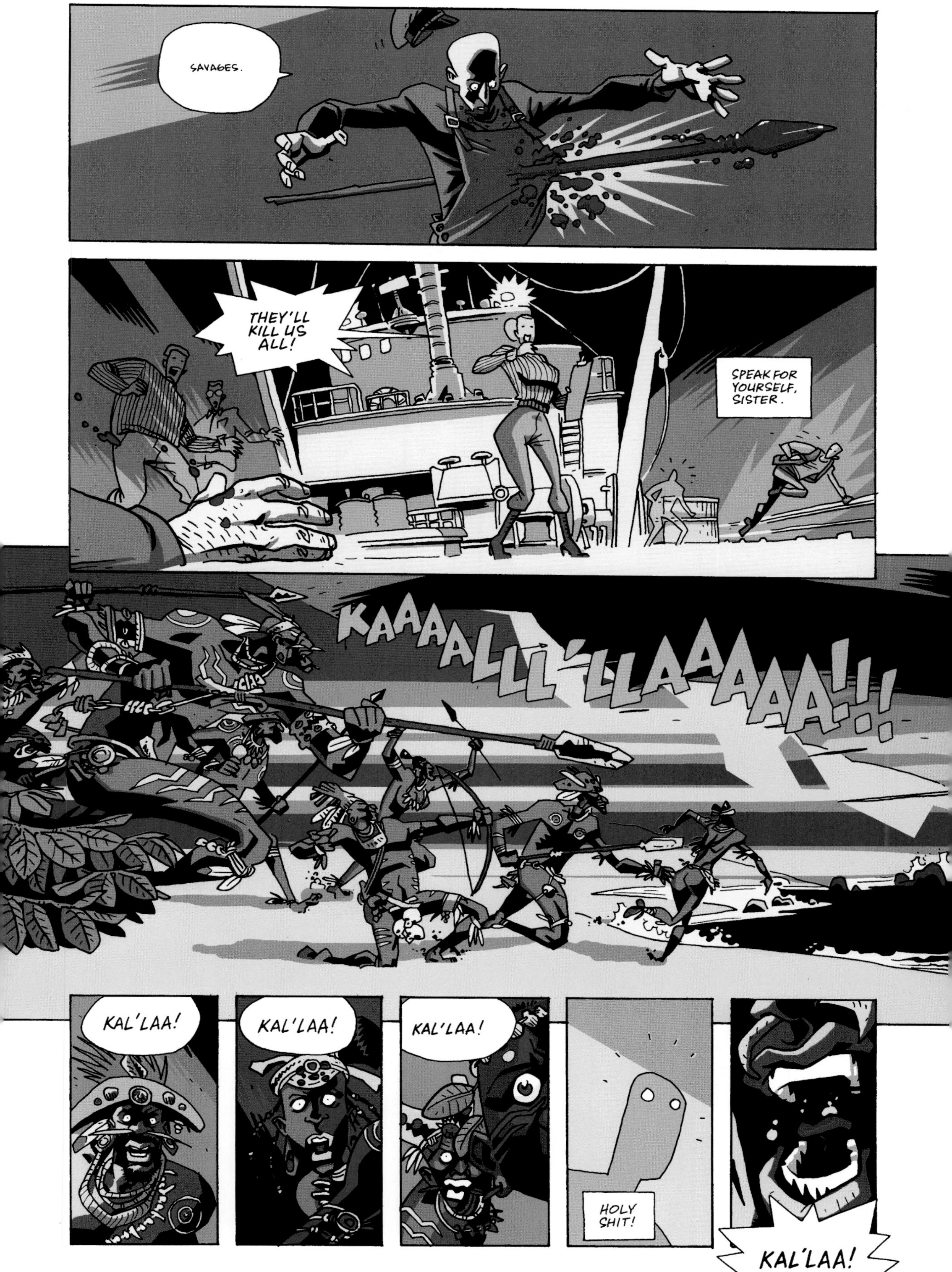
SAVAGES.
THEY'LL KILL US ALL!
SPEAK FOR YOURSELF, SISTER.
KAAAALLL'LLAAAAAA!!!
KAL'LAA!
KAL'LAA!
KAL'LAA!
HOLY SHIT!
KAL'LAA!

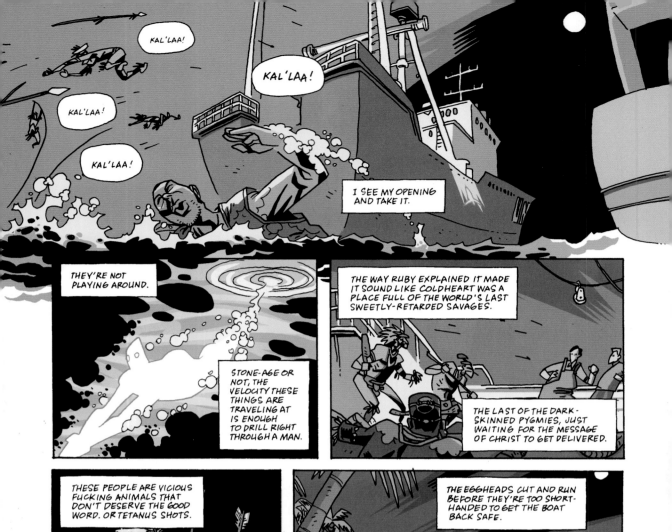

KAL'LAA!

KAL'LAA!

KAL'LAA!

KAL'LAA!

I SEE MY OPENING AND TAKE IT.

THEY'RE NOT PLAYING AROUND.

STONE-AGE OR NOT, THE VELOCITY THESE THINGS ARE TRAVELING AT IS ENOUGH TO DRILL RIGHT THROUGH A MAN.

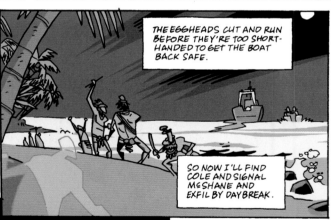

THE WAY RUBY EXPLAINED IT MADE IT SOUND LIKE COLDHEART WAS A PLACE FULL OF THE WORLD'S LAST SWEETLY-RETARDED SAVAGES.

THE LAST OF THE DARK-SKINNED PYGMIES, JUST WAITING FOR THE MESSAGE OF CHRIST TO GET DELIVERED.

THESE PEOPLE ARE VICIOUS FUCKING ANIMALS THAT DON'T DESERVE THE GOOD WORD. OR TETANUS SHOTS.

EVEN IF THEY DID DO MY DIRTY WORK FOR ME.

THE EGGHEADS CUT AND RUN BEFORE THEY'RE TOO SHORT-HANDED TO GET THE BOAT BACK SAFE.

SO NOW I'LL FIND COLE AND SIGNAL McSHANE AND EXFIL BY DAYBREAK.

KAL'LAA!

KAL'LAA!

KAL'LAA!

KAL'LAA!

AND NOT A MOMENT TOO SOON. THESE FUCKING SAVAGES CREEP ME--

HOW *WEARY* I GROW OF THIS *CHARADE.*

--OUT?

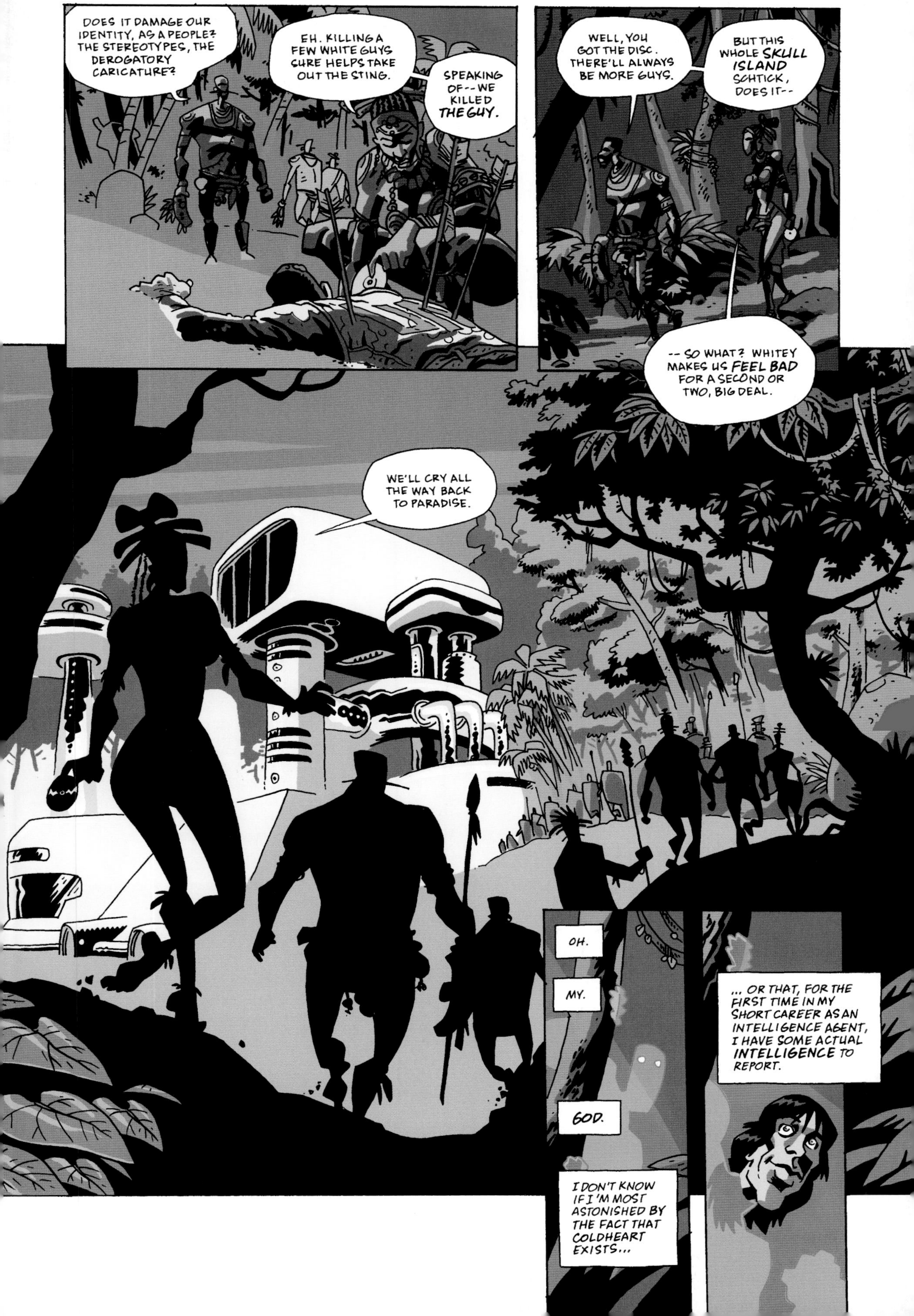
DOES IT DAMAGE OUR IDENTITY, AS A PEOPLE? THE STEREOTYPES, THE DEROGATORY CARICATURE?
EH. KILLING A FEW WHITE GUYS SURE HELPS TAKE OUT THE STING.
SPEAKING OF-- WE KILLED THE GUY.
WELL, YOU GOT THE DISC. THERE'LL ALWAYS BE MORE GUYS.
BUT THIS WHOLE SKULL ISLAND SCHTICK, DOES IT--
-- SO WHAT? WHITEY MAKES US FEEL BAD FOR A SECOND OR TWO, BIG DEAL.
WE'LL CRY ALL THE WAY BACK TO PARADISE.
OH.
MY.
GOD.
I DON'T KNOW IF I'M MOST ASTONISHED BY THE FACT THAT COLDHEART EXISTS...
... OR THAT, FOR THE FIRST TIME IN MY SHORT CAREER AS AN INTELLIGENCE AGENT, I HAVE SOME ACTUAL INTELLIGENCE TO REPORT.

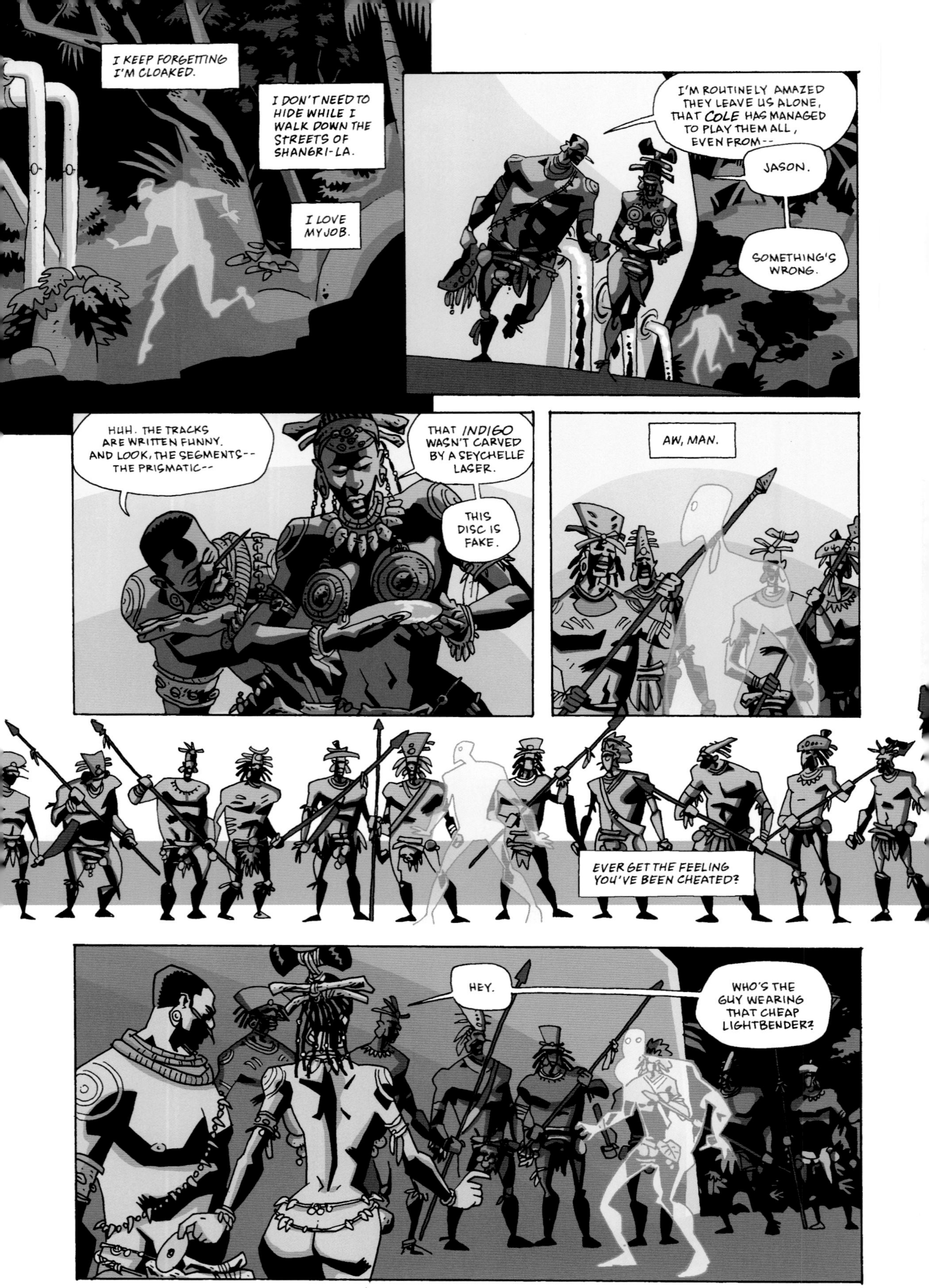
I KEEP FORGETTING I'M CLOAKED.
I DON'T NEED TO HIDE WHILE I WALK DOWN THE STREETS OF SHANGRI-LA.
I LOVE MY JOB.
I'M ROUTINELY AMAZED THEY LEAVE US ALONE, THAT COLE HAS MANAGED TO PLAY THEM ALL, EVEN FROM--
JASON.
SOMETHING'S WRONG.
HUH. THE TRACKS ARE WRITTEN FUNNY. AND LOOK, THE SEGMENTS-- THE PRISMATIC--
THAT INDIGO WASN'T CARVED BY A SEYCHELLE LASER.
THIS DISC IS FAKE.
AW, MAN.
EVER GET THE FEELING YOU'VE BEEN CHEATED?
HEY.
WHO'S THE GUY WEARING THAT CHEAP LIGHTBENDER?

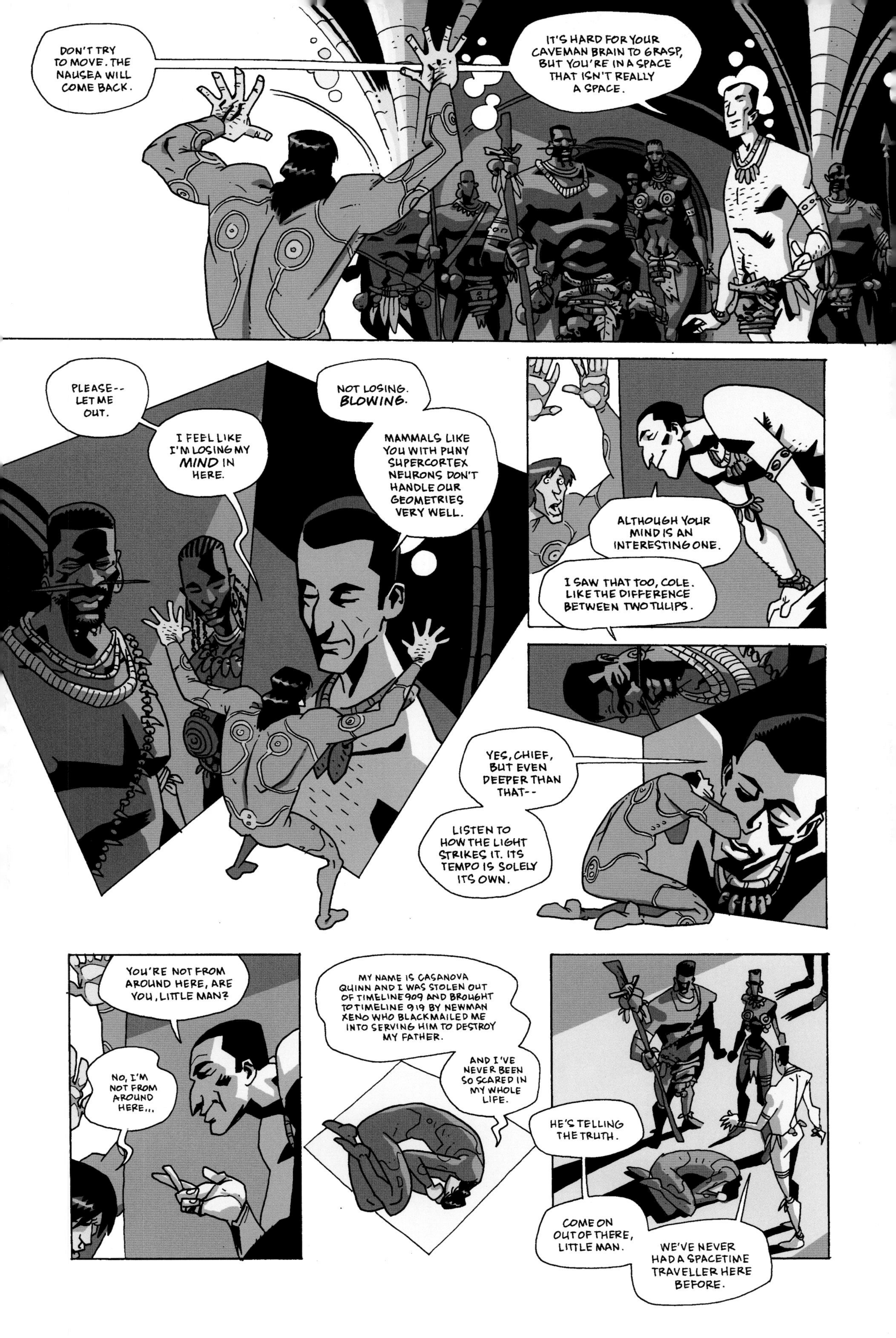
DON'T TRY TO MOVE. THE NAUSEA WILL COME BACK.
IT'S HARD FOR YOUR CAVEMAN BRAIN TO GRASP, BUT YOU'RE IN A SPACE THAT ISN'T REALLY A SPACE.
PLEASE-- LET ME OUT.
I FEEL LIKE I'M LOSING MY *MIND* IN HERE.
NOT LOSING. **BLOWING.**
MAMMALS LIKE YOU WITH PUNY SUPERCORTEX NEURONS DON'T HANDLE OUR GEOMETRIES VERY WELL.
ALTHOUGH YOUR MIND IS AN INTERESTING ONE.
I SAW THAT TOO, COLE. LIKE THE DIFFERENCE BETWEEN TWO TULIPS.
YES, CHIEF, BUT EVEN DEEPER THAN THAT--
LISTEN TO HOW THE LIGHT STRIKES IT. ITS TEMPO IS SOLELY ITS OWN.
YOU'RE NOT FROM AROUND HERE, ARE YOU, LITTLE MAN?
NO, I'M NOT FROM AROUND HERE...
MY NAME IS CASANOVA QUINN AND I WAS STOLEN OUT OF TIMELINE 909 AND BROUGHT TO TIMELINE 919 BY NEWMAN XENO WHO BLACKMAILED ME INTO SERVING HIM TO DESTROY MY FATHER.
AND I'VE NEVER BEEN SO SCARED IN MY WHOLE LIFE.
HE'S TELLING THE TRUTH.
COME ON OUT OF THERE, LITTLE MAN.
WE'VE NEVER HAD A SPACETIME TRAVELLER HERE BEFORE.

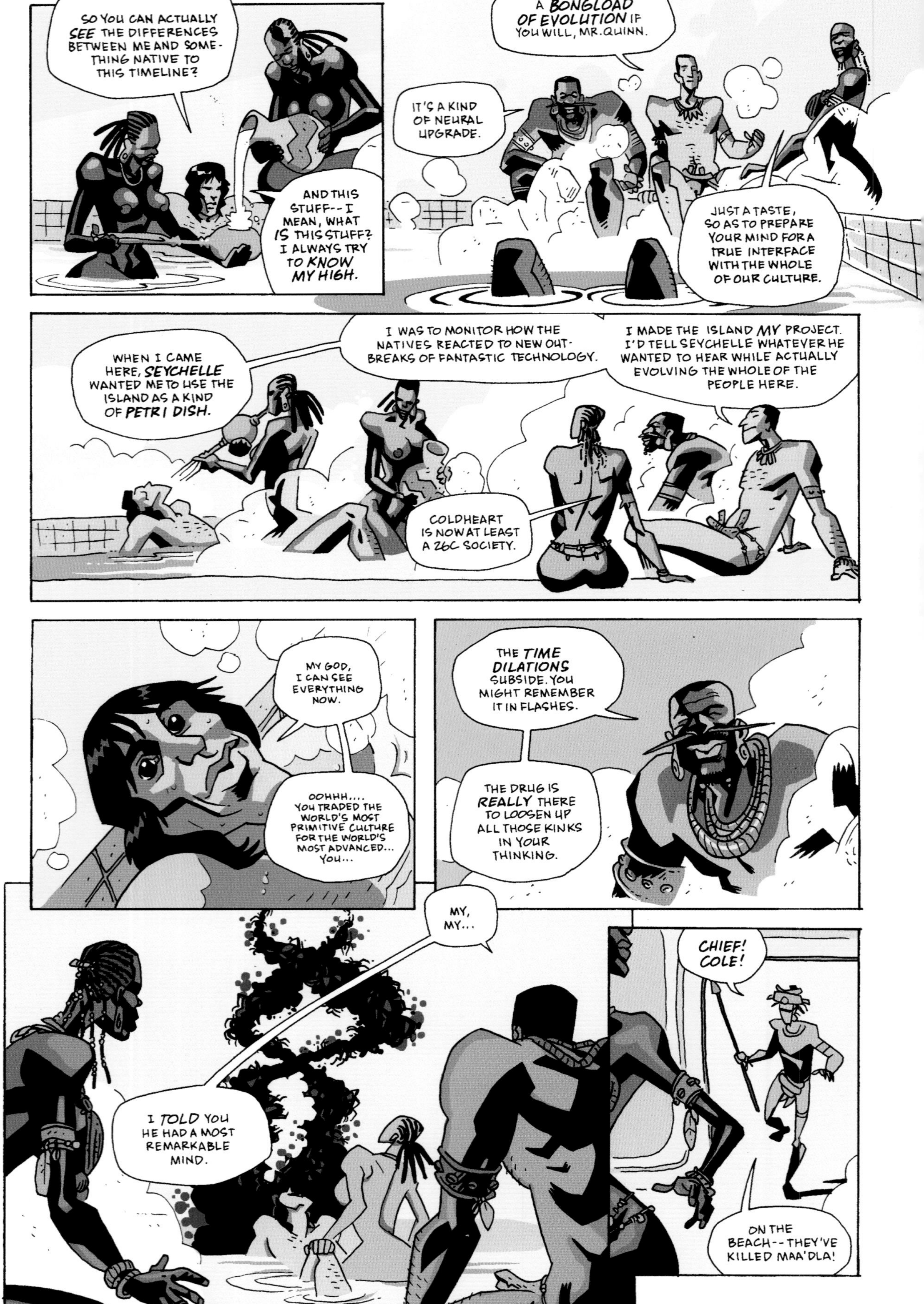
SO YOU CAN ACTUALLY SEE THE DIFFERENCES BETWEEN ME AND SOME-THING NATIVE TO THIS TIMELINE?
AND THIS STUFF-- I MEAN, WHAT IS THIS STUFF? I ALWAYS TRY TO KNOW MY HIGH.
IT'S A KIND OF NEURAL UPGRADE.
A BONGLOAD OF EVOLUTION IF YOU WILL, MR. QUINN.
JUST A TASTE, SO AS TO PREPARE YOUR MIND FOR A TRUE INTERFACE WITH THE WHOLE OF OUR CULTURE.
WHEN I CAME HERE, SEYCHELLE WANTED ME TO USE THE ISLAND AS A KIND OF PETRI DISH.
I WAS TO MONITOR HOW THE NATIVES REACTED TO NEW OUT-BREAKS OF FANTASTIC TECHNOLOGY.
I MADE THE ISLAND MY PROJECT. I'D TELL SEYCHELLE WHATEVER HE WANTED TO HEAR WHILE ACTUALLY EVOLVING THE WHOLE OF THE PEOPLE HERE.
COLDHEART IS NOW AT LEAST A 26C SOCIETY.
MY GOD, I CAN SEE EVERYTHING NOW.
OOHHH.... YOU TRADED THE WORLD'S MOST PRIMITIVE CULTURE FOR THE WORLD'S MOST ADVANCED... YOU...
THE TIME DILATIONS SUBSIDE. YOU MIGHT REMEMBER IT IN FLASHES.
THE DRUG IS REALLY THERE TO LOOSEN UP ALL THOSE KINKS IN YOUR THINKING.
MY, MY...
I TOLD YOU HE HAD A MOST REMARKABLE MIND.
CHIEF! COLE!
ON THE BEACH-- THEY'VE KILLED MAA'DLA!

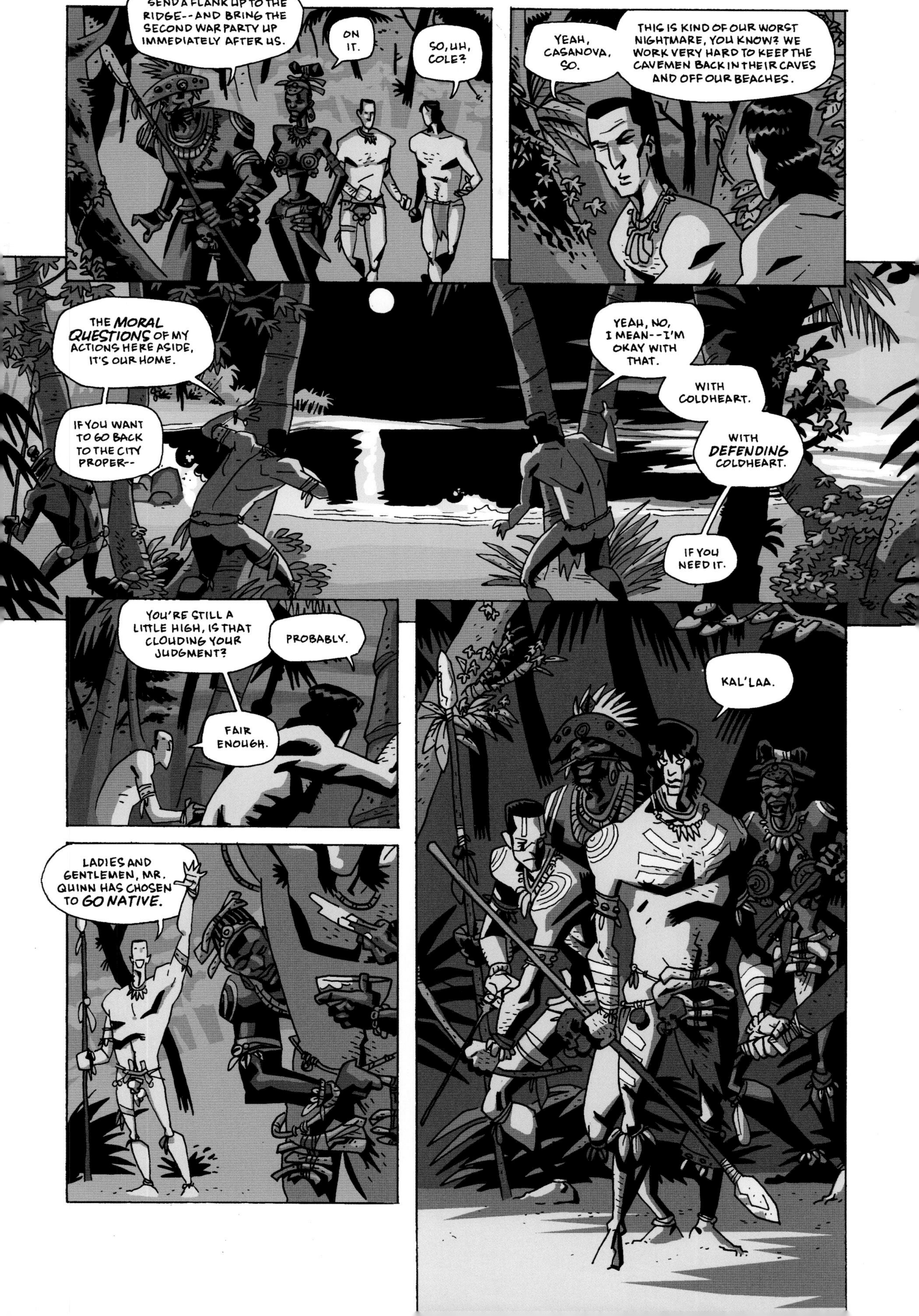
SEND A FLANK UP TO THE RIDGE--AND BRING THE SECOND WAR PARTY UP IMMEDIATELY AFTER US.
ON IT.
SO, UH, COLE?
YEAH, CASANOVA, SO.
THIS IS KIND OF OUR WORST NIGHTMARE, YOU KNOW? WE WORK VERY HARD TO KEEP THE CAVEMEN BACK IN THEIR CAVES AND OFF OUR BEACHES.
THE MORAL QUESTIONS OF MY ACTIONS HERE ASIDE, IT'S OUR HOME.
IF YOU WANT TO GO BACK TO THE CITY PROPER--
YEAH, NO, I MEAN--I'M OKAY WITH THAT.
WITH COLDHEART.
WITH DEFENDING COLDHEART.
IF YOU NEED IT.
YOU'RE STILL A LITTLE HIGH, IS THAT CLOUDING YOUR JUDGMENT?
PROBABLY.
FAIR ENOUGH.
LADIES AND GENTLEMEN, MR. QUINN HAS CHOSEN TO GO NATIVE.
KAL'LAA.

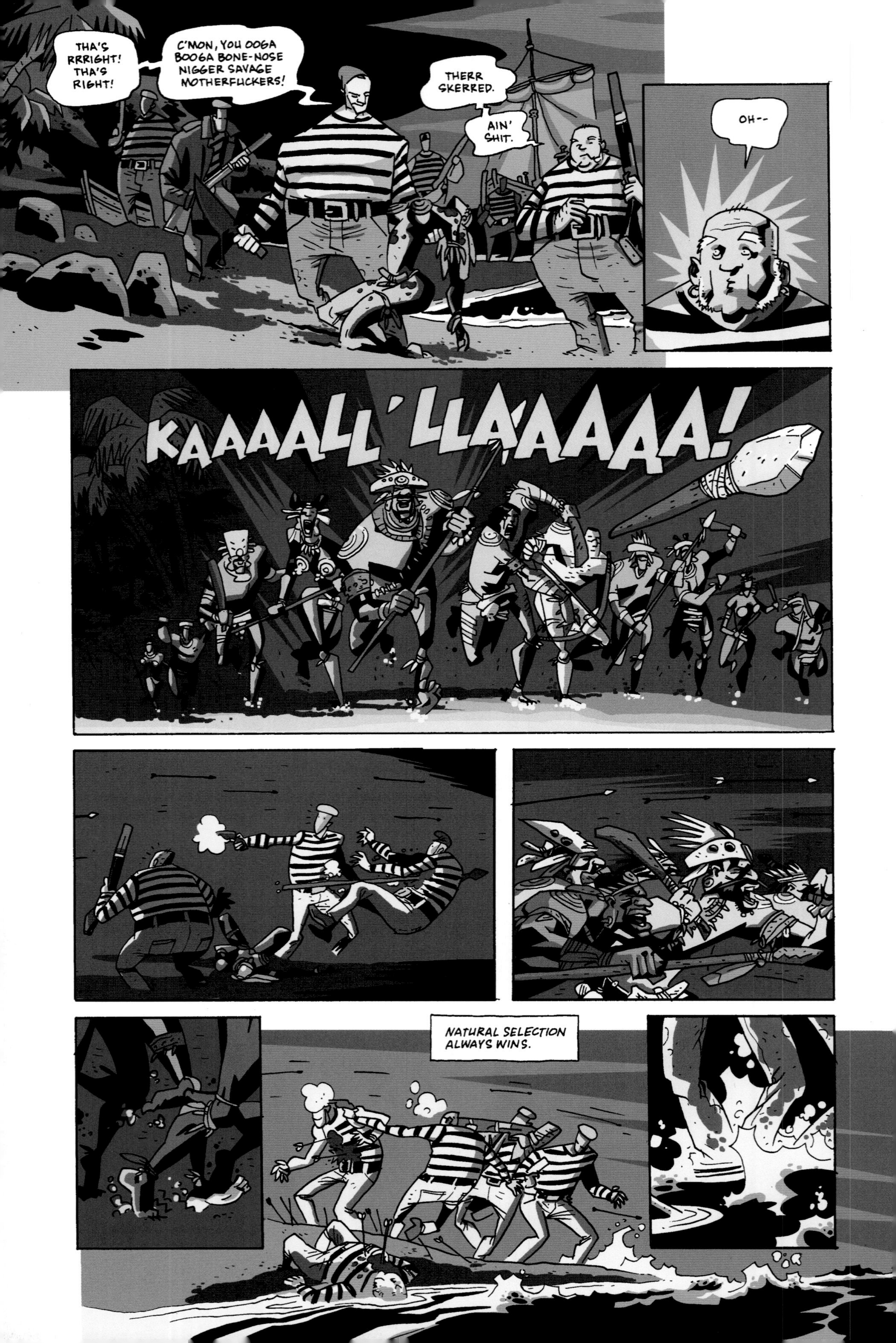
THA'S RRRIGHT! THA'S RIGHT!
C'MON, YOU OOGA BOOGA BONE-NOSE NIGGER SAVAGE MOTHERFUCKERS!
THERR SKERRED.
AIN' SHIT.
OH--
KAAAALL' LLAAAAAA!
NATURAL SELECTION ALWAYS WINS.

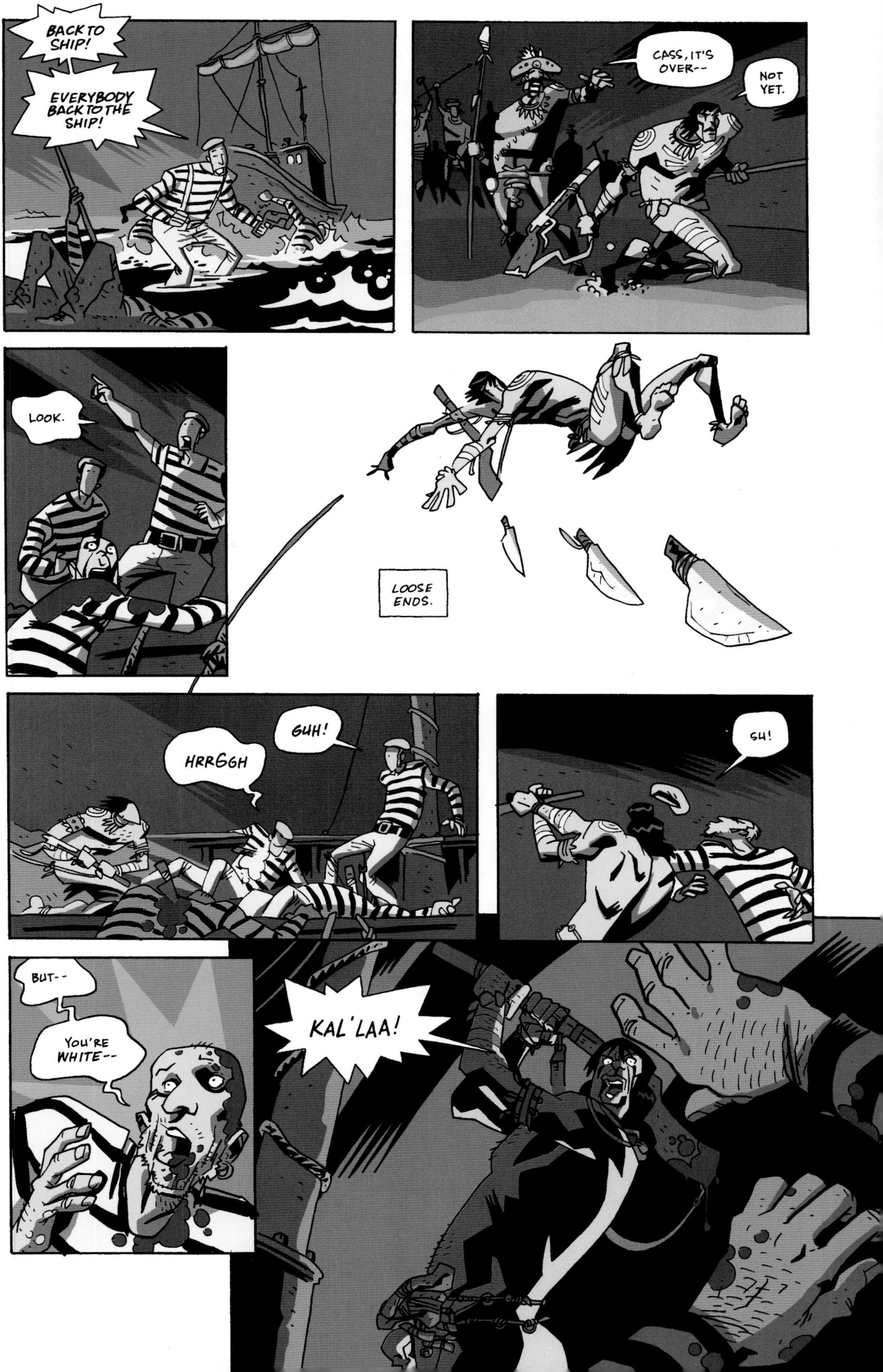
BACK TO SHIP!
EVERYBODY BACK TO THE SHIP!
CASS, IT'S OVER--
NOT YET.
LOOK.
LOOSE ENDS.
HRRGGH
GUH!
GU!
BUT--
YOU'RE WHITE--
KAL'LAA!

≡HEFF≡

≡HEFF≡

OKAY. THEY'RE DONE.

THAT WAS SWEET.

UNNECESSARILY **VIOLENT**, BUT SWEET.

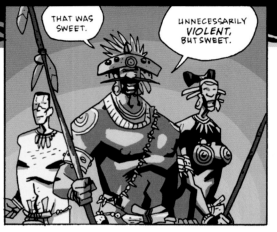

I KNOW, I JUST--

THEY WOULD'VE COME BACK AND THEY WOULD'VE **KEPT** COMING BACK.

YOU CAN'T KILL THE WHOLE **WORLD**, BOY, NO MATTER HOW MUCH YOU WISH IT TO BE.

INSTEAD I THINK WE WILL SIMPLY **GO.**

GO? GO WHERE? OUT INTO THE **WORLD?**

HA! "**THE WORLD!**"

WE'RE JUST AS OUT OF TIME NOW AS WE WERE BEFORE COLE **GREW** US.

WE HOPED TO HELP. WE **CANNOT.** SO WE'LL **GO** SOMEWHERE YOUR KIND WILL NEVER LOOK.

...

YOU'RE WELCOME TO JOIN US, LITTLE SPACETIMEMAN. FREE YOURSELF OF IT ALL.

CAN I, uh, CAN I ASK YOU GUYS FOR A FAVOR, INSTEAD?

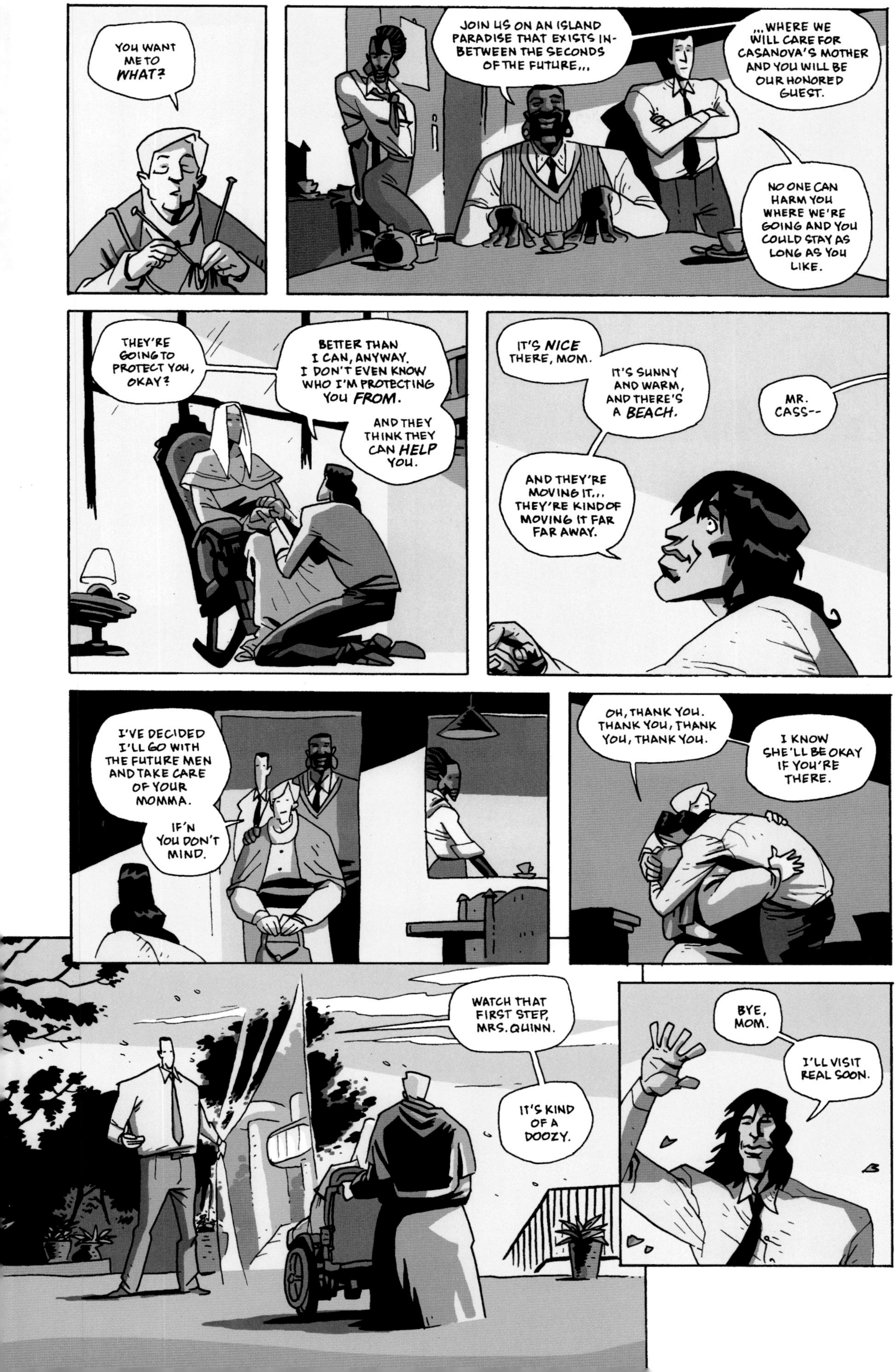
YOU WANT ME TO *WHAT?*
JOIN US ON AN ISLAND PARADISE THAT EXISTS IN-BETWEEN THE SECONDS OF THE FUTURE...
...WHERE WE WILL CARE FOR CASANOVA'S MOTHER AND YOU WILL BE OUR HONORED GUEST.
NO ONE CAN HARM YOU WHERE WE'RE GOING AND YOU COULD STAY AS LONG AS YOU LIKE.
THEY'RE GOING TO PROTECT YOU, OKAY?
BETTER THAN I CAN, ANYWAY. I DON'T EVEN KNOW WHO I'M PROTECTING YOU *FROM*.
AND THEY THINK THEY CAN *HELP* YOU.
IT'S *NICE* THERE, MOM.
IT'S SUNNY AND WARM, AND THERE'S A *BEACH*.
AND THEY'RE MOVING IT... THEY'RE KIND OF MOVING IT FAR FAR AWAY.
MR. CASS--
I'VE DECIDED I'LL GO WITH THE FUTURE MEN AND TAKE CARE OF YOUR MOMMA.
IF'N YOU DON'T MIND.
OH, THANK YOU. THANK YOU, THANK YOU, THANK YOU.
I KNOW SHE'LL BE OKAY IF YOU'RE THERE.
WATCH THAT FIRST STEP, MRS. QUINN.
IT'S KIND OF A DOOZY.
BYE, MOM.
I'LL VISIT REAL SOON.

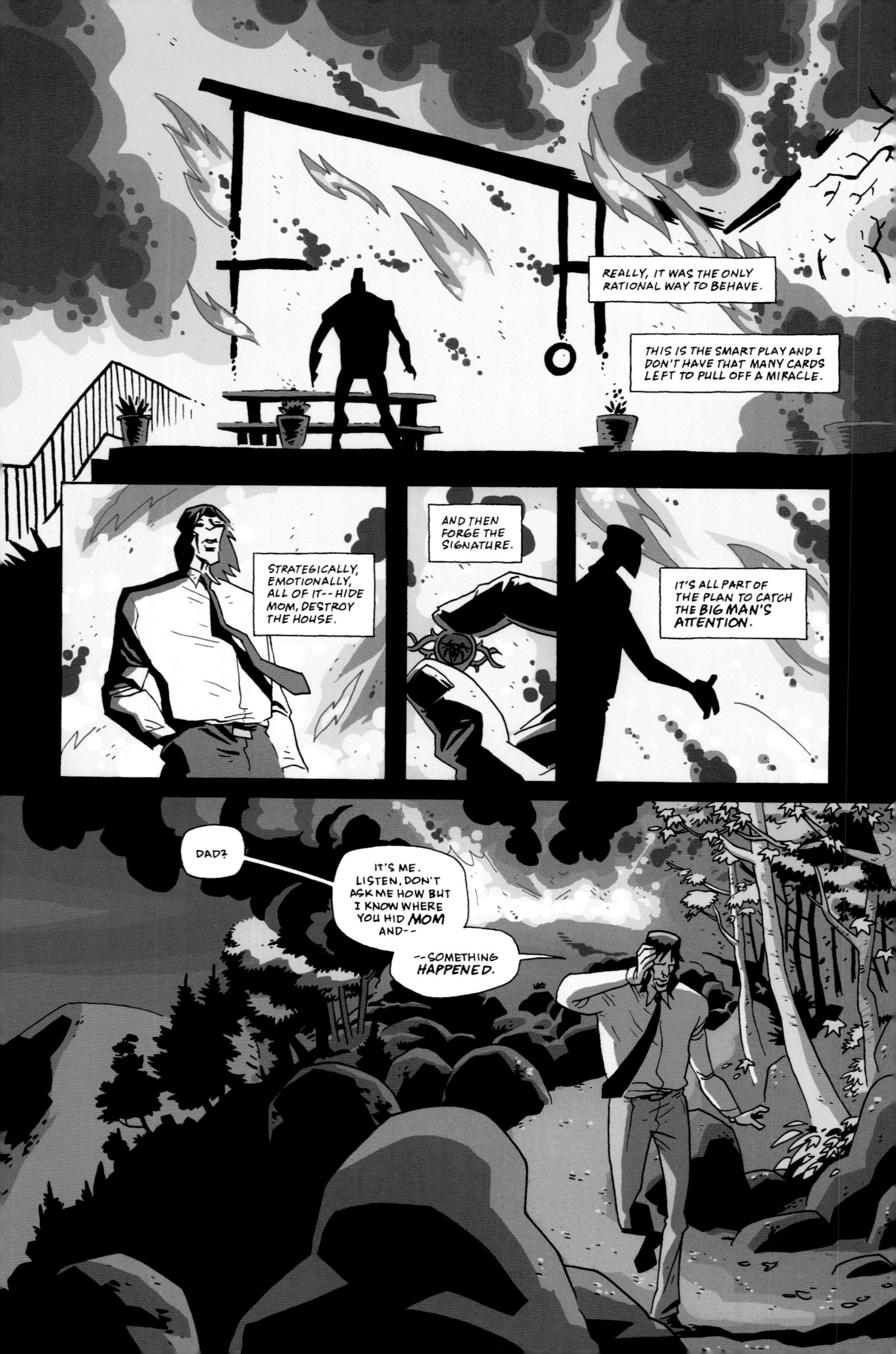
REALLY, IT WAS THE ONLY RATIONAL WAY TO BEHAVE.
THIS IS THE SMART PLAY AND I DON'T HAVE THAT MANY CARDS LEFT TO PULL OFF A MIRACLE.
STRATEGICALLY, EMOTIONALLY, ALL OF IT--HIDE MOM, DESTROY THE HOUSE.
AND THEN FORGE THE SIGNATURE.
IT'S ALL PART OF THE PLAN TO CATCH THE BIG MAN'S ATTENTION.
DAD?
IT'S ME. LISTEN, DON'T ASK ME HOW BUT I KNOW WHERE YOU HID MOM AND--
--SOMETHING HAPPENED.

WOMEN AND MEN (PART ONE)

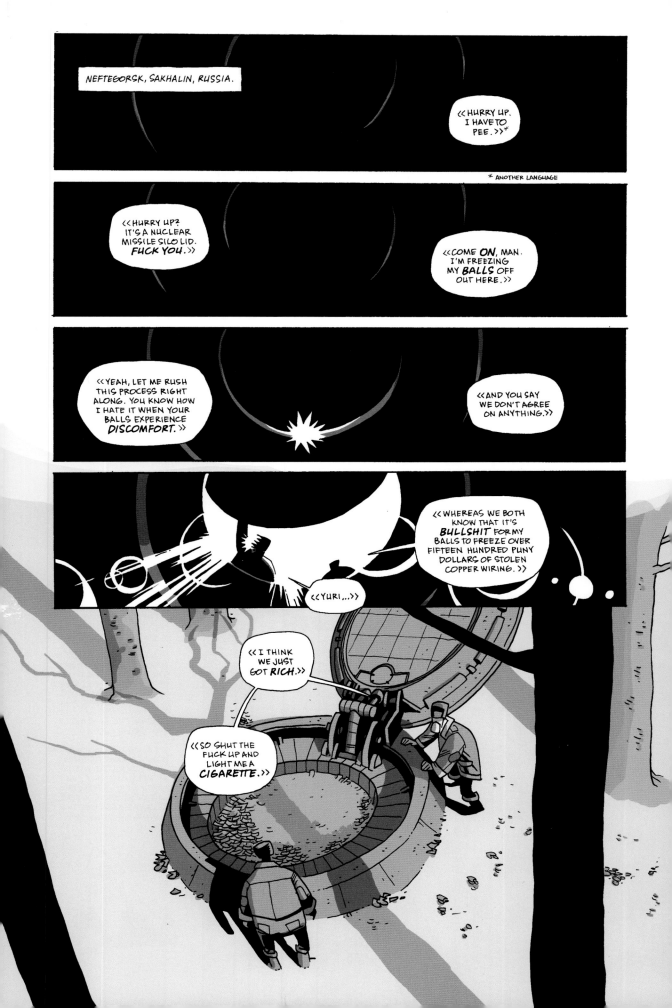

NEFTEGORSK, SAKHALIN, RUSSIA.

<<HURRY UP. I HAVE TO PEE.>>*

* ANOTHER LANGUAGE

<<HURRY UP? IT'S A NUCLEAR MISSILE SILO LID. *FUCK YOU*.>>

<<COME *ON*, MAN. I'M FREEZING MY *BALLS* OFF OUT HERE.>>

<<YEAH, LET ME RUSH THIS PROCESS RIGHT ALONG. YOU KNOW HOW I HATE IT WHEN YOUR BALLS EXPERIENCE *DISCOMFORT*.>>

<<AND YOU SAY WE DON'T AGREE ON ANYTHING.>>

<<WHEREAS WE BOTH KNOW THAT IT'S *BULLSHIT* FOR MY BALLS TO FREEZE OVER FIFTEEN HUNDRED PUNY DOLLARS OF STOLEN COPPER WIRING.>>

<<YURI...>>

<<I THINK WE JUST GOT *RICH*.>>

<<SO SHUT THE FUCK UP AND LIGHT ME A *CIGARETTE*.>>

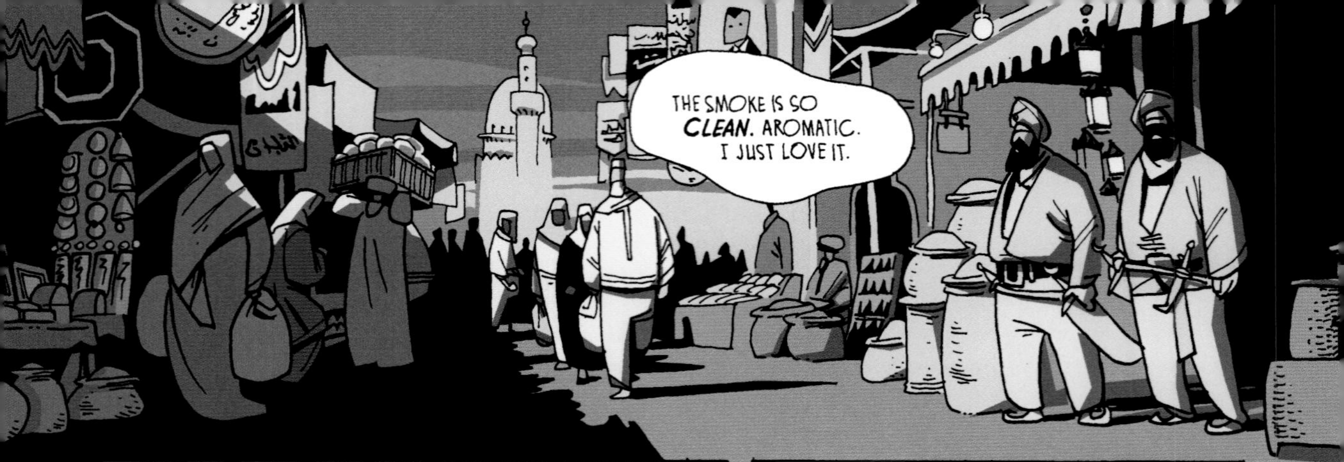
THE SMOKE IS SO **CLEAN**. AROMATIC. I JUST LOVE IT.

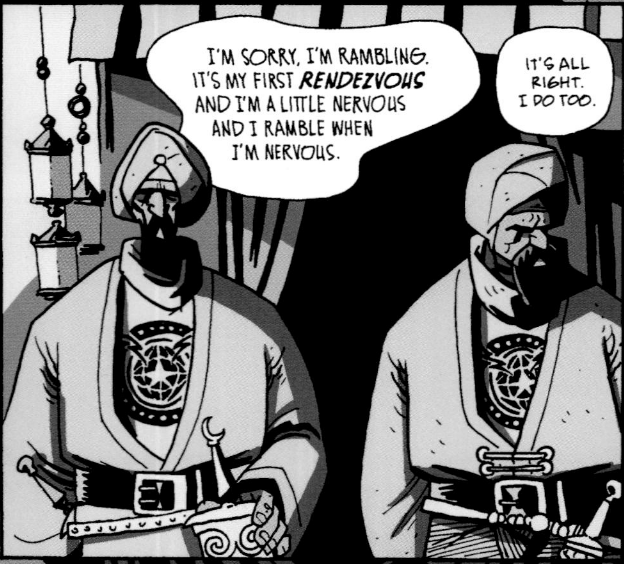
I'M SORRY, I'M RAMBLING. IT'S MY FIRST ***RENDEZVOUS*** AND I'M A LITTLE NERVOUS AND I RAMBLE WHEN I'M NERVOUS.
IT'S ALL RIGHT. I DO TOO.

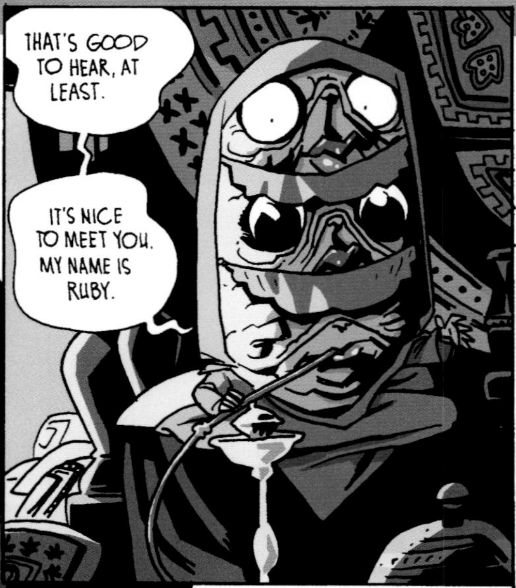
THAT'S GOOD TO HEAR, AT LEAST.
IT'S NICE TO MEET YOU. MY NAME IS RUBY.

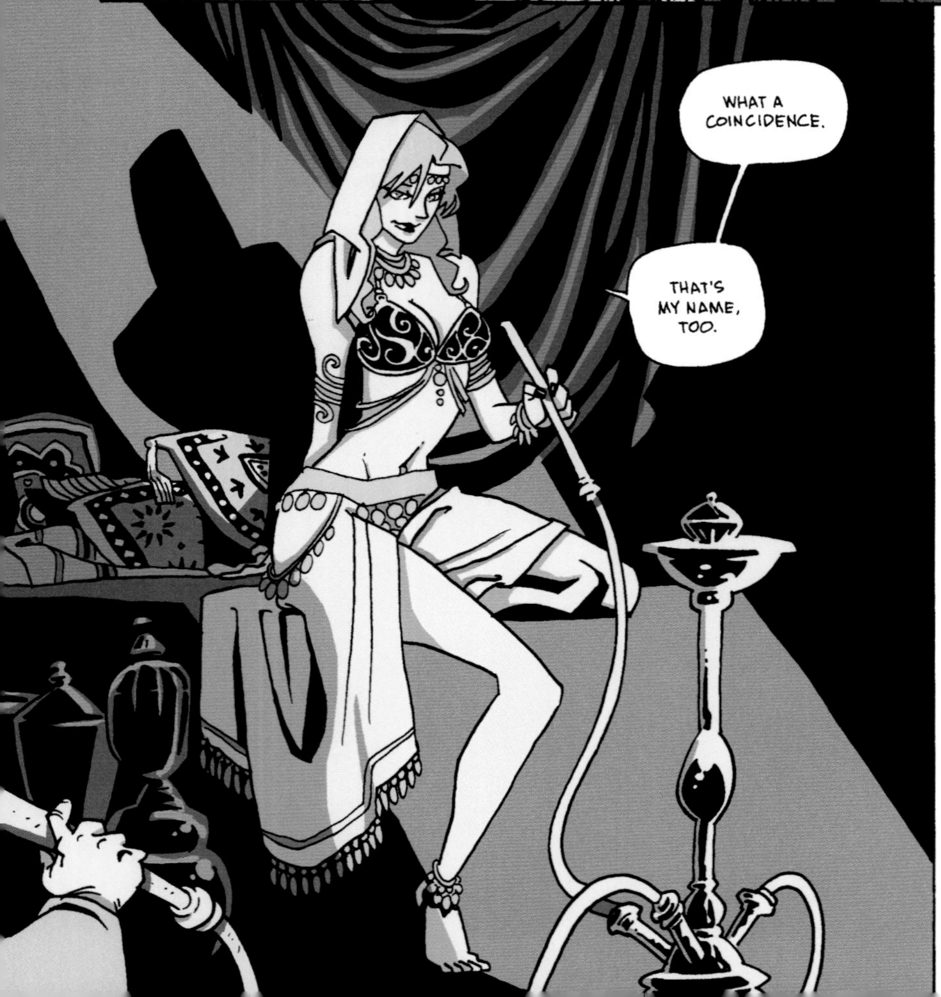
WHAT A COINCIDENCE.
THAT'S MY NAME, TOO.

RUBY SEYCHELLE MEETS RUBY BERSERKO! DUH! NUH! NUHHHH!

RUBY S. WAS LAST SEEN IN **CASANOVA #2** AS SHE FLED THE WILDS OF **ÁGUA PESADA**.

RUBY S. AND **RUBY B.** HAVE **IDENTICAL MINDS:** THE FORMER BEING A COPY OF THE LATTER, UPLOADED INTO A SEYCHELLEBOT AND FREED FROM HER LIFE OF INDENTURED SEXITUDE WITHIN THE SEYCHELLE CRIME EMPIRE.

WE ALL ASSUMED THAT SHE, LIKE SO MANY DANGLING PLOT THREADS, WOULD MERELY FADE AWAY, BUT WE WERE **WRONG!** A DIABOLICAL SCHEME SEVERAL ISSUES IN THE MAKING HATCHES NOW!

-- GOD, CREATOR OF ALL THINGS

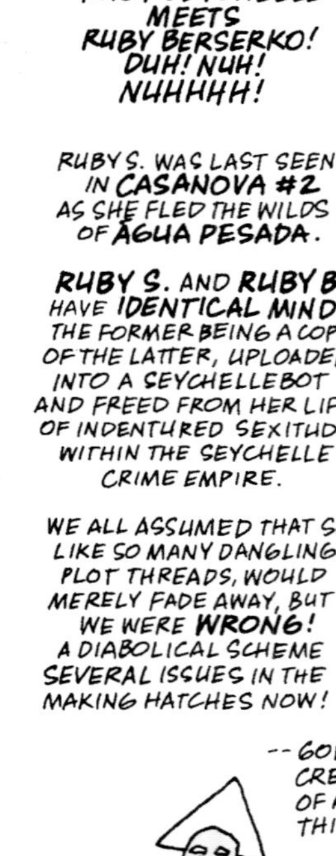

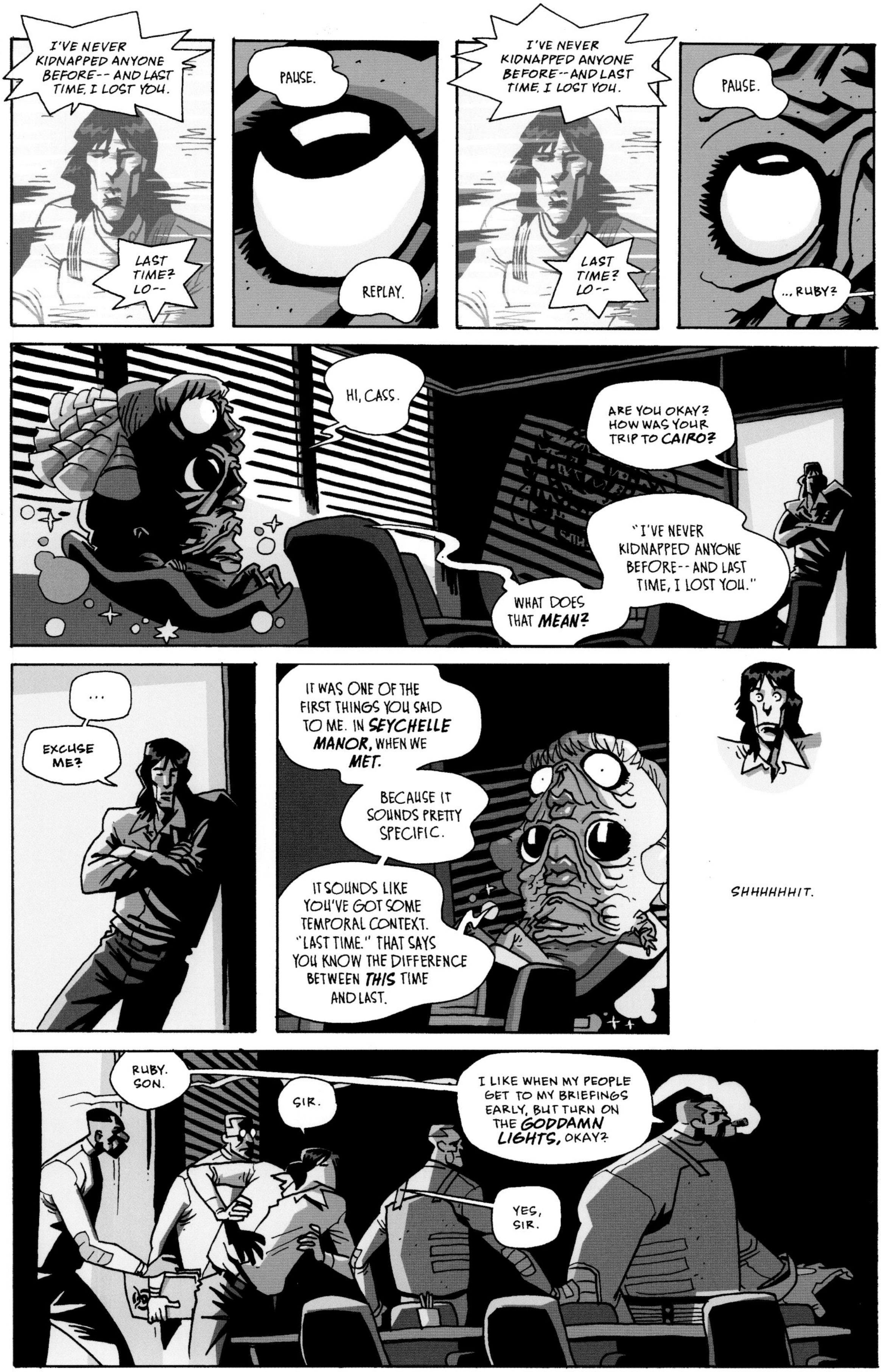
I'VE NEVER KIDNAPPED ANYONE BEFORE-- AND LAST TIME, I LOST YOU.
LAST TIME? LO--
PAUSE.
REPLAY.
I'VE NEVER KIDNAPPED ANYONE BEFORE-- AND LAST TIME, I LOST YOU.
LAST TIME? LO--
PAUSE.
...RUBY?
HI, CASS.
ARE YOU OKAY? HOW WAS YOUR TRIP TO CAIRO?
"I'VE NEVER KIDNAPPED ANYONE BEFORE-- AND LAST TIME, I LOST YOU."
WHAT DOES THAT MEAN?
...
EXCUSE ME?
IT WAS ONE OF THE FIRST THINGS YOU SAID TO ME. IN SEYCHELLE MANOR, WHEN WE MET.
BECAUSE IT SOUNDS PRETTY SPECIFIC.
IT SOUNDS LIKE YOU'VE GOT SOME TEMPORAL CONTEXT. "LAST TIME." THAT SAYS YOU KNOW THE DIFFERENCE BETWEEN THIS TIME AND LAST.
SHHHHHHIT.
RUBY. SON.
SIR.
I LIKE WHEN MY PEOPLE GET TO MY BRIEFINGS EARLY, BUT TURN ON THE GODDAMN LIGHTS, OKAY?
YES, SIR.

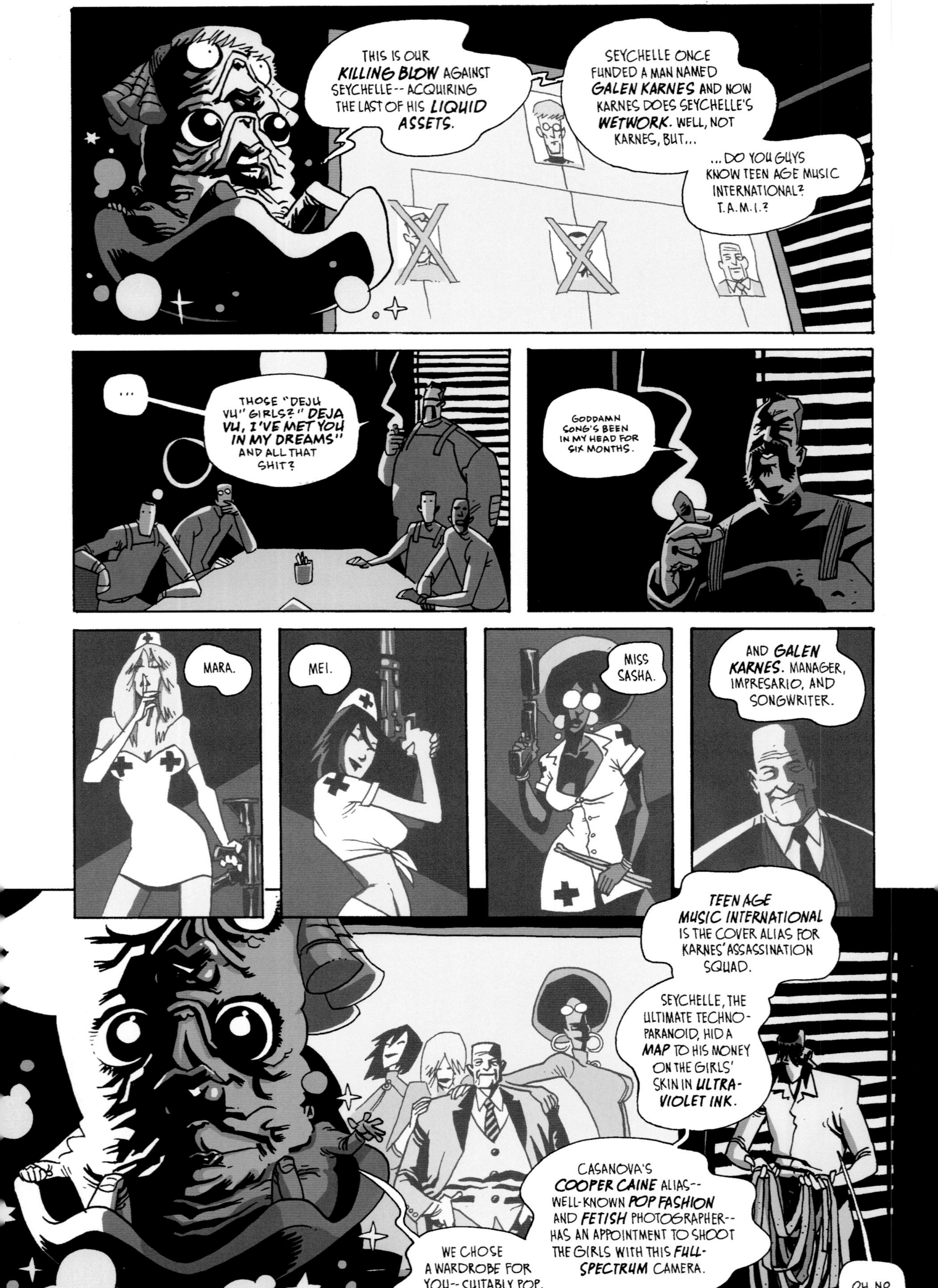
THIS IS OUR KILLING BLOW AGAINST SEYCHELLE-- ACQUIRING THE LAST OF HIS LIQUID ASSETS.
SEYCHELLE ONCE FUNDED A MAN NAMED GALEN KARNES AND NOW KARNES DOES SEYCHELLE'S WETWORK. WELL, NOT KARNES, BUT...
...DO YOU GUYS KNOW TEEN AGE MUSIC INTERNATIONAL? T.A.M.I.?
...
THOSE "DEJU VU" GIRLS?" DEJA VU, I'VE MET YOU IN MY DREAMS" AND ALL THAT SHIT?
GODDAMN SONG'S BEEN IN MY HEAD FOR SIX MONTHS.
MARA.
MEI.
MISS SASHA.
AND GALEN KARNES. MANAGER, IMPRESARIO, AND SONGWRITER.
TEEN AGE MUSIC INTERNATIONAL IS THE COVER ALIAS FOR KARNES' ASSASSINATION SQUAD.
SEYCHELLE, THE ULTIMATE TECHNO-PARANOID, HID A MAP TO HIS MONEY ON THE GIRLS' SKIN IN ULTRA-VIOLET INK.
CASANOVA'S COOPER CAINE ALIAS-- WELL-KNOWN POP FASHION AND FETISH PHOTOGRAPHER-- HAS AN APPOINTMENT TO SHOOT THE GIRLS WITH THIS FULL-SPECTRUM CAMERA.
WE CHOSE A WARDROBE FOR YOU-- SUITABLY POP, NIHILISTIC, AND PROFANE...
OH, NO WAY.

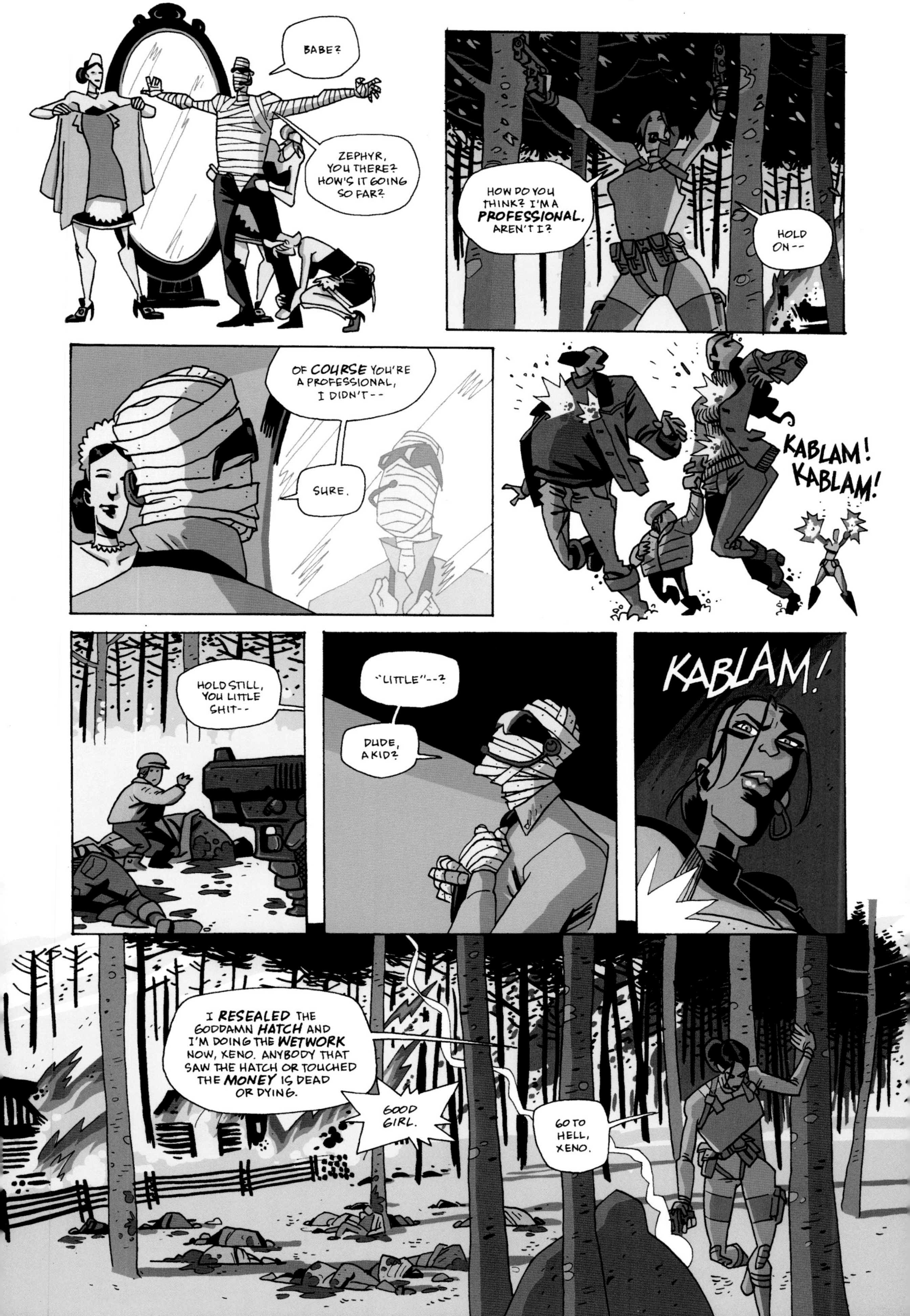
BABE?
ZEPHYR, YOU THERE? HOW'S IT GOING SO FAR?
HOW DO YOU THINK? I'M A **PROFESSIONAL**, AREN'T I?
HOLD ON--
OF **COURSE** YOU'RE A PROFESSIONAL, I DIDN'T--
SURE.
KABLAM! KABLAM!
HOLD STILL, YOU LITTLE SHIT--
"LITTLE"--?
DUDE, A KID?
KABLAM!
I **RESEALED** THE GODDAMN **HATCH** AND I'M DOING THE **WETWORK** NOW, XENO. ANYBODY THAT SAW THE HATCH OR TOUCHED THE **MONEY** IS DEAD OR DYING.
GOOD GIRL.
GO TO HELL, XENO.

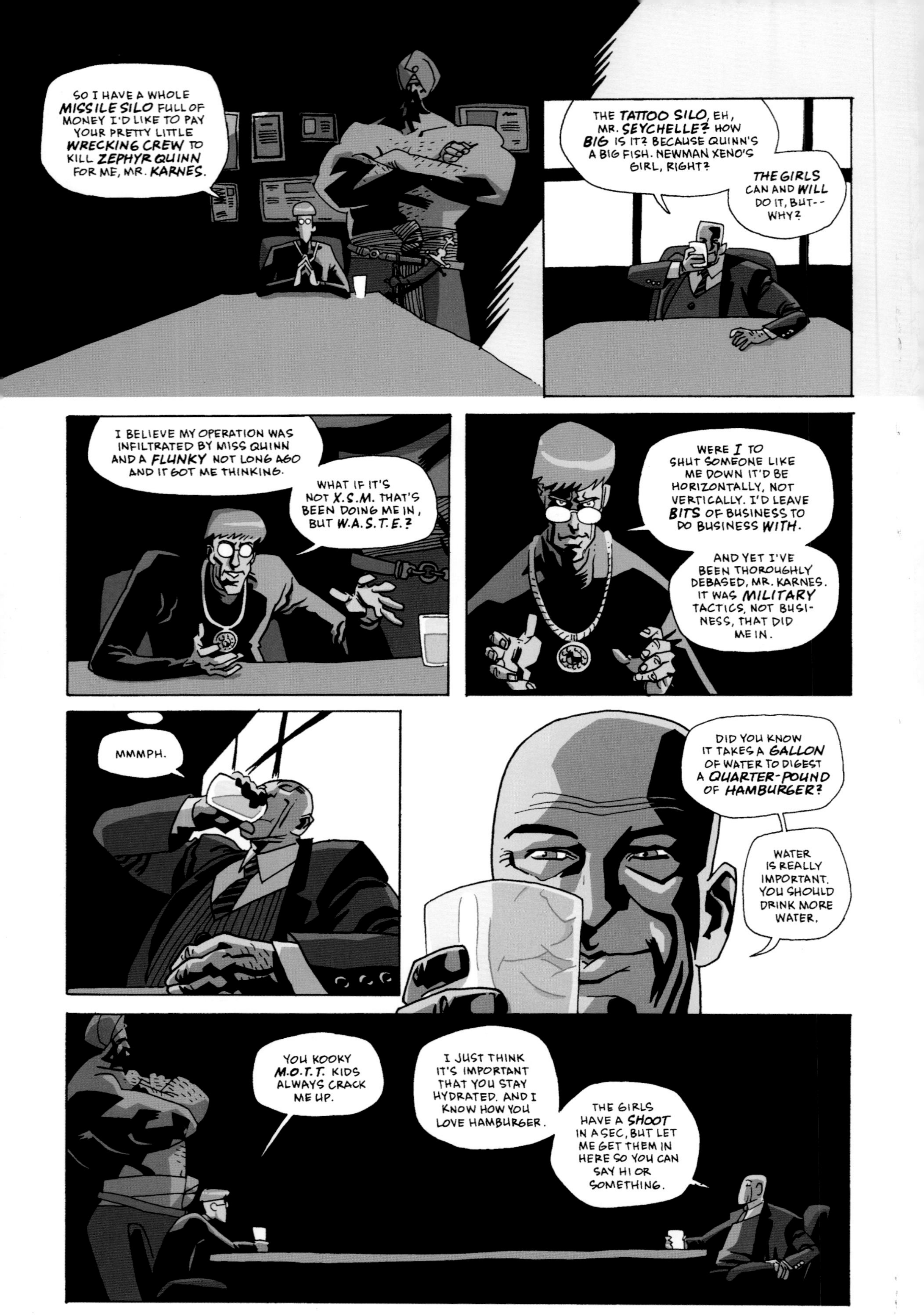
SO I HAVE A WHOLE MISSILE SILO FULL OF MONEY I'D LIKE TO PAY YOUR PRETTY LITTLE WRECKING CREW TO KILL ZEPHYR QUINN FOR ME, MR. KARNES.
THE TATTOO SILO, EH, MR. SEYCHELLE? HOW BIG IS IT? BECAUSE QUINN'S A BIG FISH. NEWMAN XENO'S GIRL, RIGHT?
THE GIRLS CAN AND WILL DO IT, BUT-- WHY?
I BELIEVE MY OPERATION WAS INFILTRATED BY MISS QUINN AND A FLUNKY NOT LONG AGO AND IT GOT ME THINKING.
WHAT IF IT'S NOT X.S.M. THAT'S BEEN DOING ME IN, BUT W.A.S.T.E.?
WERE I TO SHUT SOMEONE LIKE ME DOWN IT'D BE HORIZONTALLY, NOT VERTICALLY. I'D LEAVE BITS OF BUSINESS TO DO BUSINESS WITH.
AND YET I'VE BEEN THOROUGHLY DEBASED, MR. KARNES. IT WAS MILITARY TACTICS, NOT BUSINESS, THAT DID ME IN.
MMMPH.
DID YOU KNOW IT TAKES A GALLON OF WATER TO DIGEST A QUARTER-POUND OF HAMBURGER?
WATER IS REALLY IMPORTANT. YOU SHOULD DRINK MORE WATER.
YOU KOOKY M.O.T.T. KIDS ALWAYS CRACK ME UP.
I JUST THINK IT'S IMPORTANT THAT YOU STAY HYDRATED. AND I KNOW HOW YOU LOVE HAMBURGER.
THE GIRLS HAVE A SHOOT IN A SEC, BUT LET ME GET THEM IN HERE SO YOU CAN SAY HI OR SOMETHING.

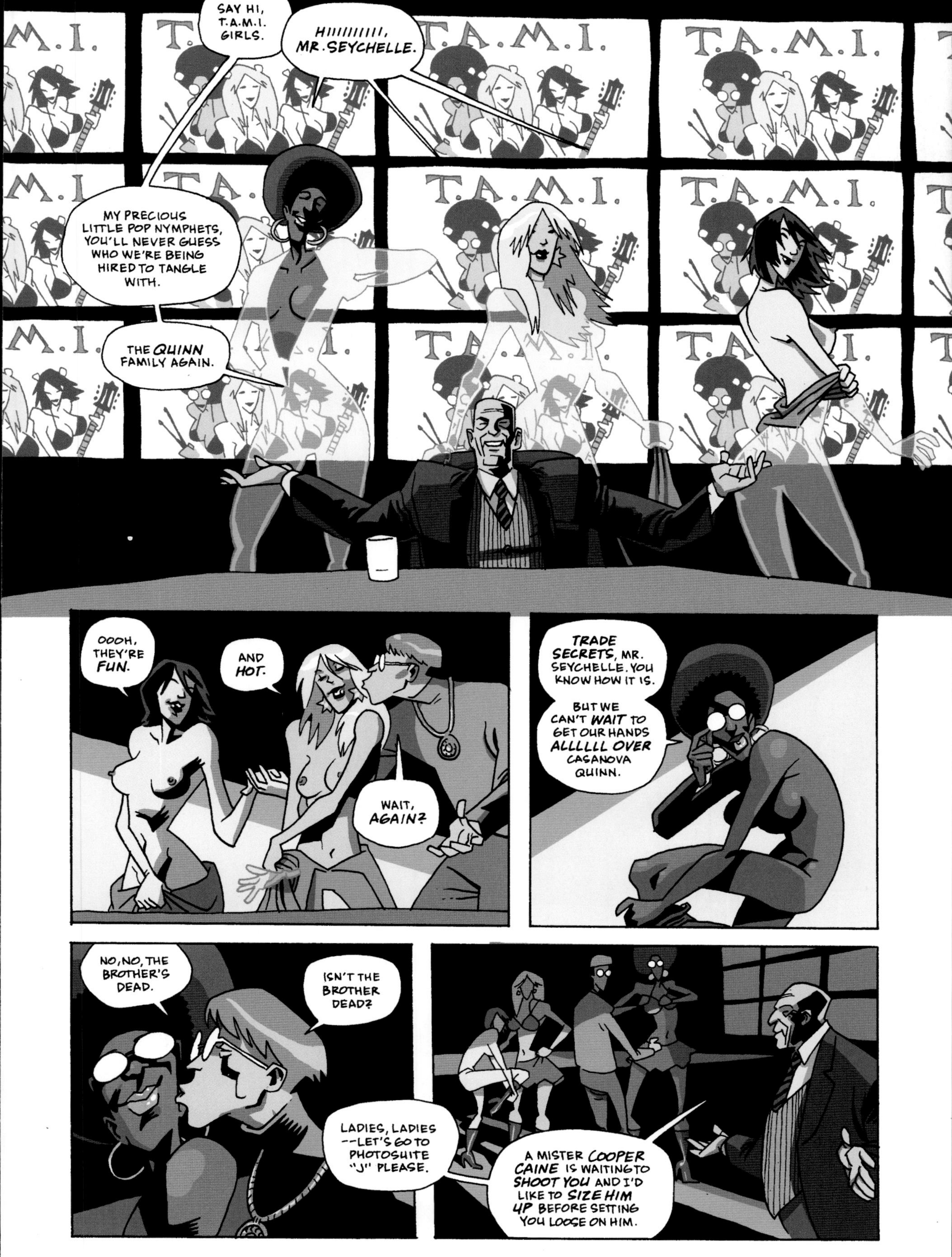
SAY HI, T.A.M.I. GIRLS.
HIIIIIIIIII, MR. SEYCHELLE.
T.A.M.I.
MY PRECIOUS LITTLE POP NYMPHETS, YOU'LL NEVER GUESS WHO WE'RE BEING HIRED TO TANGLE WITH.
THE QUINN FAMILY AGAIN.
OOOH, THEY'RE FUN.
AND HOT.
WAIT, AGAIN?
TRADE SECRETS, MR. SEYCHELLE. YOU KNOW HOW IT IS.
BUT WE CAN'T WAIT TO GET OUR HANDS ALLLLLL OVER CASANOVA QUINN.
NO, NO, THE BROTHER'S DEAD.
ISN'T THE BROTHER DEAD?
LADIES, LADIES --LET'S GO TO PHOTOSUITE "J" PLEASE.
A MISTER COOPER CAINE IS WAITING TO SHOOT YOU AND I'D LIKE TO SIZE HIM UP BEFORE SETTING YOU LOOSE ON HIM.

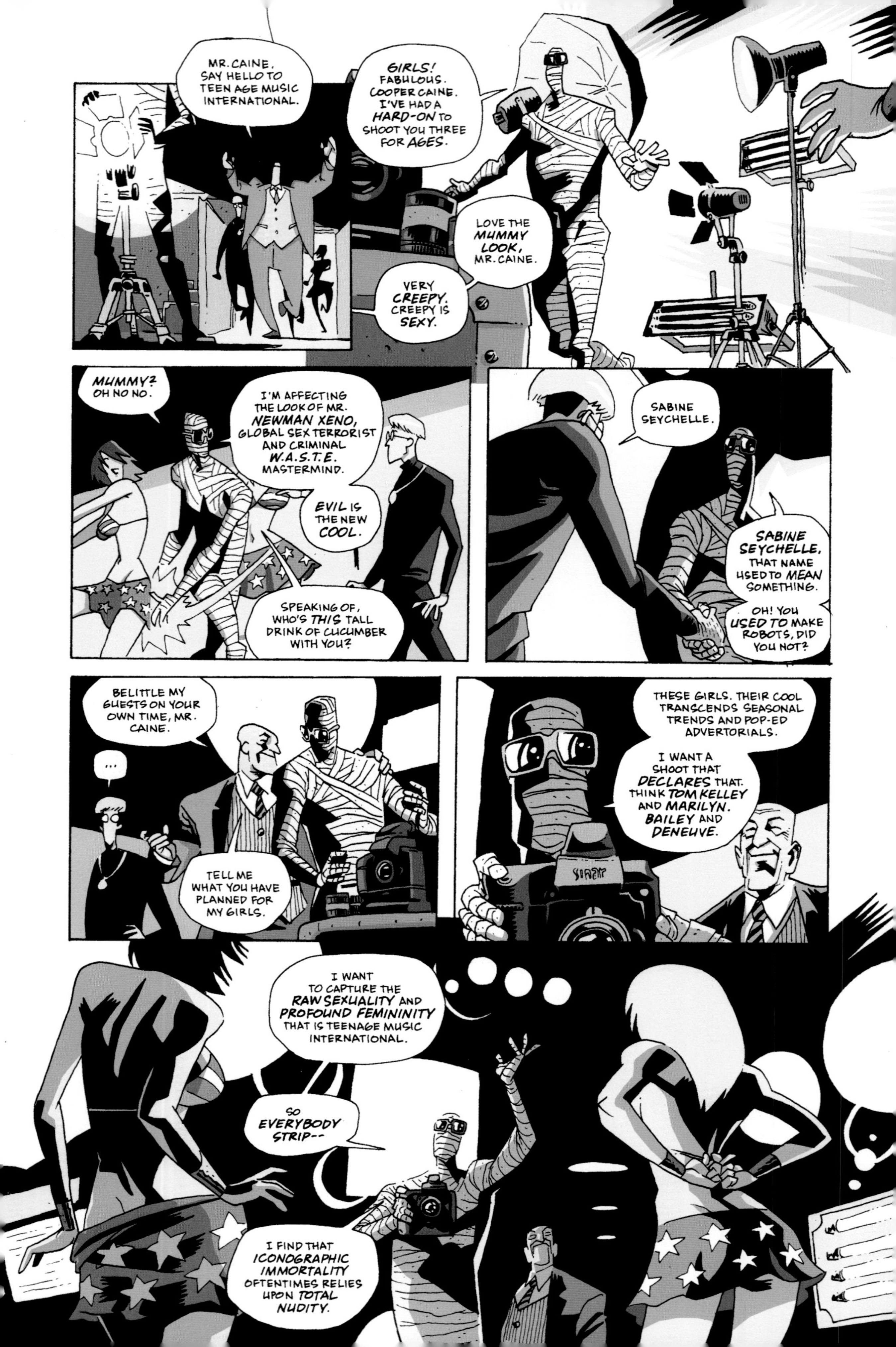
MR. CAINE. SAY HELLO TO TEEN AGE MUSIC INTERNATIONAL.
GIRLS! FABULOUS. COOPER CAINE. I'VE HAD A HARD-ON TO SHOOT YOU THREE FOR AGES.
LOVE THE MUMMY LOOK, MR. CAINE.
VERY CREEPY. CREEPY IS SEXY.
MUMMY? OH NO NO.
I'M AFFECTING THE LOOK OF MR. NEWMAN XENO, GLOBAL SEX TERRORIST AND CRIMINAL W.A.S.T.E. MASTERMIND.
EVIL IS THE NEW COOL.
SPEAKING OF, WHO'S THIS TALL DRINK OF CUCUMBER WITH YOU?
SABINE SEYCHELLE.
SABINE SEYCHELLE, THAT NAME USED TO MEAN SOMETHING.
OH! YOU USED TO MAKE ROBOTS, DID YOU NOT?
BELITTLE MY GUESTS ON YOUR OWN TIME, MR. CAINE.
...
TELL ME WHAT YOU HAVE PLANNED FOR MY GIRLS.
THESE GIRLS. THEIR COOL TRANSCENDS SEASONAL TRENDS AND POP-ED ADVERTORIALS.
I WANT A SHOOT THAT DECLARES THAT. THINK TOM KELLEY AND MARILYN. BAILEY AND DENEUVE.
I WANT TO CAPTURE THE RAW SEXUALITY AND PROFOUND FEMININITY THAT IS TEENAGE MUSIC INTERNATIONAL.
SO EVERYBODY STRIP--
I FIND THAT ICONOGRAPHIC IMMORTALITY OFTENTIMES RELIES UPON TOTAL NUDITY.

FAR BE IT FROM ME TO DICTATE YOUR *ART*, MR. CAINE.

HAVE A *GOOD SHOOT*, GIRLS.

BYYYYE, MR. KARNES!

OH COME *ON*, SABINE, HE'S RIGHT AND *YOU'VE* SAID AS MUCH FIFTEEN MINUTES AGO. YOU *DID* USED TO BE SOMEBODY.

NO, KARNES, IT'S NOT THAT. IT'S NOT THAT AT ALL...

WHEW! I THOUGHT *THOSE SQUARES* WOULD NEVER LEAVE.

LET ME CHECK JUST ONE MORE THING, LADIES. I'M GONNA TEST-FIRE THE STROBE HERE.

POP!

ЮЖНО-САХАЛИН

DID YOU SEE THAT?

MISTER CAINE--

ALL I SAW WAS *FIRE*, GIRLS.

LET ME SEE IT AGAIN.

POP!

GIVE ME MORE.

sinar

POP!

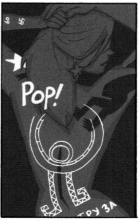

POP!

РОЛИЬ ЛАПЕ

POP!

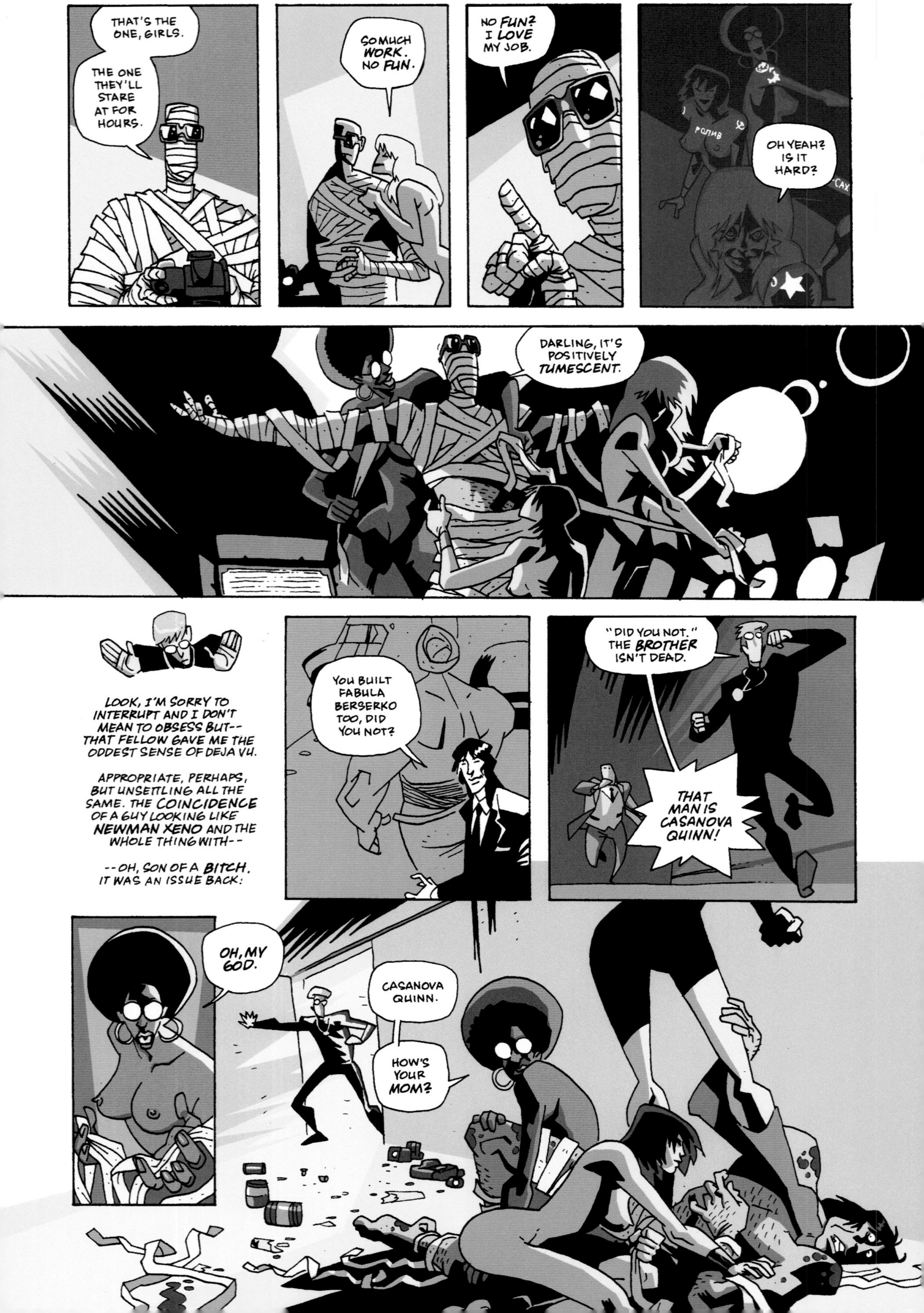
THAT'S THE ONE, GIRLS.
THE ONE THEY'LL STARE AT FOR HOURS.
SO MUCH WORK. NO FUN.
NO FUN? I LOVE MY JOB.
OH YEAH? IS IT HARD?
DARLING, IT'S POSITIVELY TUMESCENT.
LOOK, I'M SORRY TO INTERRUPT AND I DON'T MEAN TO OBSESS BUT-- THAT FELLOW GAVE ME THE ODDEST SENSE OF DEJA VU.
APPROPRIATE, PERHAPS, BUT UNSETTLING ALL THE SAME. THE COINCIDENCE OF A GUY LOOKING LIKE NEWMAN XENO AND THE WHOLE THING WITH--
--OH, SON OF A BITCH. IT WAS AN ISSUE BACK:
YOU BUILT FABULA BERSERKO TOO, DID YOU NOT?
"DID YOU NOT." THE BROTHER ISN'T DEAD.
THAT MAN IS CASANOVA QUINN!
OH, MY GOD.
CASANOVA QUINN.
HOW'S YOUR MOM?

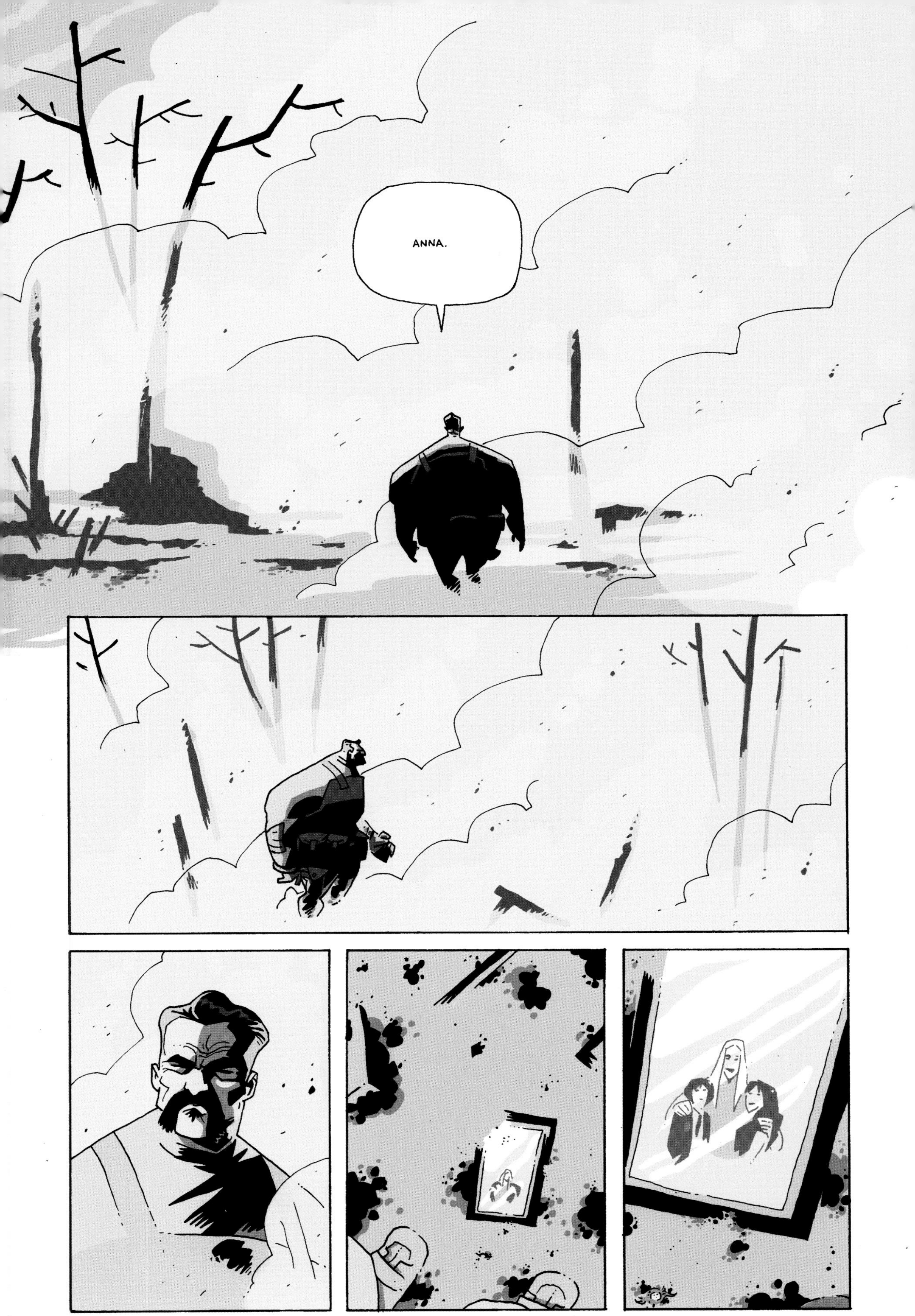
ANNA.

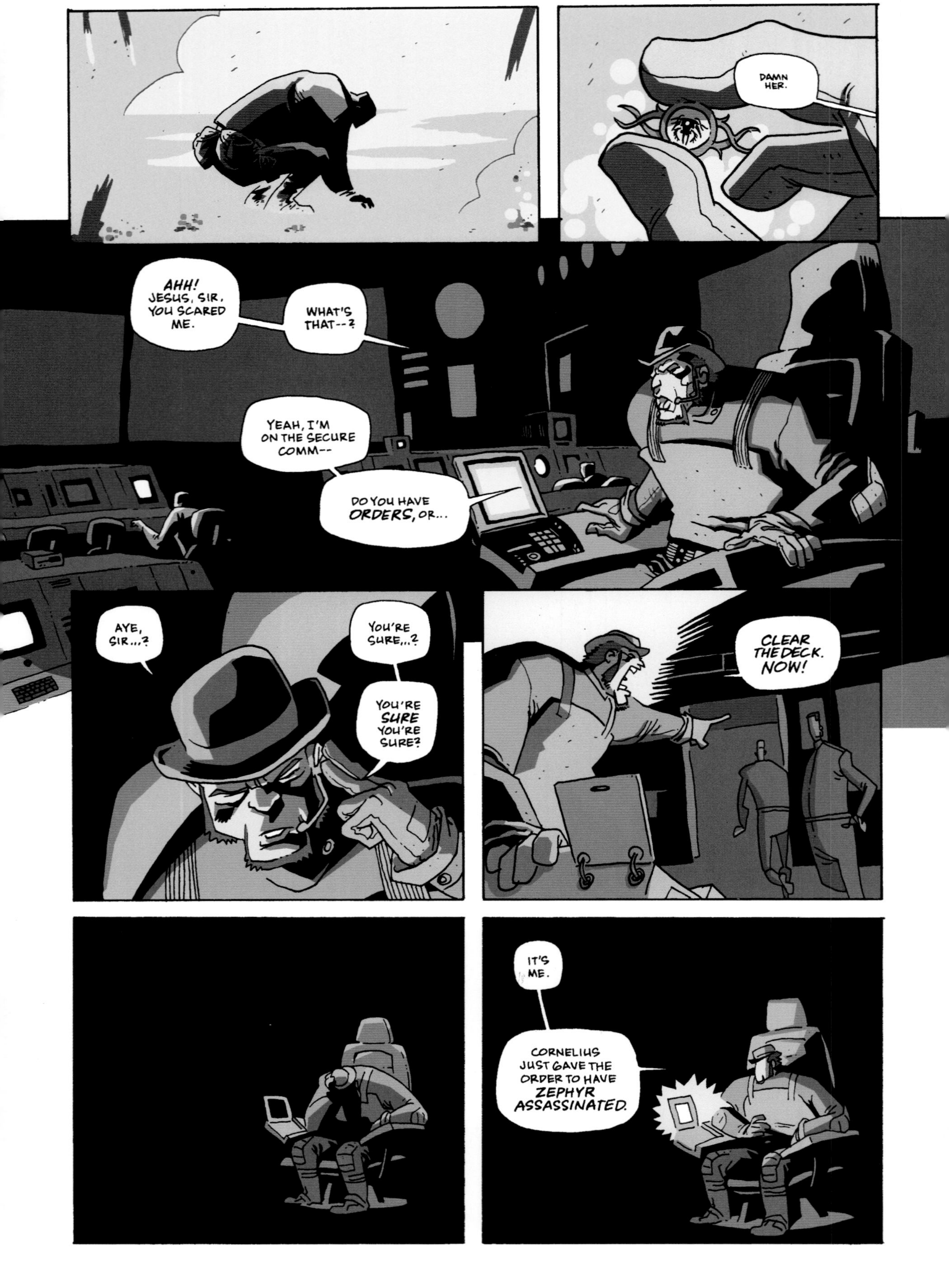
DAMN HER.
AHH! JESUS, SIR, YOU SCARED ME.
WHAT'S THAT--?
YEAH, I'M ON THE SECURE COMM--
DO YOU HAVE ORDERS, OR...
AYE, SIR...?
YOU'RE SURE...?
YOU'RE SURE YOU'RE SURE?
CLEAR THE DECK. NOW!
IT'S ME.
CORNELIUS JUST GAVE THE ORDER TO HAVE ZEPHYR ASSASSINATED.

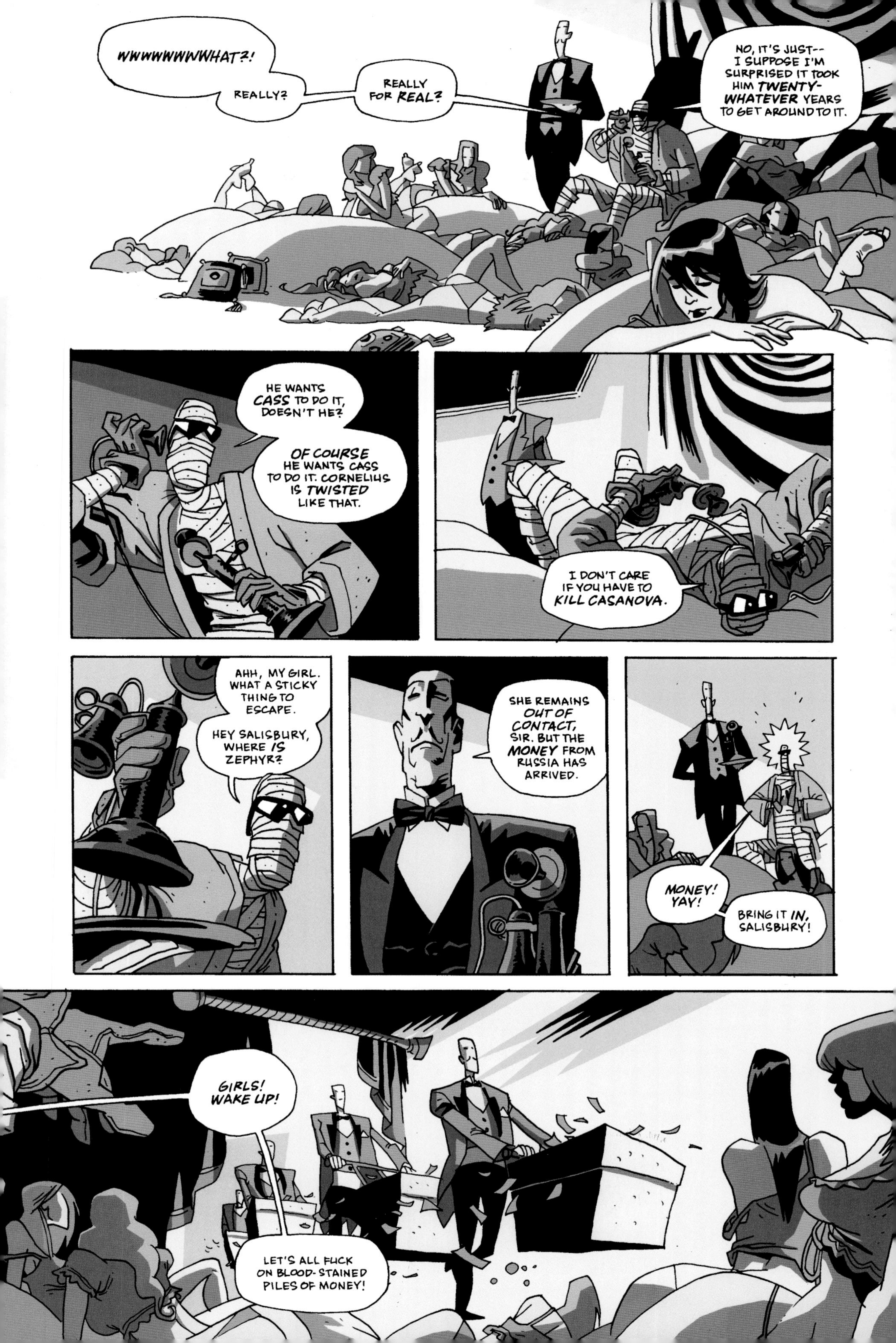
WWWWWWWWHAT?!
REALLY?
REALLY FOR REAL?
NO, IT'S JUST-- I SUPPOSE I'M SURPRISED IT TOOK HIM TWENTY-WHATEVER YEARS TO GET AROUND TO IT.
HE WANTS CASS TO DO IT, DOESN'T HE?
OF COURSE HE WANTS CASS TO DO IT. CORNELIUS IS TWISTED LIKE THAT.
I DON'T CARE IF YOU HAVE TO KILL CASANOVA.
AHH, MY GIRL. WHAT A STICKY THING TO ESCAPE.
HEY SALISBURY, WHERE IS ZEPHYR?
SHE REMAINS OUT OF CONTACT, SIR. BUT THE MONEY FROM RUSSIA HAS ARRIVED.
MONEY! YAY!
BRING IT IN, SALISBURY!
GIRLS! WAKE UP!
LET'S ALL FUCK ON BLOOD-STAINED PILES OF MONEY!

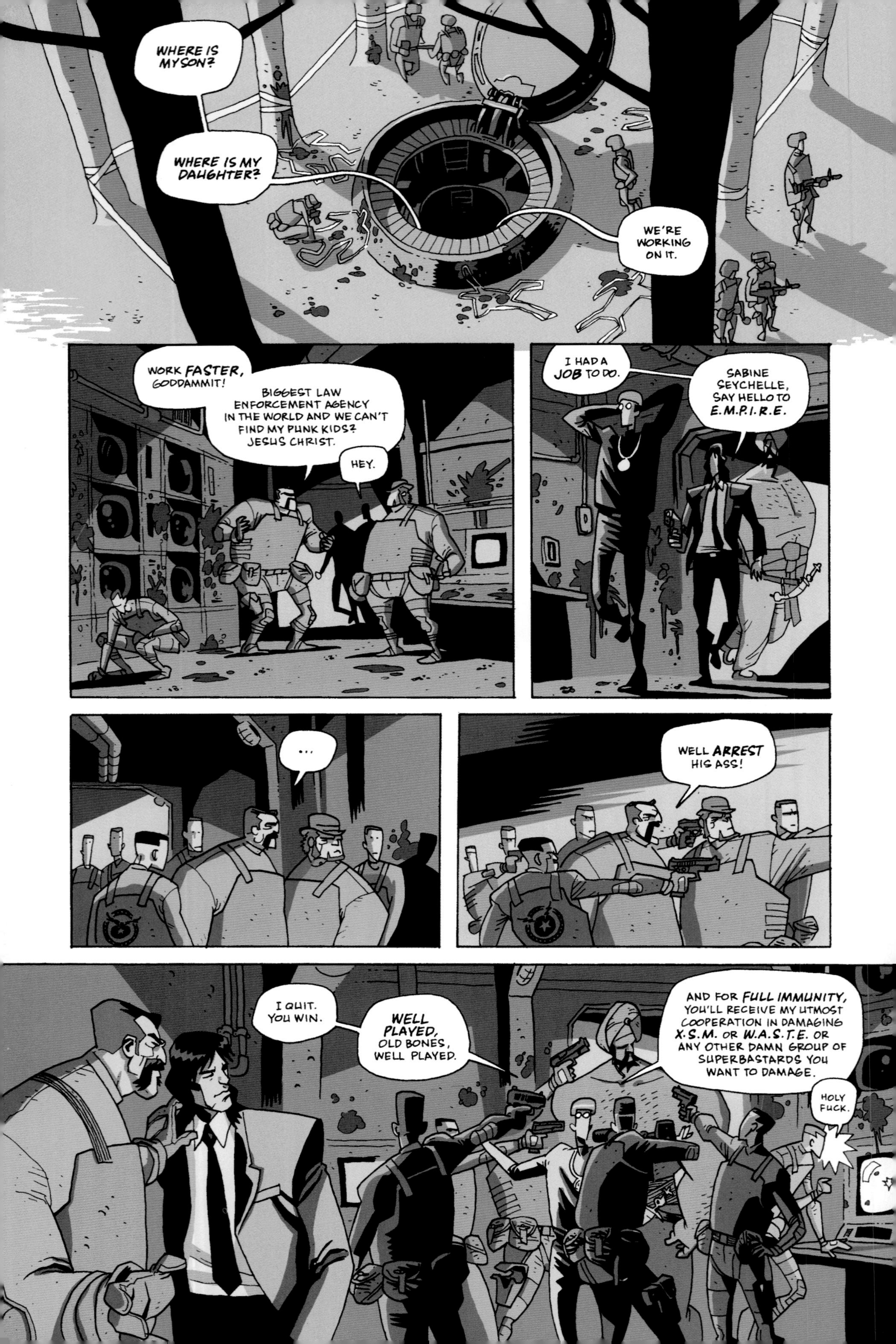
WHERE IS MY SON?
WHERE IS MY DAUGHTER?
WE'RE WORKING ON IT.
WORK FASTER, GODDAMMIT!
BIGGEST LAW ENFORCEMENT AGENCY IN THE WORLD AND WE CAN'T FIND MY PUNK KIDS? JESUS CHRIST.
HEY.
I HAD A JOB TO DO.
SABINE SEYCHELLE, SAY HELLO TO E.M.P.I.R.E.
...
WELL ARREST HIS ASS!
I QUIT. YOU WIN.
WELL PLAYED, OLD BONES, WELL PLAYED.
AND FOR FULL IMMUNITY, YOU'LL RECEIVE MY UTMOST COOPERATION IN DAMAGING X.S.M. OR W.A.S.T.E. OR ANY OTHER DAMN GROUP OF SUPERBASTARDS YOU WANT TO DAMAGE.
HOLY FUCK.

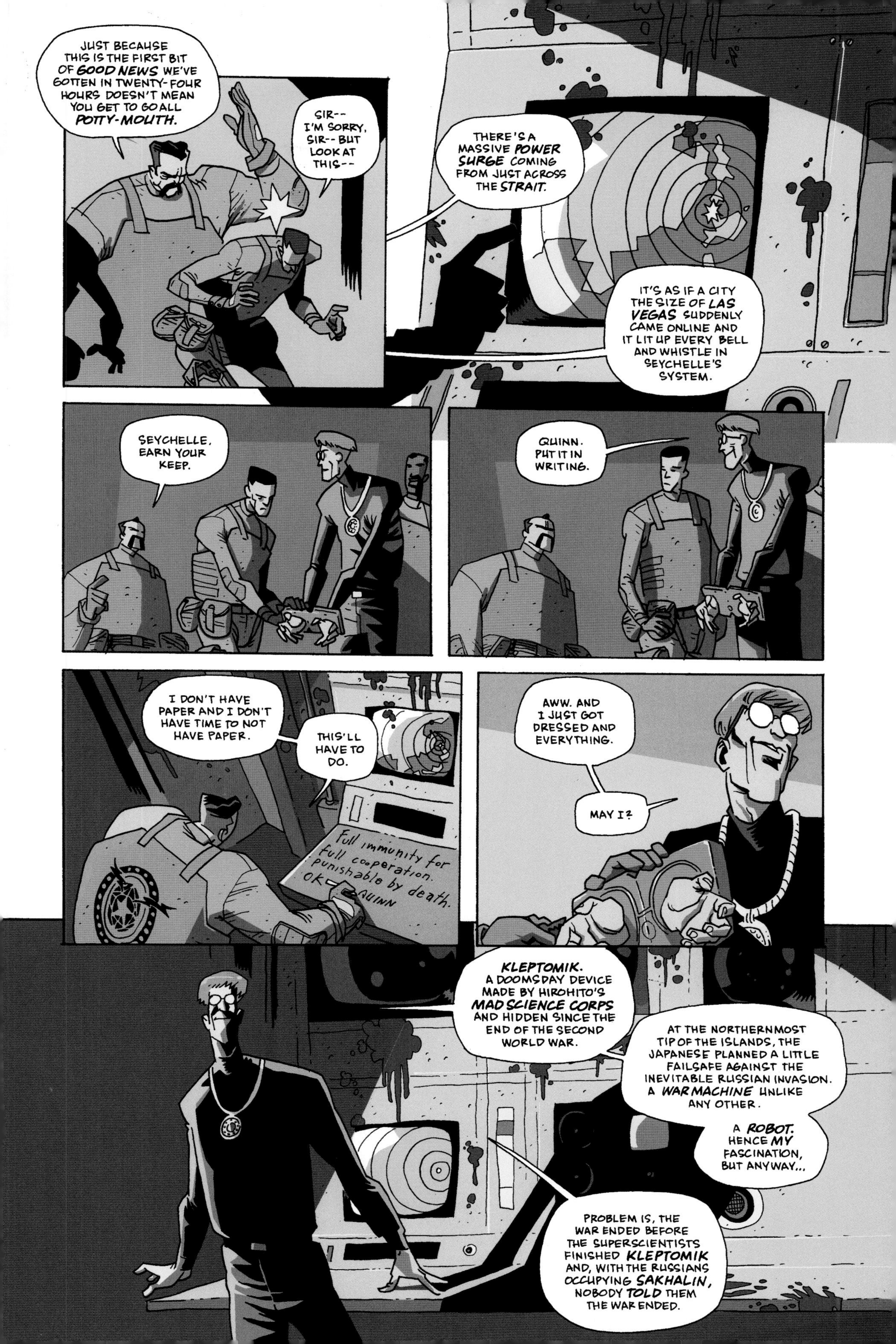
JUST BECAUSE THIS IS THE FIRST BIT OF GOOD NEWS WE'VE GOTTEN IN TWENTY-FOUR HOURS DOESN'T MEAN YOU GET TO GO ALL POTTY-MOUTH.
SIR-- I'M SORRY, SIR-- BUT LOOK AT THIS--
THERE'S A MASSIVE POWER SURGE COMING FROM JUST ACROSS THE STRAIT.
IT'S AS IF A CITY THE SIZE OF LAS VEGAS SUDDENLY CAME ONLINE AND IT LIT UP EVERY BELL AND WHISTLE IN SEYCHELLE'S SYSTEM.
SEYCHELLE. EARN YOUR KEEP.
QUINN. PUT IT IN WRITING.
I DON'T HAVE PAPER AND I DON'T HAVE TIME TO NOT HAVE PAPER.
THIS'LL HAVE TO DO.
Full immunity for full cooperation. punishable by death.
OK QUINN
AWW. AND I JUST GOT DRESSED AND EVERYTHING.
MAY I?
KLEPTOMIK. A DOOMSDAY DEVICE MADE BY HIROHITO'S MAD SCIENCE CORPS AND HIDDEN SINCE THE END OF THE SECOND WORLD WAR.
AT THE NORTHERNMOST TIP OF THE ISLANDS, THE JAPANESE PLANNED A LITTLE FAILSAFE AGAINST THE INEVITABLE RUSSIAN INVASION. A WAR MACHINE UNLIKE ANY OTHER.
A ROBOT. HENCE MY FASCINATION, BUT ANYWAY...
PROBLEM IS, THE WAR ENDED BEFORE THE SUPERSCIENTISTS FINISHED KLEPTOMIK AND, WITH THE RUSSIANS OCCUPYING SAKHALIN, NOBODY TOLD THEM THE WAR ENDED.

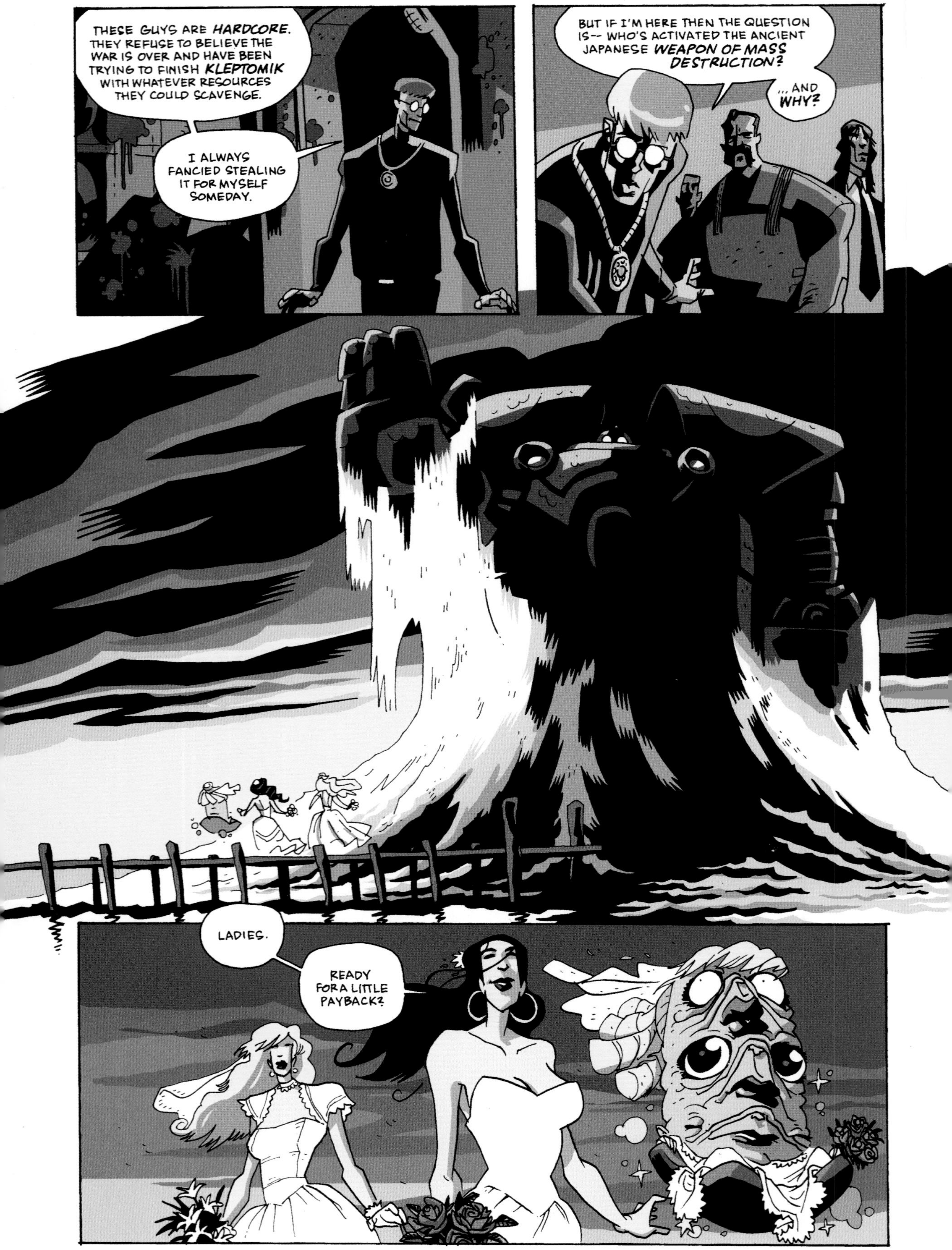
THESE GUYS ARE HARDCORE. THEY REFUSE TO BELIEVE THE WAR IS OVER AND HAVE BEEN TRYING TO FINISH KLEPTOMIK WITH WHATEVER RESOURCES THEY COULD SCAVENGE.
I ALWAYS FANCIED STEALING IT FOR MYSELF SOMEDAY.
BUT IF I'M HERE THEN THE QUESTION IS-- WHO'S ACTIVATED THE ANCIENT JAPANESE WEAPON OF MASS DESTRUCTION?
...AND WHY?
LADIES.
READY FOR A LITTLE PAYBACK?

EXECUTION DAYS

PRETTY LITTLE POLICEMAN

MISSION TO YERBA MUERTA

DÉTOURNEMENT

COLDHEART

WOMEN AND MEN (PART ONE)

WOMEN AND MEN (PART TWO)

I THINK I ALMOST LOVED HIM

IS THIS IT? (REDUX)

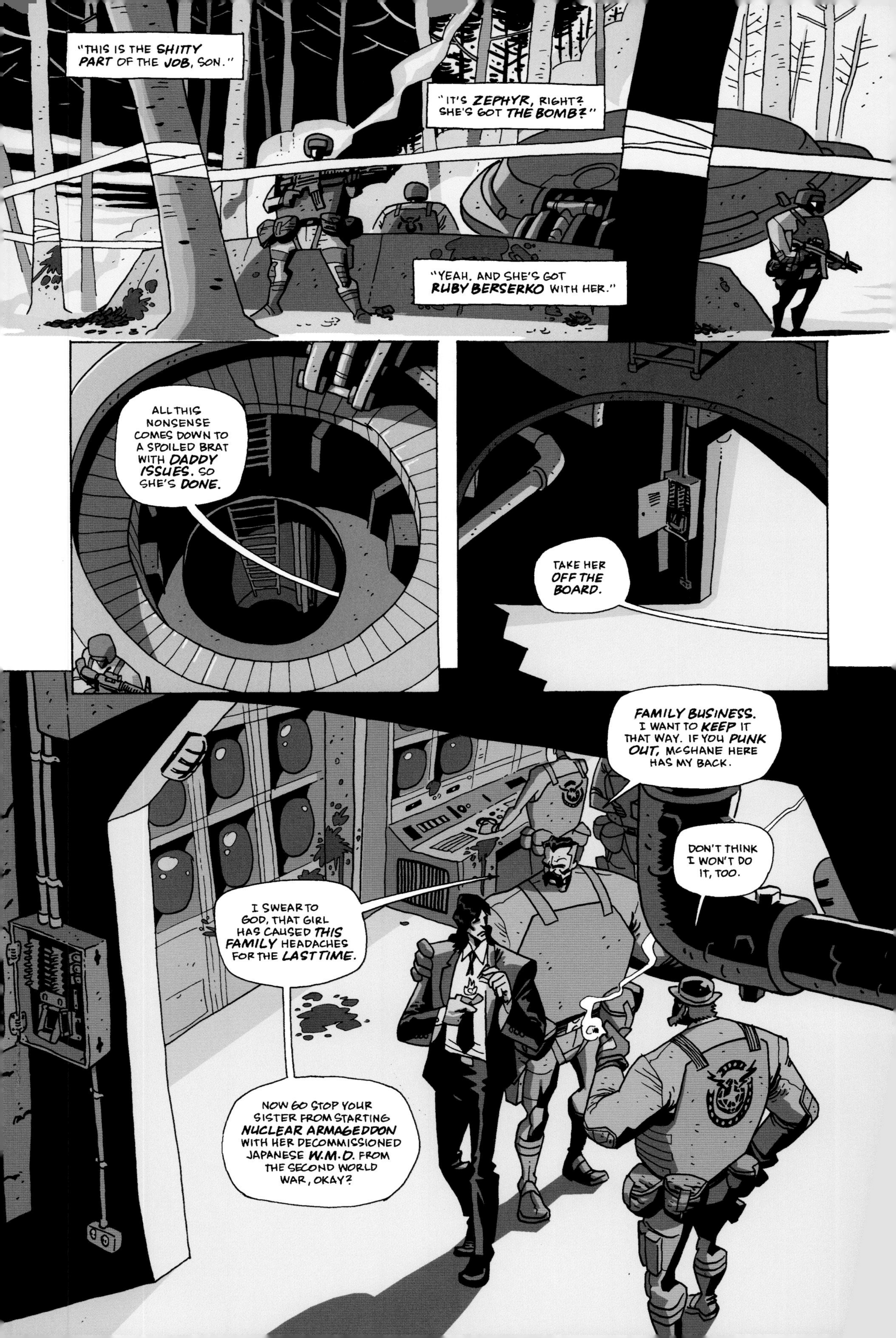
"THIS IS THE SHITTY PART OF THE JOB, SON."
"IT'S ZEPHYR, RIGHT? SHE'S GOT THE BOMB?"
"YEAH. AND SHE'S GOT RUBY BERSERKO WITH HER."
ALL THIS NONSENSE COMES DOWN TO A SPOILED BRAT WITH DADDY ISSUES. SO SHE'S DONE.
TAKE HER OFF THE BOARD.
FAMILY BUSINESS. I WANT TO KEEP IT THAT WAY. IF YOU PUNK OUT, McSHANE HERE HAS MY BACK.
DON'T THINK I WON'T DO IT, TOO.
I SWEAR TO GOD, THAT GIRL HAS CAUSED THIS FAMILY HEADACHES FOR THE LAST TIME.
NOW GO STOP YOUR SISTER FROM STARTING NUCLEAR ARMAGEDDON WITH HER DECOMMISSIONED JAPANESE W.M.D. FROM THE SECOND WORLD WAR, OKAY?

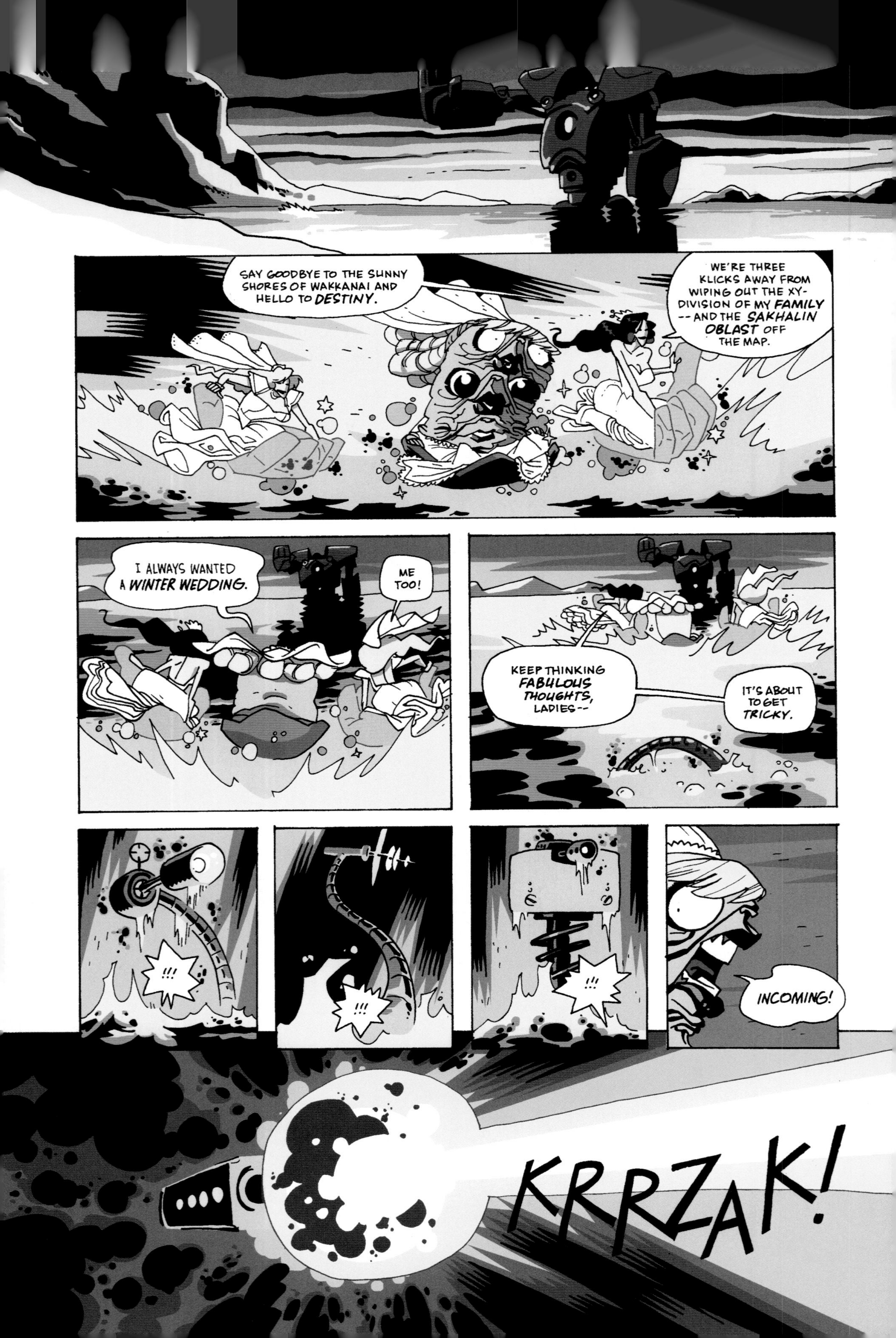
SAY GOODBYE TO THE SUNNY SHORES OF WAKKANAI AND HELLO TO DESTINY.
WE'RE THREE KLICKS AWAY FROM WIPING OUT THE XY-DIVISION OF MY FAMILY --AND THE SAKHALIN OBLAST OFF THE MAP.
I ALWAYS WANTED A WINTER WEDDING.
ME TOO!
KEEP THINKING FABULOUS THOUGHTS, LADIES--
IT'S ABOUT TO GET TRICKY.
!!!
!!!
!!!
INCOMING!
KRRZAK!

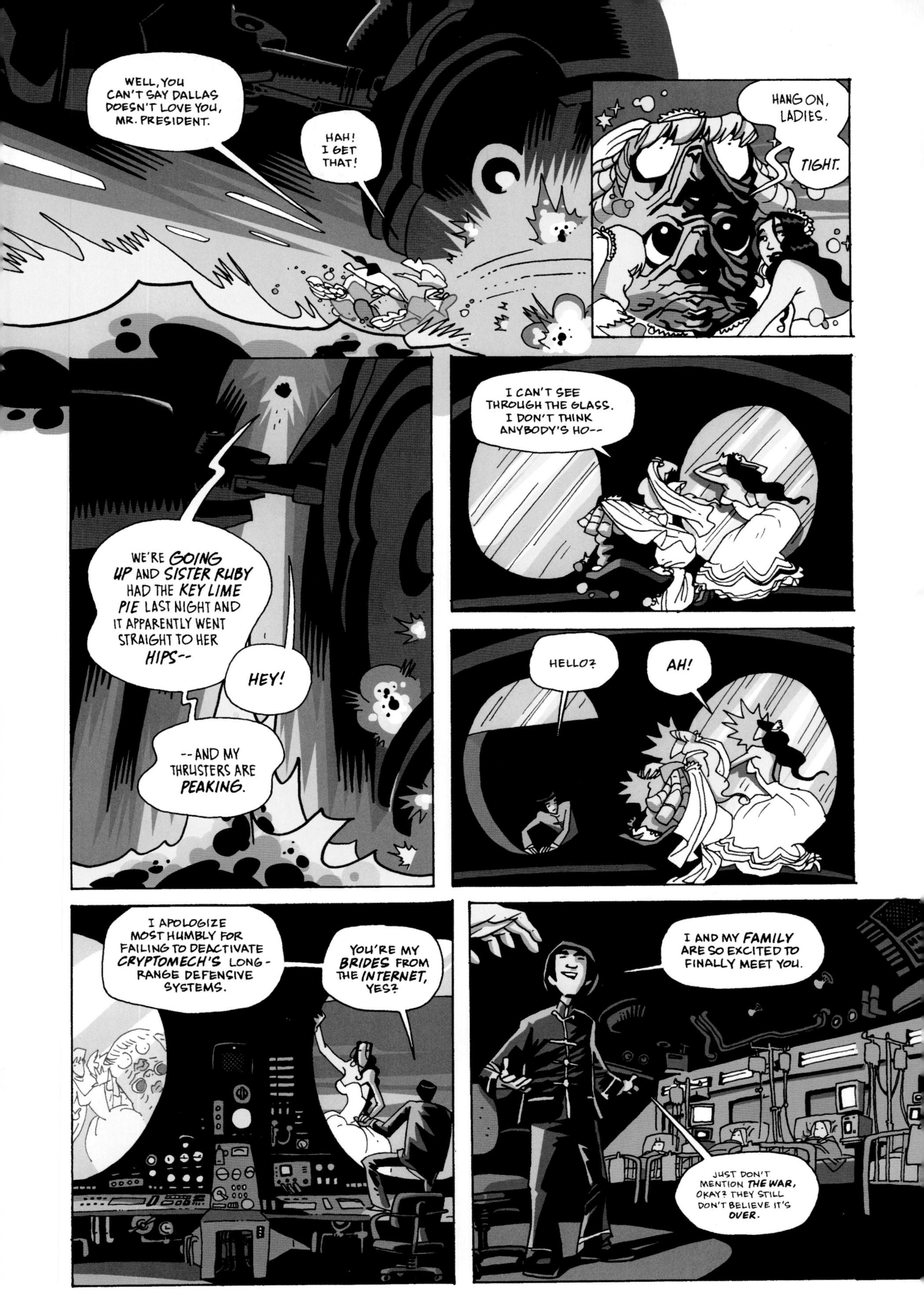
WELL, YOU CAN'T SAY DALLAS DOESN'T LOVE YOU, MR. PRESIDENT.
HAH! I GET THAT!
HANG ON, LADIES.
TIGHT.
WE'RE GOING UP AND SISTER RUBY HAD THE KEY LIME PIE LAST NIGHT AND IT APPARENTLY WENT STRAIGHT TO HER HIPS--
HEY!
--AND MY THRUSTERS ARE PEAKING.
I CAN'T SEE THROUGH THE GLASS. I DON'T THINK ANYBODY'S HO--
HELLO?
AH!
I APOLOGIZE MOST HUMBLY FOR FAILING TO DEACTIVATE CRYPTOMECH'S LONG-RANGE DEFENSIVE SYSTEMS.
YOU'RE MY BRIDES FROM THE INTERNET, YES?
I AND MY FAMILY ARE SO EXCITED TO FINALLY MEET YOU.
JUST DON'T MENTION THE WAR, OKAY? THEY STILL DON'T BELIEVE IT'S OVER.

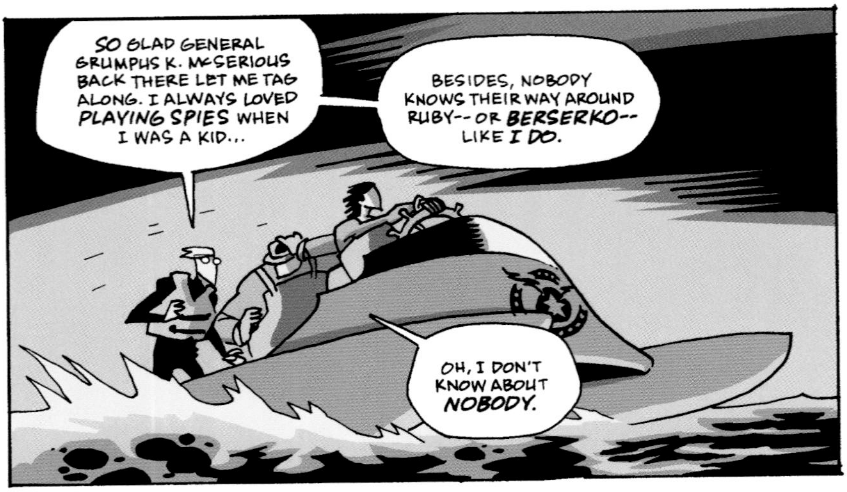
SO GLAD GENERAL GRUMPUS K. McSERIOUS BACK THERE LET ME TAG ALONG. I ALWAYS LOVED PLAYING SPIES WHEN I WAS A KID...
BESIDES, NOBODY KNOWS THEIR WAY AROUND RUBY--OR BERSERKO--LIKE I DO.
OH, I DON'T KNOW ABOUT NOBODY.

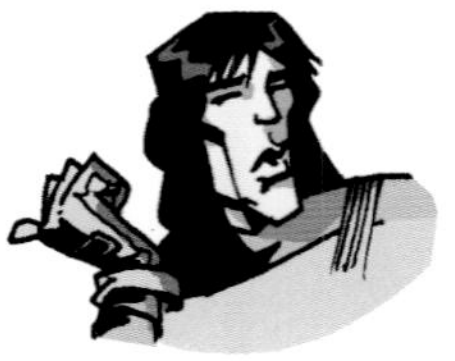
STUCK IN LA PEROUSE STRAIT ON A SILENT-RUNNING E.M.P.I.R.E. HYDRO-FOIL WITH RUBY'S TWO BICKERING EX-BOYFRIENDS?
YEAH, NO, THAT'S NOT AWKWARD FOR ME AT ALL, THANKS FOR ASKING.

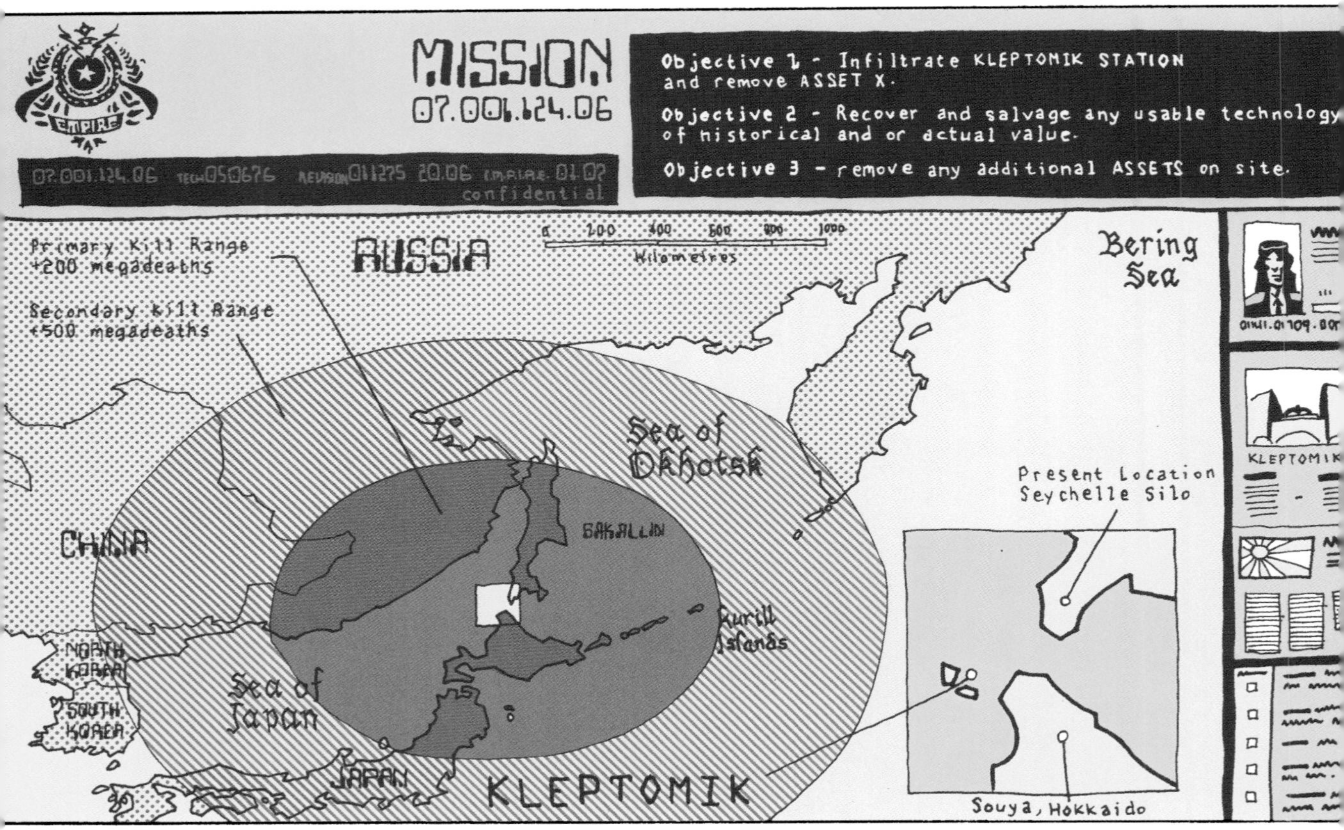
EMPIRE
MISSION
07.001.124.06
07.001.124.06 TECH050676 REVISION011275 20.06 E.M.P.I.R.E. 01.02
confidential
Objective 1 - Infiltrate KLEPTOMIK STATION and remove ASSET X.
Objective 2 - Recover and salvage any usable technology of historical and or actual value.
Objective 3 - remove any additional ASSETS on site.
Primary Kill Range +200 megadeaths
Secondary Kill Range +500 megadeaths
RUSSIA
0 200 400 600 800 1000
Kilometres
Bering Sea
Sea of Okhotsk
CHINA
SAKHALIN
Kurill Islands
NORTH KOREA
SOUTH KOREA
Sea of Japan
JAPAN
KLEPTOMIK
Present Location Seychelle Silo
Souya, Hokkaido
KLEPTOMIK

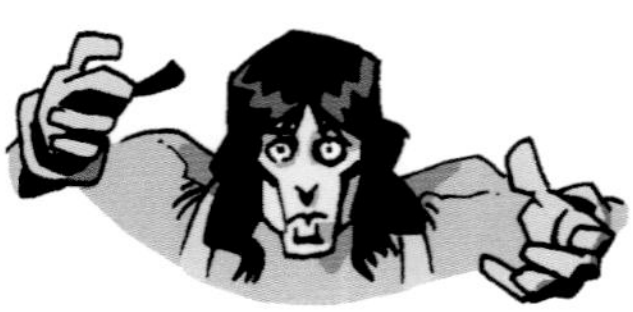
FOUR-HUNDRED-SOME KLICKS OF THIS SHIT. WE'RE ROCKETING TOWARDS A DECADES-OLD WEAPON WITH A SEVEN-HUNDRED-PLUS MEGADEATH CAPABILITY AND I HAVE TO LISTEN TO McSHANE AND JOHNNY CRANK ARGUE DICK SIZE.
I'M GONNA BEAT ST. PETER'S ASS WHEN I SEE HIM.

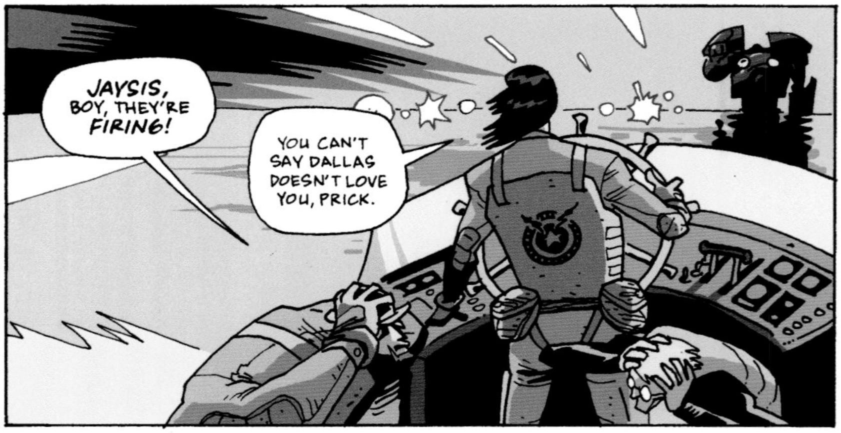
JAYSIS, BOY, THEY'RE FIRING!
YOU CAN'T SAY DALLAS DOESN'T LOVE YOU, PRICK.

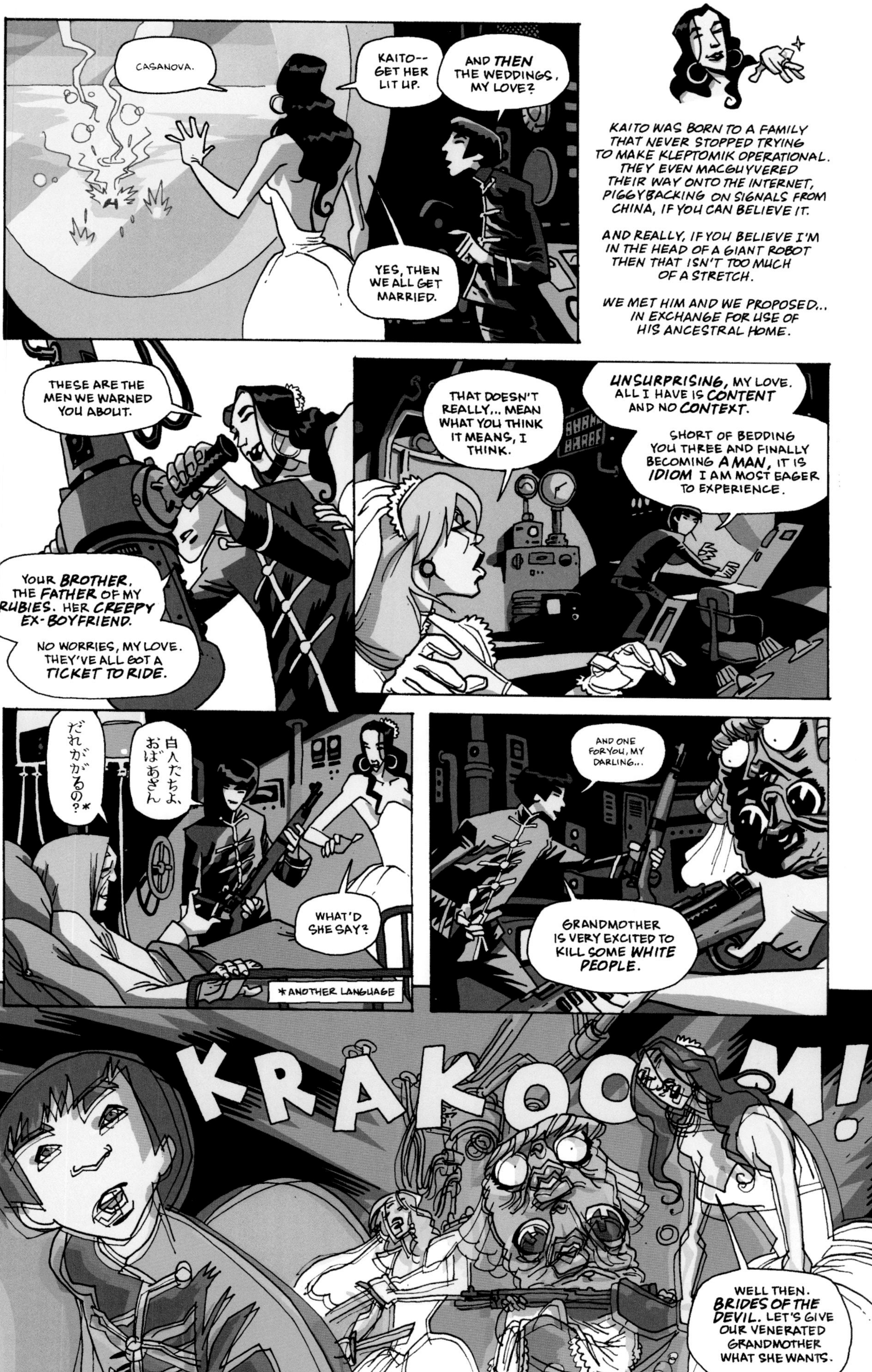

CASANOVA.
KAITO-- GET HER LIT UP.
AND THEN THE WEDDINGS, MY LOVE?
YES, THEN WE ALL GET MARRIED.
KAITO WAS BORN TO A FAMILY THAT NEVER STOPPED TRYING TO MAKE KLEPTOMIK OPERATIONAL. THEY EVEN MACGUYVERED THEIR WAY ONTO THE INTERNET, PIGGYBACKING ON SIGNALS FROM CHINA, IF YOU CAN BELIEVE IT.
AND REALLY, IF YOU BELIEVE I'M IN THE HEAD OF A GIANT ROBOT THEN THAT ISN'T TOO MUCH OF A STRETCH.
WE MET HIM AND WE PROPOSED... IN EXCHANGE FOR USE OF HIS ANCESTRAL HOME.
THESE ARE THE MEN WE WARNED YOU ABOUT.
YOUR BROTHER. THE FATHER OF MY RUBIES. HER CREEPY EX-BOYFRIEND.
NO WORRIES, MY LOVE. THEY'VE ALL GOT A TICKET TO RIDE.
THAT DOESN'T REALLY... MEAN WHAT YOU THINK IT MEANS, I THINK.
UNSURPRISING, MY LOVE. ALL I HAVE IS CONTENT AND NO CONTEXT.
SHORT OF BEDDING YOU THREE AND FINALLY BECOMING A MAN, IT IS IDIOM I AM MOST EAGER TO EXPERIENCE.
だれがかるの？*
白人たちよ、おばあさん
WHAT'D SHE SAY?
*ANOTHER LANGUAGE
AND ONE FOR YOU, MY DARLING...
GRANDMOTHER IS VERY EXCITED TO KILL SOME WHITE PEOPLE.
KRAKOOOM!
WELL THEN. BRIDES OF THE DEVIL. LET'S GIVE OUR VENERATED GRANDMOTHER WHAT SHE WANTS.

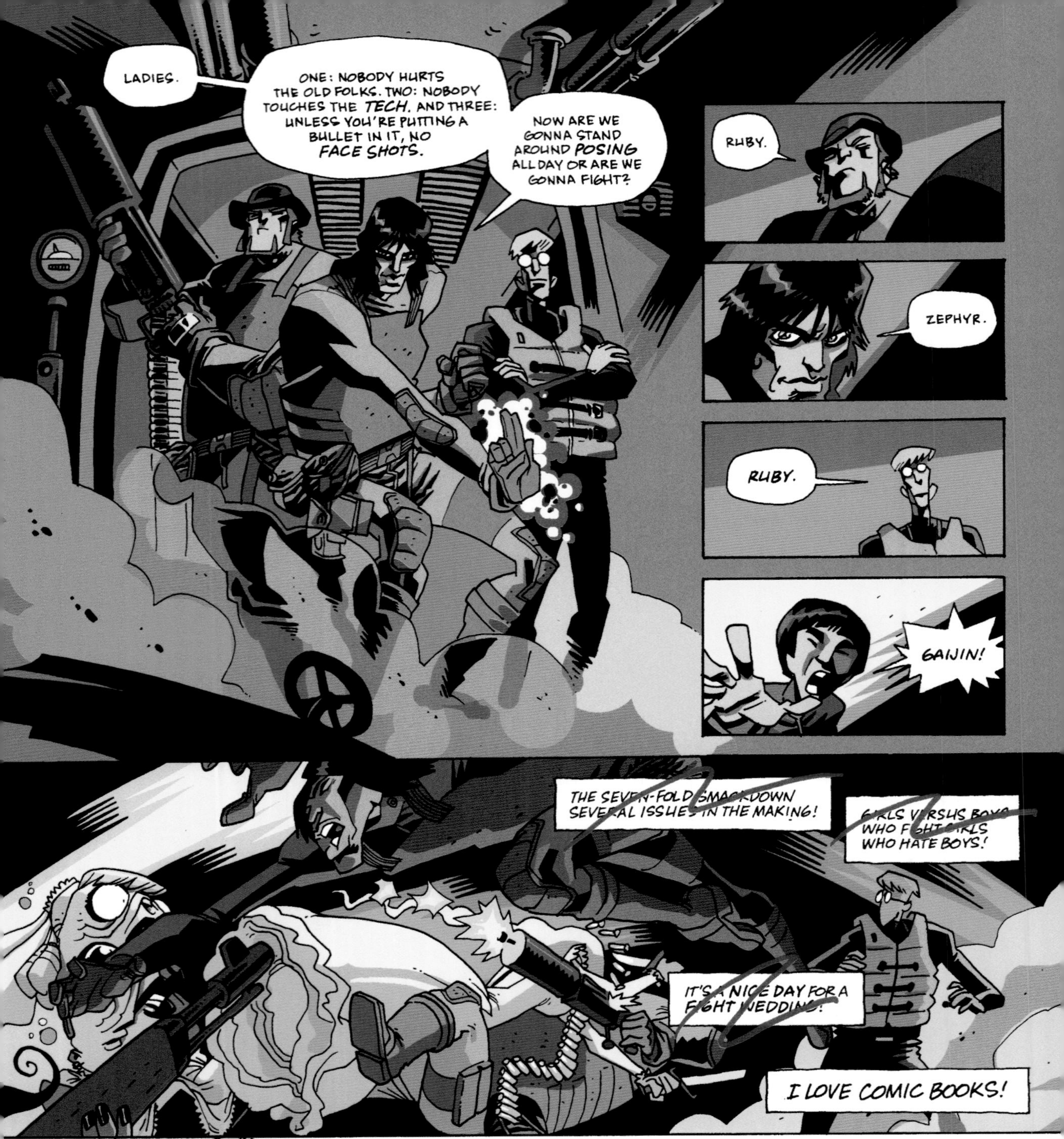
LADIES.
ONE: NOBODY HURTS THE OLD FOLKS. TWO: NOBODY TOUCHES THE TECH. AND THREE: UNLESS YOU'RE PUTTING A BULLET IN IT, NO FACE SHOTS.
NOW ARE WE GONNA STAND AROUND POSING ALL DAY OR ARE WE GONNA FIGHT?
RUBY.
ZEPHYR.
RUBY.
GAIJIN!
THE SEVEN-FOLD SMACKDOWN SEVERAL ISSUES IN THE MAKING!
GIRLS VERSUS BOYS WHO FIGHT GIRLS WHO HATE BOYS!
IT'S A NICE DAY FOR A FIGHT WEDDING!
I LOVE COMIC BOOKS!

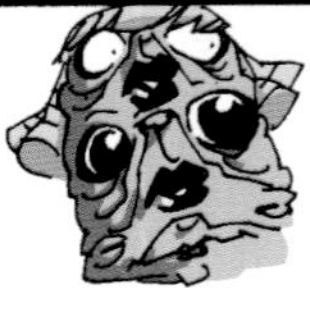

GOSH I DON'T KNOW--SEEING SABINE AGAIN? I THOUGHT I WAS READY. I THOUGHT--OH, GOD, I THOUGHT I WAS OVER HIM.

I KNOW--I KNOW HOW MUCH THINGS HAVE CHANGED. AND I KNOW I'M--I KNOW I'M DIFFERENT NOW. I KNOW... I MEAN, I KNOW HOW I LOOK, OKAY? I KNOW.

GOD, I JUST DON'T WANT HIM TO LAUGH AT ME.

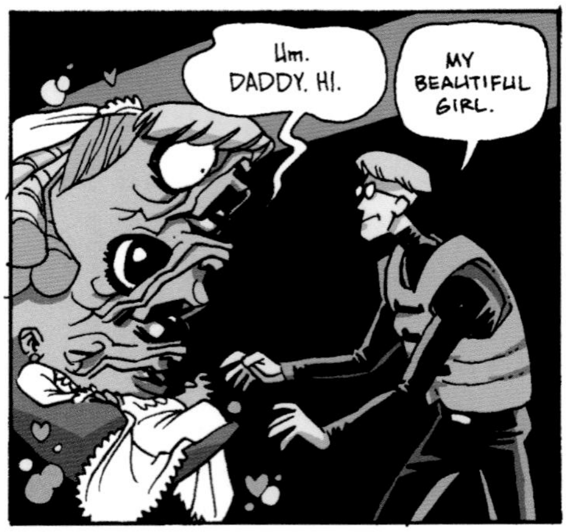
Um. DADDY. HI.
MY BEAUTIFUL GIRL.

RUBY WAS MY A.I. MASTERWORK. DOTING, DARLING, SUBSERVIENT IN PUBLIC AND A STRAP-ON BITCH IN THE BOUDOIR. **BERSERKO** WAS MY ROBOTICS MASTERPIECE--HE **SHITS** NOBEL PRIZES, THAT'S HOW GOOD HE IS.

TOGETHER THEY'RE BOTH MONUMENT AND MIRROR, THE SUM OF MY SKILLS AND THE MEASURE OF MY DREAMS.

SO OF COURSE I STILL LOVE HER. **SAMIR** WON'T BE HAPPY, BUT FUCK THAT GUY.

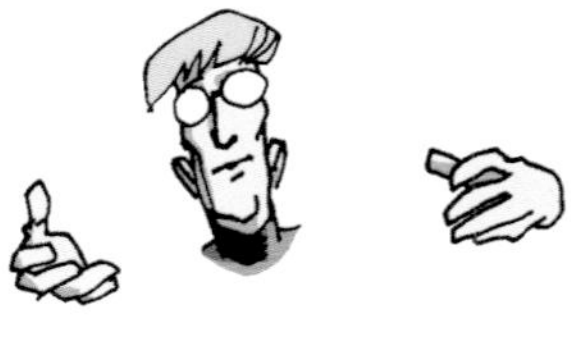

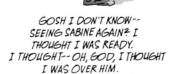

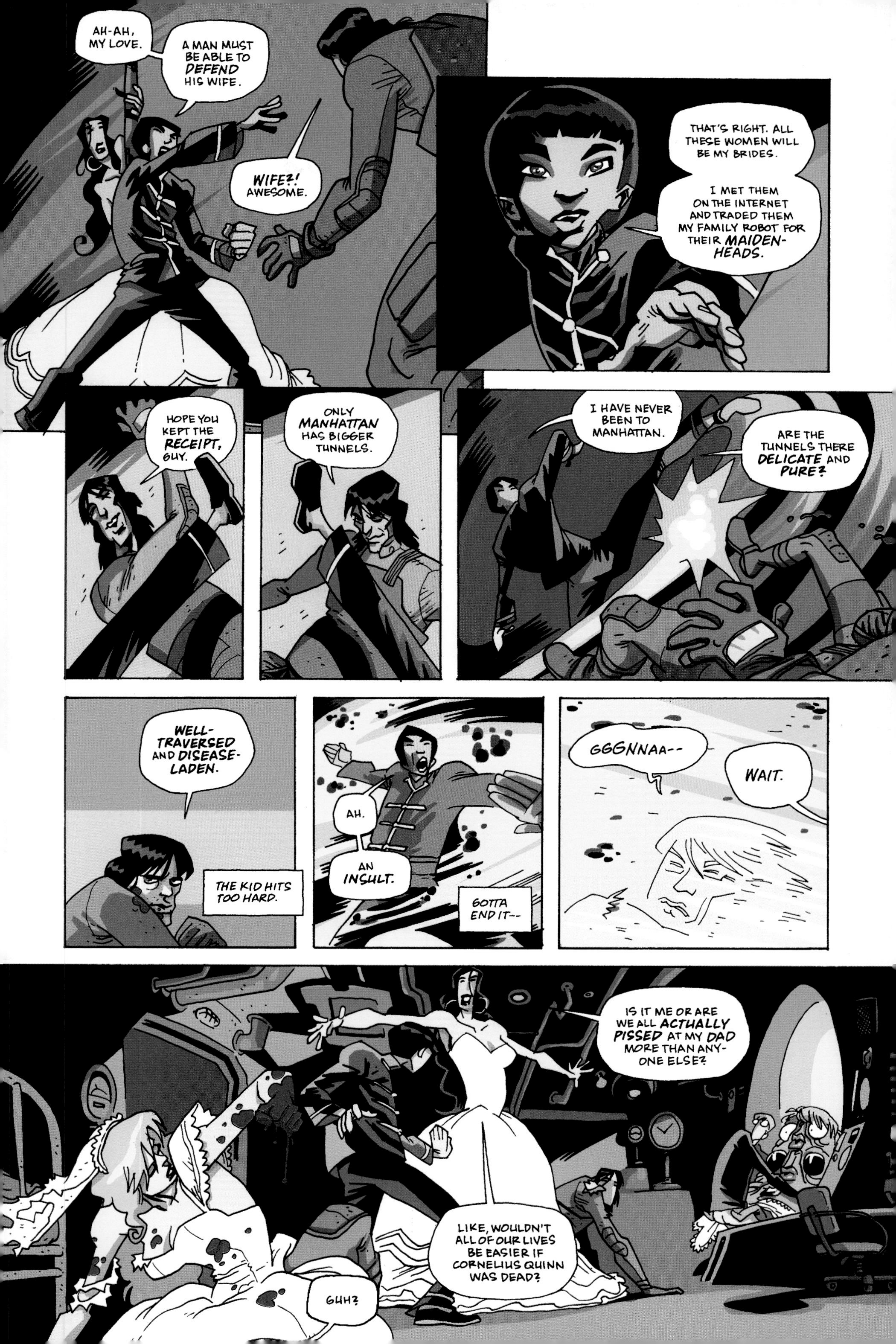
AH-AH, MY LOVE.
A MAN MUST BE ABLE TO DEFEND HIS WIFE.
WIFE?! AWESOME.
THAT'S RIGHT. ALL THESE WOMEN WILL BE MY BRIDES.
I MET THEM ON THE INTERNET AND TRADED THEM MY FAMILY ROBOT FOR THEIR MAIDEN-HEADS.
HOPE YOU KEPT THE RECEIPT, GUY.
ONLY MANHATTAN HAS BIGGER TUNNELS.
I HAVE NEVER BEEN TO MANHATTAN.
ARE THE TUNNELS THERE DELICATE AND PURE?
WELL-TRAVERSED AND DISEASE-LADEN.
THE KID HITS TOO HARD.
AH.
AN INSULT.
GOTTA END IT--
GGGNNAA--
WAIT.
IS IT ME OR ARE WE ALL ACTUALLY PISSED AT MY DAD MORE THAN ANY-ONE ELSE?
LIKE, WOULDN'T ALL OF OUR LIVES BE EASIER IF CORNELIUS QUINN WAS DEAD?
GUH?

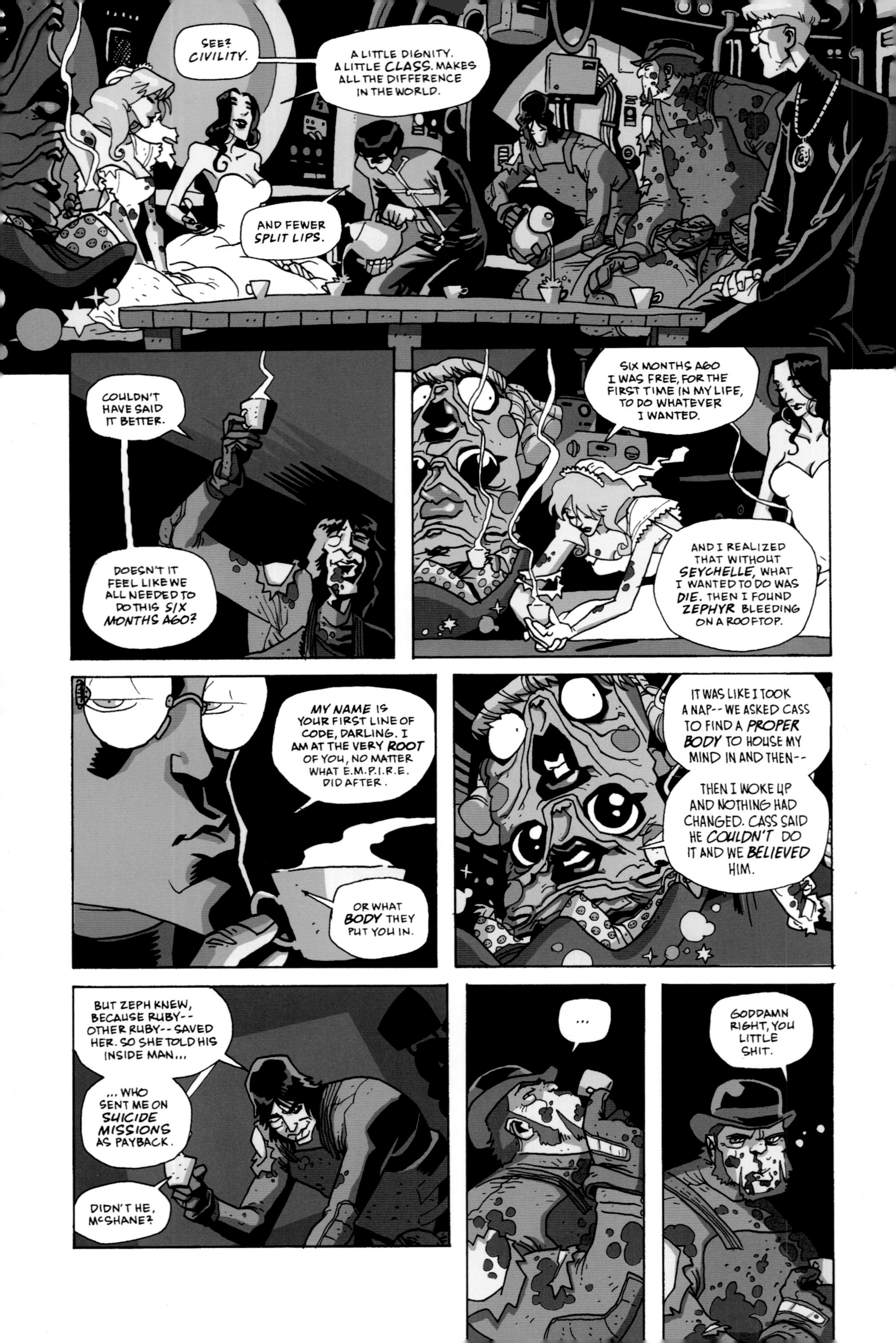
SEE? CIVILITY.
A LITTLE DIGNITY. A LITTLE CLASS. MAKES ALL THE DIFFERENCE IN THE WORLD.
AND FEWER SPLIT LIPS.
COULDN'T HAVE SAID IT BETTER.
DOESN'T IT FEEL LIKE WE ALL NEEDED TO DO THIS SIX MONTHS AGO?
SIX MONTHS AGO I WAS FREE, FOR THE FIRST TIME IN MY LIFE, TO DO WHATEVER I WANTED.
AND I REALIZED THAT WITHOUT SEYCHELLE, WHAT I WANTED TO DO WAS DIE. THEN I FOUND ZEPHYR BLEEDING ON A ROOFTOP.
MY NAME IS YOUR FIRST LINE OF CODE, DARLING. I AM AT THE VERY ROOT OF YOU, NO MATTER WHAT E.M.P.I.R.E. DID AFTER.
OR WHAT BODY THEY PUT YOU IN.
IT WAS LIKE I TOOK A NAP-- WE ASKED CASS TO FIND A PROPER BODY TO HOUSE MY MIND IN AND THEN--
THEN I WOKE UP AND NOTHING HAD CHANGED. CASS SAID HE COULDN'T DO IT AND WE BELIEVED HIM.
BUT ZEPH KNEW, BECAUSE RUBY-- OTHER RUBY-- SAVED HER. SO SHE TOLD HIS INSIDE MAN...
...WHO SENT ME ON SUICIDE MISSIONS AS PAYBACK.
DIDN'T HE, McSHANE?
...
GODDAMN RIGHT, YOU LITTLE SHIT.

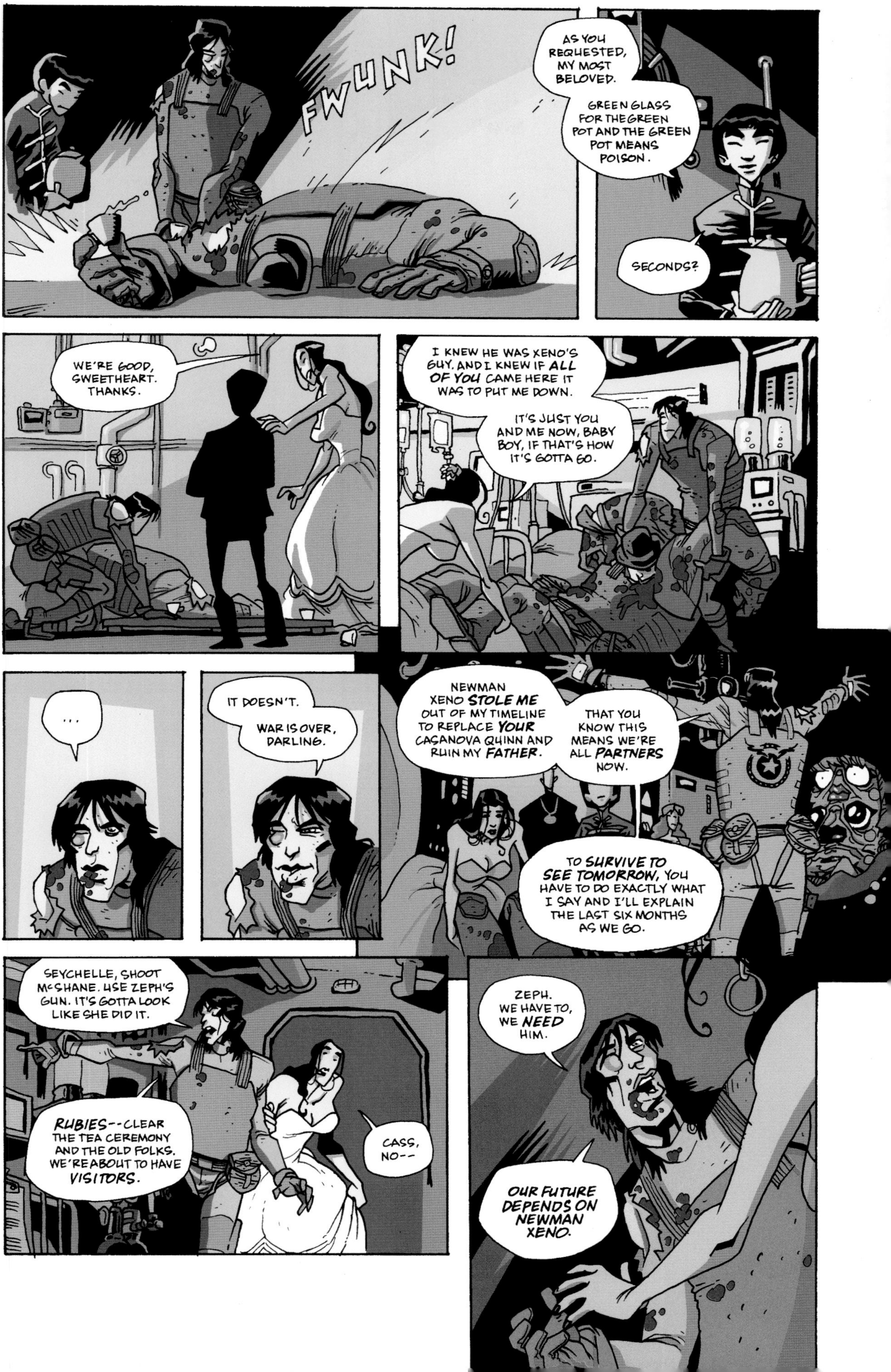
FWUNK!
AS YOU REQUESTED, MY MOST BELOVED.
GREEN GLASS FOR THE GREEN POT AND THE GREEN POT MEANS POISON.
SECONDS?
WE'RE GOOD, SWEETHEART. THANKS.
I KNEW HE WAS XENO'S GUY. AND I KNEW IF ALL OF YOU CAME HERE IT WAS TO PUT ME DOWN.
IT'S JUST YOU AND ME NOW, BABY BOY, IF THAT'S HOW IT'S GOTTA GO.
...
IT DOESN'T.
WAR IS OVER, DARLING.
NEWMAN XENO STOLE ME OUT OF MY TIMELINE TO REPLACE YOUR CASANOVA QUINN AND RUIN MY FATHER.
THAT YOU KNOW THIS MEANS WE'RE ALL PARTNERS NOW.
TO SURVIVE TO SEE TOMORROW, YOU HAVE TO DO EXACTLY WHAT I SAY AND I'LL EXPLAIN THE LAST SIX MONTHS AS WE GO.
SEYCHELLE, SHOOT McSHANE. USE ZEPH'S GUN. IT'S GOTTA LOOK LIKE SHE DID IT.
RUBIES--CLEAR THE TEA CEREMONY AND THE OLD FOLKS. WE'RE ABOUT TO HAVE VISITORS.
CASS, NO--
ZEPH. WE HAVE TO, WE NEED HIM.
OUR FUTURE DEPENDS ON NEWMAN XENO.

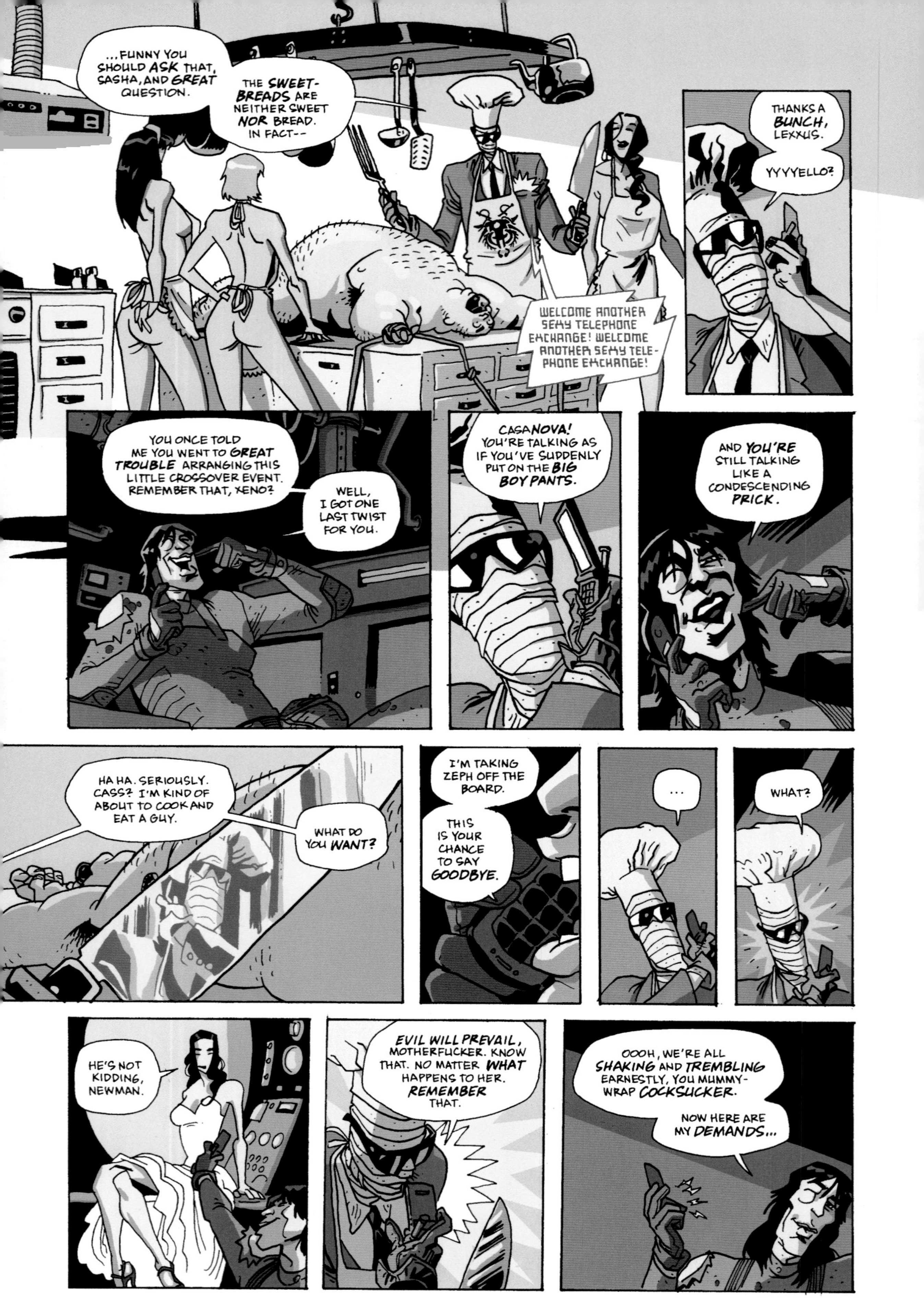
...FUNNY YOU SHOULD ASK THAT, SASHA, AND GREAT QUESTION.
THE SWEET-BREADS ARE NEITHER SWEET NOR BREAD. IN FACT--
WELCOME ANOTHER SEXY TELEPHONE EXCHANGE! WELCOME ANOTHER SEXY TELEPHONE EXCHANGE!
THANKS A BUNCH, LEXXUS.
YYYYELLO?
YOU ONCE TOLD ME YOU WENT TO GREAT TROUBLE ARRANGING THIS LITTLE CROSSOVER EVENT. REMEMBER THAT, XENO?
WELL, I GOT ONE LAST TWIST FOR YOU.
CASANOVA! YOU'RE TALKING AS IF YOU'VE SUDDENLY PUT ON THE BIG BOY PANTS.
AND YOU'RE STILL TALKING LIKE A CONDESCENDING PRICK.
HA HA. SERIOUSLY. CASS? I'M KIND OF ABOUT TO COOK AND EAT A GUY.
WHAT DO YOU WANT?
I'M TAKING ZEPH OFF THE BOARD.
THIS IS YOUR CHANCE TO SAY GOODBYE.
...
WHAT?
HE'S NOT KIDDING, NEWMAN.
EVIL WILL PREVAIL, MOTHERFUCKER. KNOW THAT. NO MATTER WHAT HAPPENS TO HER. REMEMBER THAT.
OOOH, WE'RE ALL SHAKING AND TREMBLING EARNESTLY, YOU MUMMY-WRAP COCKSUCKER.
NOW HERE ARE MY DEMANDS...

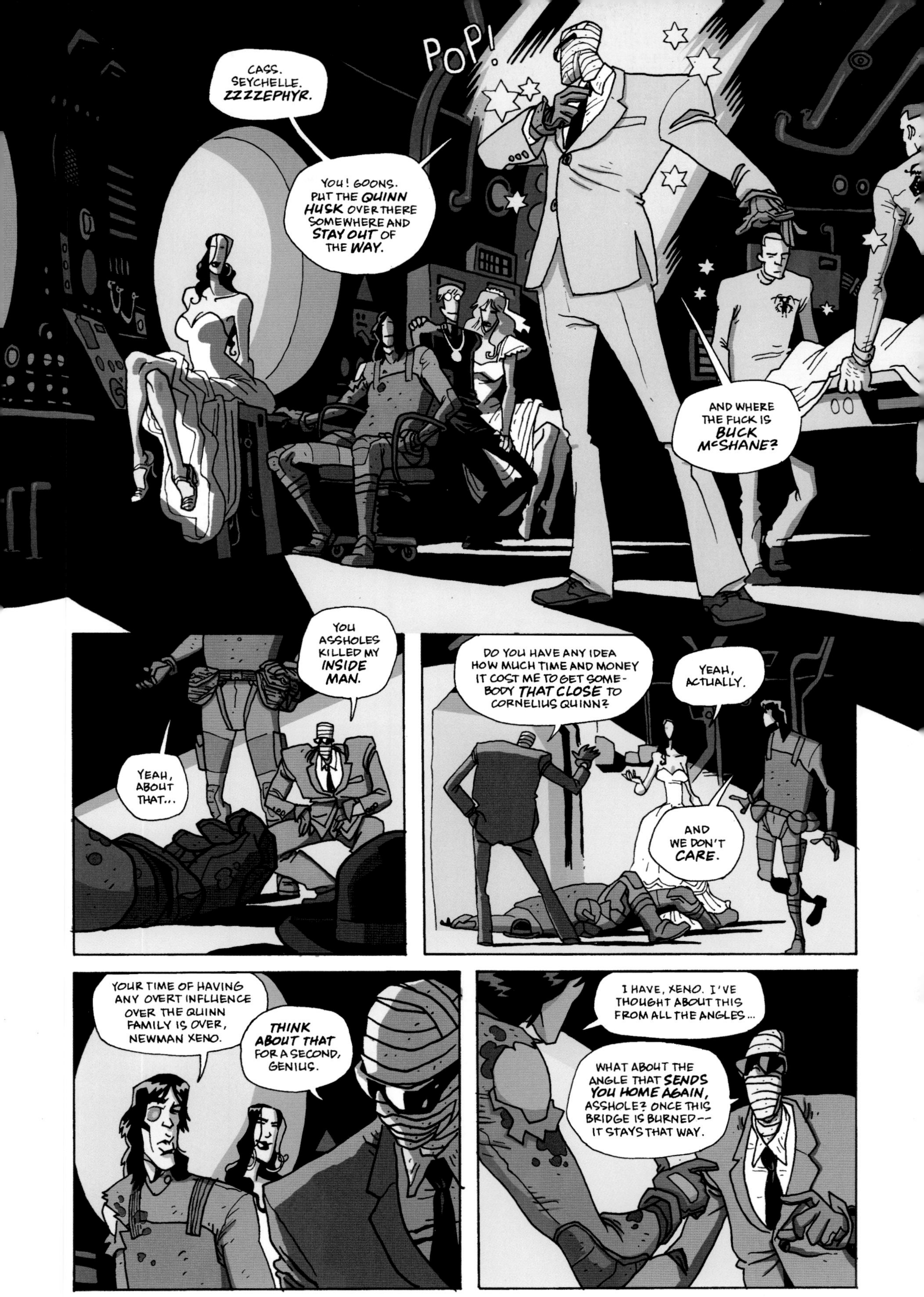
POP!
CASS. SEYCHELLE. ZZZZEPHYR.
YOU! GOONS. PUT THE QUINN HUSK OVER THERE SOMEWHERE AND STAY OUT OF THE WAY.
AND WHERE THE FUCK IS BUCK McSHANE?
YOU ASSHOLES KILLED MY INSIDE MAN.
YEAH, ABOUT THAT...
DO YOU HAVE ANY IDEA HOW MUCH TIME AND MONEY IT COST ME TO GET SOME-BODY THAT CLOSE TO CORNELIUS QUINN?
YEAH, ACTUALLY.
AND WE DON'T CARE.
YOUR TIME OF HAVING ANY OVERT INFLUENCE OVER THE QUINN FAMILY IS OVER, NEWMAN XENO.
THINK ABOUT THAT FOR A SECOND, GENIUS.
I HAVE, XENO. I'VE THOUGHT ABOUT THIS FROM ALL THE ANGLES...
WHAT ABOUT THE ANGLE THAT SENDS YOU HOME AGAIN, ASSHOLE? ONCE THIS BRIDGE IS BURNED-- IT STAYS THAT WAY.

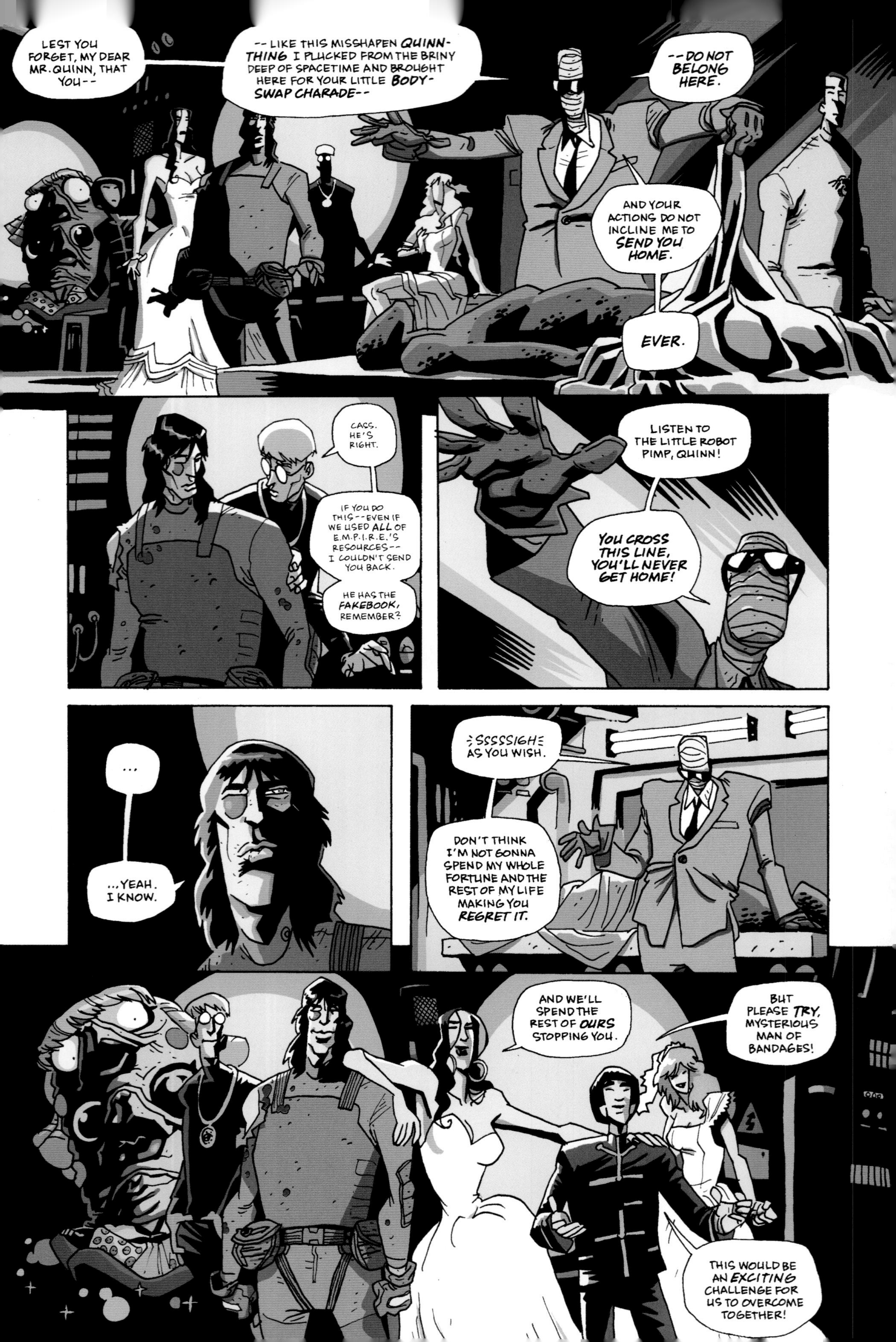
LEST YOU FORGET, MY DEAR MR. QUINN, THAT YOU--
--LIKE THIS MISSHAPEN QUINN-THING I PLUCKED FROM THE BRINY DEEP OF SPACETIME AND BROUGHT HERE FOR YOUR LITTLE BODY-SWAP CHARADE--
--DO NOT BELONG HERE.
AND YOUR ACTIONS DO NOT INCLINE ME TO SEND YOU HOME.
EVER.
CASS. HE'S RIGHT.
IF YOU DO THIS--EVEN IF WE USED ALL OF E.M.P.I.R.E.'S RESOURCES--I COULDN'T SEND YOU BACK.
HE HAS THE FAKEBOOK, REMEMBER?
LISTEN TO THE LITTLE ROBOT PIMP, QUINN!
YOU CROSS THIS LINE, YOU'LL NEVER GET HOME!
...
...YEAH. I KNOW.
SSSSSIGH AS YOU WISH.
DON'T THINK I'M NOT GONNA SPEND MY WHOLE FORTUNE AND THE REST OF MY LIFE MAKING YOU REGRET IT.
AND WE'LL SPEND THE REST OF OURS STOPPING YOU.
BUT PLEASE TRY, MYSTERIOUS MAN OF BANDAGES!
THIS WOULD BE AN EXCITING CHALLENGE FOR US TO OVERCOME TOGETHER!

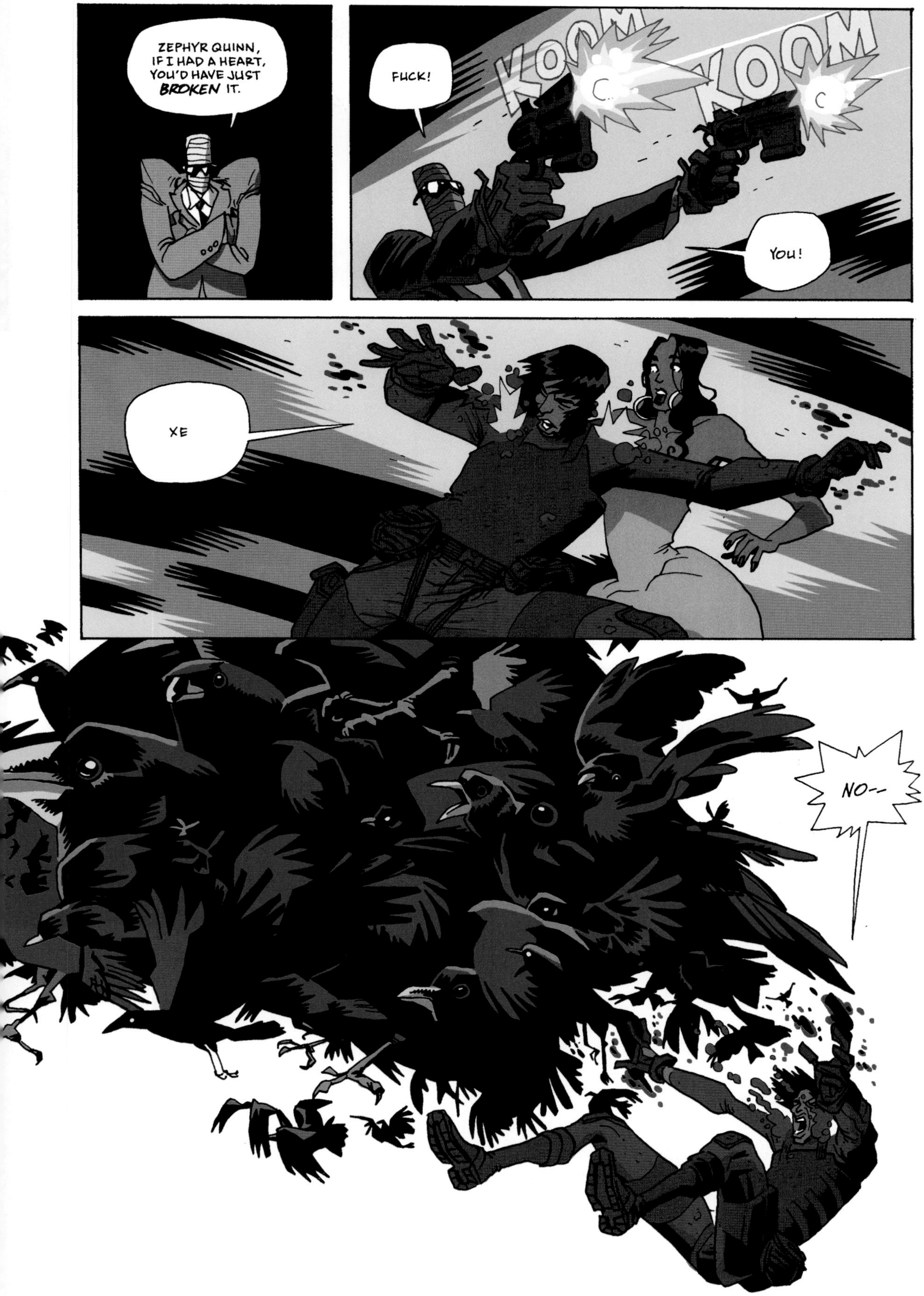
ZEPHYR QUINN, IF I HAD A HEART, YOU'D HAVE JUST BROKEN IT.
FUCK!
KOOM
KOOM
YOU!
XE
NO--

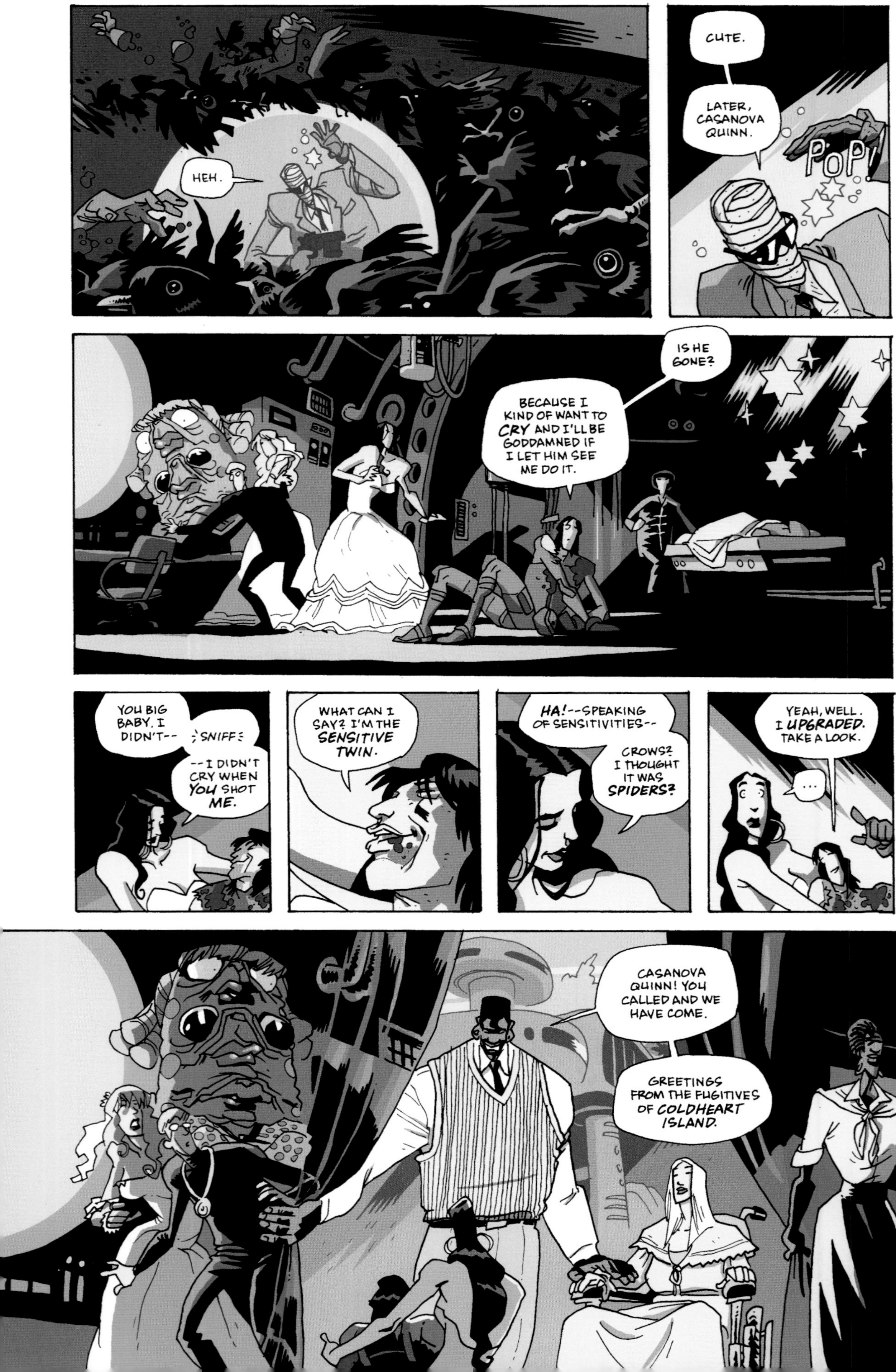
HEH.
CUTE.
LATER, CASANOVA QUINN.
POP!
IS HE GONE?
BECAUSE I KIND OF WANT TO CRY AND I'LL BE GODDAMNED IF I LET HIM SEE ME DO IT.
YOU BIG BABY. I DIDN'T--
SNIFF
--I DIDN'T CRY WHEN YOU SHOT ME.
WHAT CAN I SAY? I'M THE SENSITIVE TWIN.
HA!--SPEAKING OF SENSITIVITIES--
CROWS? I THOUGHT IT WAS SPIDERS?
YEAH, WELL. I UPGRADED. TAKE A LOOK.
...
CASANOVA QUINN! YOU CALLED AND WE HAVE COME.
GREETINGS FROM THE FUGITIVES OF COLDHEART ISLAND.

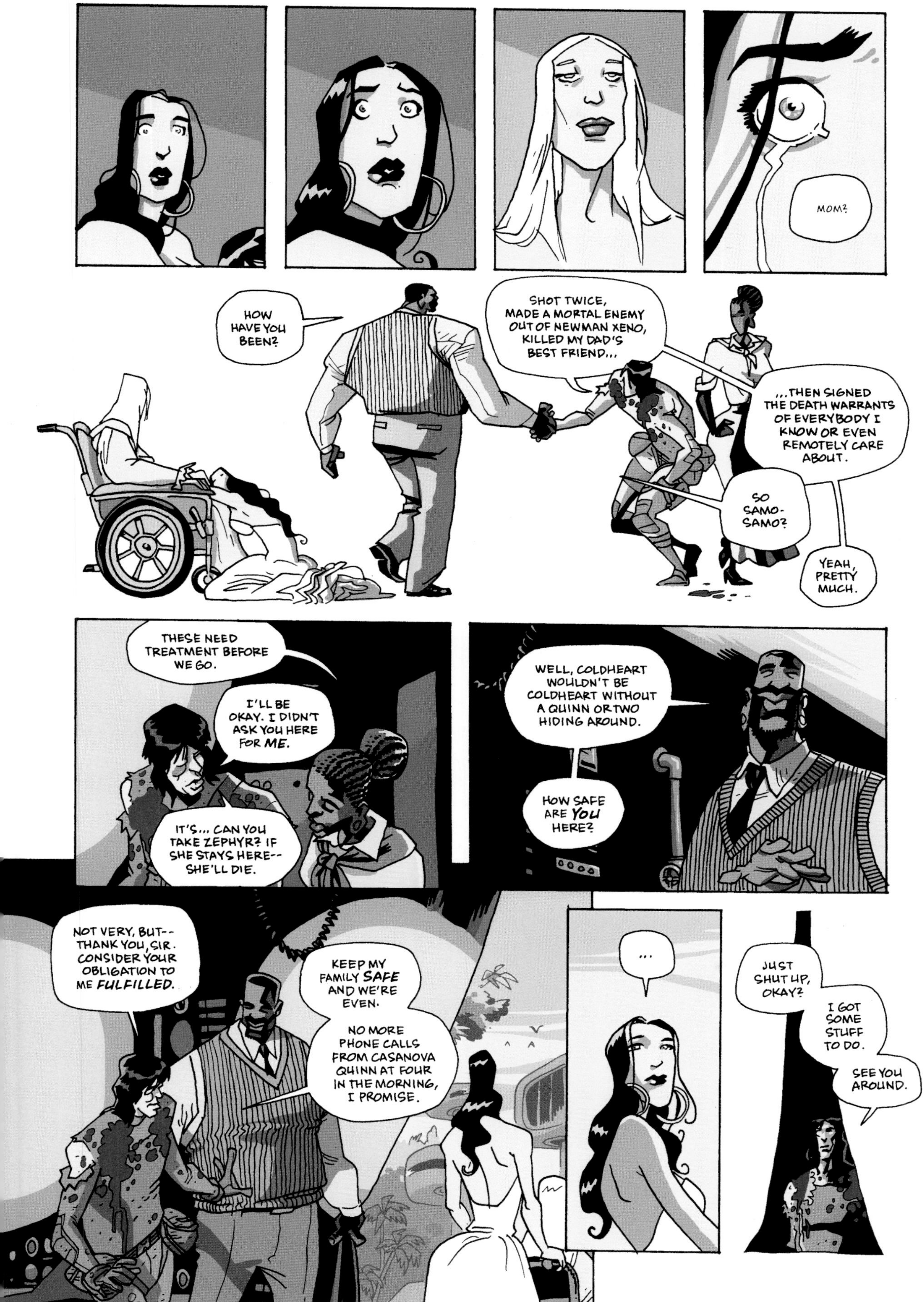
MOM?
HOW HAVE YOU BEEN?
SHOT TWICE, MADE A MORTAL ENEMY OUT OF NEWMAN XENO, KILLED MY DAD'S BEST FRIEND...
...THEN SIGNED THE DEATH WARRANTS OF EVERYBODY I KNOW OR EVEN REMOTELY CARE ABOUT.
SO SAMO-SAMO?
YEAH, PRETTY MUCH.
THESE NEED TREATMENT BEFORE WE GO.
I'LL BE OKAY. I DIDN'T ASK YOU HERE FOR ME.
IT'S... CAN YOU TAKE ZEPHYR? IF SHE STAYS HERE--SHE'LL DIE.
WELL, COLDHEART WOULDN'T BE COLDHEART WITHOUT A QUINN OR TWO HIDING AROUND.
HOW SAFE ARE YOU HERE?
NOT VERY, BUT--THANK YOU, SIR. CONSIDER YOUR OBLIGATION TO ME FULFILLED.
KEEP MY FAMILY SAFE AND WE'RE EVEN.
NO MORE PHONE CALLS FROM CASANOVA QUINN AT FOUR IN THE MORNING, I PROMISE.
...
JUST SHUT UP, OKAY?
I GOT SOME STUFF TO DO.
SEE YOU AROUND.

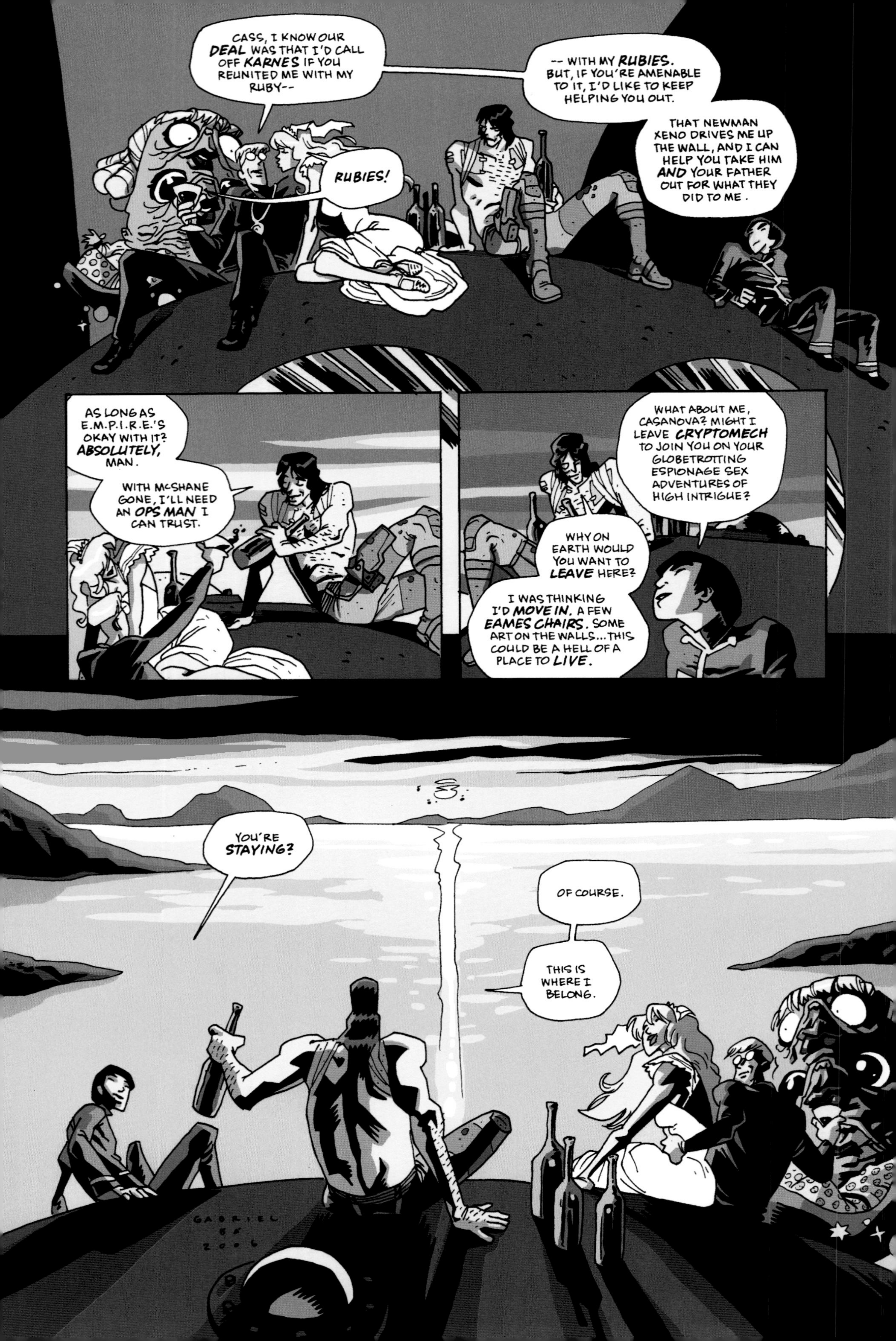
CASS, I KNOW OUR DEAL WAS THAT I'D CALL OFF KARNES IF YOU REUNITED ME WITH MY RUBY--
RUBIES!
-- WITH MY RUBIES. BUT, IF YOU'RE AMENABLE TO IT, I'D LIKE TO KEEP HELPING YOU OUT.
THAT NEWMAN XENO DRIVES ME UP THE WALL, AND I CAN HELP YOU TAKE HIM AND YOUR FATHER OUT FOR WHAT THEY DID TO ME.
AS LONG AS E.M.P.I.R.E.'S OKAY WITH IT? ABSOLUTELY, MAN.
WITH McSHANE GONE, I'LL NEED AN OPS MAN I CAN TRUST.
WHAT ABOUT ME, CASANOVA? MIGHT I LEAVE CRYPTOMECH TO JOIN YOU ON YOUR GLOBETROTTING ESPIONAGE SEX ADVENTURES OF HIGH INTRIGUE?
WHY ON EARTH WOULD YOU WANT TO LEAVE HERE?
I WAS THINKING I'D MOVE IN. A FEW EAMES CHAIRS. SOME ART ON THE WALLS... THIS COULD BE A HELL OF A PLACE TO LIVE.
YOU'RE STAYING?
OF COURSE.
THIS IS WHERE I BELONG.
GABRIEL BA 2006

EXECUTION DAYS

PRETTY LITTLE POLICEMAN

MISSION TO YERBA MUERTA

DÉTOURNEMENT

COLDHEART

WOMEN AND MEN (PART ONE)

WOMEN AND MEN (PART TWO)

I THINK I ALMOST LOVED HIM

IS THIS IT? (REDUX)

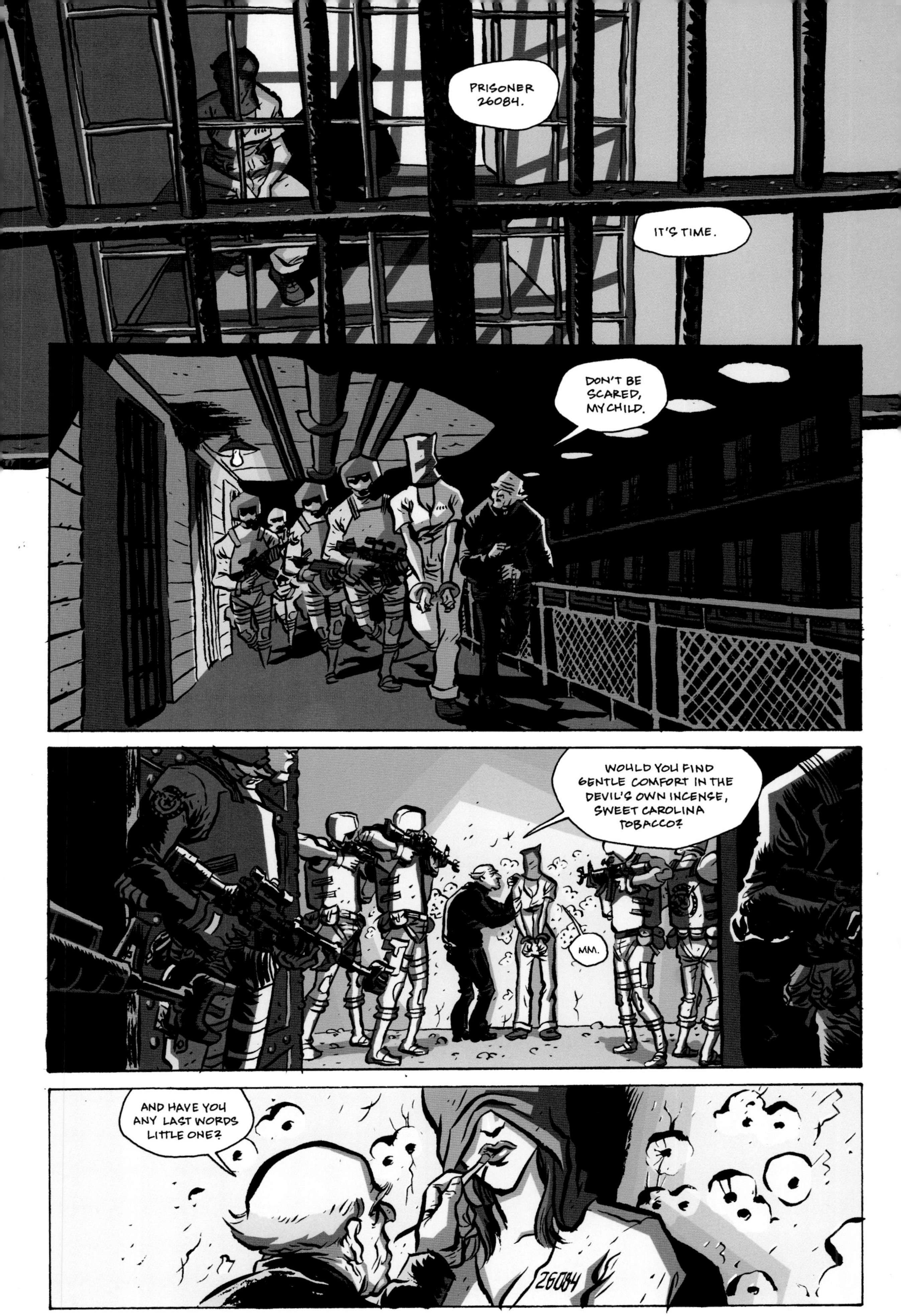
PRISONER 26084.
IT'S TIME.
DON'T BE SCARED, MY CHILD.
WOULD YOU FIND GENTLE COMFORT IN THE DEVIL'S OWN INCENSE, SWEET CAROLINA TOBACCO?
MM.
AND HAVE YOU ANY LAST WORDS LITTLE ONE?
26084

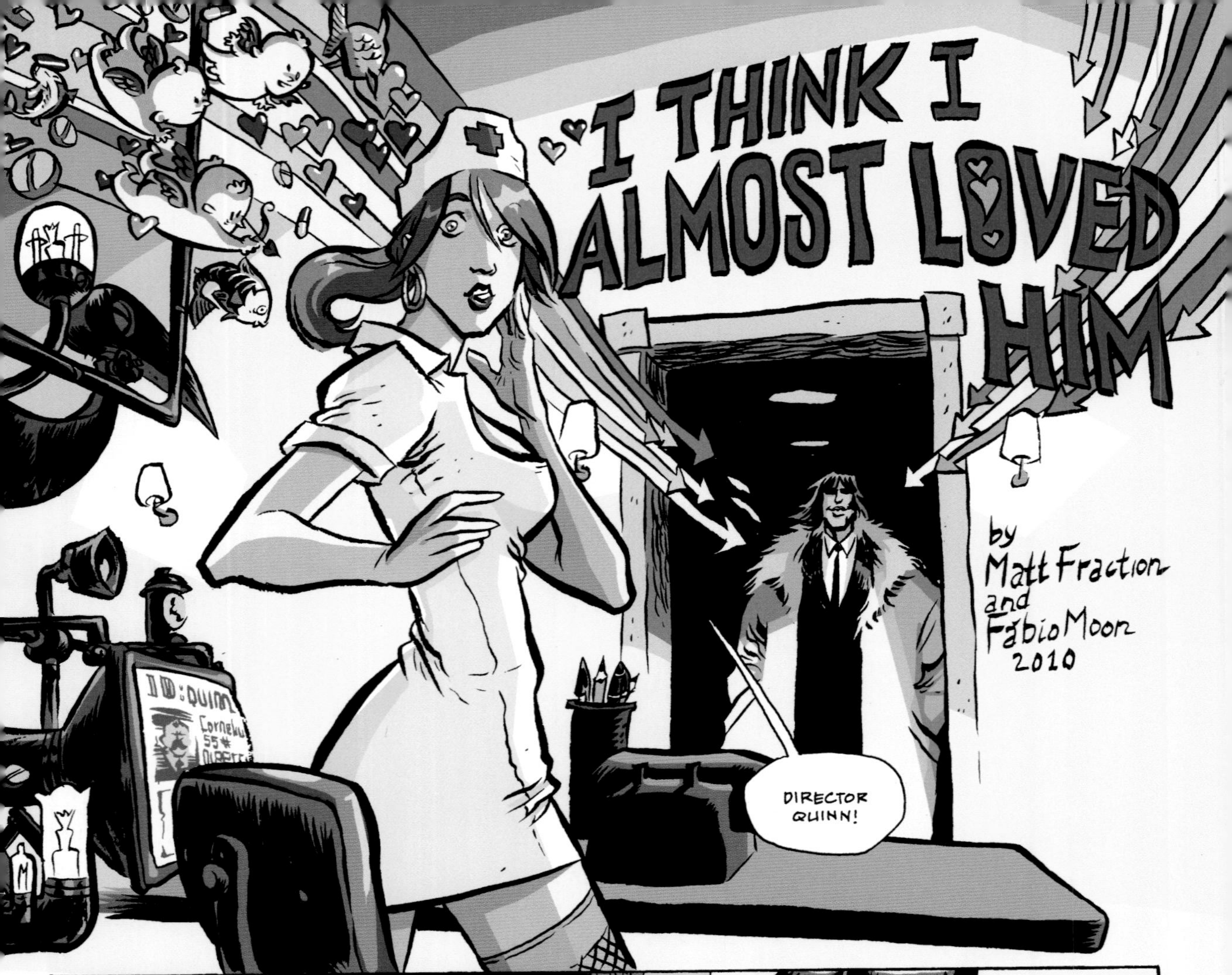
I THINK I ALMOST LOVED HIM
by Matt Fraction and Fábio Moon 2010
DIRECTOR QUINN!

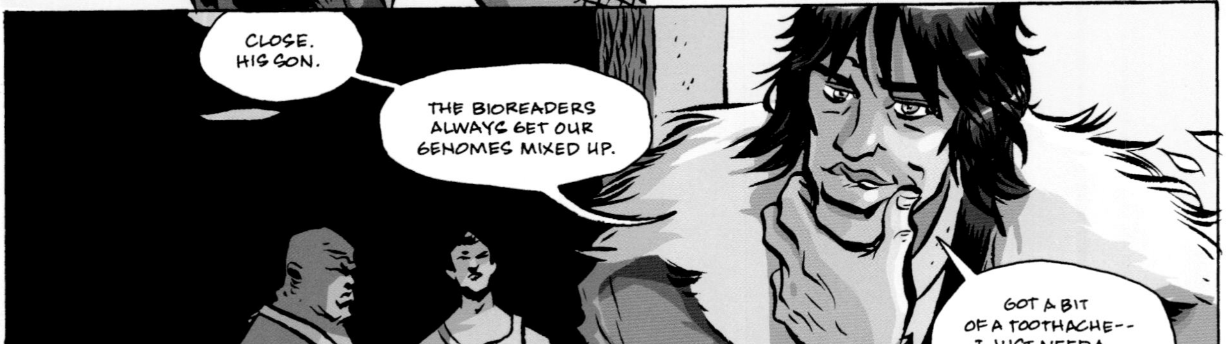
CLOSE. HIS SON.
THE BIOREADERS ALWAYS GET OUR GENOMES MIXED UP.
GOT A BIT OF A TOOTHACHE-- I JUST NEED A LITTLE SOMETHING TO GET ME THROUGH THE NIGHT.

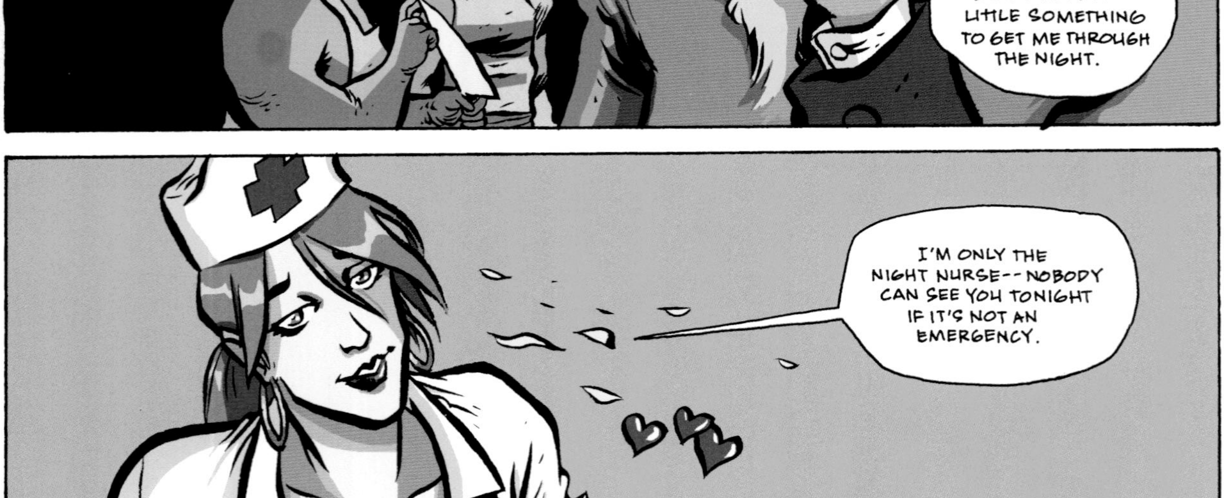
I'M ONLY THE NIGHT NURSE-- NOBODY CAN SEE YOU TONIGHT IF IT'S NOT AN EMERGENCY.

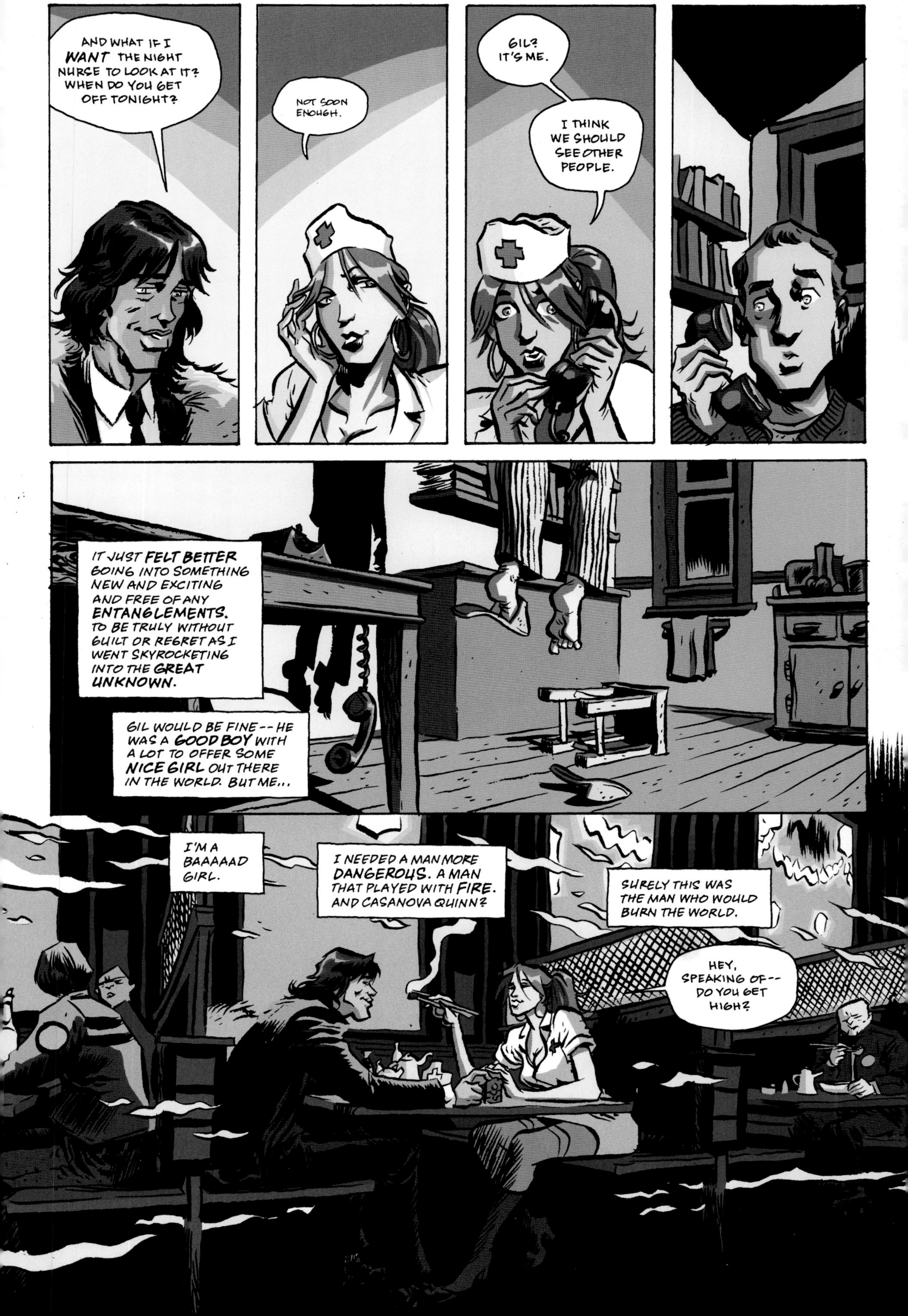
AND WHAT IF I WANT THE NIGHT NURSE TO LOOK AT IT? WHEN DO YOU GET OFF TONIGHT?
NOT SOON ENOUGH.
GIL? IT'S ME.
I THINK WE SHOULD SEE OTHER PEOPLE.
IT JUST FELT BETTER GOING INTO SOMETHING NEW AND EXCITING AND FREE OF ANY ENTANGLEMENTS. TO BE TRULY WITHOUT GUILT OR REGRET AS I WENT SKYROCKETING INTO THE GREAT UNKNOWN.
GIL WOULD BE FINE -- HE WAS A GOOD BOY WITH A LOT TO OFFER SOME NICE GIRL OUT THERE IN THE WORLD. BUT ME...
I'M A BAAAAAD GIRL.
I NEEDED A MAN MORE DANGEROUS. A MAN THAT PLAYED WITH FIRE. AND CASANOVA QUINN?
SURELY THIS WAS THE MAN WHO WOULD BURN THE WORLD.
HEY, SPEAKING OF -- DO YOU GET HIGH?

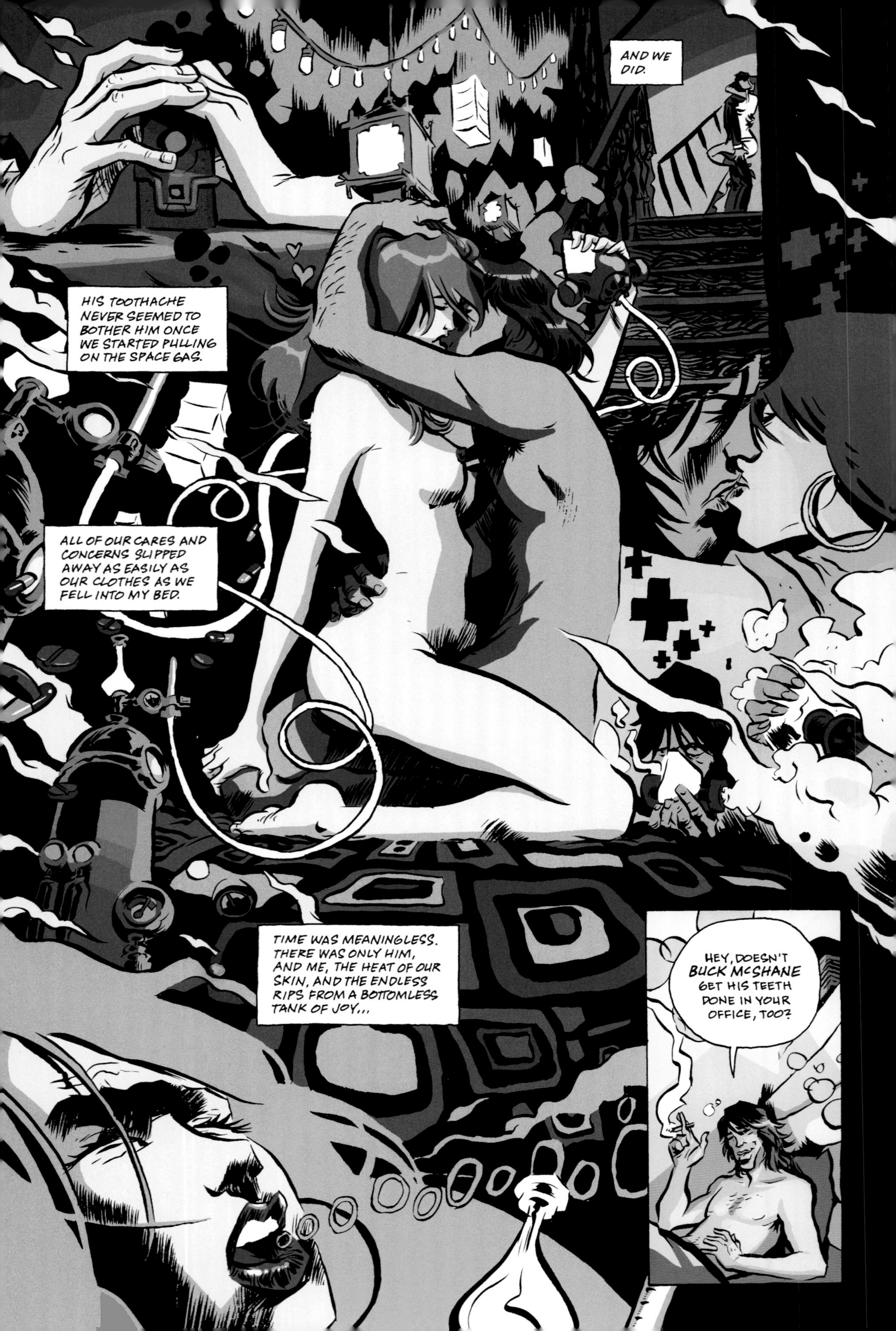
AND WE DID.
HIS TOOTHACHE NEVER SEEMED TO BOTHER HIM ONCE WE STARTED PULLING ON THE SPACE GAS.
ALL OF OUR CARES AND CONCERNS SLIPPED AWAY AS EASILY AS OUR CLOTHES AS WE FELL INTO MY BED.
TIME WAS MEANINGLESS. THERE WAS ONLY HIM, AND ME, THE HEAT OF OUR SKIN, AND THE ENDLESS RIPS FROM A BOTTOMLESS TANK OF JOY...
HEY, DOESN'T BUCK McSHANE GET HIS TEETH DONE IN YOUR OFFICE, TOO?

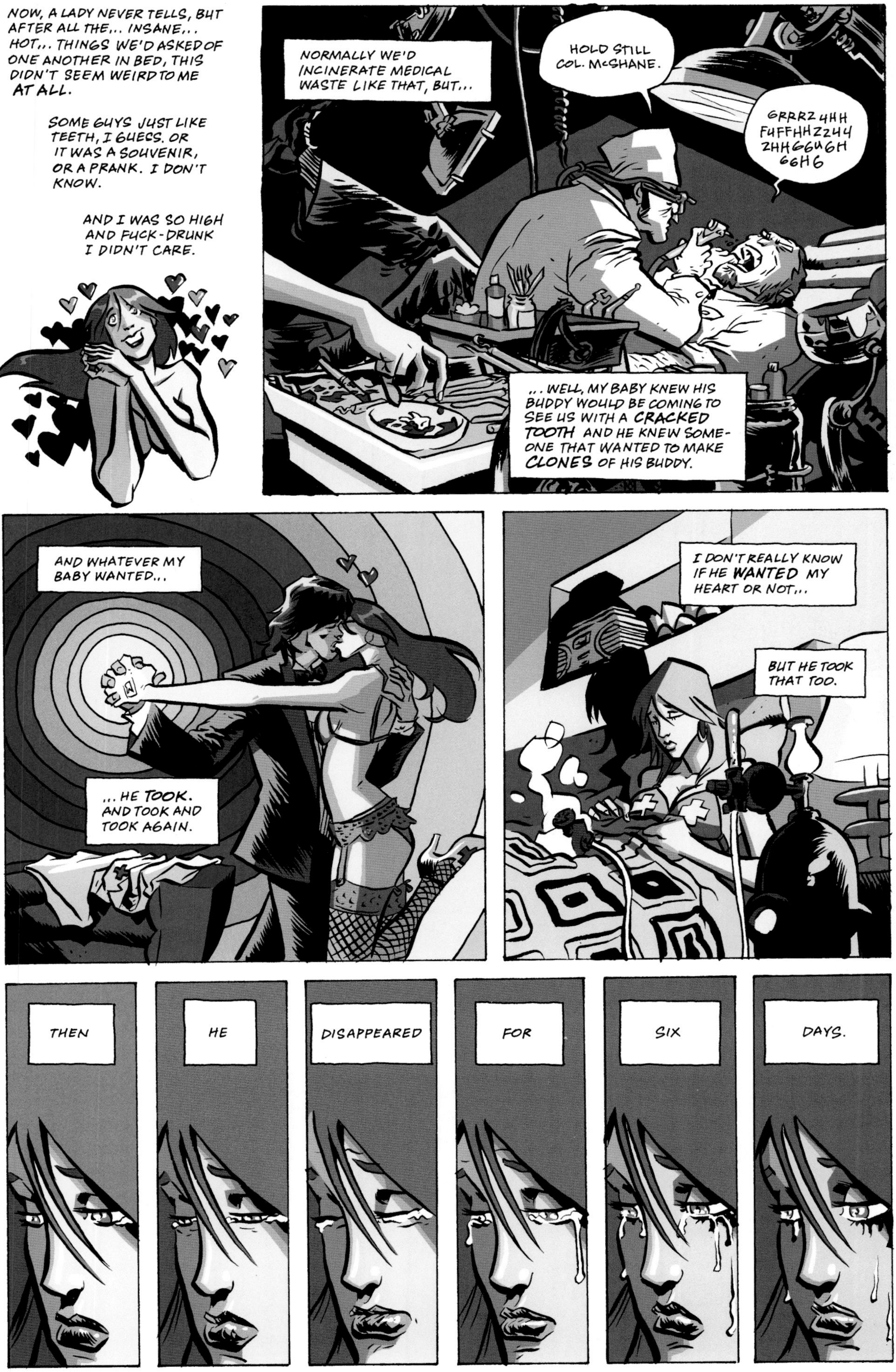
NOW, A LADY NEVER TELLS, BUT AFTER ALL THE... INSANE... HOT... THINGS WE'D ASKED OF ONE ANOTHER IN BED, THIS DIDN'T SEEM WEIRD TO ME AT ALL.
SOME GUYS JUST LIKE TEETH, I GUESS. OR IT WAS A SOUVENIR, OR A PRANK. I DON'T KNOW.
AND I WAS SO HIGH AND FUCK-DRUNK I DIDN'T CARE.
NORMALLY WE'D INCINERATE MEDICAL WASTE LIKE THAT, BUT...
HOLD STILL COL. McSHANE.
GRRRZ4HH FUFFHHZZ44 ZHH66U6H 66H6
...WELL, MY BABY KNEW HIS BUDDY WOULD BE COMING TO SEE US WITH A CRACKED TOOTH AND HE KNEW SOME-ONE THAT WANTED TO MAKE CLONES OF HIS BUDDY.
AND WHATEVER MY BABY WANTED...
...HE TOOK. AND TOOK AND TOOK AGAIN.
I DON'T REALLY KNOW IF HE WANTED MY HEART OR NOT...
BUT HE TOOK THAT TOO.
THEN
HE
DISAPPEARED
FOR
SIX
DAYS.

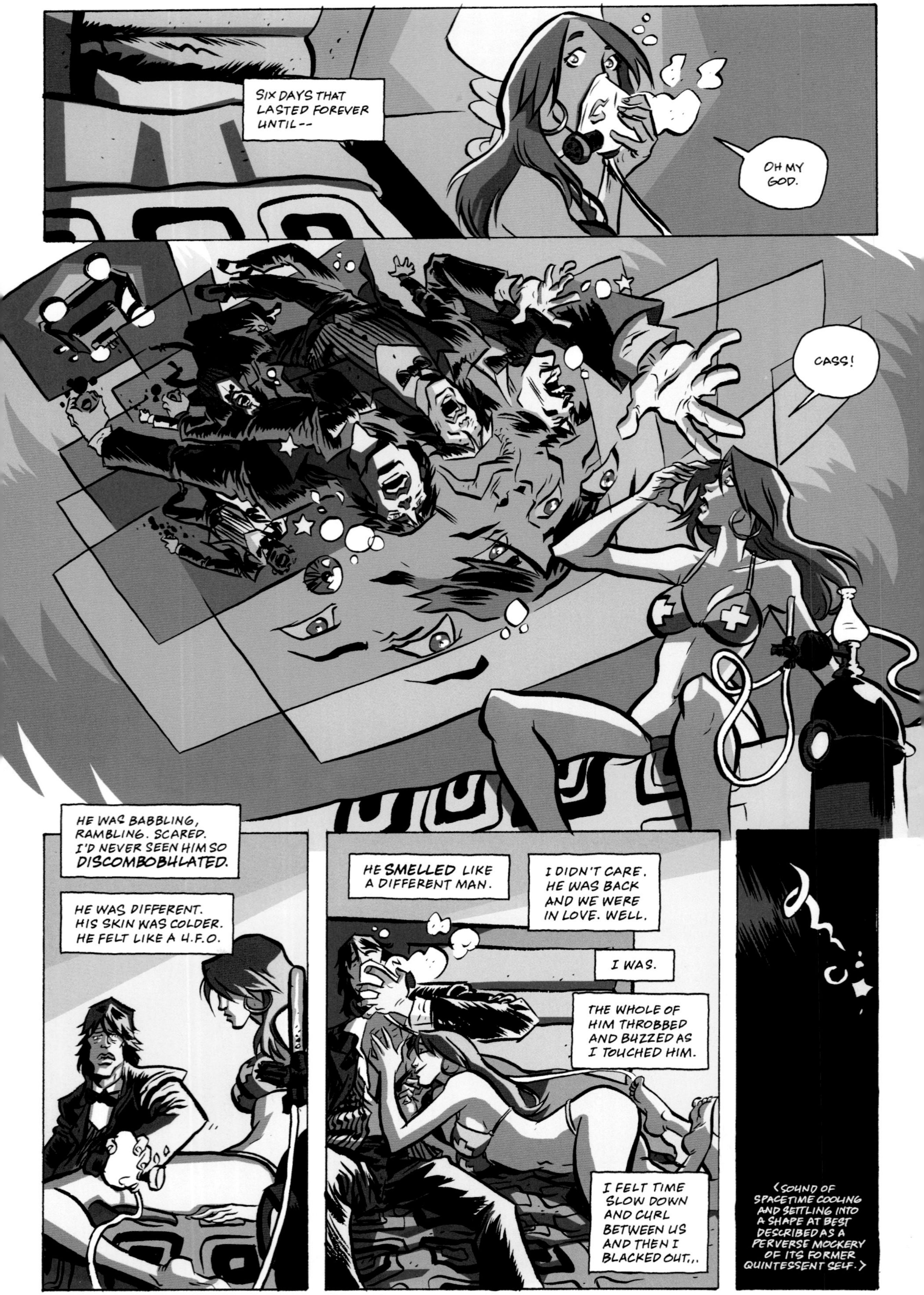
SIX DAYS THAT LASTED FOREVER UNTIL--
OH MY GOD.
CASS!
HE WAS BABBLING, RAMBLING. SCARED. I'D NEVER SEEN HIM SO DISCOMBOBULATED.
HE WAS DIFFERENT. HIS SKIN WAS COLDER. HE FELT LIKE A U.F.O.
HE SMELLED LIKE A DIFFERENT MAN.
I DIDN'T CARE. HE WAS BACK AND WE WERE IN LOVE. WELL.
I WAS.
THE WHOLE OF HIM THROBBED AND BUZZED AS I TOUCHED HIM.
I FELT TIME SLOW DOWN AND CURL BETWEEN US AND THEN I BLACKED OUT...
<SOUND OF SPACETIME COOLING AND SETTLING INTO A SHAPE AT BEST DESCRIBED AS A PERVERSE MOCKERY OF ITS FORMER QUINTESSENT SELF.>

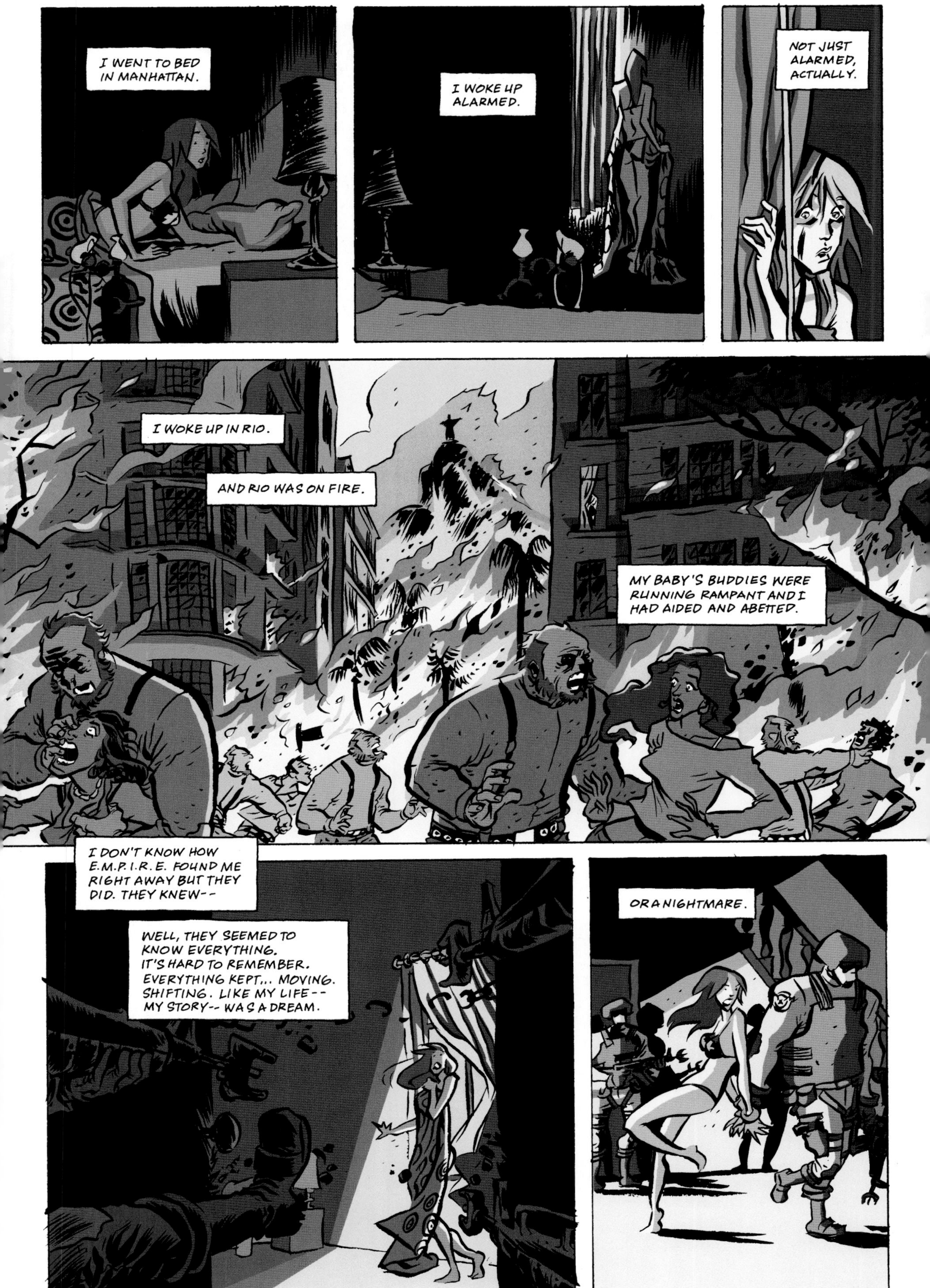
I WENT TO BED IN MANHATTAN.
I WOKE UP ALARMED.
NOT JUST ALARMED, ACTUALLY.
I WOKE UP IN RIO.
AND RIO WAS ON FIRE.
MY BABY'S BUDDIES WERE RUNNING RAMPANT AND I HAD AIDED AND ABETTED.
I DON'T KNOW HOW E.M.P.I.R.E. FOUND ME RIGHT AWAY BUT THEY DID. THEY KNEW--
WELL, THEY SEEMED TO KNOW EVERYTHING. IT'S HARD TO REMEMBER. EVERYTHING KEPT... MOVING. SHIFTING. LIKE MY LIFE-- MY STORY-- WAS A DREAM.
OR A NIGHTMARE.

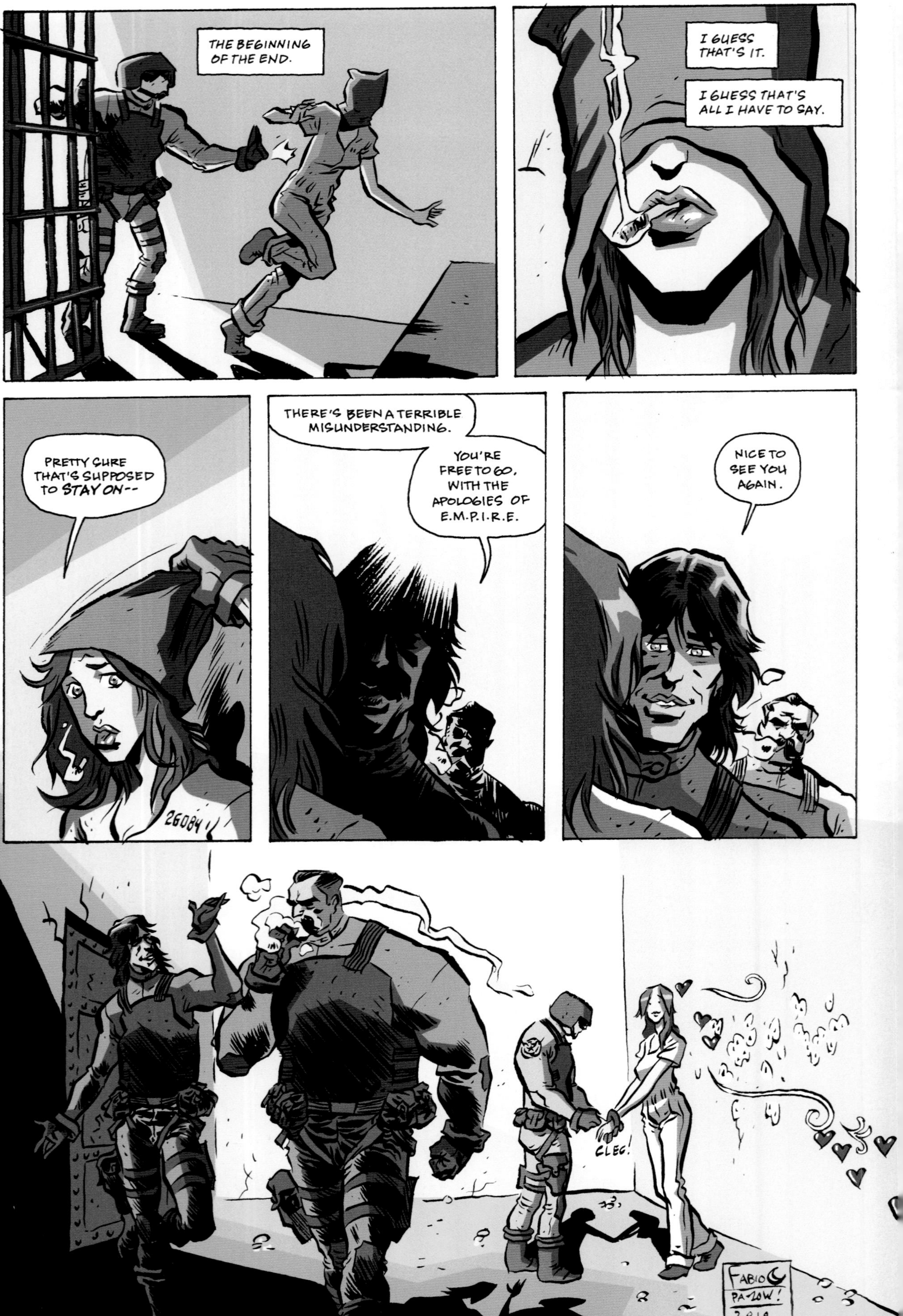
THE BEGINNING OF THE END.
I GUESS THAT'S IT.
I GUESS THAT'S ALL I HAVE TO SAY.
PRETTY SURE THAT'S SUPPOSED TO STAY ON--
26084
THERE'S BEEN A TERRIBLE MISUNDERSTANDING.
YOU'RE FREE TO GO, WITH THE APOLOGIES OF E.M.P.I.R.E.
NICE TO SEE YOU AGAIN.
CLEG!
FABIO PA-ZOW! 2010

EXECUTION DAYS

PRETTY LITTLE POLICEMAN

MISSION TO YERBA MUERTA

DÉTOURNEMENT

COLDHEART

WOMEN AND MEN (PART ONE)

WOMEN AND MEN (PART TWO)

I THINK I ALMOST LOVED HIM

IS THIS IT? (REDUX)

BACKMATTER[1]
1 (Image Comics, 2007)[2]

What up, earthmen? Welcome to the first issue of Casanova.

This book cooked in my head like a white-hot star my whole life. Kind of a weird thing to say and mean, but—there you go. I said it. I mean it. For thirty years, this book waited. Its heart, anyway. The soul of the thing. The specifics came much more recently. And like all pop trash, it started with Phil Spector.

Before becoming a one-man tabloid circus indicted for murder and sporting an afro defying logic and gravity, Spector produced records. And Hemingway wrote and Hitchcock made movies, right? Anyway, Spector called his trademark production techniques the WALL OF SOUND. It meant *layers*. Layers and layers and layers of music. A half-dozen guitars playing the same riff all at once, or ten different back-up singers jammed into a small room hollering to God while Phil caught it all and mixed it down to mono. Phil hated records. He loved singles. Listen to BE MY BABY or RIVER DEEP, MOUNTAIN HIGH—two singles so dense I bet those little 45s *vibrated*.

"Little symphonies for the kiddies," he called them. And they were.[3]

So late January, early February '05. Warren Ellis, tyrant-raconteur and creator of FELL (our big sister book in format) got FELL off the ground while I read and thought about Spector. I had just looked at the classic Claremont/Byrne run of UNCANNY X-MEN[4]. Most of those issues in our neighborhood, length-wise [PH]. And Ellis and I got back and forth about FELL and Spector and Andrew Long Oldham and Bryan Talbot[5] and what writing a 16-page comic means, what it demands, what it *needs*.

Anyway. Ellis, and METAL EDGE enthusiast/full contact GØDLAND auteur Joe Casey[6], egged me towards writing a monthly. And when I started, it was Spector I carried with me. 16 pages means none of that languid mage pacing—no 7 pages of a sword coming out of a sheath—and no "writing for the trade" stuff that's turned today's comics into watered down sketches. It meant little symphonies.

What would a comic read like if you were going to produce it WALL OF SOUND-style, if you were going to try and translate one technique from one medium into another technique in another medium? I don't mean just overwriting, cramming every page and panel full of words—I want to write like a DJ and collage little bits of everything, repurposing it all to suit CASANOVA. Song lyrics turn into lines of dialogue[7], plot points. Shots from films translated into whole-page stanzas.

So. Like I said. Welcome to the first issue of CASANOVA.

Does any of that matter? Does any of that add up to anything at all? Did a single one of you read CASANOVA #1 and think, gee, I bet Matt was thinking about Phil Spector? Or, now that you know, does it change anything?

God no; of course not. But I think comics are perfect little epiphanies of trash culture, of pop decadence and confection. And I think if you're doing a superspy book of ambiguous timeframe and deliberate homage, then you're inviting conversation about these things. All the bits of CASANOVA'S DNA, from Diabolik and Jerry Cornelius, to David Bailey and Paco Rabanne, Bob Peak and Jim Steranko[8]—all of them play a part in this little symphony.

Team CASANOVA can be contacted at casanovaquinn@gmail.com. Or pop by our forums and say hi at www.imagecomics.com/messageboards and click on "Matt Fraction" under the CREATORS heading.[9]

This has been CASANOVA #1. My brilliant collaborator and partner is Mr. Gabriel Bá. It was lettered with aplomb and patience by Mr. Sean Konot[10], and designed by the inimitable Ms. Laurenn McCubbin[11].

---

1   CASANOVA has always had a backmatter section after the comics proper. The purpose has shifted and changed over the years and I've gone from enjoying it to outright resenting it; it's collected here, however, in the interest of presenting the complete—*compleat*—LUXURIA for the first time, less some typos. These footnotes are whatever occurs to me as I reread it all again for the first time since sending it off to print.

2   CASANOVA existed at Image Comics, in 2007, then was reprinted in color at Icon Comics, starting in 2010, before returning to Image in 2015. There were seven Image issues of LUXURIA and GULA. These were colored, reprinted, and relettered in four issues at Icon (reprinting issue 1 plus the bonus story "I Think I Almost Loved Him," 2 & 3, 4 & 5, and 6 & 7, respectively). Those four issues had all-new backmatter and will be collected here in sequence.

3   Essential reading: WALL OF PAIN, D. Thompson; TEARING DOWN THE WALL OF SOUND, M. Brown; LOOK! LISTEN! VIBRATE! SMILE!, D. Priore; 2STONED, A. Loog-Oldham.

4   Zillions of reprints abound but the simplest, most value-packed, would be the black and white ESSENTIAL X-MEN VOLUME 2. Should run you about fifteen bucks. Worth reading not only for the density but for the thinly-veiled perversion; CASANOVA pales in comparison.

5   THE ADVENTURES OF LUTHER ARKWRIGHT, last published, I think by Dark Horse Comics, stands as one of the great (and, in America, largely unknown if not unsung) masterpieces of science fiction, and comics, literature.

6   My career has many fathers. Predating CASANOVA, I co-wrote a column with Joe Casey from the perspective of a guy-trying-to-break-in asking questions and talking about the medium with a guy-that'd-been-around-the-block-a-few-times-and-was-over-it. Joe, instrumental in encouraging me and my career in the early days when writing comics was what I did when I wasn't at work, probably has regretted it ever since. GØDLAND, by Casey and Tom Scioli, exists as six trade paperbacks from Image and remains as fun, funky, and irreverent now as it did then.

7   I remember once hearing or reading an interview with Tom Petty, who had upset Eddie Murphy by including the latter's name in the former's song "Jammin' Me." Petty confessed it didn't mean anything; Bob Dylan had suggested turning everything around him into lyrics – newspaper headlines, magazines, cereal boxes. And Petty, writing the song, looked down at the paper and saw an article about Murphy and his then-SATURDAY NIGHT LIVE costar Joe Piscopo and just put their names into the couplets because they fit the meter. And it struck me then—as now, as it's still a thing I do frequently—as a kind of... a kind of way to place a pin-drop on a map, an anchor to memory. A way of geotagging your location in time if not space? I do it constantly. If for no other reason than it tricks my fingers into moving.

8   Google. Google, google google. Go to the library. Pillage Amazon. Plunder back issue bins. Feed yourself everything.

9   I haven't looked at either of these in literally years.

10   Sean lettered the first iteration of CASANOVA; Dustin Harbin the second and subsequent. Dusty, who I've known since my teens and who I worked with in comics retail, letters by hand, and it gives the text a warm chaos and shimmer digital lettering erases with its vectored perfection.

11   Now Mrs., it turns out; she married the "Johnson" of issue #3 in 2008.

1 (Icon Comics, 2010)

With love to our many mothers and fathers without whom we could not be:

I wailed in my office like a baby. Not just for the friend I'd never get to speak to again, for his daughter he didn't get to see grow or the wife he didn't grow old with, not for the memento mori he'd become in my own memory, not for the grey hair I named for him. It was for all the things we didn't do together because our lives diverged. The unshared discoveries lost forever.

For the short time we were intertwined, Jay and I discovered the most important music and films of our lives, copied and memorized, dubbed-down and studied. We grew our tastes together and learned to not worry about cool. Believe me: nothing was more uncool than Queen and glam-Bowie in Concord, NC, circa 1991.

When I learned he was gone I ached for that otherwise-awful time of my life, for the first time, ever. Jay was the good of that rotten year: finding Queen, finding Bowie, finding The Velvet Underground the same day Sam Hefferon wore those damn boots and that damn skirt. Jay and I were dorky rock archeologists, revelation led to revelation, and all of those revelations eventually led me here.

Discovery inspired creation.

Falling in love with art empowers its creation. There is far too much subtraction surrounding us. Snark and derision have consumed discourse; contempt is bred from the entitlement borne of access. Mockery and meh-menship are tolerated, somehow, and treated as being more valid than the purported abominations at which they are aimed[12].

I am tired, I am exhausted, I am repelled, by the subtractive. It is cheap and it is easy and it is so very far beneath what we are capable of creating. Do not be cheap. Do not be easy. You diminish yourself; you diminish us all.

These are works of art that moved and inspired me beyond measure. Without them there would be no CASANOVA. Without them there would be no me. I hope you find something new mentioned here; I hope you take from these things the same energy, the same urge to create, that I did.

Good night, Daniel Jay Poore[13]. I wish we could've listened to IN THE AEROPLANE OVER THE SEA together just once.

•

HOWARD CHAYKIN'S AMERICAN FLAGG!
Howard Chaykin with Ken Bruzenak[14]
Image Comics/Dynamite Forces

If Casanova Quinn has a father it isn't Jerry Cornelius, James Bond, Diabolik, or Luther Arkwright: it's Reuben Flagg. (True story: CASANOVA started off as a pitch based on another Chaykin character, Dominic Fortune). It's nearly impossible to describe the effect this book had on my head when I first encountered it—as resonant, deforming, and unforgettable as the first time hearing Pixies or reading Pynchon, maybe. Alternately profane, profound, scathingly intelligent and ra-ra-explosion-time comic-book exciting. The storytelling techniques on display here, too—the world that Howard Chaykin and Ken Bruzenak create—are unparalleled. Maaaaybe MAX HEADROOM came close. Or VIDEODROME. Maybe. What vexed me most, as a kid, about this book beyond the sci-fi stuff, beyond the bountiful big asses and stocking-and-garters on display—and, believe me, this is maybe the sexiest comic of all time— and beyond the wildly inventive graphic design and quality of the art itself, is the way it teaches you to read it as you go. I'd never encountered a comic that respected my intelligence before. Back in print and gorgeously remastered after too many years gone. If you want a real treat, though, track down the twelve first issues from FIRST COMICS. AMERICAN FLAGG! was a comic that pushed printing itself to the very edge of its capabilities. Literally, you can see the presses fail on the page as they struggle to keep up with the magnitude of Chaykin's vision.

DANGER: DIABOLIK![15]
(d. Mario Bava, 1968)

One of my go-to responses when doing press about CASANOVA is that "as a kid most guys working in comics had heroes that put on capes; mine put on suits," which sounds good, maybe, even if it's not 100% true. DANGER: DIABOLIK is the movie I've chosen to reflect the superspy genre that I do so dearly love; all the same, I don't think Diabolik ever actually wears a suit-and-tie suit anywhere in the film. Still, this is maybe as amazing and trashy a cinematic experience as the genre can offer. If watching John Phillip Law and Marisa Mell fuck on a pile of money doesn't make you wish you lived inside a volcano, I can't help you and god can't either, son—you're done. Was on DVD for a time but is now out of print, so take to the internet, monkeys, and find your treasure. I live in impotent hope for the CRITERION edition. Other gems, if you want to take your superspies beyond THUNDERBALL: THE IPCRESS FILE, DEPARTMENT S, DEADLIER THAN THE MALE, THE GIRL FROM RIO. Only watch the first FLINT, and only watch the dance scene. Avoid Matt Helm like a wet hacking cough in an elevator. The genre's apotheosis is almost McGoohan's THE PRISONER but for its Ken-doll sense of sex. If only No. 6 would've taken off his shirt once in a while…

THE ADVENTURES OF LUTHER ARKWRIGHT
Bryan Talbot
Currently reprinted by Dark Horse Comics

---

12   This pissed a lot of people off who thought I'd turned traitor and now put on airs, having myself come up through the comics commentariat. Fuck 'em. *Fuck 'em all.*

13   The first of many no longer with us. Getting old is a bitch. I miss my friend. Friends. I miss my friends so goddamn much.

14   I currently enjoy the strange fortune of making a comic with these men called SATELLITE SAM.

15   I think this is out of print. Unthinkable. Obscene.

I named "Cornelius" after Jerry Cornelius because I know, on some level, that respect to the Cornelius Quartet and to Moorcock must be paid, but, if I was telling the truth about where the influence really came from, I'd have named him 'Luther.' Warren Ellis said this book is "probably Anglophone comics' single most important experimental work," and he is absolutely sight. Another thing Ellis was right about, for my money, is that Talbot here is something like filmmaker Nick Roeg or novelist Cortázar, maybe, in that the techniques, tricks, and tools they either singularly invented or perfected are passed along and enter the popular argot with very little recognition for them or understanding by us. It's stunning how much stuff was done here first. What I'm saying is: this book is the root text of so many things it will destroy you to read it for the first time. You can draw a very straight, very short line from here to FLAGG!, too, if you're interested in drawing lines between things. This book is like SLAUGHTERHOUSE FIVE for me—I cannot casually engage it. It engulfs me and rivets me every time, cover to cover. I finally made myself go talk to Bryan Talbot at a show in New York a couple years back; he was one of a handful of guys I'd not been able to make myself talk to for fear of...well, being revealed to be the mewing and mawkish child I am, I suppose. I didn't tell him who I was or what I did, but said that if my house was on fire and my family was safe, THE ADVENTURES OF LUTHER ARKWRIGHT would be the book I'd go back in for. And I would, too.

THE TESTMENT OF DR. MABUSE
(d. Fritz Lang, 1933)
Criterion Collection

More so than Moore, Kirby, Kurtzman, or Los Bros. Hernandez, the guy I've learned the most from in terms of how to tell a story with pictures was Fritz Lang. "M" is good, too—look at the way he uses sound the first time he has sound to use as a tool—but this, man... it's creepy and pulpy and brilliantly done. Watch Lang for how he cuts—how he goes from one location to another, one plot thread to another plot thread. Watch how he opens the film—how he paces it and how it relies on you to watch it, to pay attention, and to be bright enough to put two and two together. And then remind yourself this was 1933. You can see a lot of Fritz Lang in Alan Moore, I think. I'm not one of those guys that believes comics and film share an identical grammar—in fact there's nothing more boring than a film committed to paper, unless it was Al Williamson committing it—but there are filmic techniques that work even more beautifully on the page if you just think to take them and try. And whenever I watch Lang, I assure you, I am watching with the intent of taking and trying everything I can. The story behind the MABUSE cycle is almost as good as the movies themselves—this was the flick that made Goebbels invite Lang to make movies for the Nazis. Oh, and also—watch DR. MABUSE, THE GAMBLER, which was the first Mabuse film and a portrait of Weimar, then THE 1,000 EYES OF DR. MABUSE, Lang's final film, and the 'Cold War' entry in the series. Mabuse was Lang's...well. Lens, I guess. Through it he viewed Germany itself.

GRENDEL
Matt Wagner and others
Dark Horse Comics

Grendel is Matt Wagner's Mabuse. This is the thing about GRENDEL: there's...if you try to figure out a reading order, you need a stellar abacus and some graph paper. It's worth it, though. Story is, "Grendel" is an evil entity—well, and entity, anyway—that spans generation after generation; each storyline, each arc, tells the story of another era of Grendel. Sometimes Matt Wagner writes and draws; other times he just writes; each GRENDEL is different. Each story, each world, the techniques and tools Wagner uses...every time, it's a brand new comic. The sheer invention on display across the course of the book's not-inconsiderable lifespan is staggering. My first recollection of encountering Grendel was the first issue of what is now collected as DEVIL'S LEGACY. I had never seen anything that looked like Arnold and Jacob Pander's art before. I literally remember staring at the first issue. Literally: it's 1986 in a WAL-MART of all places, on a spinner rack, and...and I'm just staring. Like Richard Dreyfus looking at his mashed potato mountain. It wasn't like any book I'd even seen before in my life. Its true genius is that whatever Wagner's moment-to-moment obsessions are, whatever his leitmotifs may be, GRENDEL gives him the venue to address them. And when he's done he can blow it all up and start over somewhere else. The idea that a comic could do that! Like an A-bomb in my head. Start with DEVIL BY THE DEED and DEVIL'S LEGACY.[16]

2 (Image Comics, 2007)

Hiyah, earthmen.

I finished writing CASANOVA #1 in New York City, before Thanksgiving, 2006. It was a Saturday, my first day off in a month. I was tired, cranky; I missed my wife. Waiting for an interminable 4 train, the RZA's awesome LIQUID SWORDS record came on.[17][18]

It opens with a sample from SHOGUN ASSASSIN, an Americanized bastardization of the first two or three LONE WOLF & CUB movies. In my notebook, my first notes I wrote down for CASS 2 was LIQUID SWORDS. You can see the monologues in the background of the first page.

And that was it—that was what the issue was about. Fathers and sons. Or—a son being over-awed by his father, and then having to adjust reality to perception. And vice-versa.

•

So I got home and decompressed and recompressed for the holidays again. In the lead-in to Christmas, I helped a friend assemble all the Beatles albums for his ten-year-old daughter on an iPod nano. At ten, and already a Beatlemaniac!

Guess what her name is?

---

16   This staggeringly important slab of comics history has, since this writing, been reprinted in four essential omnibus books in story-chronology from Dark Horse. Save yourself the nightmare of trying to parse the story chronology or chase down long out-of-print collections and just get those four beautiful volumes.

17   The 4 train, southbound; 23rd Street Station. Sunday afternoon.

18   I was art directing and cutting commercials for a printer and camera manufacturer in my past life. We took the job to pay for a friend's cancer treatment.

Ruby.

Totally coincidental.

•

On the flight to North Carolina to visit my family, I thought about Ruby and her Christmas present and how great it would be to have a Christmas where you listened to nothing but the Beatles. So that's what I did—loaded up all the Beatles stuff in sequential order and started listening.

So Cass jumps out of an airplane to the bass-line of TAXMAN and the Fab Four become, I dunno, this issue's patron saints? One can hope.[19]

•

I jotted down bits of lyrics thinking they'd find a home as dialogue; some made it in and some didn't. I'm a new and better man. Pretty little policeman [in a row-ow-ow]. The line about test tubes from "Maxwell's Silver Hammer," [PH—most song titles seem to be ALL-CAPS, not quotes] but that didn't make it.

I wrote a whole thing on John vs. Paul that got cut for space. I thought about making the, erm, Casanoverse one where it was Paul that got assassinated. None of that made it out of the notebook though.

By the time I did the final rewrite, I'd moved on to The Flaming Lips. They creep in around the edges, but I dunno that anybody'll catch it. I cut the biggest reference; it just sat there like a parade float.

•[20]

Words can't express how awesome I think Gabriel makes Ruby Berserko. During the first issue, Gabriel couldn't believe we'd killed Fabula off (after he had to design and draw the bizarre little fucker). I promised him we hadn't. I didn't get specific.
The wig! The eyelashes! Those puppy-dog eyes. So great. Who can blame McShane for falling in love?

AGUA PESADA means "Heavy Water" in Portuguese. Just liked the sound of it. And I liked how it echoed off Paul Pope's superb HEAVY LIQUID, Pope being a favorite of both Bá's and mine.

•

The city itself—the old, weird stones it's built on top of—come from a story I started writing about five years ago about fucked up kids going nowhere. At Christmas, like Heath says, I sat in a little room in my parents' house and jotted out longhand notes, absolutely drowning in nostalgia and "If I knew then what I know now," and everything else. The story never got published and by the time I was done, the stones were written out anyway; the only think left were the fucked up kids going nowhere.[21]

I lived outside of Charlotte, North Carolina for a while, growing up between it and a little town called Concord. Scattered throughout Concord are these massive and ancient volcanic rocks. They've just—I dunno, they've just been there since Concord, North Carolina, had volcanoes, I guess. The story I wrote them, with the fucked up kids, was supposed to play against the age of the stones—these things we actually used to drive by every day, these things we'd stand on or spray-paint or whatever—was what interested me. These ancient, timeless things, just waiting around and letting us dumb kids stand on 'em and paint 'em and whatever the hell else. Long after we're dust and bones, those stones'll still be waiting. In the early drafts they were statuary; that got changed back to just stones[22].

When I was in France, I saw walls that were build in 40-something BC. The oldest things I'd ever seen, I thought.

Hm. Not quite. We forget, sometimes, you know?

In our supreme arrogance we behave as though we're the oldest things here, and that it actually means something.

Anyway, I wanted a city build on old weird stones that radiated some kind of crazy magic. Both then, and now. I liked the symmetry. Maybe I could finally put those particular little ghosts to bed, you know?
•

Since everything in this arc is about lust and sex, the energy had to be Orgone.

•

---

19 This book feels more decoupaged than written, filled with weird aggregate memories like this upon rereading. I don't or haven't thought of it since I wrote the stuff but the second I reread *this* stuff it all comes back. I was trying to quit smoking and gnawing this goddamn gum, listening to the Beatles, stuck on a plane home for Christmas that I wanted to jump out of. So in my notebook, I wrote *Cass jumps out of a plane* because I couldn't and I wanted to so very badly...

20 Deleted from this section were faux-excerpts and contextual captions from "Heath's" comic. Mr. Steven Sanders, with whom I made the Image comics graphic novel THE FIVE FISTS OF SCIENCE, drew the panels as "Heath." Originally conceived to appear *on page* in a kind of WATCHMEN/"Tales of the Black Freighter" metafictional conceit, the comic panels were commenting on the above action while providing textual transitions or visual and conceptual links with Bá's stuff, to Sanders' stuff, and then back *out* to Bá's again... it was a little much to reach for, especially for a second issue. Anyway we just ended up excerpting a few panels in the backmatter. Better that reach exceed grasp, yes; that's still no reason to go around *commemorating* it, eh?

21 This is a little dishonest; there was more to the story than this. Someone I'd admired at the time, a grown-up I'd looked up to, did something wildly disappointing and I was dealing that feeling of betrayal, of being confident and secure enough in my own morality and ethical code to realize someone I'd admired didn't measure up, in the end. I didn't include their name or the explicit mention of it then because I was afraid they were reading; I don't include it now because I realize it's one of several now. Part of the pain of growing up, right? Realizing the infallible are, in fact, quite fallible; that we were looking up not because these mentors were great, but because, quite simply, they were taller than we were. I think this occurred to me in the writing; I think I see traces of different people being thought about and reevaluated, when I look back at the issue. Who knows? Life's too short to carry grudges like that around that long.

22 Maybe some Gilbert Hernandez in this, too. See HUMAN DIASTROPHISM.

That'll take you at least to the Wilhelm Reich entry in Wikipedia, which isn't that far away from how much I know about the guy. Fascinating guy. In that Phil Dick/inevitable tragedy kind of way[23].

*

Let me interject here to say my relationship with own father is great.

*

Paco Rabanne is a fashion designer. You know him best as the guy that designed the costumes in BARBARELLA. He's still working, still designing, still crafting incredibly impractical and extraordinarily _hot_ fashion for extraordinarily hot women. Would that we could've filled this section with photographs of the man's work.

(When we first talked about making CASANOVA the one-color book it is, I immediately thought—OH! Like Forest's BARBARELLA[24]. In fact, in the Bible, I scanned maybe a half-dozen pages from my ancient collection of the BARBARELLA strips[25].)

*

Mary Quant literally turned Mondrian designs into miniskirts. They're very Sixties, you know?
Until you see Rabanne's work[26].

*

That's really a Leslie Gore song Zeph's singing. It's called WHAT AM I GONNA DO WITH YOU? and that's a real lyric.[27]

*

The "sweetmint milk of the polanut." There's this gum I like? Orbit? And there's a flavor called "Sweetmint"? I dunno. It's real good. When I quit smoking, I chewed about ten million pieces of it; maybe the sea-foam green of the package was the right kind of opposite to break my habit of having those fire-engine red packs of Marlboros in my pocket all the time.

Like I said. Its' all just snatches of signal pulled out of noise.

*

Take the outfits that Heath makes his guests wear—with the Dr. No suits and the hoods and shit. I got to the scene and looked up from my laptop and there they were, on the TV. They came from the outfits these prisoners wore in some random episode of GIGANTOR. It doesn't mean anything—I was just grabbing a snippet of something out of the air as it floated by.

This whole book is becoming that. Fusing all these little things together to see what the new shapes look like on the other side. The references don't lead to anywhere, the same way that using, like, a Lee "Scratch" Perry sample in a beat doesn't mean anything other than—hey, cool sound.

It must be said that, in GIGANTOR, they had these giant single buttons on the jackets. Like, the size of pancakes. I tried drawing it for Bá—the first time he drew them, all of Health's guests looked like hostages—and he made fun of me.

*

"Winston Heath." More Beatles there—the lines, "Ha ha, Mr. Wilson/Ha ha, Mr. Heath," from TAXMAN. But "Winston" sounds better.

*

And of course somewhere around here it occurs to me that I'm riffing on APOCALYPSE NOW.

I've never even read HEART OF DARKNESS. My frame of reference is shallow and flickers.

*

---

23 This is where this shit starts to rub me the wrong way. I sound like someone more interested in being interviewed about writing than actually _writing_. You know what I mean? I'd published like 30 pages at this point.

24 Oh, jeez, the color. Did I talk about this? The first iteration of CASANOVA was black, white, and a kind of olive green. A lima bean green. That's it. That's all. We thought it would knock our production cost down but, since we were printing a full color cover, it was like we were printing a full color book, cost wise, but only showing two of those colors. Ha ha.

BARBARELLA did that—one color per four-page signature, changing every four pages. We wanted to emulate that look. And hopefully save money. We are very bad at saving money here at Team: CASANOVA.

25 Weirdly enough, my wife, the writer Kelly Sue DeConnick, has done a new adaptation of BARBARELLA that sees print from Humanoids in Fall 2014. First time since its initial U.S. publication that's happened. Check it out. It's a glorious and gorgeous edition.

26 Before I wrote a word of CASANOVA I produced what's called a "Bible." It was big—thirty pages? Seventy? A millionty?—and full of... well, everything but script. It was how I figured out what the book was about, basically; I don't know that anyone but I needed to read it but I inflicted it on people all the same. There was a substantial visual section full of reference and inspiration—all produced before I knew I was writing for Bá and Moon. Lots of Quant and Rabanne there as I recall. Film stills, character biographies, a map of the first series, a broad-strokes outline of the whole thing... crazy stuff. If you're reading this with an eye towards getting a job writing comics, don't ever write something like that and show it to a publisher or an editor. They don't have time or, honestly, interest. If it's important to write for your process, like it was, at least for CASANOVA, to mine, by all means write it, go nuts—but keep it to yourself. A huge thing I had to learn was that just because I wrote something didn't mean it deserved to be _read_...

27 Check out GIRL GROUP SOUNDS: ONE KISS CAN LEAD TO ANOTHER from Rhino Records if you can find it. Essential girl group listening, lovingly curated.

Oh! This was weird. On Page 10, there's another mention to a Cassnoverse band called TEEN AGE MUSIC INTERNATIONAL. They came up on the edges of CASANOVA #1. I swear to GOD I thought I made it up, back in the Bible days when I was just coming up with as many anagrams as I possible could for the various agencies and organizations in the book.

As it turns out, there's a movie called THE T.A.M.I. SHOW from 1965. Guess what T.A.M.I. stands for?

T.A.M.I.—our T.A.M.I., I mean—will show up down the road, in either CASANOVA #6 or #7 or both, I think, but there's still time for those scripts to surprise me.[28]

•

"What I really need now is ideas," is The New Pornographers. They were the soundtrack band for the first issue and our series Bible. There's a lot of them in these early bits—the song "Jackie," off of their debut record MASS ROMANTIC, has the line, "There's been a break in the continuum," and there was out big twist in the first issue. On TWIN CINEMA, their latest record, there's a sequel song called, "Jackie, Dressed in Cobras," that has the lyric, "Left on the jungle floor/Jackie's dressed in cobras/Giving me ideas/What I really need now is ideas."

Yoink.

While it'll be a while before we see Zeph dressed in cobras (issue #4, if you wanna know), I liked the song for her, and I liked that plaintive wail for me. A lot of CASS got written or planned out on an elliptical trainer with headphones on—*what I really need now is ideas* seemed as much a prayer to the muses than anything else and I clung to it.

•

And hey—fight scene. Fathers and sons; creators and creations. Oedipus MAX!

First, with regards to the full frontal dude-ity: we're an equal-opportunity naughty-bits-show-er here at Team CASSANOVA. And after all the objectification of women we've been trucking in (come ON—! They're all ROBOTS! Not the subtlest pen, mine), I wanted the real flesh and blood thing we're talking about stripped down. Literally. I liked how it turned expectations on its ear. I liked how it embraced—tut tut—all the homoerotic clichés of scenes like this, be they in superhero comics or spy movies.[29]

And most of all, I liked how it leveled the comics playing field, if only for a couple pages, if only for a little bit.

A little dangly bit.

•

Whatever the lesson of this issue was—a lesson about fathers and sons, or creators and creations, more to the point—seemed like an important lesson for Cass to learn early in the series. The creation doesn't owe its creator anything—it lives its own life, regardless of what we plan.

So: lesson learned. Moving on.

3 (Image Comics, 2007)

Hiyah, earthmen.

This one started in San Francisco. I was there for a couple days at the tail end of a business trip, staying with my friend (and CASANOVA book designer) Laurenn McCubbin and her fella, Alex Getchell. We had a day to kill and wanted to hang out, but I needed to get CASANOVA #3 nailed down and, as it stood, I had nothing. Work? Play? Meh. We needed food and coffee.

We went to Lois the Pie Queen. It's at 851 60th Street at Adeline (cue Elliott Smith's "Sweet Adeline") in Emeryville, just outside of Oakland. Or maybe it's just still Oakland, I dunno. Not my town. And while Ms. Lois Davis, know to young and old as Lois the Pie Queen, has passed on, her son Chris ("Chris, the Prince of Pies" doesn't have the same ring as "Lois the Pie Queen," does it?) runs the place now.

We had to sit at the bar, which sits before a wall filled with the pictures and autographs of some of the Pie Queen's fans, including, but not limited to, Reggie Jackson (who has His Meal named for his on the menu), and, as Cass asks Chris, Morris Day AND Jerome Benton. And while I didn't have the "Reggie Jackson" (eggs and pork chops, as I recall), what I did have was quite possible the best breakfast sausage of my life, and a slice of pie so nuked with spice that I actually did consider marrying it until Getchell pointed out it was that old slut nutmeg that had me in a tizzy.

Anyway, so we're eating at the bar and I'm inhaling sausage and eggs and I suggest a road trip down to Big Sur. Wholly pointless. Just a thing to do, a thing to see. I'd never been and always wanted to go. It was the right amount of time and space apart. We'd eat and split, arriving just in time for the sun to set, and then we'd turn around and come home.

---

28   They do. Also, THE T.A.M.I. SHOW came out on DVD in 2010.

29   There's a riff from THE DARK KNIGHT RETURNS here, too, like a straight lift of how Miller stages a fight scene on a 4-tiered, 1/16th paneled page. When you gotta learn, steal from the best, right?

Also maybe the homoeroticism of the scene was a reaction to the unfortunate places Miller's work and public persona has gone in the 21st century. Reinforces the theme of the issue too, now that I think about it.

Anyway. Turns out Miller's not our Eisner after all; he's our Lindbergh. What a shame.

And the bastard writer in my that's horrible company more obsessed with his own work than his friends knew that I could sit in the back and write. in a notebook the whole time.

Everything about CASANOVA has been a leap of faith. I've giving myself over to whatever brings it forth and however it chooses to come. A kind of holism of process, maybe, I dunno. I leap and have faith there'll be a mattress below. This might result in a book more sizzle than steak, but that's for you to decide and not me, but it's the path we're on and so far and, so far, it's the path on which I'm staying.

I made a deal with myself before that first cup of coffee was gone: I would throw the entire issue off the cliff of this wholly ridiculous thing to do. When we got home, I would have the issue broke one-way or the other.

Going in, the only think I knew about the issue was what it meant to our status quo—it has to be about Cass paying the price for the reckless independence he showed in issue 2—and we were going to end with the beatific smile of Anna Quinn. The story would start at Lois the Pie Queen. I'd record the rest of the day, refracted through the lens of CASANOVA, and on the other end I'd pray we'd end up with Anna still waiting.
• [30]

Here's how I write a CASANOVA script: it starts with lists. Or lines. Random bits and pieces of ideas. Images. Doodles. Notes, right? And those notes get written and rewritten and arranged into sentences. The sentences are sometimes whole sentences, but mostly they're putting one "And then" after the next until the story has some kind of logical shape[31].

Looking for anything to build the story around, I grabbed the idea of "3" and ran with it. With a ticking clock over the affair, I needed something, anything, to build story around. So I went with a trick of structure and built the third issues around the number 3.

As I sat in the back of Laurenn's car, I made a list. 1-18.

Right. 18. Because 18 is a multiple of 3.

We're a 24-page book with 16 pages of comic and 4 of cover. 16 pages of content! Gah. Don't be fooled by that 6—it's not a multiple of 3, even though it feels like it should be. It's a rip off. So here's my genius idea, Casanovanauts, and I'm gonna tell all of YOU about it here and now so that, one day, when I convince someone to actually do it, you'll bask in the glow that it's that handy shtick I've been scheming about since CASANOVA #3.

VARIANT ENDINGS!

What I wanted to do was write THREE different epilogue pages. One with Cass and Anna. One with Cornelius and McShane. And one where we actually meet Sabine Seychelle. And we'd print three different versions of CASANOVA #3, where whatever copy of the book you got, you'd randomly get. We wouldn't tell ANYONE. Just a weird little thing we'd slip out into the world and hope to create cute little pieces of confusion.

You know that when APOCALYPSE NOW opened, in New York there was one ending and in L.A. there was another? That was where I got the idea.

So there'd just be three different epilogues. And you might get ending A and your pal would get ending B. And maybe if you guys talked, you'd realize what happened. Otherwise…it'd just be a bit of strangeness for strangeness' sake.

Needless to say, financially, this was one of my many Bad Ideas. One day, Casanovanauts. One day, one day, one day[32].

•

So the idea of telling an issue in threes was implemented. Three major scenes existing in three timelines, dealing with the three sides of Cass' persona in his new timeline—E.M.P.I.R.E, W.A.S.T.E., and his own. And I'd gank what I could from my favorite episode of the late, lamented show FIREFLY by Joss Whedon and Tim Minear.

There's an episode called "Out of Gas." In it, a think on the titular spaceship our intrepid heroes travel on breaks, leaving them more or less "Out of Gas." And it opens with our main intrepid hero bleeding to death in a de-powered, dark, and otherwise abandoned ship. The credits come up.

BEST! OPEN! EVER![33]
What follows is a story that's fractured into three timelines, each one feeding into and informing the next. It's a bit of narrative bravura, a piece of writings that's pure art for art's sake and I know that, as a novice, I learned a hell of a lot from studying it some. So we interwove between Cass' three faces in some kind of…dumb[34] obscure tribute to OUT OF GAS.

---

30   Omitted here and subsequently throughout are captions and pencil excerpts of Bá's pages, not because I don't think it's worth seeing but because it was filler, something to look at, some way for me to not feel guilty for how much self-important blather I was doing.

31   This still holds true, largely. I've likened it, with far more poetic license, to trying to catch numbered butterflies in sequence on a stick covered with honey.

32   I still want to do this. Oh, GOD, do I want to do this. We almost did, at Marvel, with the final issue of FEAR ITSELF, of all things—it was editor Tom Brevoort's idea and I jumped on it. Then the powers that be decided we had to run something like all six epilogues/previews of series spinning out of that last FEAR ITSELF issue and so it became the RETURN OF THE KING of event books with ending after ending instead. It would've been the most transgressive thing I'd ever done, if we got away with it.

33   I realize I'm talking out of both sides of my mouth here but, I kind of admire, looking back at this now, just how open a work-journal I was willing to make this section, just how fuck-it-all-let's-talk-about-the-process-as-we-make-it-up this all is. I've done pretty much nothing professionally since writing it BUT write comics for a living and I think that's maybe been beaten or ground out of me. Or maybe I've just outgrown it. As a reader I remain fascinated by process pieces, by commentary tracks and how-tos, even if I don't like the final product itself. I love to talk and learn about technique. Just, y'know. Not *mine*.

34   Before, I used a different word here, a word I'd not use now. The only apology I can offer for the insensitivity of past is to live right in the present and future. This is me trying.

•

So I needed a way to differentiate between timelines. Changing Cass' appearance was a visual way to do that.

Also? The long hair and beard thing? I have long hair. And a beard. And, dammit, since the issue was based on our day, why shouldn't I wear Casanova's skin for the same time? Like, inverted method writing. If for no to her reason, then because I got to put Getchell's line to me—the gothic hobo bit—into the book.

•

The opium den. What can I say? I was on the Barbary Coast.

•

The plot for Timeline C, the graveyard, came as we passed Pacifica, right outside of San Francisco on our way to Big Sur. It made Laurenn talk about the Pescadero cemetery, one of her favorite sites on the that trip down Route 1. Since I knew I had only 5 pages for Cass' mission to unfurl and resolve (since the other two timelines had 5 pages each, and then there was our mystery Last Page), I knew the mission needed to be light. No heavy infiltration and exfiltration, just lean and mean and fast. So: digging up a grave. Why? It was a spy grave. Okay. So there's the "plot."

At the top of my list, I wrote the following:

CASS RETRIEVES A THING FROM A BODY INTERRED ON AN ISLAND IN THE BAY FULL OF JOHN DOES. HE GOES TO BIG SUR TO CLEAR HIS HEAD CONCURRENT TO THIS, MAYBE SOMETHING ELSE HAPPENS.

See? Writing is FUN! And very ADULT!

•

The Oakland Cranes. I've dreamt about them breaking loose from their moorings and going running like a stampede every since I first saw them. I've pitched the idea as a music video three, maybe four times and it always gets shot down. I don't know if it's the kind of thing that only affects me or if I do a lousy job articulating the vision to music video commissioners. Whatever. It's my comic, so here: the Oakland Cranes[35] stampede through D.U.M.B.O. in Brooklyn[36]. Ta-da.

•

We passed a sign for YERBA BUENA. "Pretty Grass," right? More or less? So our graveyard would be called YERBA MUERTE. Dead grass. WRITING!

•

"BAD GRASS NEVER DIES." I'm a fan of linking scenes with little things like this, especially when a time and scene location changes on a page-flip. Some kind of comment to create a bridge between pages, panels. A little attempt at unity, whether verbal (like here) or visual or whatever.

I suppose these get attributed to Alan Moore a lot of times (he's certainly big on the visual effects), but I first remember seeing it (and thinking, ooh, there's a tool to use) in Fritz Lang movies[37].

But most of all, I liked the line because I first heard it as the title of Chuck Barris' follow-up to his autobiography CONFESSIONS OF A DANGEROUS MIND. How perfect! It's a book by a guy pretending to be a spy-assassin.

•

Can I just say I love Zeph's W.A.S.T.E. bra? I didn't script it. Gabriel added it. Hello, merchandising![38]

•

The list got filled in after dinner and in the dark, driving home with the dome light inside the car on. And alternate endings aside, this real important event here was that Cass ended up in Big Sur, confessing to his catatonic mother. So: Cassanovanauts, meet Anna Quinn. Mission fucking accomplished.

Oh! So, in the end, we got to Big Sur as the sun was setting. We stood on a series of cliffs together and watched it, the wind whipping the shit out of us. It's a magnificent piece of earth to see. And as we stood there and just watched the light change, I realized...

...You know, this far out, this far up? I could totally kill them both and nobody'd know. Shove 'em each onto the rocks and the water

---

35   I guess this is where the AT-ATs in EMPIRE STRIKES BACK come from, too?

36   The late Maggie Estep, an acquaintance of mine and dear friend of my wife, had an amazing place in D.U.M.B.O. we used to stay at, when Maggie was out of town. The whole area has been transformed by money and privilege now; back then, it was much different. Back then, Maggie was alive. It goes by so fast, it all happens so suddenly, doesn't it? Enjoy every sandwich. Send every note. Hug absolutely everyone one last time.

37   There's... there's David Lean in this, too. There's a cut in DR. ZHIVAGO where you think you're going to hear two train-car hitches clink together but on the cut you hear glass clinking in the Doctor's lab... I probably saw ZHIVAGO before I saw anything from Lang. And when I think back on DR. ZHIVAGO, I remember that cut more than anything else. Watch everything. Read everything. Steal everything. Repurpose it all.

38   We made shirts and stickers but never W.A.S.T.E. bras. Now's as good a time as any to point out the W.A.S.T.E., E.M.P.I.R.E., and X.S.M. logos were designed by my friend Ben Radatz.

disappear them forever.

So as the air turned cold, I had the whole issue in my head, its twists and turns, the sizzle and the steak. However much of each is yours to decide.

Laurenn, Alex: thanks. Sorry I thought about shoving you off a cliff.

2 (Icon Comics, 2010)

If I had to point to the two books that, for whatever reasons, made me think cogently and coherently for the first time that I wanted to be a writer, they were A SCANNER DARKLY by Philip K. Dick and WONDER BOYS by Michael Chabon[39].

That you could scarcely find two better warnings AWAY from what the life of a writer can look like than those two books is another matter entirely, I suppose, but there you are.

I was lucky enough to meet Chabon through my work and ever since we've been more or less geeking out over one damn thing or the other whenever possible. This time it was about superspies.

•

Matt Fraction: So I've made it a habit of, when talking about CASANOVA, saying something along the lines of that, when I was a kid, my heroes didn't put on capes, they put on suits. And while not 100% true, it's...y'know, 75% true. But: aside from the globetrotting, the women, the volcano bases...the appeal of the genre, to me—of Bond and beyond—*was that he knew what wine to order with fist and how to play baccarat.*

This is, I realize, the superspy equivalent of reading PLAYBOY for the charticles or whatever, but it's true: I wanted to know what buttons on a three-button blazer to button as badly as I wanted to aquacar and Marissa Mell and copious applications of the Union Jack to my escape pathology. So you can imagine how insane I went when gifted THE BOOK OF BOND, OR, EVERY MAN HIS OWN 007, which is LITERALLY a how-to guide for Bond-wannabes...

Michael Chabon: So, do you order your cigarettes for Morland's, the Macedonian blend with the three gold rights? You know how Macedonia is basically synonymous with a really good smoke.

It was the card-playing for me, I'm terrible at games. But more than that, I think the thing I loved most about the whole Bond thing, especially in the books, was the weird modesty of the British spy service, the way everything pretended to be these poky little Import/Export companies and they were always scrapping with Bond over his expense sheet, spackling percussion bombs together inside of an old talcum powder can. All way more lo-fi than in the films, with the idea of the shrinking and therefore somehow more benevolent, homier Empire than ours or the Russians...You read the books now, Bond's always like, really tired, he had bad breath, he hasn't turned in his expense sheets...

MF: I don't, alas. But I did smoke Dunhills for a little bit because that's what John Constantine smoked...

Y'know now that I think about it, the entire...what, *mise en scène* of the literary Bond world, is whatever the opposite of awesome and envious is. I always marvel, if that's the word, over all the food he's eaten, the cigarettes smoked, drinks consumed. Bond would be dead by fifty and they'd find seven empty bottles of Tums in the back of his beat-up old Aston Martin. The Bond books radiate *heartburn* and *tooth-grinding exhaustion.* I don't know what you do for morning breath on Crab Key but Bond was most certainly doing it daily.

Weirdly enough—maybe it's just being hung over from the Bondian decadence, the Terence Young of it all—that's precisely the thing I love about THE IPCRESS FILE. How beat down Harry Palmer is (who apparently didn't even have a name in the novels?), how nine-to-five the job is. The lousy apartment, boiling the water for coffee in the morning, the glasses from the public health. The profound LACK of glamour. The entire GOLDFINGER team made the movie though so it all looks great anyway...

MC: HAVE to see that one again. I was just watching the Steve McQueen THOMAS CROWN again and was struck by how much it chimed with the Steranko S.H.I.E.L.D. stuff[40], which are an obvious source/homage in CASANOVA, the split screen in that film breaking down like a page of Steranko but also the unlikely and marvelous warm/cool blend that you get with McQueen, and find in Nick Fury, too, and in our friend JC. A deep, profound cool that still, somehow, encompass foolishness, bemusement. Also by all the TELEPHONE BOOTHS! They were as plentiful as bison!
Also struck by how much more appealing and interesting and complicated the Faye Dunaway character was than what you find in the Bond women. Something much closer to a Fraction Woman, vice and virtue, heart and brain, curiosity and confidence and self-doubt all folded around a basic kick-ass attitude...

MF: Hah! I swoon.

That's really the ultimate disappointment of the Bond books, isn't it? The dismay-evoking women, save for ON HER MAJESTY'S SECRET SERVICE. It's as good as it gets I think. And a huge part of that is Tracy. I mean—she's the only Bond woman worthy of Dame Diana Rigg, y'know?

---

39   Listen: this is my experience with things. You make things sometimes, you put them out into the world, and somehow, through some extraordinary and weird chain of events you can neither control nor predict, you sometimes get to meet the people that made the work that inspired you in the first place. And then? It happens again, and again, and again. This is one of those things and I cannot tell you what it means to me.

40   Run don't walk to acquire IDW'S STERANKO: NICK FURY AGENT OF S.H.I.E.L.D. ARTIST'S EDITION right now.

My favorite bit in a film FULL of favorite hits is where Lazenby is sitting on a bench at the chalet and he looks like he's about to lose his mind. He's fucked, everything's fucked, and Blofeld is going to be on him in an instant and everybody's going to die—and then there she is saving him. We get to see Bond trapped and panicked like an animal and Diana Rigg as his saint and savior and, in that moment, his better. Of COURSE he had to marry her. She made him real and he made her a hero on his level. Warm to his cool in every way. So of course she was doomed.

Have you ever tried explaining OHMSS to anyone that's not a, uh, not a giant nerd? First, that film is rather treated like the fanfic piece of the canon. People don't see it. It had the guy who was Bond only once so, somehow, it doesn't count...

Anyway, every time I try to make the case to a civilian it sounds like I'm making it up. OHMSS is the Bond film too good to be true.

She's the shining exception that proves the rule about the superspy genre's treatment of women. What are the exceptions? MODESTY BLAISE? God save you from having to WATCH that damn thing. BARBARELLA? Um...and it just gets worse outdie of Bond: the Matt Helm is just clownish and grotesque and by the time you get to the two Bulldog Drummond films of that era its misogyny is just profane. I love Elke Sommer but I never want to see DEADLIER THAN THE MALE again.

It's interesting, too, to think that in 1967 you've got both that and Faye Dunaway in BONNIE AND CLYDE. Alpha and Omega.

MC: That is such a weird movie, though. I love Diana Rigg so much, and god she looks beautiful, but I always think Lazenby looks like a stand-in for somebody else, and TELLY SAVALAS as BLOFELD, I dunno, if you came up watching Kojak every week...He always seems to be having too much of the wrong kind of fun with the part.

Dunaway is also totally amazing and hard-as-steel (with a couple of great catfights) in the Lester MUSKETEERS films. Now that I think about it, she is a seriously underappreciated actress...And her surname rhymes with her first name, too.

We need tough, strong, smart kickass female characters...Mrs. Peel bing the prime example, I think...my daughter would probably toss Buffy in there...but is there anything lamer and more embarrassing than the generic Lara Croft "tough-bitch" character with the spandex pants and the blazing Glocks and the hollow plaster heart?

MF: Let's be honest, wasn't Telly Savalas always the guy in THE DIRTY DOZEN you didn't really think was acting?

But: yes. Tracy. Tracy Tracy Tracy.

It's funny you bring up your daughter: when we were first pregnant, but before I knew if we were having a boy or a girl, I was doing work on a couple Marvel books—IRON FIST had started and I was in Los Angeles doing research stuff on what'd become THE ORDER and I realized that if this was going to be what I did for a living, and if we had a daughter, then one day I was going to have an awful lot of explaining to do. Comics—really most genre fiction when I think about it—don't treat its female characters terrifically well almost as an immutable rule. Whether it's the clichéd Bond girl, Lois Lane who sits across a desk her whole life from the story of the century, or any of the be-thonged and high-heeled David Lee Roth video girl nightmares that pass as comic heroines most days, I realized that if I had a little girl one day she was going to want to know, if nothing else, why comics weren't better to girls.

It's embarrassing to say, but it's true. *One day I'll have to justify Power Girl to her.* Or Whatever Girl. I'd have to explain how I could work in a medium that fetishes her gender so often and so profusely that it's all just a given most times. "Here's why sexualized violence is okay, honey."

So that's where the pirate queen Iron Fist came from, the direction Pepper Potts has gone, and where so much of Zeph and who Sasa Lisi will end up becoming came from. That weird, sinking, shameful realization that for all of my well-placed intentions or so-called progressiveness, the greatest sin comes from just *not thinking about that stuff*...like, basic intellectual carelessness. Does that make sense? My awareness was dimmed. Bond damage.

Anyway, it was time to think about that stuff. Did the idea of your daughter one day reading your work affect how you produced it? And does genre fiction keep perpetuating its own worst stereotypes? Why is Mrs. Peel or Buffy the exception and not the rule?

MC: Yes. When I wrote SUMMERLAND I was writing for her, and so I worked very hard to create a strong, competent, independent, appealing female heroine for that book, although Jennifer T. Rideout is not the central character. But I knew Sophie would not go for it otherwise.

In the end she didn't love the book anyway...Too much baseball. Or too many words.

I prefer my adventure stories to feature either a strong, active, intelligent female character whose agency is essential (TERMINATOR 2, the Whedonverse) or no females as all (THE GREAT ESCAPE, MASTER AND COMMANDER). Helpless, weak, simpering, idiotic, passive eye-candy needing to be rescued or "a strong hand" spoils the whole thing. And, so, yes, I have trouble watching the early Bond films now[41].

My whole life has been, in some measure, a process of struggling to recognize, overcome and finally, hopefully, combat the great western heritage of misogyny...

Now, where were we? Cool spy cars? Top 5 ultracool vehicles in film or comics, did you say?

1) The Whiz Wagon, Kirby's JIMMY OLSEN
2) Bullitt's Mustang
3) The Aston Martin
4) Lady Penelope's FAB-1

---

41   Michael wrote me not long ago to say he and his son now felt DIAMONDS ARE FOREVER to be the greatest film ever made so, y'know. Everything changes.

5) The Saint's Volvo P-1800

I feel bad not having Starsky and Hutch's Gran Torino, though. And the FF's Pogo Plane.

MF: I thought it was swankiest boudoirs of the young and espionage-y?

1) Diabolik's rotating room-size three-level circular platform bed of larceny
2) Fury's New York Pad, NICK FURY AGENT OF S.H.E.I.L.D. #2
3) Barbarella's fur floor bed
4) Bonnie Parker's wrought-iron bedframe from the first two minutes of BONNIE AND CLYDE
5) Blofeld's private digs inside Piz Gloria

And between Eva, the Contessa, Barbarells, Bonnie, and Tracy, there's not a soft sister in 'em.

•[42]

4 (Image Comics, 2007)

Hiyah, earthmen.

Some time last summer, a sixteen-year-old Nepalese boy named Ram Bahadur Banjan sat beneath the tree and began meditating. He'd go nonstop, allegedly without food and water, for the next ten months.

Miracle? Hoax? Scam? Performance Art?

The part of my brain that cheapens everything suspected it was an issue of CASANOVA waiting to happen.

•

Every was fast to call Ram Bahadur Banjan the…not "reincarnated" Buddha, but…I guess it'd be the new Buddha? I'm not a Buddhist so forgive me if I misunderstand how this works. But he was exhibiting certain Buddha-esque behaviors. People were getting excited. Now he had attendants. Now he had pilgrims.

What's more important is that Ram insisted he wasn't Buddha. He allegedly awoke back in November and told an attendant as much. He said he didn't have Buddha's energy. And he said he needed six more years of meditation.

So under his tree he sat. And then came more attendants and pilgrims. Word spread, slowly at first, and people began to come see the Boy Buddha (Can't you hear a petulant sixteen-year-old insisting, "But I'm NOT the Buddha! GOD!" before storming off to his…uh…hut?).

Doctors were not allowed to approach him, for fear of his meditation being disturbed. A kind of curtain was set up at night, shielding him from view. It's a hoax, right? They're slipping him food at night. They're taking care of him in the dark.

It's a scam. It's gotta be a scam.

But word spread. The people came.

And the press, too. Which is where I came in, a tourist to Ram Bahadur Banjan's drama.

•

George Saunders, the brilliant author of CIVILWARLAND IN BAD DECLINE, PASTORALIA, and IN PERSUASION NATION, wrote about the Buddha Boy for the June 2006 issue of GQ. It has Christina Aguilera and her pillow on the cover, but if you can find it you should buy it, or at least read it, anyway.

Saunders went to Nepal and surveyed the scene, as it were. He stared at Ram Bahadur Banjan. He spent time with his friends. He spent time with the attendants and the pilgrims. He took pictures. He spent time with and took pictures of Ram Bahadur Banjan's parents.

And any questions you might have about Ram Bahadur Banjan are probably answered in his article.

So you should read that. [43]

•

Here's the thing—shortly after Saunders finished his article (but still months before it was published), Ram Bahadur Banjan vanished.

Sort of the ultimate good news/bad news, isn't it? There's a Teenage Buddha! Annnnnnnnd he's gone missing.

At least I knew what the CASANOVA story would be about.

•

42   Omitted here was a bibliography of everything we talked about. You're smart people. You can use the internet to find things.

43   Or read George Saunders' excellent THE BRAINDEAD MEGAPHONE (2007), which collects many of his essays, this included.

Ram Bahadur Banjan came back, momentarily.

He came back long enough to tell the Chairman of the Village Committee that watched over him that he was going away to complete his six years of meditation. There was no peace beneath his tree, so he was going into the woods. Like any good teenager, he was running away.

"Tell my parents not to worry," he said.

My god.

If I were a sixteen-year-old runaway, I would've told my parents to go fuck themselves.

This kid really IS holy.

•

I was fascinated. Double fascinated, even. Not, you know, as a Buddhist or a cynic or anything else, but as a fan of...spectacle? Hope? I don't know what you'd call it.

The world should be more special. The world should be more interesting. This I believe and lament.

And so maybe a sixteen-year-old sitting under a tree and waking up as a god is just the kind of magic that's missing in the world; that missing magic means the loss that's robbed us of jetpacks and rocketcars, of maglev skateboards and Paco Rabanne lines at Target—in short, everything that makes up the dumb little details and the superficial gleam of CASANOVA.

•

So, Ram Bahadue Banjan goes missing in March.

Then, David Blane stated talking about his spring stunt, where he'd put himself inside a bubble of water in New York City for like a week.

Apparently that's what passes for spectacle, television, and magic these days.

And between these two boys, the character of David X presented himself. It made the idea of Cass absconding with something holy somewhat palatable. And it made the whole thing kind of funny.

Messiahs or Gods or whatever kinds of miracle workers then and now are demarcated maybe only by dint of having a press agent.

•

Which brings me to maybe my biggest misgiving about this issue—who was doing the narration on the first page there? New Buddha's PR guy?

THAT'S a character I'd like to get back to writing.

•

So here we also get to meet Sabine Seychelle.

I liked the idea of Johnny Quest, all adult and crooked. The son of an adventure scientist and his be-Polo'd sidekick would grow up... how, exactly? Bent, I supposed. Weeeird. The kind of guy that would create these phenomenal machines...and then sleep with them three at a time[44].

A lot of times I just kind stare off into space, and sometimes people will ask me what I'm thinking about, and I'll demure and say nothing and try to move the conversation along.

But really, sometimes, I'm thinking about a growed-up Johnny Quest sticking it in a robot.

•

I'd like to add that this giant Hashshashin guy—where goes Johnny Quest, so would go Hadji, right?—that looks like the genie from ALADDIN gone bamboo is one of my favorite moments of cartooning in the book thus-far.

Gabriel Bá, ladies and gentlemen.

I say this every month, but this is my favorite issue of CASANOVA so far.

From our very earliest days, I knew I'd be writing and planning CASANOVA in a four-tiered page and that our pacing would be dictated by an 8-grid. In the fight scene at the end of our second issue I tried a 16-grid. I love it, and when Bá drew it, I loved it even more. The economy of his cartooning, smashed into the 4:4 time signature of an 8-grid, punctuated by those snare-drum cracks that the little 16th panels give the page...I just loved it. It felt like comics should feel to me. Subjective as that sounds.

---

44 The writing of this predates literally the same character appearing on THE VENTURE BROTHERS by a few months but still stunned me. Between that show and ARCHER there's now maybe a dozen CASANOVA bits that never saw the light of day.

I couldn't wait to get to do it again, even though it takes me twice as long to write.

There's an array of Bá's pencils from this issue presented here. I hope you folks will love seeing them and comparing them to the final product as much as I do.

●

We've started getting letters from our readers. As I write this, the first issue of CASANOVA has been out about a month, and the second one is on its way to stores as I type.

The response has been, to put it mildly, overwhelming. Flattering, effusive, generous, encouraging…in all ways off both hook and chain. So much so that running them makes me feel funny.

They've meant the world to us here at Team CASANOVA. Than you for your kindness and encouragement—that we've struck a chord with so many of you is beyond flattering. And it's not just ME, although, you know, those are always totally the best letters. You people are falling in love with Bá's work; you people are seeing how vital a contributor Sean Konot and his divine lettering is to the book. And then you're telling us as much.

So, thanks, Casanovanauts. Drop us a line at casanovaquinn@gmail.com, or visit us at the Image Comics forum at: http://www. imagecomics.com/messageboard/viewforum.php?f=31. Or don't. No pressure. We're all cool either way[45].

●

Speaking of Team CASANOVA, this issue sees Designatrix Laurenn McCubbin head off to Viz and the starry climes of SHOJO BEAT, where she's now the Managing Editor.

She'll be marshaling the forces of Japanese Schoolgirls that dictate what everybody'll be wearing in three years. Congrats, Laurenn, and thanks. We wouldn't have made it this far without you.

Filling those mighty tall shows that serve only to augment the giantess McCubbin is the Mighty Drew Gill, sure to be our very own Sir George Martin.

Welcome, Drew[46].

●

Oh, so, Ram Bahadur Banjan turned seventeen a week or so after I finished this script.

I only noticed when rereading all of my notes on the kid. He'd come and gone, a human interest story with a question mark for a punchline, and unless he's found running a hot dog cart outside of Madison Square Garden, I doubt very much anyone will hear of him, or from him, ever again.

I find myself transfixed by the thought of all those people that gathered around him…the cluster of open-hearted followers that prayed with him and watched his hair grow for ten months. Are any of them still there, still starting at Ram Bahadur Banjan's tree, waiting for him to come back? Did they take the dirt he sat on, carve bark off of his tree and hold them in tight, cold fists? It gets cold in Nepal, you know? How are they staying warm, now that the Buddha Boy has gone away? When did they give up? What was the straw, I wonder, that broke the backs of their faith?

Or are they still waiting?

Ram Bahadur Banjan's birthday passed while we was allegedly meditating somewhere under a tree in the heart of Nepal, far away from his followers and his faithful.

Surely, he had more important things on his mind.

5 (Image Comics, 2007)

Hiyah, earthmen.

On February 9th, 2006, the Daily Telegraph out of London reported that two fishermen, dangerously off-course and equally as drunk, drifted onto the shores of Sentinel Island and were, erm, arrowed to death by the last tribe of Stone Age man on Earth.

The Sentinelese are indigenous to the Andaman Islands, specifically North Sentinel Island, off of the Great Andaman archipelago in the Bay of Bengal. They have defended themselves from incursions from the Outer World as long as the Outer World has attempted to incur upon them. As such, they remain untouched by history. Fiercely so. These are the savages that refused to bow down before a world that would break them.

The bodies of the fishermen have not been recovered.

Because, you know. The arrows and stuff.

●

---

45   Again: long since abandoned. I stopped checking the email after issue 7's commentary. Come to think of it that might have… well, keep reading.

46   Drew, in fact, designed the book you're reading right now.

I love the 1933 KING KONG—it's a pulp magazine come to life, a lean and mean 104 minutes that pass in a fever-dream heartbeat. Like CASABLANCA, it's one of those movies that can surprise you the first time you see it, as a someone with some degree of pop-culture experience, and you realize that it's a colossal pop-cultural touchstone. It's fun and silly and sexy and naïve and ridiculous and dramatic and exciting and goddamn, there's a beautiful chaos in Willis O'Brien's animation work, something warm and throbbing in the Uncanny Valley, something that ten million orcs CGI-ing across New Zealand will never have.

Is "orc" spelled with a C or a K?

I digress. So, last Christmas, like dozens of you, I went to go see the vanity remake of KING KONG. Guh, I dunno. I had a bad day and wanted to watch the monkey spike that bi-plane out of the sky, right? I'm only human. I'm not made of stone. I have needs and weaknesses just like the rest of you.

Anyway. New KING KONG. It's not so good. You probably heard that from, y'know, the rest of the whole world.

They get to Skull Island where savages feed virgins to King Kong. And, while remaining faithful to every aspect of the '33 KONG, bajillionaire director Peter Jackson populates the place with, as our fisherman in CASANOVA calls the citizens of Coldheart, "ooga booga bone-nose nigger savage motherfuckers."

Now, I'm about as sensitive to race issues as the next middle-class white guy. But—really, Peter? Really? That's the best you could do? You can show us the money and the girl ice-skating in Central Park, but you can't manage to update the D.W. Griffin-level of stereotypical Savage Negro Monster? Were there no assistants or friends, colleagues or freakin' P.A.s that took the His Grande Hobbitness aside to point out that, hey, maybe we're spending two hundred million dollars and short of top hats and canes, we've just filled Skull Island like it was the Isle of Misfit Al Jolsons?[47][48]

It wasn't re-envisioning, re-mastering, reinventing or re-presenting anything but bigotry; Jackson and Co. trucked in racism and wrote it off as an act of fidelity and faithfulness to flawed and ignorant source material.

And anyway it just pissed me off. So when, a few months later, I read about North Sentinel Island for the first time, the two thoughts collided with one another.

Fuck that guy. Here are savages to save the world[49].

•

This was originally supposed to be CASANOVA #4; in fact, it was on the Big Sur trip that inspired the third issue that we saw an island of some sort and started talking about it. In my notebook I wrote the following as we drove by:

> An island that's accesible once every 20 years.
>
> Waters receed & the pop. of the island reintegrate with the world for a few days.
> Cass gets on & gets off again?

That's right. "Accesible." "Receed." I write English good A LOT.

•

This story got moved from #4 to #5 when I realized we needed to threaten Cass through Anna and I needed to get Anna off the board safely for a little while. So we had to establish the threat, establish that even Cass realized how fucked he was, and put Cass on the road from playing defense to offense.

It made sense that Cass would hide her on Coldheart, given our conceit, and so that was that.

I felt bad about the shuffle, because I'd run Gabriel through the whole story and the, when the time came to deliver the script, send a wholly new script in its place.

•

Johnny Blame writes:

Oakland is my town so I loved this last issue of Casanova especially. Very Happy Lois the Pie Queen is in Berkeley I'm pretty sure, right outside of Oakland. My sisters ultimate team at CAL is called the Pie Queens because of that restaurant actually. Keep up the good work. You ever think about adding a letter column to Casanova?

Johnny,

Sweet—does your sister's team have T-shirts? And thanks.

Also, re: letters. Nah.

•

---

47 Jesus, this still bothers me. I haven't let my kid watch the film because of this shit.

48 I also think I could've – should've – made this point better. I wish I'd found a different way of putting it.

49 And, as has been pointed out to me, to pass straight into the *magic Negro* category. The embarrassment of growing up and learning in public pales before the pain of ignorance.

I love this issue. Mostly because it was the first one I'd written after seeing Bá and Konot's work on CASANOVA #1, soup to nuts. I had a whole, finished book in my hands and could write for the two of them[50].

So, in the interest of keeping these pages as process-oriented as possible, I thought this month I'd show y'all, step by step, how some of our favorite shots came together this issue.

The way we work, Bá gives us penciled pages, I rewrite the dialogue if needed and break down lettering guides for Sean; Sean starts his lettering process over the raw pencils' Bá sends inks, then a few days later, tones. Sean gets the lettering over to Drew Gill, who stitches the whole book together.

•

Here's the script for Page 5, Panel 1[51]:

5.1 SAME
WIDE PANEL: PULL BACK to reveal a SPEAR throbs dead center in the guy's chest, blood spreading slowly outward. Everyone else near him freezes in shock, staring at the spear.

Maybe give the spear some jiggle lines so we get the feeling like it's throbbing up and down with his heartbeat.

> *1 U.N. GUY   Savages.*

See how I screwed that up? I wrote a filmed moment, something that needed more than a few cartoon-y jiggle lines to pull the moment off. The explosion of, erm, U.N. Guy, the rushing spear, the hat flying backwards—that's the shot and Bá knew it. He knew what the right moment was and gave it to us.

Dropping the background out of works to rack-focus the moment. Sometimes Bá leaves background details out of his pencil roughs and other times he delivers tightly rendered pages. This was one of those times where I hoped he'd leave the background out and, save for some stylization in the tones, he did.

There's unending joy, working on this book. Every moth is makes me a smarter[52], better[53] writer.

Or at least that's what I tell myself.

•

Here's Page 7, Panel 1:

7.1 SAME.
The SAVAGES all turn from the shore, heading towards the vegetation at the beach's edge. They remove headdresses or nosebones and every other affectation like the stage props they are. We're angling on THE CHIEF as his ADVISOR (a woman) bends over PUKEY'S BODY and takes a DISC out of a pocket; the CASS SHAPE hides behind a tree off to the side in the back somewhere.

> *1 CHIEF   DOES IT DAMAGE OUR IDENTITY, AS A PEOPLE? THE STEREOTYPES, THE DEROGATORY CARICATURE?*
>
> *2 ADVISOR   EH. KILLING A FEW WHITE GUYS SURE HELPS TAKE OUT THE STING.*
>
> *3 ADVISOR   SPEAKING OF—WE KILLED THE GUY.*

I load these panels up with stuff sometimes. We have a big, rotating cast every issue and, working at the page number we have, every beat counts. A lot of times that means every cast-member on-panel needs to be doing something very, very specific so we can keep moving forward.

God help Bá, you know? Here's how he pulls it off—

First, all the information is there in the pencils. Foreground, middle, and back, each action clear and concise, the framing not only establishing the space we're in, but each of our three narrative lines.

There's a freedom and energy to Bá's pencil work that his precision with ink doesn't suggest.

At the same time, he even marks down those little hatches on the dead guy's back. The ink I always assume was unplanned and wholly spontaneous are, like every other mark he puts down, considered with elegance and exactitude.

And you don't miss a think in the staging. The flow still whips your eye down the panel's diagonal; the grounding is made more real by the blacks.

Check in the Advisor's hand—he tones her in green so we don't miss the pure white of the CD.
Page 7, Panel 3:

---

50   The first and last time I was ever this far ahead of the art team much to the consternation of said art team.

51   The art samples have been removed from this sequence for space; you can flip back to see what Bá drew.

52   Ha.

53   HA.

7.3
BIG PANEL: through a clearing that THE NATIVES walk down, angling down a hill, we see a glorious city in the middle of Coldheart Island.

It's a thriving, otherworldly paradise, almost literally a thousand years beyond anything humans have achieved elsewhere. A combination of Mayan-style stone architecture and fantastic forms of liquid, organic metals. INn essence, Coldheart is a combination of the distant past and the far future.

> 6 ADVISOR   SO WHAT? WHITEY MAKES US FEEL BAD FOR A SECOND OR TWO. BIG DEAL.

> 7 ADVISOR   WE'LL CRY ALL THE WAY BACK TO PARADISE.

Like I said above, this is the first issue where I had a whole book in my hand, so I was willing to stanch my raging, obsessive, controlling ego and let my partners do their thing.

I mean, here's a whole CITY that I don't describe beyond the most vague of platitudes. Were this a scene in CASANOVA #1, I suspect I'd have written about every piece of glass, every blade of grass.[54]

This is, I think, the most overtly Kirby-esque art from Bá to date. In fact, Coldheart City kind of looks like H.E.R.B.I.E. from the old FANTASTIC FOUR cartoon, doesn't it? Which is maybe some Toth, smashed up on Kirby.

Anyway. I had NO idea what Bá was going to draw when we got here. But I knew he was going to deliver the goods, and that I was embarrassed almost by how overwritten the earlier scripts were.

There's Mignola in Bá's stuff, no doubt. That Bá is unafraid of slinging down lots of black is my favorite bit. The one-color thing Bá and I decided on literally the moment we decided to work together. But, at one point, the question of color came up and Bá effectively shut the discussion down with this glorious declaration:

COLOR IS EVIL![55]

Looking at panels like this, and seeing what Bá does with black and green and while, I tend to agree.

●

Page 9, Panels 2-4

9.2 LIMBO
Time to show off a little bit. CASS is in a prison that exists OUTSIDE OF THE PANEL. So it's white space with NO BORDERS. In fact, we see two planes that intersect and form an angle, the surfaces are what he presses his hands against. Through each we see two different angles of the COLDHEART MEN that interrogate him, as though CASS was a prisoner of two conjoining panels. Remember the effect of CASS being plucked from one timeline to the next? Now he's a prisoner between those planes.

I can doodle this for you, so it makes better sense, if the above loses you.

> 3 CASS   PLEASE—LET ME OUT.

> 4 CASS   I FEEL LIKE I'M LOSING MY MIND IN HERE.

9.3 INT. HOLDING ROOM. SAME.
NORMAL SPACE: COLE LEANS UP TO CASS, who goes BUG EYED inside his invisible cell.

> 5 COLE   OH, YOU ABSOLUTELY ARE. MAMMALS LIKE YOU WITH SUCH PUNY
>   SUPERCORTEX NEURONS DON'T HANDLE OUR GEOMETRIES VERY WELL.

> 6 COLE   ALTHOUGH YOUR MIND IS AN INTERESTING ONE.

9.4 LIMBO
CASS drops to his knees, covering his face with his arms. PLANES ABOVE AND
TO THE SIDE show the MASSIVE FACES of COLE and the CHIEF.

> 7 CHIEF   I SAW THAT TOO, COLE. LIKE THE DIFFERENCE BETWEEN TWO TULIPS.

> 8 CHIEF   YES, CHIEF, BUT EVEN DEEPER THAN THAT—LISTEN TO HOW THE LIGHT STRIKES IT.
>   ITS TEMPO IS SOLELY ITS OWN.

Just what every artist wants to read, huh? "Let's show off a bit."

These pages had every right to be utter disappointments, collapsing beneath the weight of their own pretension. Were it not tethered to reality by Bá's sense of place and staging, they would have.

There's no point that we can't follow the flow and timing. Bá never loses us and never sends up astray. And for a page layout that forces a 2-D space to pretend it's 3-D, that's saying something.

---

54   Bá and Moon have said to me "The first line of a panel description in a CASANOVA script is for us. The rest is for you." And they're right.

55   Clearly they've come around since then. A section about the coloring of CASANOVA follows the commentary for LUXURIA's finale.

My favorite detail in the page? Look at how Cass looks from outside his holding cell—all line work, no spot blacks there at all. Even in the final version, the green exists purely outside the cell, creating a sense of spatial difference in the panel—two different spaces with two different...qualities of air, almost, presented within the same panel/metapanel construct.

Good times.

3 (Icon Comics, 2010)

Mike Doughty, who was in a band once called Soul Coughing, and who now performs as just Mike Doughty, played for my wife and I a cover of the Magnetic Fields' "Book of Love" at our wedding. It was his gift to us. It was the single greatest piece of musical performance I have ever been lucky enough to see. He put a version of it out not long ago that'll suggest, maybe, the majesty and triumph and beauty of that moment. Maybe if you listen to it with my wife all in white and all of your friends crying all around you? I dunno.

Anyway. That was the first of two impossible things for which I owe Mike thanks.

On September 10th, 2001, I drank my last drink; I hadn't gotten high in nearly a year at that point I think but who knows. That was the date I got clean. I entered a recovery program on December 29th, 2007. That was the date I started to learn how to live sober and it's from that date I count my days. I am clean and I am sober and I live the life I live and have the hob I have and I am a father and I am the man I am and I have not set myself on fire or ruined my marriage or died in a car crash. That one could mark those two lines on a matching curve is not, I believe, coincidence.

I am an alcoholic and an addict[56]. I stopped drinking and getting high because I could not say no to drinking or getting high, ever, under any circumstance, and I did not know how to live without them.

I was able to white-knuckle *not-using* and *not-drinking* by swapping addictions one for the next. This is not healthy. I started writing my first graphic novel like nine days after I quit, slept an hour a night, and a week later had banged it all out—for an example, I smoked like ten trillion cigarettes and stopped sleeping for days and went bonkers until I no longer bit my lip when I thought about drinking; I could not stop burning. I could not stop the rage or the anxiety or the feeling like I was in a restaurant for the first time but had no idea what a menu was. I could not contain or correct or address the endless loathing that bubbled out of me and could, and usually did, ruin everything. I did not have the grammar that allowed me to ask anyone for *help*.

And the panic attacks weren't going away[57].

I went into recovery because I learned what recovery was. I went into recovery because I didn't want to feel like I was on fire all of the time and I wanted to make a living as a writer and I could not for the life of me reconcile those two things.

I met Mike. We had mutual friends; I was a fan. They say that when you look for a sponsor you look around the room for someone that has what you want; I did and saw that Mike did. He had left the relative security of a successful collective experience to go on his own, cleaned up, and was by any measure successful at doing what he loves to do and paying his bills by doing it. I say myself, or my history and desires, reflected in that. When I entered program and stayed in program, what Mike had was what I wanted more than anything.

I wanted to be alive and I wanted to write and I wanted to not feel like I was on fire all of the time.

I knew how to ask for help a while before I actually asked. One of the biggest fears I had about getting sober—and make no mistake there is very a much a difference between being clean and being sober—was that recovery would inflict capital-G-God upon me and would dull whatever creative instruments I had in my arsenal. I do not believe in any kind of supreme organized intelligences that I can petition with my wants or desires and I did not want to be sober if that meant having to bow down before such a thing.

It was Mike who at a glance showed me that wasn't true. That there was no shame in sobriety, no mandatory Judeo-Christian believe system one had to swear to, and no end to creativity or productivity that came with sobriety.

And to that end I am as atheistic, manic, and hard-working as I ever was. Only now it doesn't feel like I'm on fire all the time and I don't get drunk or high anymore.

Today I don't even miss it.

Anyway what I'm saying is I asked Mike to be my sponsor and he agreed and that's the second impossible thing to repay.

He's writing a recovery memoir and <u>that</u> inspired me wanting to try <u>this</u>; to talk to this guy I so very highly admire about how sobriety integrates itself into the life of a working musician, or writer, or artist, or whatever. It's a paramount concern of mine. It kept me out for a long time, y'know? And it keeps friend of mine out.

I've never outed myself as being in recovery before now. It's not terribly hard to read between the lines of my work and see it but, at the same time, it's not terribly hard to assume I'm a drugged-out lunatic from reading my work, either, judging by the sheer volume of amazing and wonderful readers who offer to get me drunk or high at shows.

(If you've ever offered to buy me a drink or get me high at a show and I've refused, no matter how often you tried, how diligent your

---

56 This ended up being one of the most important things I've ever written. To everyone that's come up to me, at literally every show or signing I've done since then, who brought this up, who thanked me, who through trembling voice told me that you read this and it helped you, thank you. Thank you for keeping me sober.

57 Hey, uh... so, mental health is a process. And a long, winding one, at that. Don't shy away from asking for help. Don't be afraid to reach out. You're not alone.

approach, or how determined you were that the little bit of Humboldt County[58] you were hiding in your glove compartment would be awesome—now you know why. It just seemed easier to demur as politely as I could at the time instead of going into all of this stuff. Which, trust me, would've made you extremely uncomfortable.)

Most recovery programs—at least the ones I frequent—rely on the tradition of attraction rather than promotion and placing the principles of those programs before the personalities that ascribe to them; I'm not entirely sure, then, how to reconcile what I'm writing with that.

I am, however, entirely sure that without program—without recovery, without sobriety, without Mike, without the hundreds of meetings I've been to in rooms that were haunted, illuminated, or somewhere in between—I would not have the panoply of lucky starts that hangs over my head tonight. And if there's any way that I could ever possibly thank Mike for what he's done, it's by maybe saying that out loud and living by example.

Somewhere out there is somebody like I used to be that thinks cleaning up means a mandatory god, involuntary boredom, and a career in self-publishing wold-and-crystal books.

There is a third option.

I am clean and I am sober and I am a husband and I am a father and I write like a motherfucker and I am telling you I do not burn.

It was the hardest thing I've ever done. But it works.

•

Matt Fraction: Were you afraid that getting sober would damage your ability to write? Because I thought I needed to feel crazy all the time to do anything worthwhile. I thought I needed to feel like I was on fire or like I was going to die all the time.

Mike Doughty: I had a hard year right after I got clean where I didn't write any songs worth a damn. Very frightening. But I was journaling constantly, just scrawling crazy stuff. At some point I started going though the craziness and picking out phrases or sequences of words that were beautiful or resonant for me. I was writing a lot about my junkie ex—a lot of it, though I didn't know it, metaphors for drugs—and when September 11 happened, she was working down near Ground Zero, and that was a catalyst to start tying these notebook fragments into melodies and chord progressions. Once I was rolling, I found my songs to be a lot truer and vibrant to me than they'd ever been before.

I guess this is along way of saying that the craziness is still present, and that I draw from that. In terms of living in pain, living in depression, in active addiction, actual debilitating craziness, I was freed when that subsided to write more and better.

MF: How is the writing process different for you then and now? Was getting fucked up ever a part of your, ah, creation strategy?

MD: I thought getting high inspired me—and I guess, initially, it really did—but by the end of it, when I got high, I could stop hating myself just long enough to do a few things, though I was way disoriented and partially incapacitated. Nearly everything I wrote for the latter half of the 90s sounds half-finished t me because of that. One key difference is that now I actually finish songs, and can be satisfied with them.

MF: There were a lot of reasons I came to you and asked if you'd be my sponsor, but a big part of it was your professional life: you'd gotten out of an unhealthy creative collective and found a way to live your life sober and to make your living off of your art—which, y'know, in all my years in art school we were taught that kind of thing is the exception and not the rule. So you, as they say, had what I wanted. There's another sort of similarity between us, I think, in that we both had to figure out how to produce work not-high and to do it alone. Was that recalibration—getting out a bad group dynamic and figuring out how to do what you do—tied into the first year of getting it together or was that a different kind of thing for you?

How did you learn to NOT be in a band is, I guess, what I want to know.

MD: It wasn't a recalibration, really, in terms of leaving a group dynamic: the band was dead, dead, dead years before it split. I felt so freed to be able to make creative decisions unhindered. I had to put a lot of pretty insanely hard work in—heavy and lonely touring—to make a living with my art, but I didn't really have a choice.

Writing not-high was indeed daunting.

MF: Have you found that getting sober, being sober, living sober—that any part of the sober pancake—has found its way into your work itself? I don't' think I've done a particularly inspired job of hiding my involvement in the program—I haven't really tried, I guess—but I do consciously have to be aware of some of the traditions, namely keeping what's in the rooms in the rooms, as it were. It's been a line I've not been sure how to walk and it feels weird to censor myself but...well, it's a line. It's a big part of who I am now—surely as big as drinking or getting high ever was—so it feels weird to not be absolutely open about it.

As I've typed this line I've realized that I've not really, uh, 'outed' myself to my parents. So that's I thing I need to do soon. (HI MOM)

MD: The world of meetings or the steps hasn't made its way into the songs, though I've certainly written about god stuff. I'm writing a memoir in which I openly speak of going to meetings, though I'm being a little coy, not identifying the program, just calling it, "the rooms."

---

58 I... I think this is a phrase from Chabon's WONDER BOYS. Cryptomnesia!

It's a technicality though, really, and I'm worried and doubtful about it. The anonymity principle is most important to me as a principle of humility, of Everyman-ness, and also I take keeping others' presence in the rooms secret. That's sacred, although, again, I'm riding a fine line in this memoir.

MF: That makes me want to ask a couple things, actually. First, was there backlash, hipster or otherwise, that came from writing "god stuff"? And…well, this is more broad than a proper question, I guess, but what can you tell me about the memoir?

MD: You know, there wasn't really a hipster backlash. Some people asked me if I was Christian, and I explained my belief in god; a belief in a god that was also not-god. One of the funniest things was on email from the director of a church choir who was angry that I said, "fucking" in my song "His Truth is Marching ON," which he wanted to arrange for his group. I wrote back politely, saying that I was speaking to burning heathens like myself. He thought that was funny.

The book's[59] just a compendium of the good drug and music stories I have, really.

MF: Do you find writing a memoir a more straightforward/confessional/exposed kind of writing than your songs? What's the internal journey been like—oh god I just typed 'internal journey'—as you've cranked along through the book? I suppose that's predicated on a few assumptions about what your memoir might be like vs. what your songs are like and for all I know the process is the same.

MD: Yeah, prose being straightforward just by its very nature. With the songs, I'm putting together phrases that make a certain kind of ineffable sense, without really knowing what they signify until the song's done, at which point it often becomes obvious that I'm dealing with come memory very directly—or sometimes the revelation doesn't happen until I've been playing it live for a year or two or three, and it'll smack me in the face.

I wrote the first hundred pages in a few months, and then my editor told me there was no set deadline, at which point it became very easy to put it down until he gave me a deadline! But, truthfully, it was the most difficult part I was avoiding—the experience of the band. Just telling the stories was traumatic enough, but, having been in an abusive relationship, it was difficult to face that I stayed in it in the first place—even recognizing that I was being abused, I stayed, something deep stopped me from leaving. And, in turn, I'm angry at myself that, in the face of all the abuse I received, my biggest reaction is shame for staying in the relationship!

MF: So leaving the band and getting sober—was one a function of the other? Were they separate events, unrelated? If they were related, how? What was that chronology, if nothing else?

MD: I quit the band, went out on my first solo tour, either drunk or jittering the entire time—I paid a guy to drive me around in a rented white Buick—and while I was out there, emailed an old girlfriend who was in the rooms to being me to a meeting. Part of just abandoning myself to being drunk and high was that I hated being in the band, so I'm not sure that if I were still in the band, my reaction wouldn't be, what the fuck, what's the point in being sober? But I don't know. I was so beat up, so hurting.

MF: Can I, uh, fan out on you for a second? You spoke really recently on twitter about how you feel about the work you produced during those years—to say you felt divorced from it is maybe being kind—how does your first solo piece SKITTISH fall into that continuum? It predates the end of the band bus it so unlike anything else you were making during that time.

MD: Making our second album, the one with "Super Bon Bon" on it, was just a horror of spite. When it was done and dusted, I wanted to make something that was pure art, no personalities. I was a fan of the producer Kramer, who did albums with Low and Galaxie 500 that I loved. I had a bunch of songs that I was too proud of to bring in to Soul Coughing-and besides, they would've sneered at them for being too emotional, I think. I wanted to make a stark record, in a very short time period (so many months making that Soul Coughing record, sheer drudgery) completely unlike Soul Coughing, and Kramer was down to do it on spec. I thought it'd be a snap to get Warner Bros. to pay him, but they weren't interested in the least, predominately, I think, because they'd spent a lot of money setting up Soul Coughing, and they didn't want me to quit. I was crushed.

MF: Also: is it true you made more by hand-selling CD-Rs of SKITTISH out of the trunk of your car, sitting on the stage after shows, meeting folks and shaking hands, than you ever did as a part of the Warner Brothers family of recording artistes? What was it like to go from Reality A to Reality B? Any advice you have for those that may find themselves on the cusp of a shifting paradigm like that[60]?

MD: I did—my income, like, doubled when I went solo. Conversely, my fame level dropped, and that was a slap in the face: I still get, five albums into a solo career, "Oh, you're that guy? What have you been doing?" Believe me, I'm making a good living, and I have a fabulous audience, so no complaints.

The money thing wasn't really a function of Warner Bros. dicking us, but that we spent so much money touring, on buses, lights, a hug crew. We'd come back from a tour playing to 2,500 people a night and I couldn't pay my rent—but then there were things, like, Warner Bros.

---

59   Called THE BOOK OF DRUGS, released in 2012, and is a great rock book, a great drug book, and a great recovery book, all at the same time. Then listen to Mike's musical reconciling with his Soul Coughing work, CIRCLES (2013), the recording of which was crowdfunded in hours by fans like me. I told him he needed to write about that for a new afterword because, Jesus, what a thing.

60   I'm not a particularly money-driven guy—I mean, I like money, it's nice, it buys stuff and puts my kids in clothes and such—so I don't mean to sound all, like, Mr. Money Guy. The meridian that divided writing-as-hobby and writing-as-job was an important one for me to cross, psychologically. I forget that some people aren't motivated by that, or let the art take them different places for different reasons sometimes.

would pay for me to stay at the Paramount Hotel for six weeks without batting an eye. The other things were that I signed my songwriting rights over to my bandmates; they told me it was that or they'd dump me. I was 23, and felt like my life's dream was on the line, so I signed.

It is very true, though, that if you make your CDs directly available to the listener and they hand you $15 cash, you'll make more money on your CDs.

As for advice: I was crazy at the time, just out of my gourd. And I didn't have any options—there's nothing else I can do, really, as a career. Being crazy and desperate is helpful for making big changes, maybe?

MF: The myth of the artist, or writer, or creator, or maker—scratch that, the myth of the TORTURED artist writer creator maker, is inexorably intertwined with using—drinking, getting high, getting fucked up. I know that kept me from getting clean; I know that kept me from getting sober. That inescapable belief that using, that chemical sidekicks, were essential to…well, doing work, period, let alone doing good or great work. Like, when I was a kid, I knew I wouldn't be an astronaut because my math wasn't strong. I thought I wouldn't or couldn't be a wrier if I didn't, from time to time, wrestle Ol' Grandad into submission. So many great pieces of art, music, film, whatever, are linked forever with someone behind the wheel being fucked up. It's hard to escape. It feels like a mandatory uniform.

Does that ring familiar to you? Was that something you had to deal with?

MD: Bill Hicks said, "Drugs are bad, but they sure didn't hurt my record collection." Well, sure, but I'd reply, "yeah, especially all those great recordings Jimi Hendrix made in the late 70s."

I definitely thought I couldn't write without weed, at least, to spark inspiration, though when I quit I realized I wasn't writing weed, either. So sure it rings familiar. I think what really helped me is pain. Drugs were a way of managing that pain, so in that sense they were indeed essential, so I could channel the pain without being destroyed by it. I still draw on that pain, and much much less obliquely, now. I've worked by ass off and gone through a lot of shit being able to deal with that pain without a palliative, and on the other side, I feel like a better artist now.

MF: At what point and how did you decide to 'out' yourself as being in recovery? A friend of mine rejects the notion of anonymity entirely, for example—not privacy, but his personal anonymity in the rooms—and in meetings identified himself by his first and last name. His first sponsor, he told me, said that somebody in that room would, some night, have to find somebody's name in the phonebook and they won't have a phone list on 'em and you can't just look up BILL W or whatever. So…yeah, so. So how did you come out to the world, and why, and were you scared or worried or happy or…or what? What was it like?

MD: I've pretty much always been out. I'm quasi-famous, so at least in meetings, I didn't have a choice. I imagine you don't have a choice, either, when you bump into comics people. I've never talked about meetings directly from the stage, but when this book comes out, it'll be like I might as well have. But people in my crowd know; I get a lot of email from people struggling with drugs, and I tell them to go to meetings, sometimes send them links to their local 12-Step websites. We're not talking about a lot of people, but I was glad to help them anyway. Like I said, the most important parts of anonymity, to me, are the principle of humbleness, and protecting other people. The anonymity tradition was invented circa 1940. And remember, it says, "We maintain personal anonymity at the level of press, radio, and films." It says nothing about TV or the internet. (jay kay jay kay jay kay)

MF: Sausage patty…or sausage links?

MD: I'm a bacon man, unless I'm in the UK, where the sausage is just amazingly delectable[61], especially the Cumberland sausage. The Limeys possess mystic knowledge of sausage creation.

•

Learning how to ask for help, for me, started with people who had been helped and I found them in meetings. Find one by going to AA.ORG or NA.ORG. Find the link that says, "How to find A.A. Meetings" or "Find a meeting." Also there's probably free coffee. And people who can save your life.

6 (Image Comics, 2007)[62]

Hiyah, earthmen.

In March sometime, I came across an article out of Russia.

A group of thieves had broken into a decommissioned nuclear missile silo to harvest it for salable scarp, and found that is was packed full of money. The wind swept the money across the countryside, and the story got out.

Now: there are nine kinds of stories to tell, right there. These guys had to know what they were doing—how many other silos have they raided? Did any radioactivity or toxins get out? What happened to the missile? Where'd the money come from? Who could arrange

---

61   Holy shit, is this ever true. I went to Dublin and Leeds subsequent to writing this and ate my weight in sausage every morning—as I was no doubt awake at 4, because I can no longer travel east without turning into an insomnia-wracked goon starved for pork in pre-dawn light.

62   This was the first issue I wrote as a full-time, no-other-job, writing-is-what-I-do-and-all-that-I-do, writer. I wrote it in a library off of the Plaza in Kansas City, Missouri in July of 2007.

such a thing? How did they arrange it? Are there more money silos? What happened to THIS money, after the wind blew? What happened to the thieves?

Literally—you could just go on and on. I put the story into the CASANOVA queue, certain that some day it'd come to something.

•

Cut to May, I guess. Browsing around through some old movie posters—I have a bookmark cluster marked FUEL full of page after page of visual junk to trawl for inspiration—I found the poster for a movie called, depending on your source, BLOOD MONEY, THE STRANGER AND THE GUNFIGHTER, or LÁ DOVE NON BATTE IL SOLE, amongst others.

A Spaghetti-Sockey synthesis of the Shaw Brothers and Italian genre hack, Antonio Margheriti, the poster had a glorious painting of Lee Van Cleef, Lieh Lo, and four naked women with a map tattooed across their backs.

Like any of you, I immediately wrote to that noted appreciator of the willfully obscure and Lee Van Cleef aficionado Warren Ellis:

From: matt fraction
Subject: well this just has to be the greatest film of all time
Date: May 3, 2006 3:19:29 PM CDT
To: Warren Ellis

http://www.dvdmaniacs.net/Reviews/A-D/blood_money.html

"Ho reveals to Dakota that there are four clues that, when compiled, will tell them where to find it.
One catch though—each piece of the puzzle is tattooed on a woman's ass."

YOINK.

•

From: Warren Ellis
Subject: Re: well this just has to be the greatest film of all time
Date: May 3, 2006 3:20:51 PM CDT
To: matt fraction

What issue of CASANOVA do you figure that is?

•

From: matt fraction
Subject: Re: well this just has to be the greatest film of all time
Date: May 3, 2006 3:32:52 PM CDT
To: Warren Ellis

6.

(#4 is the one where he kidnaps the new Buddha, and then has to replace him with a ringer before Buddha's scheduled reawakening; #5 is where he has to find the guy hiding out on the island where the last stone-age tribe has lived undisturbed. So #6 is at least the soonest, and that's if I don't do the russian missile silo full of money thing.)

•

And look! I managed to do them both.

Of course, I had to order the film immediately. And so allow me to offer up a few notes by way of review: it is not the greatest film of all time. It never really—as we used to say in art school—transcends its own character. Lee Van Cleef, though, wears a tremendous hat and soldiers through the film with this bemused grin on his face that says, "Sure beats workin'."

And it probably did.

(This is the part of the rambling on about Lee Van Cleef that Warren would want me to remind you all that Lee Van Cleef always had the best hats, and that is what makes him so very worthy of, I dunno, worthiness.

It's kind of true, too.)

•

Around when I was idly looking at kung-fu posters, I came across UV tattoos for the first time. I'd never seen them! I never even imagined it was possible. But I fell in love with the idea of a tattoo being some kind of visual shibboleth or something, permanent ink hidden and invisible, and knew I had to shoehorn it in somewhere. There's a kind of glory in that irony, to me. It's the living embodiment of a proud secret.

(And it gave us the chance to use a different color. So, you know. Hurrah!)

In fact, when I made the CASANOVA t-shirts (What's that? CASANOVA t-shirts? You didn't know? Are you on the CASANOVA emailing list? Drop a line to casanovaquinn@gmail.com and let us know. The Casanovanauts got first dibs on the shirts—some sizes still available. PayPal-ready! 25 bucks! Drop a line! Ask! Buy! Love! What?), I designed the art to be near-invisible, black logo on a black shirt (or grey-on-grey). Same urge, same attraction. Invisible advertising. Maybe it speaks to my time working in advertising? Dunno.

I don't have any tattoos—my wife does, but I don't. The one I came closest to getting would've been the Hitchcock profile doodle on my right arm somewhere. It seemed really important back when I was in film school, I dunno. I lived in Chicago for a while, on a block at Belmot and Sheffield, and there was a bar called HITCHCOCK'S at the other end. I don't think it's there anymore. Chicago is forever entangled with poverty and drunkenness and bad decisions for me. And film, too, which I somehow lost sight of amidst all that drunk drama.

One of my roommates—Bowls (Because he smoked bowls and bowls and bowls of pot.)—had a MATT HELM obsession. In our living room for the longest time—aside from everybody's girlfriend's luggage—was a vintage poster for THE WRECKING CREW, the fourth Matt Helm movie. I think I saw about three or four minutes of it once, and thought it was really sad and stopped watching. Sad old drunk Dean harshed my boner for awesome[63]. But the poster—four hot girls, one of whom was Sharon Tate, all four of whom were riding wrecking balls, and Dean Martin with a gun—always stayed in my mind.

So many movies of that era are better in poster form than movie form, I swear to god.

Anyway. WRECKING CREW. Drunk, in love with movies, and staring at the poster for THE WRECKING CREW. The visual stays with me, even when everything else does not.

Cut to a decade later, and CASANOVA is coming together. I'm listening to a lot of The New Pornographers. Their latest record, TWIN CINEMA—that link to film again—opens with the track, "Use It." There's a line in it—"You better send the Wrecking Crew after," that made me think of those painted girls that I imagined where a team, going after a secret agent.

And and and, Phil Spector's team of session musicians in L.A. were called "The Wrecking Crew[64]." These hardcore pros sat in on sessions for everybody from the Beach Boys to Bing Crosby and back. Carol Kaye, Glen Campbell, Tommy Tedesco, Hal Blaine, conductor Jack Nitzsche…these men and women would put in 10, 12, 15-hour sessions, laying down track after track of classic pop. You dad worked at the office. These guys worked in rock. They were the pulp novelists of AM radio, churning out classical trash under fake names, sweating out the jams like fevers, then going for drinks and doing it all over the next day.

I knew, very very early on, that we would be introducing a teenybopper group of girls that were actually assassins. I don't know where it came from, other than I just thought it was a funny cover story for a group of killers.

Sometimes I feel like writing this book is a bit like playing one of those old-school computer quest games, where in the first room you're in you find, like, a feather, and you hold onto it the whole game until the very last level where you have tickle someone's foot and use that feather, finally. All these bits of detritus that I line my nest with one day become useful.

That was the only easy thing about this issue.

I got late. REAL late. Luckily I was well ahead of Bá, so I had the time to burn, but my goal of having the book wrapped by July fell to shit. The book meaning 6 AND 7, not just 6. I went into convention season without a finished CASANOVA volume under my belt and felt crushing weight come down.[65]

I blocked it out ten, twelve times. Plotted it backwards and forwards and stared at the notebook for, literally, a couple months. I have pages and pages and pages of false starts and miscues. I went until the list failed, then I'd start a new list and repeat until it failed.

•

I made more lists. I kept trying to put it all together and failing. Without blowing where we're gonna end up next month, there's maybe not so much more I can say. But this took me forever to figure out. Even with the knowledge we were doing a two-parter, even knowing the giant robot was waiting in the water, even after mapping out what part of Russia would lead to what part of Japan. You think you have a hard time following the ins and outs of this book? Try planning them sometime. Even though I knew where I wanted it all to go, when we got down to the wrap-up I was paralyzed as to how I'd make it happen.

•

I've scanned mort all of the pages from my notebooks, embarrassing doodles and all, in the interest of making the process transparent. I don't know why, exactly, but it feels like the right thing to do. These pages have been about how the hot dog got made, so in the interest of full disclosure, this is how my thought process ordered itself onto paper. If you can read my handwriting, you can see me get to desperate that I start questioning everything about what I'd written so far. You can feel the panic as I start to doubt my own premise and kept flailing about in too deep waters.

(Anything that you might be able to interpret as a spoiler for the next issue or next arc has been blacked out.)

In the end, the key was Ruby Berserko. Somehow, once I figured out she needed to go undercover—in what is maybe my favorite panel of the series to date, where she's in Cairo, with the veils—everything clicked into place. Everybody was where they needed to be and knew what they needed to know. The endgame was in place, all the pieces were on the board and their roles were locked.

I love Ruby Berserko.

I should get HER tattooed over my heart in invisible ink.

Keep the torrents seeding[66].

---

63   Still does. Read Tosches' DINO to completely disabuse yourself of your Ratpack love and admiration.

64   Read THE WRECKING CREW: THE INSIDE STORY OF ROCK AND ROLL'S BEST-KEPT SECRET by K. Hartman.

65   At HeroesCon, in Charlotte, that summer, I sat next to Jonathan Hickman, who had the first issue of NIGHTLY NEWS with him; I had the first CASANOVA issue and THE FIVE FISTS OF SCIENCE with me, and we sat there, alone, for three days, noodling around in our notebooks and getting to know one another. I only stopped carrying notebooks with me to shows last year.

66   Lifted from the end credits of any MYSTERY SCIENCE THEATER 3000 episode that implored viewers to "Keep Circulating the Tapes."

7 (Image Comics, 2007)

Hiyah, earthmen.

None of this should matter to any of you, but I loved writing—and finishing—this first CASANOVA album (That's right. "Album." Not volume or arc or season or anything else—album. As in, literally, "a collection in book form of short literary or musical pieces or pictures." That's really what this whole thing is to me, looking at it all…and it ties everything back to that Phil Spector stuff and everything else. So fuggit. Album. I'm taking it back!). And now I'm gonna talk about it. And I mean actually talk about the writing of the thing; not what any of it might mean to me, necessarily, or to just, you know, drop names or dork or whatever.

I recognized that there existed some sort of sealed covenant between me and The Process/The Powers That Be/The Big Whatever when someone broke into our house on The Worst Christmas Eve Ever, 2005, just after I wrote the scene where Casanova Quinn broke into Winston Heath's house. Payback's a motherfucker, y'know?

I got robbed one-on-one before, but this whole violation-of-my-space-and-there-were-bad-guys-rooting-through-my-shit thing felt all-new and all-shitty. Add to that the holiday; add to that we found out from 1100 miles away at the time; add to that the *will-somebody-please-find-the-goddamn-cats* terrors; add to that the weird fingerprint power ghosts lying in wait for us to return, my wife's scattered clothes on the floor, the antique cameras these shitfuck thieves carried from one room to the next before deciding them un-pawn-worthy, and…

And I felt colder and crueler towards my lead character. I wanted to punish Casanova Quinn for his transgressions. I knew this arc— Album! Shit! Sorry!—would see Casanova gradually realizing the world was larger, more important and, in some small way, more satisfying than his own hedonism. But, burglarized after romping through two chapters of freewheelin' good times, I now wanted to blacken Casanova's blood a little bit, to punish the little shit, and most of all, I wanted to show The Big Whatever that I gave and got in equal goddamn measure. Okay, I thought to Casanova Quinn, *bring your weak ass on.*

The point, Gentle Reader?

I takes a tremendous amount of magical thinking—ice cold and shaken up with three fingers of ego—to correlate a random act of poverty-inspired crime with a bare-knuckle fistfight with your own creative process and, indeed, fate itself…the kind of magical thinking and ego, Gentle Reader, *that I have in spades.*

When the last line sat there, finally written, I got to sit back and see the whole game-board for the first time. CASANOVA gave me a lens, and through it I bent the strange light of this strange year as it fell all around me in whatever weird way felt appropriate. I look back at these seven issues and see that year (really, a bit longer, but not by much) broken up and re-encoded amongst the pages. There's a part of me astonished at how naked my life looks in CASANOVA…then I remember it's all Superbuddhas and three-faced Ruby and whatnot and all that emotional blood-and-guts stuff makes no sense to anyone but me. I made CASANOVA *my* semaphore, you know? Not yours or anybody else's (I bet Gabriel and Sean can look back and see the same things. Christ! As much work as those two put in, I sure hope they can.).

•

Writing the first issue burned a molten hole through my head. When I finished, I realized that, holy shit, *this changes everything.* Sitting back and seeing the whole shape now, it occurs to me that maybe—maaaaaaaybe—that understates it a little bit.

Get ready to learn the secret ingredient, the special sauce, the thing I couldn't articulate until now…the mystery key to this whole Imagine Slimline™© Format. I think you gotta bleed for it. You gotta wail away in these pages as hard as you can and believe in what you do like what you do means saving the world. You can approach it however you like, but when you stick that goddamn landing and come arms-up for the world to see, the look on your face has to sell it. Even if nobody else believes—or cares, or even reads the thing— when you fight in this ring, you gotta fight like you mean it.[67]

(Shit, just look at FELL, our sister book, to see what I mean. Has Warren Ellis every written a more Ellis-ian character than poor old Richard Fell? Has Ellis ever put himself or his concerns, fears, and interest down onto the page so nakedly (Maybe with John Cain in SCARS…but that's a guy tied to Richard Fell by a very short line)? Add to that the haunted and hungry career-best work (FUCKING KILLS ME TO SAY IT[68]) Ben Templesmith bleeds into that book and you begin to understand that what makes FELL so fantastic all happens inside, beneath, and under what any of us actually get to read…)

That's the sauce of this particular chaos, maybe. Belief, faith, sincerity, whatever you want to call it. You gotta fucking ache for it, sometimes; whatever you feel, feel big. Nobody else pays for this ticket but you. Nobody else can pay for it. You gotta put it all out there and let your dick hang in the breeze with such fearless conviction that *you can write obnoxiously sad shit like this thing right here* and *not care at all.*

What have I learned, Charlie Brown? This format kills fakers.

Now here's the tricky part: that runs antithetical to the way I live and work. I keep my shit wired tight, or I try to, anyway. My wife, born in a strange and alien land called Toomuchinformationsburgh, rolls a little differently. But me? What happens to me stays with me. And yet, the deal meant that to whatever or wherever this book wanted to take me, I had to allow myself to get taken. To stomach seeing it, I made it an intimate and personal code. So: you see seven issues about a spoiled hedonist and criminal finding secret science fiction islands and three-headed transgendered robots, I see an emo-factor 10 *Dear Diary* engagement with my personal creative process.

Like I said before, none of that should matter to anybody; I only offer it up in the interest of full disclosure here at the end of our time together.

---

67 I don't know what all this "you" shit is all about. *I* needed to do it this way.

68 Because Ben and I did a 30 DAYS OF NIGHT story together called JUAREZ and I loved working with him, and his work on FELL was even better, and I was envious.

Something austere and holy hid inside CASANOVA for me, waiting to be hatched, and I knew it from Jump Street. Every pathetically little bit of instinct I have screamed something when I started writing, and that usually means *pay attention, Fuck-O*. Once its shell cracked—once I bolted upright from a catnap I was taking on my couch, the first page with the CITIZEN KANE gage in my head—I knew I became the parent of a child way more powerful than me. I bought the ticket; I took the ride; I would put it all down on the page or the page would break me in two. Even if only I see it, I swear to god that, across these seven issues, I held up my end of the deal[69].

•

At some point it became impossible for me to not see the details of my life perpetually intertwined with the fictional details of Casanova's life, whether I planned it or not. Everything I went through got predicted or reinterpreted here. I went to San Francisco, so Cass could go to San Francisco. I wanted to punish a burglar so Cass got punished. As my own long-hibernating work began to awaken, so did David X wake up from his nap. And on and on.

Then, after I quit my day-job, we lost the baby.

Let me back up.

I knocked up my wife. We found out on June 15th. My friend Chris played a piano recital that night, so we kept it to ourselves.

For like a day.

Our exuberance overwhelmed the first trimester caution-watch and we told more people than we should. My wife's breasts became magnificent.

A couple weeks before that, I celebrated the sixth birthday of the company I helped start with some school friends after we graduated or just plain old dropped out. It functioned as my primary creative outlet and source of income, first professional priority, and, now that I look back on it, the band of my existence. Faced with the notion of a child on the way, I realized I didn't love my job anymore. I didn't want to work the kind of hours it, on occasion, demanded; I didn't want the responsibility it could, with no notice, drop upon me. I realized I didn't want to live life as an absentee father, and, as my wife's breasts kept becoming more magnificent, I started to think seriously about exit strategies. And boobs. But mostly exit strategies.

Then I got in a fight with my co-partners and just quit spontaneously. For right or for wrong, I ripped the fucking band-aid right off and got on a plane with my wife to visit my parents and attend HeroesCon in Charlotte, NC. That way, I could break the news to my parents in person that, while they were becoming grandparents, I had not regular employment.

Just like that, the whole *I love my job* theme that Cass fought through over these seven issues took on a new context. I saw, for the first time, what I really wrote about. Cass, me, the jobs and the identities we chose to identify ourselves with...I hadn't been writing about free-spirited Cass not wanting anybody to tell hi what to do—*I wrote about me*. I dunno, maybe a shrink could nail that from 100 meters but sure as shit, *it blew my mind*.

It was the big stuff, right? Not the dumb little *I'm on a Beatles kick* lagniappe. In one weird heartbeat I realized just how deep The Big Whatever had taken me.

Oh! So. The night of July 1st, Kelly Sue (my wife) felt a sharp pain in her belly. She suspected the worst; I denied and sang "Hang on Little Tomato" until I stopped feeling scared. Cramping started by Sunday. By Tuesday morning, the miscarriage passed, and we got on the plane taking us home (HeroesCon does not cause miscarriages. Neither do spoken-word events with Warren Ellis).

In the Minnesota airport, where we had a layover, I implored her to buy a lottery ticket. "C'mon—it's your lucky day," I said. She did. She won a hundred bucks. SUCK IT, MISCARRIAGE (You laugh because otherwise you cry. Miscarriages happen with ridiculous frequency—1 in 5, some counts even suggest 1 in 4—and people don't realize it. We can put a man on the moon, and I lived 30 goddamn years in mortal terror that just the sight of my un-latex-wrapped penis by a naked woman could cause spontaneous pregnancy, but the second we pull the goalie and TRY for kids, it becomes a minor miracle that anybody gets pregnant, ever.).

•

I don't really know what else to say here, but I can't tell where I should stop. I held it in my hands. I wrapped it in my Mom's yellow hand-towel and sealed it in a Ziploc freezer bag to bring with us, because the doctors on the phone asked me. I cried so hard I thought my lungs would burst. I would suffocate, when nobody else could see—I would go into dark and empty rooms where I took deep, gulping panic breaths but no air came. You ever want to feel helpless? Watch your wife miscarry. It hurts like a motherfucker.

I had to deal with it. Annnnd, as petty and small and ridiculous and inappropriate and absurd and embarrassing as it all sounds, the place I had chosen (or was chosen for me) to deal with all stuff great and small was this goddamn book.

I dealt with it by not killing Zephyr Quinn.

Originally, I intended Zephyr to buy it in the process of making a noble sacrifice, giving up her botched and blackened life to save her maybe-brother, hoping that he could find his redemption in her redemption.

And yet, when the time came, I felt like I'd seen enough blood; indeed, I *had* enough blood on my hands for one summer. So I got home from con season and, instead of finishing this book as a father-to-be with a meaningful and secure job, I sat down to write it as a terrified freelance writer for the first time in my life, struggling, with my wife, to keep our minds, our spirits, and probably even our marriage intact.

---

69   Ellis once said to me that my writing process was like I had one day fell on a nail and, with my shinbone, drove it through a plank and now that's just how I think nails go into wood. He's not wrong. I could make this easier on myself. I really could.

Through that, Zeph got her second chance.

Zeph commits heinous, senseless, meaningless acts of violence. She breaks hearts and spills blood everywhere she goes. She leaves people crying so hard their lungs hurt. And last issue? *She killed a kid.*

Still. I forgave her. *You* don't have to, but I did. I had to so I could hold up my end of the deal, so I could move on, and so Cass could follow suit.

Now I'm sweeping up and putting the chairs on the tables, right back where I started—staring The Big Whatever right in the face, thinking, *bring your weak ass on.*

•

And so as Casanova Quinn discovers some sense of chastity for the first time in his life (By which I mean the classical sense of chastity—courage and moral strength through sacrifice. Not the sexual kind of chastity that, uh, remains wholly undiscovered by Cass.), the curtain closes on CASANOVA: LUXURIA (That's Latin for "lust." Maybe naming your book after your theme is a little too on-the-nose. I don't know. Who cares? Yes.). As planned, we take a hiatus and then will return.

The second album, CASANOVA: GULA, beings in late summer of fall of 2007. I wish I knew a firmer date than that. For up-to-the-minute updates, though, you can subscribe to the CASANOVANAUTS newsletter by sending an email to casanovaquinn@gmail.com.

My esteemed colleague, collaborator, co-conspirator, and constant inspiration, Mr. Gabriel Bá, will next publish work in Dark Horse's upcoming series THE UMBRELLA ACADEMY. It's co-created and written by Gerard Way, he of the band MY CHEMICAL ROMANCE. Their epic rage-against-the-darkness album THE BLACK PARADE rightfully landed on a lot of Best-Of lists this year, and I can't wait to see what these two cook up together.

To you, sir, and to the others in our little murder of crow: To Sean Konot, with your infinite fucking patience in dealing with me; to Laurenn McCubbin, who I could never, ever throw off a cliff, no matter how much I thought I'd get away with it; to Drew McGill, who redefines grace under pressure on a regular basis; to Eric Stephenson at Image for clearing us for take-off in the first place; and to all the CASANOVANAUTS, whether you wrote to me the second you saw the FELL ad or tonight as I wrote this (Hi Paul E.! Hi John C.!)—to all of you I can only offer my unending gratitude.

See you next year, motherfuckers. Keep the torrents seeding.

4 (Icon Comics, 2010)

One of the towering monuments of my development as a comic writer...as a comic reader...hell, just as a person...was Howard Chaykin's AMERICAN FLAGG! It remains, to this day, one of my very favorite comics ever published. I've read the fist issue eighty-nine thousand four hundred times. I love it.

The epoch-defining and groundbreaking first year of Howard Chaykin's AMERICAN FLAGG! is, after decades of exile to back issue bins and long boxes, reprinted by Dynamic Forces and Image Comics at the moment.

Without FLAGG! there is no CASANOVA; in a way, without FLAGG! there is no me. Howard Chaykin's AMERICAN FLAGG! was the comic that showed me what comics could do.

•

Matt Fraction: Now that Dynamic Forces has put out a remastered collection of AMERICAN FLAGG!—the first time in at least, what, 20 years that the material has been readily available?—I was wondering if you had a chance to go back and look at it again. Not for typos or quality control or for editorial purposes but rather...as a reader, as a guy that made it however many years on. When you look at FLAGG! today, what do you see?

Howard V. Chaykin: It feels a bit presumptuous and hubristic. I believe a major flaw in my thinking has often been a mistaken assumption that my tastes, beliefs, and sensibilities are at least common, and frequently universal. This certainly plays out in FLAGG!—but comes to a head in TIME(SQUARED).

That said, I've had more than one twinge of bitterness at a number of elements of graphic design applied to narrative that seem to have been absorbed into the modern vocabulary without any acknowledgment.

In sum, it feels reasonably clever and mildly smutty—and I wish I'd been a more sophisticated draftsman, because many of the graphic ideas and nuances might have been better served by more evolved drawing.

MF: When I was a part of MK12 and I'd see our work ripped off—subtly or blatantly, and always for more money than we ever made, and at far greater profiles—I got to a point where I couldn't handle how angry it'd make me, so I just started repeating, "It's an honor to be part of the global design discussion," like a mantra while praying for the screaming hot death of my enemies.
HVC: I usually go right for the ass cancer.

MF: Where were you, in your life, when work started on FLAGG? How old were you, what were you up to, what was your life like away from the drawing table? What fueled something as ambitious as FLAGG?

HVC: I was 31, soon to be 32. Married to my second wife, Leslie, living a very typical life of a young childless couple in Manhattan. We had a pretty good time, in a terrific apartment, hanging with my pals and hers—entertaining at home—ours and theirs—and in saloons.

FLAGG! was inspired by the offer of what was, at the time, a shitload of money—that would subsidize a personal vision, created for FIRST COMICS, a company with no baggage or history whatsoever.

Here was an opportunity to pull out the stops and see what I could do with my limited toolkit, without the governor of preconceptions. I felt that most comics were lazy at best, patronizing at worst, so I tried to create a book that assumed you weren't an idiot, and would be willing to work a bit harder on a potentially more rewarding dense product.

I wish I'd anticipated the hate mail and death threats.

MF: FLAGG! was my first encounter with a comic that refused to accept I was so dumb as to NEED a story told in a six-panel grid or whatever. It's that old saw that "it teaches you to read it as you read it," but goddamn, it did. From there to TIME(SQUARED) thought BLACKHAWK and, and I guess up through your retirement/exile (your first retirement/exile?), your work never ever ever treated me like a dumb kid. If I didn't get it, I kept fucking reading until I did. And, y'know, coming from the world of six-panel grids...that was a revelation.

Anyway, you'll be happy to hear that's still the way things are, and I don't think I've done anything REMOTELY as aggressively intelligent as FLAGG! When I get "rage" as a response to CASANOVA, it's...I'm sure the French or the Germans have a word for "amusing and yet depressing"...but that's what it is, to see the build-in self-contempt that some comics readers have for themselves laid so bare like that. How dare you try, etc., etc. God forbid you aspire; god forbid your reach exceeds the most rudimentary of grasps.

What kind of stuff were you reading and watching and listening to going into FLAGG! and during? Any recall? When did you start... you're the first modern cartoonist I can think of that has a vested interest in fashion and the fashionable—that might not be accurate but anecdotally it is, so fuck it—so where does that come into your toolkit? What other comics? Were you at Upstart by this point?

HVC: I honestly can't recall what I was reading at the time. What was worth watching on TV was Bochco's stuff—as well as other material from MTM.

As for music, a lot of Van Morrison, Ry Cooder, the Band, Procol Harum...some of the San Francisco psychedelic stuff...Gram Parsons, Poco, Michael Nesmith—and I was just beginning to get a grasp of jazz—mostly through vocalists like Sarah Vaughn, Billie Holiday and Lee Wiley.

I became a Eurotrash wannabe clothes whore in the mid-70s, when all the fuckwads who'd called me a faggot for having long hair all of a sudden looked like the Allman brothers. I cut off my hair, started pomading and changed my presentation from freak slob to well cut and well tailored oil bag.

This led me to give a serious shit about clothes, and in turn informed my drawing of both clothing and costume.

I might add that as you well know, those days are gone, and I'm back to being a complete slob—go figure.
And yes, I was at Upstart—from late 1978 to October 1985.

MF: I know you were a comic guy as a kid; were you a science fiction guy, too?

Who was working in Upstart as you were cranking on FLAGG! around that time?

HVC: Gifted as I legendarily am for the recollection of the irrelevant and utterly trivial, I'm embarrassed to admit that I have no memory of what I was reading, beyond Chandler, Hammett, Cain, and their imitators. By the time I did FLAGG!, I'd had my interest in SF beaten out of me by Archie Goodwin—and the only material in that genre that I'd read back then was stuff for which I was providing cover art. Upstart was originally Simonson, Starlin, Mayerik, and me. Mayerik decided to leave, and asked Jim Sherman to take his place—significantly never bothering to ask any of the three of us whether this was okay.

Starlin then decided to move upstate, and he brought in Frank Miller as his replacement—which we all signed off on.

In my last two years working there, I brought Larry O'Neil and Dean Haspiel in as assistants.

MF: I just want to point out—because not many people know this that Frank's DAREDEVIL and RONIN, Walter's STARSLAMMERS and THOR, and your FLAGG! were all being produced in the same room at the same time.

Hey, so what was Archie like? He's one of those guys most folks of my wave, and at least a couple waves prior, never got a chance to work with and we still hear about. One of the legendary guys, y'know? He and Mark Gruenwald...

HVC: I could be crazy, but Archie always struck me as a guy who was committed to playing the hand he was dealt—in a sanguine manner beyond the men of my generation, and certainly impossible to consider for those guys who came up after me.
A brilliant talent, and an unnervingly patient man, blessed with an enviable dignity.

Gruenwald I barely knew, but he struck me as an odd guy—in an odd man's field. He and a number of other guys tried to create a side career as comedians, but it never came to anything.

MF: So was there any editorial oversight with FLAGG! beyond what you yourself put on the page? Had you worked much outside of the big two at that point, had you worked much without an editorial boot on your neck?

HVC: Most of my contact with First was with Mike Gold, who clearly, in retrospect, felt comfortable giving me enough rope to hang myself. I don't recall any wrangles with him—as opposed to the constant wrestling matches with Rick Oliver—where the hell he is—on TIME(SQUARED).

The last time I'd worked with that much freedom had been on the STAR-REACH stuff but by the time I did FLAGG!, I was far more disciplined and organized.

MF: I should've asked this earlier, but I'm callow and dull. What can you tell me about the look of FLAGG!, in terms of how the graphic idea came to be executed? Do you recall if there was a lot of experimentation on your part to get to the look of the thing, did it come fairly effortlessly? And that visual density—that had to be monstrous to create on a monthly schedule. Was there burnout for you on FLAGG! along the way?

HVC: Nothing came easy. It was all about roughs, analysis, failure, redoing—along with all the accidental solutions that become vocabulary.

It also took all my time, seven days a week, a minimum of ten hours a day, and terminally damaged my second marriage—which came to an end a few months after we'd relocated to Los Angeles in 1985.

MF: Christ, man. That's awful.

What was the reaction to that wave of independent, creator-owned books like FLAGG! like? You said you got death threats and hate mail, so there's that but I'm curious about what reaction was like from your peers, from folks that were both working in an independent idiom and those still doing work for hire stuff...I know that's kind of an unfair and broadly diffuse question; that wave of books, that era, set the mold for the creator owned stuff guys like me do today. And I don't just mean aesthetically but as an entity in the direct market.

HVC: Actually, I considered the death threats a badge of honor—at least I was pissing somebody off.

As for the reaction, cat yronwode, who never seemed to understand that being an independent publisher, and thus competition, reviewed and hated the book. But then again, she worshipped Eisner, who as you know, I believe had utter contempt for her and those like here—so what did she know?

Kim Thompson saw black and whites at a small press expo, loved it, and gave it big play in AMAZING HEROES, for which I've been forever grateful.

Shooter at Marvel was completely indifferent—not the sort of thing that interested him, or, frankly, that he'd understand.

Jenette Kahn at DC seemed peevish that I hadn't published with them, but I said then and believe now that the lack of history at First was a direct contributor to FLAGG!'s otherness.

Most of my colleagues seemed to like it, and it generated the first positive response to my work from Gil Kane.

MF: Gil did what's arguably the first American graphic novel with BLACKMARK in 1971—was he into where comics were going with the kind of work you guys were doing?

HVC: Actually, he predated that with what most of my generation regard as the first American graphic novel, HIS NAME IS SAVAGE, in 1966. He, along with Alex, was a huge fan of Richard Corben—who pointed the way for a lot of us. Gil grudgingly respected the work I did on FLAGG!, and was open to new stuff. He had no taste for Sienkiewicz, for example, unlike Alex, who was a fan—while Gil was in awe of Michael Golden.

MF: I know you STILL get backlash on FLAGG! by...I don't know what to call it exactly, "the establishment" or whatever. I'm thinking of your cover piece and story in ALTER EGO recently where the brief 'History of HFCF!' piece diverted onto a tangent regarding the outrage to the sex and violence and language that appeared in the book, only for an editor's not where the editor of the magazine itself revealed that it was HE who objected then in the letter column and now as *the editor of the fucking magazine* to the content FLAGG!... was that reaction common? Surely there had to be weirdoes like me who thought it hung the moon, too, right?

HVC: Fuck them. ALTER EGO? Did I miss something?

MF: Shit, maybe I got the wrong magazine title. One of those Two Morrows deals. I dunno, you did the cover. Captain America and Reuben Flagg back to back...?

HVC: I had plenty of positive response, resulting in a lot of people showing up at shows dressed as Rangers, or in lingerie.

MF: Okay, that's the best fucking thing ever.

What can you tell me about how you and Ken Bruzenak worked together? It's so seamless on the page, you guys made work both in FLAGG! And again in TIME(SQUARED)...it's impossible to think of the work without him. How did you two manage to work—or at least make it look like you worked—in such syncopation?

HVC: In retrospect, I'm astonished at how well everything worked out. I lived and worked in Manhattan, Ken was in Reading PA. We spoke frequently but rarely got together. FedEx was our connection. He'd letter directly on the page and I'd move and adjust their location with xerography and spray mount.

Same with logos and signage. Xeroxes and paste-ups. The pages were a filthy mess, but camera ready.

Needles to say, I love working with Ken Bruzenak, who I level is an unsung giant, a major contributor to the graphic language of comic book lettering and type design. He's been picked over and borrowed from without acknowledgement from word one by nearly everybody who came along after him—

—And he's an award-winning ballroom dancer, as well.

MF: …Now I think you're just fucking with me.

HVC: Absolutely god's honest truth. Ken is a great dancer—and has done serious time on the circuit. Not for a few years, however.

MF: So, okay—last bit, I swear. Absolutely everything I love about your work—everything I love about YOU, even—is in FLAGG! (And if FLAGG! Is the Rosetta stone of "you," and I think you could argue the case, then TIME(SQUARED) is that shone compressed down like a goddamn diamond, but that's another show, Oprah…) Not just visually, although that's as true as anything else, but as a piece of writing it's all there at some point. The pulp stuff, the political stuff, the sex, the cynicism, it's funny as fuck…So I'm wondering, when considered as a piece of writing, as removed from its visual techniques as one can…what do you see in it now when you read it as a story? And what does the write you are now, what do you make of FLAGG?

HVC: It's astonishingly difficult to separate the visual from the textual—because in a FLAGG!, I felt I'd finally found a series of keys to the language of comics that could compete on their own terms with preexisting graphic narrative systems. Fuck—does that sound pretentious, or what?

That said, I feel there's a snarky wit and some cleverness to the dialogue, and the plots, as convoluted as they get, still seem structurally sound. In retrospect, I've come to believe the book did better in the southeast and Midwest than on the coasts, because the readers there had more of an appetite for smut—and in England because of the above mentioned snarkiness.

It never translated particularly well into foreign languages, which hurt its international sales.

And TIME(SQUARED) was too fucking oblique, not to say opaque, for its own good—but I still can reread it with relish. The best thing I can say about both books, and ultimate the thing that let them slip through the cracks, was that neither could be summed up in one line.

What I'm proudest of in these books was the broader comedy—an aspect of comics writing sorely lacking in modern comics.

When I write today, I can't help myself—I still always look for laughs—because I may not be the smartest guy in the room, but I might be the cleverest.

Does that make me sound like too much of an asshole?

MF: Have you read CASANOVA? That kind of reach vs. grasp argument is the coin of the fucking realm.

HVC: Unlike the currently dead Will Eisner, who passed judgment on everything despite his awareness of whatever being discussed or the lack thereof, I'm embarrassed to admit I have not—and of course, now I have to in order to stay in you and your wife's good graces.

Shame on me.

MF: Well, it's all downhill from here.

•

COLORS

Three different stages of the colors on our book.

First we have the original black and green art.

Second is the first rendering Cris delivered.

Finally, we have the final version, with the colors from the palette.

CASANOVA is a comic from another time. That's the whole concept behind its craziness and for all my artistic choices. When I first decided to make it black, white and green, it was a way to make it look like an old comic, with all the production and printing limitations of the past, things that would force creators to make artistic choices in order to achieve what they meant to.

Personally, I love the black and green look.

When we decided now it was time to go full color, the concept behind the colors was still the same as before and that's what I had to explain to Cris.

We still want every story arc to have a dominant color and LUXURIA would still be green. That's all I told her before she sent me the first samples, just so we could see what she did right and what was wrong and which way we would go from there.

We are really old school when it comes to comic book art, so we like to make stuff by hand, work in black and white and, if need be, flat colors. Whatever goes outside these borders doesn't really fit with our art style, so we banned all the gradients, airbrushes and smooth, shining areas on the first batch of colors. I wanted it all flat, and of course it's harder to make everything flat, because you have to make decisions

when to break one color with the other, how to combine these colors. A smooth transition is always easier, but we're making a comic book and we need all our creativity focused on the graphic aspect of the process.

After we established that, I took her samples and selected some colors she used, mixed some others and created the "CASANOVA PALETTE" for her to use. These 45 colors (and I still think it's too much) were all the colors she could use on the pages.

The last step of the process was choosing the combination of colors, how to use one or the other to enhance the mood of a scene, how to create more drama, how to help the story. Making the foreground pop up a little more, get the focus on the right point of the scene, make clear which panel is the most important one of the page, these kinds of things.

As with everything else about this comic, it's a very difficult process and it takes a lot of back and forth between us and Cris, but in the end it looks great. We are so happy with the results that sometimes we forget there was a time the comic was not in full color.

Gabriel Bá

CASANOVA PALETTE

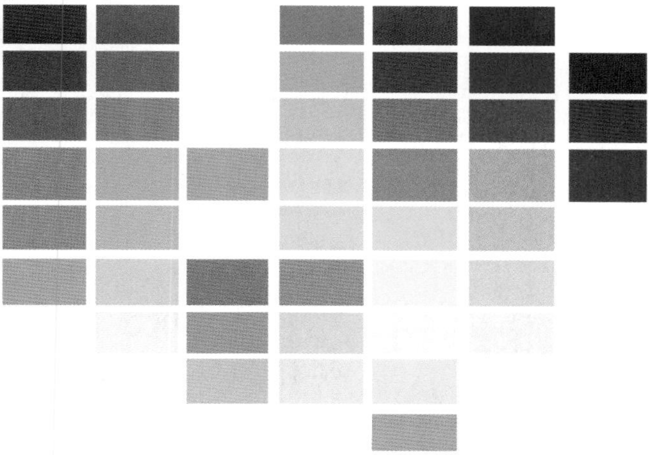

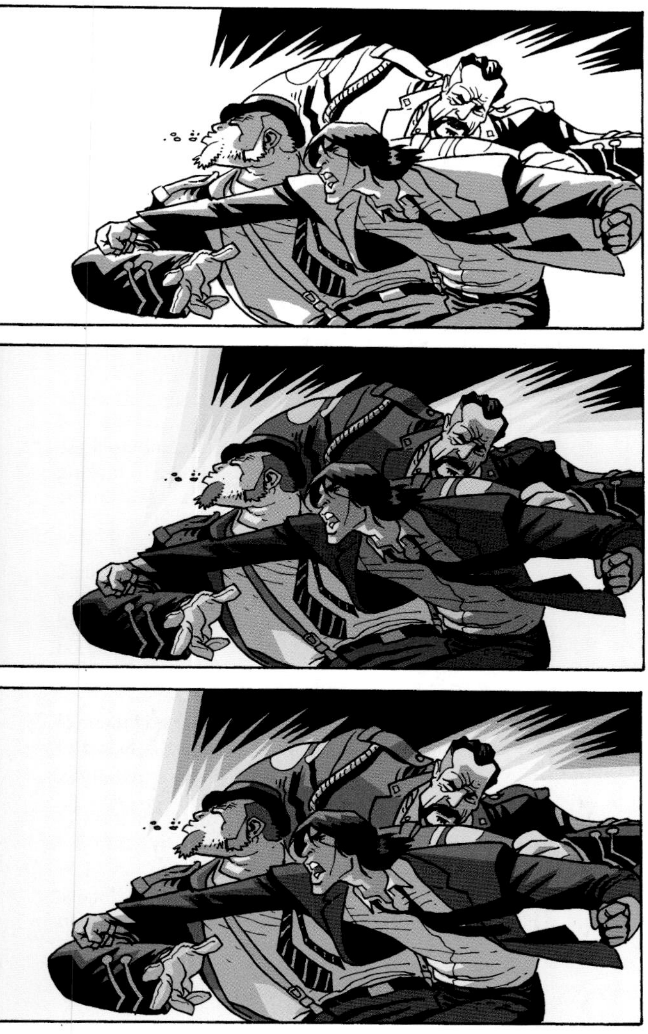

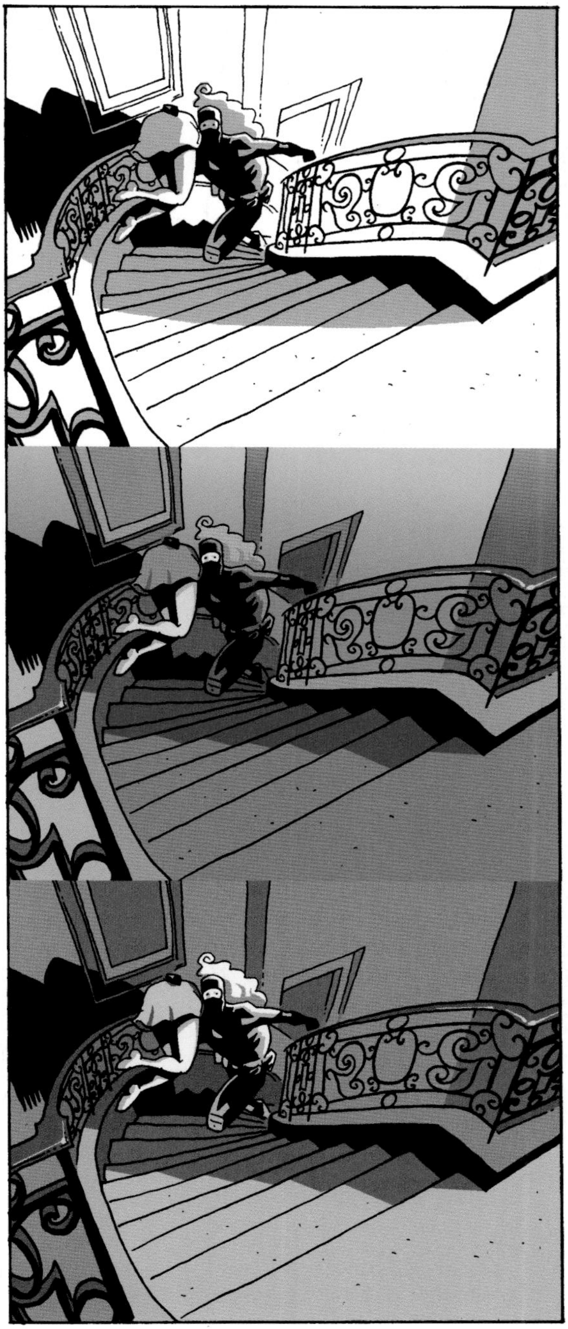

When you first start doing digital colors, you know that you have all the colors you can imagine to work with. After Gabriel set that 45-color palette, I was actually thrilled! It is this kind of thing that forces you to really use your head to color.

In this business, with the short deadlines and pressure, after a while a colorist can start doing combinations and rendering almost automatically, without really thinking about what you're doing to the storytelling, but challenges like these make you grow as a professional, make you start thinking about doing the best work you can, to be a part of an awesome project.

Working with CASANOVA it's been a real learning experience, it made me remember why I got into coloring comics in the first place.

Cris Peter

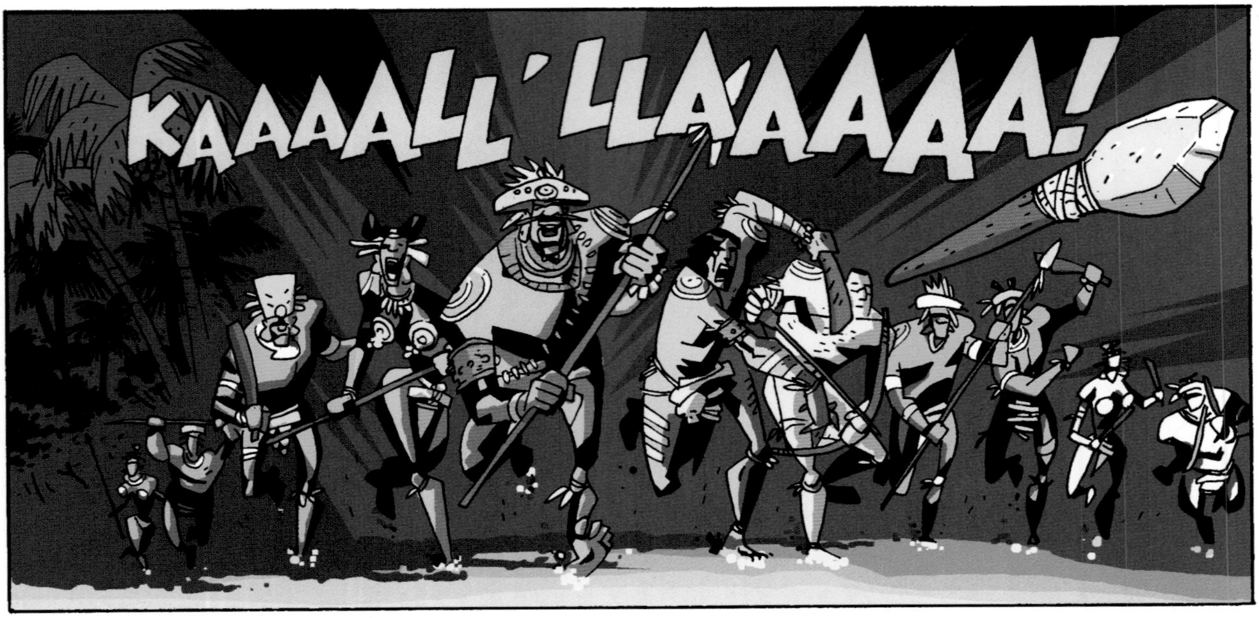
KAAAALL' LLAAAAA!

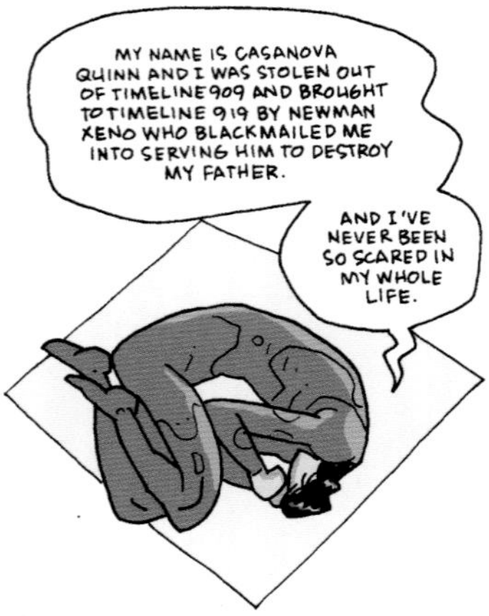
MY NAME IS CASANOVA QUINN AND I WAS STOLEN OUT OF TIMELINE 909 AND BROUGHT TO TIMELINE 919 BY NEWMAN XENO WHO BLACKMAILED ME INTO SERVING HIM TO DESTROY MY FATHER.
AND I'VE NEVER BEEN SO SCARED IN MY WHOLE LIFE.

LETTERS

Hand-lettering is kind of a weird animal in the digital age. I could go on for days about it, and argue both sides of a digital-vs-analog discussion with passion and zeal. At the end of the day hand-lettering and computer-lettering are just different tools, the application is always in the hands of the artist. But real honest-to-gosh hand-lettering has a certain feel to it that can be hard to replace with a font. In my case, that "feel" is comprised of sloppiness, blobby inscrutability, and typos.

But since I started working on CASANOVA I've been refining my process, trying to get faster—oh boy, lettering by hand is a time consumer of Galactus-ian (comic book reference) proportions—by using a mishmash of analog and digital tools. By the time I was lettering CASANOVA #4, I was penciling the letters on legal size pieces of bristol board. I'd print the art, blown up by about 115%, in black and white, then use a lightbox to plan the balloons out: where they'll go, how many/how long the lines will be, where their little tails will point. I'd pre-print the boards with very light gray guidelines on my trusty b&w laserjet printer, so I could just move any old where to stick a balloon.

Once I fill up the board with infinitesimal pencil marks, usually about eight comics pages worth per board, depending on the script, I shut down the retina-scalding lightbox and ink everything up with Rapidograph pens. I work REALLY small—I think the blown-up letters are still smaller than most sane people's handwriting—so the Rapidographs help me keep everything consistent. Then everything gets scanned in to the computer, fiddled with, corrected, and sharpened up, and the pasteup work begins, moving each individual balloon into place over Cris's gorgeous colors.

As of this writing, I'm working on the second issue of the sextastic GULA story-arc, and now I have a Wacom Cintiq tablet as part of my process. I'm actually drawing the letters right on the screen, then I print out very light bluelines and ink those. Saves a ton of time and makes the planning a lot easier.

If all this sounds super-boring, don't worry, it is! The real calling of the letterer is to be mostly invisible. A letterer is like a bass player—great to have in the band, but you don't want him soloing or anything. So most of this stuff is just the web of supports and cables and litter and hobos under a really gorgeous awesome bridge or something. You can check it out if you like, but really, the bridge is the cool part. Although CASANOVA is like the most sexiest, righteousest bridge to work under, let me tell you.

Dustin Harbin

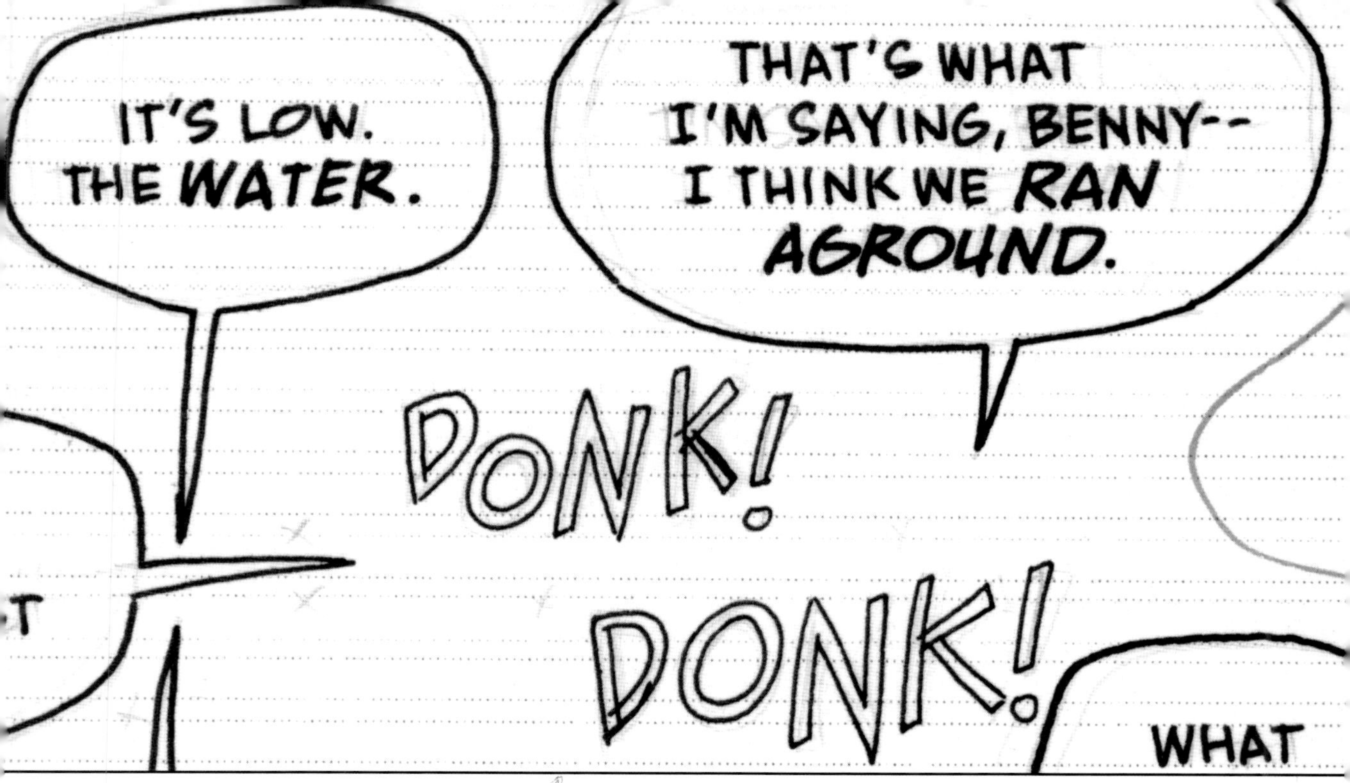
IT'S LOW. THE WATER.
THAT'S WHAT I'M SAYING, BENNY-- I THINK WE RAN AGROUND.
DONK!
DONK!
WHAT

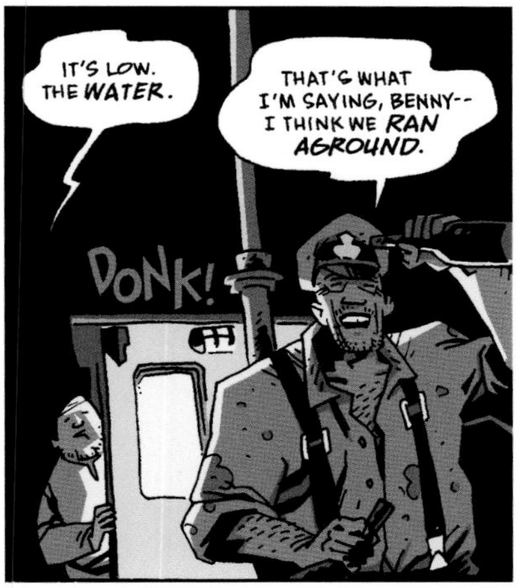
IT'S LOW. THE WATER.
THAT'S WHAT I'M SAYING, BENNY-- I THINK WE RAN AGROUND.
DONK!

On the right, a page filled with Dustin's letters and balloons, a crazy mash of shapes, words, sounds on a maze only he can get his way around. It's actually really organized visually.

On the top, a close up on some balloons and sound effects that will go on the finalized colored panel right above this text.

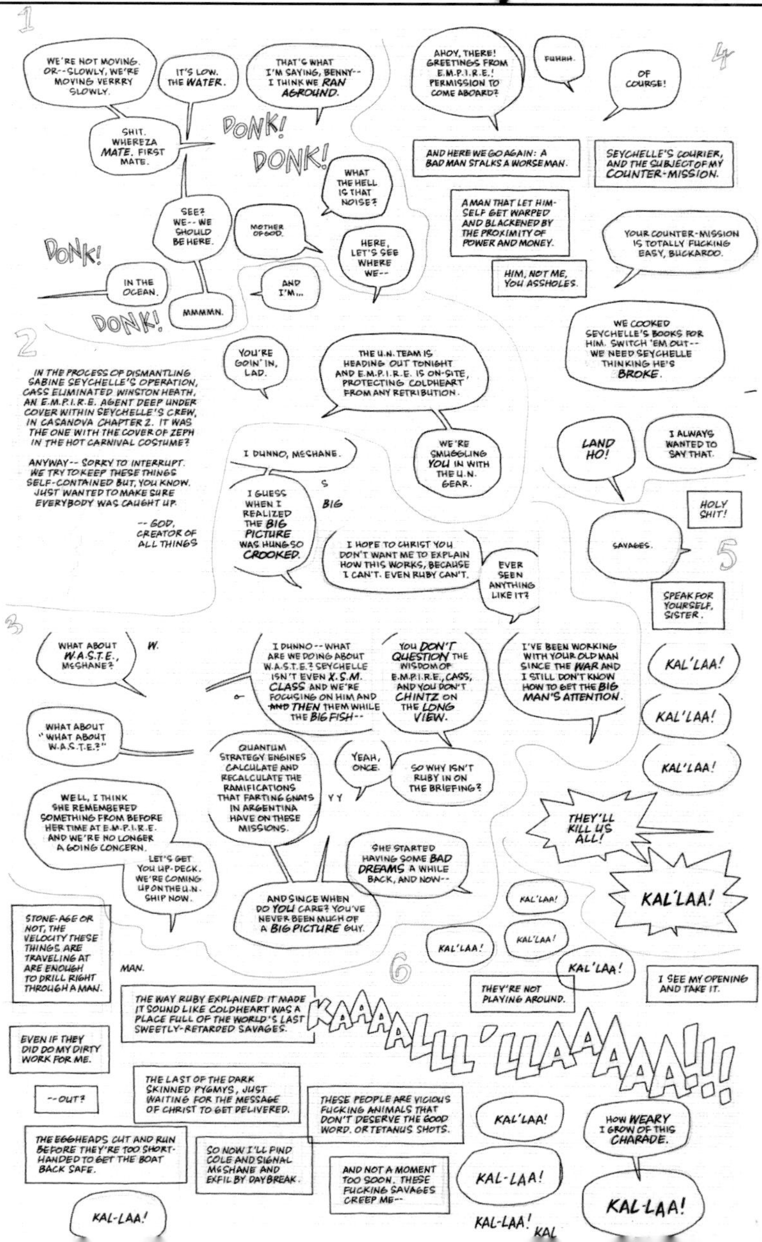
1
WE'RE NOT MOVING. OR--SLOWLY, WE'RE MOVING VERRY SLOWLY.
IT'S LOW. THE WATER.
THAT'S WHAT I'M SAYING, BENNY-- I THINK WE RAN AGROUND.
SHIT. WHEREZA MATE. FIRST MATE.
DONK!
DONK!
WHAT THE HELL IS THAT NOISE?
SEE? WE--WE SHOULD BE HERE.
MOTHER OF GOD.
HERE, LET'S SEE WHERE WE--
DONK!
IN THE OCEAN.
AND I'M...
MMMMN.
DONK!
AHOY, THERE! GREETINGS FROM E.M.P.I.R.E.! PERMISSION TO COME ABOARD?
FUHHH.
4
OF COURSE!
AND HERE WE GO AGAIN: A BAD MAN STALKS A WORSE MAN.
SEYCHELLE'S COURIER, AND THE SUBJECT OF MY COUNTER-MISSION.
A MAN THAT LET HIMSELF GET WARPED AND BLACKENED BY THE PROXIMITY OF POWER AND MONEY.
YOUR COUNTER-MISSION IS TOTALLY FUCKING EASY, BUCKAROO.
HIM, NOT ME, YOU ASSHOLES.
WE COOKED SEYCHELLE'S BOOKS FOR HIM. SWITCH 'EM OUT-- WE NEED SEYCHELLE THINKING HE'S BROKE.
2
IN THE PROCESS OF DISMANTLING SABINE SEYCHELLE'S OPERATION, CASS ELIMINATED WINSTON HEATH, AN E.M.P.I.R.E. AGENT DEEP UNDER COVER WITHIN SEYCHELLE'S CREW, IN CASANOVA CHAPTER 2. IT WAS THE ONE WITH THE COVER OF ZEPH IN THE HOT CARNIVAL COSTUME?
ANYWAY-- SORRY TO INTERRUPT. WE TRY TO KEEP THESE THINGS SELF-CONTAINED BUT, YOU KNOW. JUST WANTED TO MAKE SURE EVERYBODY WAS CAUGHT UP.
-- GOD, CREATOR OF ALL THINGS
YOU'RE GOIN' IN, LAD.
THE U.N. TEAM IS HEADING OUT TONIGHT AND E.M.P.I.R.E. IS ON-SITE, PROTECTING COLDHEART FROM ANY RETRIBUTION.
WE'RE SMUGGLING YOU IN WITH THE U.N. GEAR.
LAND HO!
I ALWAYS WANTED TO SAY THAT.
I DUNNO, MCSHANE.
I GUESS WHEN I REALIZED THE BIG PICTURE WAS HUNG SO CROOKED.
HOLY SHIT!
I HOPE TO CHRIST YOU DON'T WANT ME TO EXPLAIN HOW THIS WORKS, BECAUSE I CAN'T. EVEN RUBY CAN'T.
EVER SEEN ANYTHING LIKE IT?
SAVAGES.
5
SPEAK FOR YOURSELF, SISTER.
3
WHAT ABOUT W.A.S.T.E., MCSHANE?
I DUNNO--WHAT ARE WE DOING ABOUT W.A.S.T.E.? SEYCHELLE ISN'T EVEN X.S.M. CLASS AND WE'RE FOCUSING ON HIM AND THEN THEM WHILE THE BIG FISH--
YOU DON'T QUESTION THE WISDOM OF E.M.P.I.R.E., CASS, AND YOU DON'T CHINTZ ON THE LONG VIEW.
I'VE BEEN WORKING WITH YOUR OLD MAN SINCE THE WAR AND I STILL DON'T KNOW HOW TO GET THE BIG MAN'S ATTENTION.
KAL'LAA!
KAL'LAA!
KAL'LAA!
WHAT ABOUT "WHAT ABOUT W.A.S.T.E.?"
QUANTUM STRATEGY ENGINES CALCULATE AND RECALCULATE THE RAMIFICATIONS THAT FARTING GNATS IN ARGENTINA HAVE ON THESE MISSIONS.
YEAH, ONCE.
SO WHY ISN'T RUBY IN ON THE BRIEFING?
WELL, I THINK SHE REMEMBERED SOMETHING FROM BEFORE HER TIME AT E.M.P.I.R.E. AND WE'RE NO LONGER A GOING CONCERN.
THEY'LL KILL US ALL!
LET'S GET YOU UP-DECK. WE'RE COMING UP ON THE U.N. SHIP NOW.
SHE STARTED HAVING SOME BAD DREAMS A WHILE BACK, AND NOW--
AND SINCE WHEN DO YOU CARE? YOU'VE NEVER BEEN MUCH OF A BIG PICTURE GUY.
KAL'LAA!
KAL'LAA!
KAL'LAA!
KAL'LAA!
KAL'LAA!
STONE-AGE OR NOT, THE VELOCITY THESE THINGS ARE TRAVELING AT ARE ENOUGH TO DRILL RIGHT THROUGH A MAN.
MAN.
6
THE WAY RUBY EXPLAINED IT MADE IT SOUND LIKE COLDHEART WAS A PLACE FULL OF THE WORLD'S LAST SWEETLY-RETARDED SAVAGES.
KAAAALLL'LLAAAAA!!!
THEY'RE NOT PLAYING AROUND.
KAL'LAA!
I SEE MY OPENING AND TAKE IT.
EVEN IF THEY DID DO MY DIRTY WORK FOR ME.
--OUT?
THE LAST OF THE DARK SKINNED PYGMYS, JUST WAITING FOR THE MESSAGE OF CHRIST TO GET DELIVERED.
THESE PEOPLE ARE VICIOUS FUCKING ANIMALS THAT DON'T DESERVE THE GOOD WORD. OR TETANUS SHOTS.
KAL'LAA!
HOW WEARY I GROW OF THIS CHARADE.
THE EGGHEADS CUT AND RUN BEFORE THEY'RE TOO SHORT-HANDED TO GET THE BOAT BACK SAFE.
SO NOW I'LL FIND COLE AND SIGNAL MCSHANE AND EXFIL BY DAYBREAK.
AND NOT A MOMENT TOO SOON. THESE FUCKING SAVAGES CREEP ME--
KAL-LAA!
KAL-LAA!
KAL-LAA!
KAL-LAA! KAL

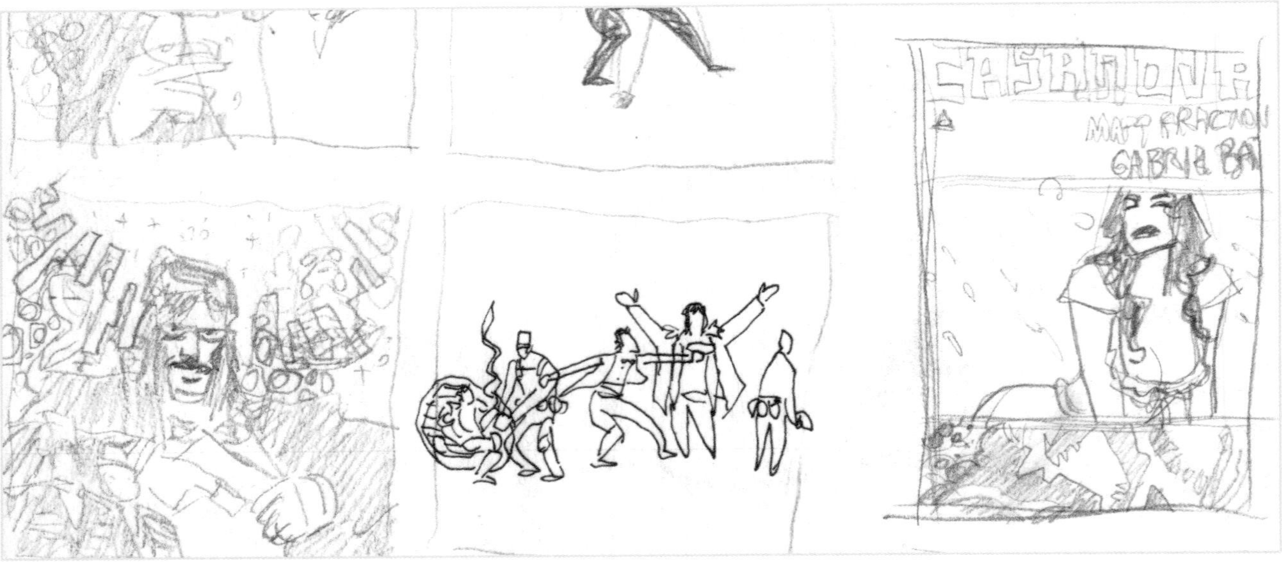

COVERS

One of the worst things about making a cover is that it is NOT a comic book page. It has no panels, no storytelling, it's one single image (usually) telling something about the book. Well, one of the best things about making a cover is that it is NOT a comic book page. Actually, when I'm working on a cover, I try to forget about comics entirely. I think about movie posters, fine arts, photography and everything else that is graphic and awesome. Because that's what I want for the covers of CASANOVA: graphic awesomeness!

Nothing inside this book is like any other book on the stands, so the covers need to be as unique as the story, as psychedelic as Matt's writing. One thing I learned working on this book is that it has no boundaries, no limits. So why should I restrain the covers?

I really like covers with stripes, different sets of images. They remind me of old pulp magazines or movie posters and I always go back to the "stripe formula" when I start thinking about covers. I also really like to create a set of covers that will work together as a group, that will have a unity, a template so when you put all of them together, you see they belong together. Whenever I work with covers, I try to establish rules or set parameters to guide my work. This time, I tried to create a pattern that would also allow me to work on a vast range of techniques and use different renderings on our covers.

People usually think covers that follow patterns will become boring over time and that was my challenge for the covers of LUXURIA.

Gabriel Bá

PS: My new challenge is to make the covers of my next arc look better than the ones Fábio is doing for GULA.

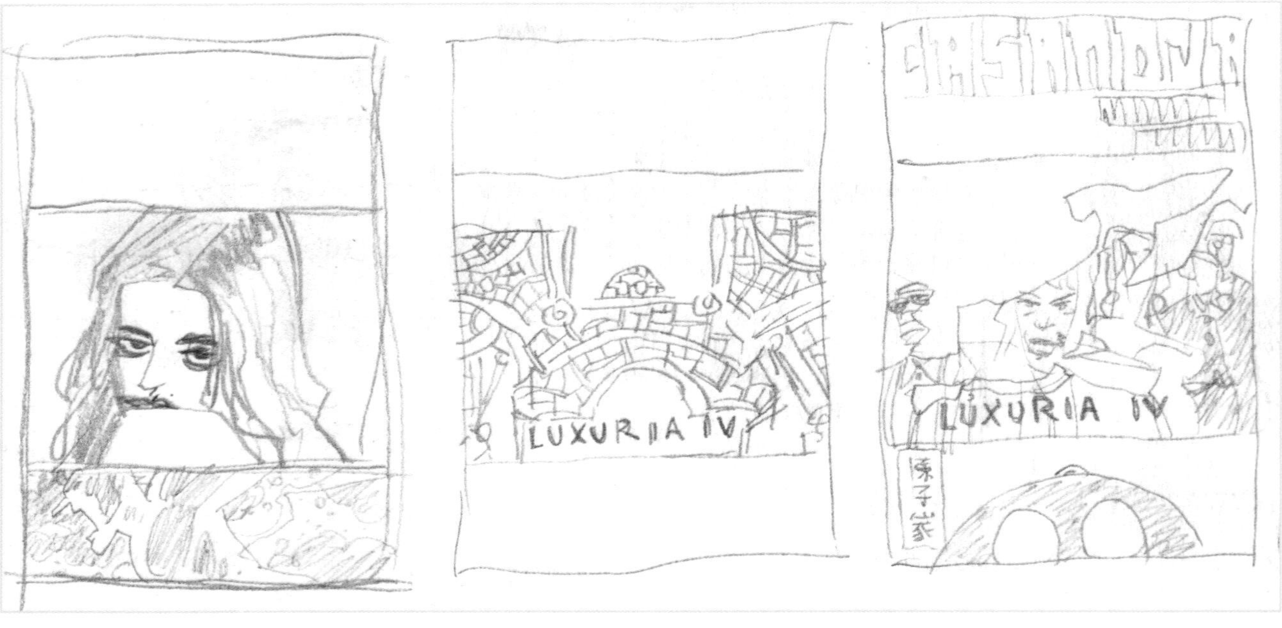
LUXURIA IV
LUXURIA IV

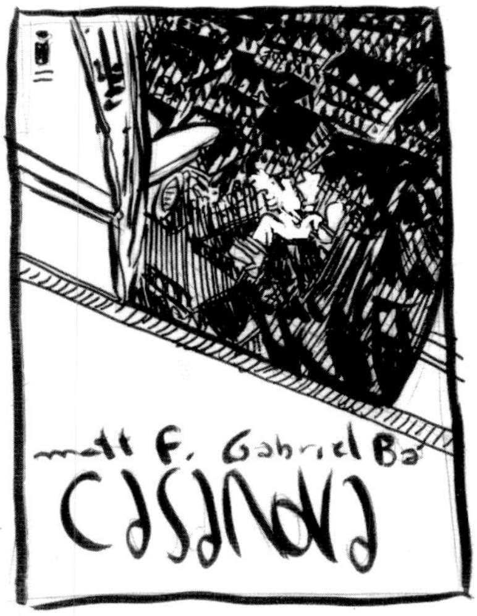
matt F. Gabriel Bá
Casanova

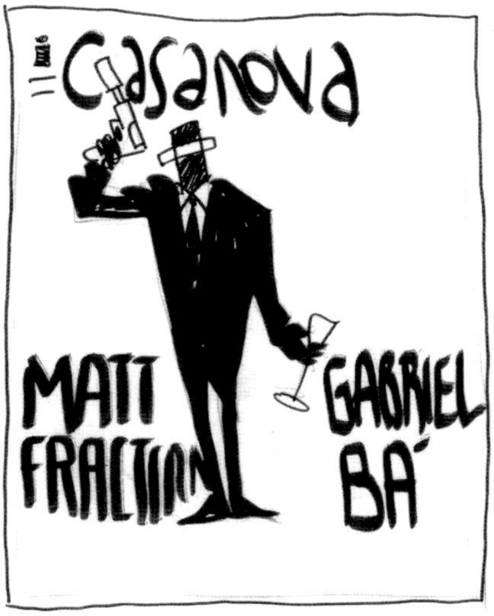
Casanova
MATT FRACTION
GABRIEL BÁ

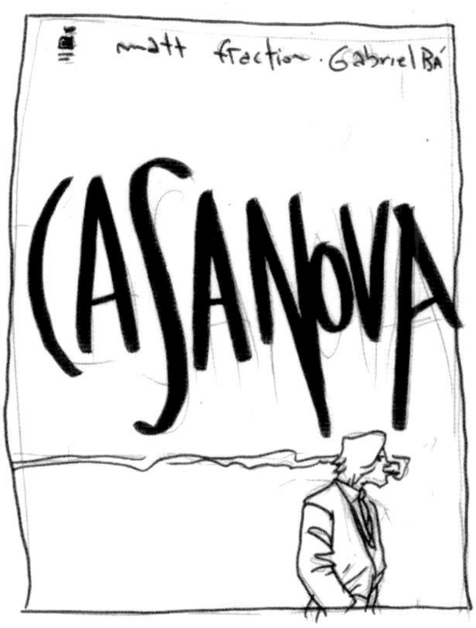
matt fraction · Gabriel Bá
CASANOVA

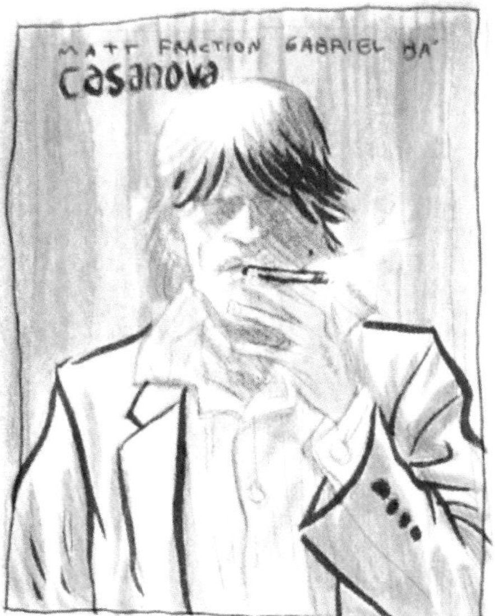
MATT FRACTION GABRIEL BÁ
Casanova

misterious guy

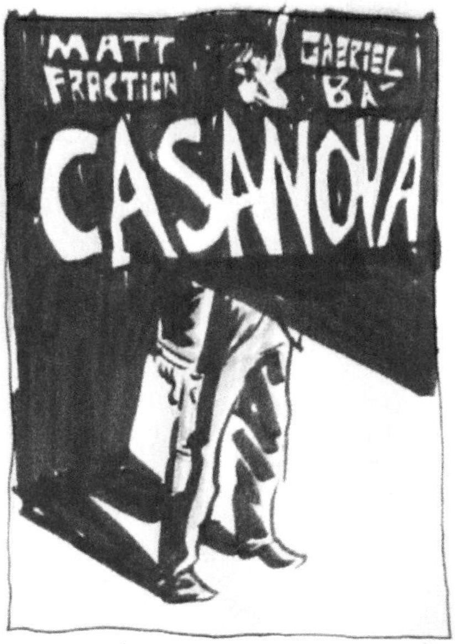
MATT FRACTION
GABRIEL BÁ
CASANOVA

misterious thief

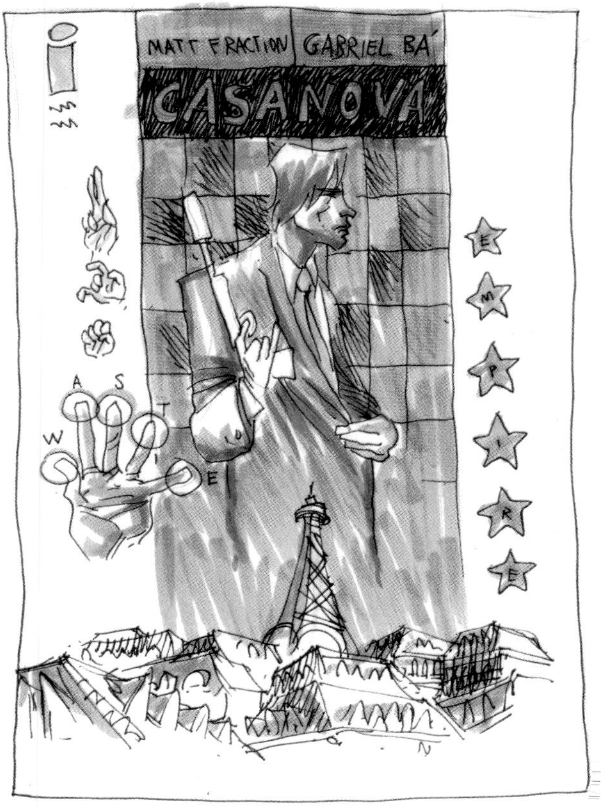
MATT FRACTION
GABRIEL BÁ
CASANOVA
WASTE
EMPIRE

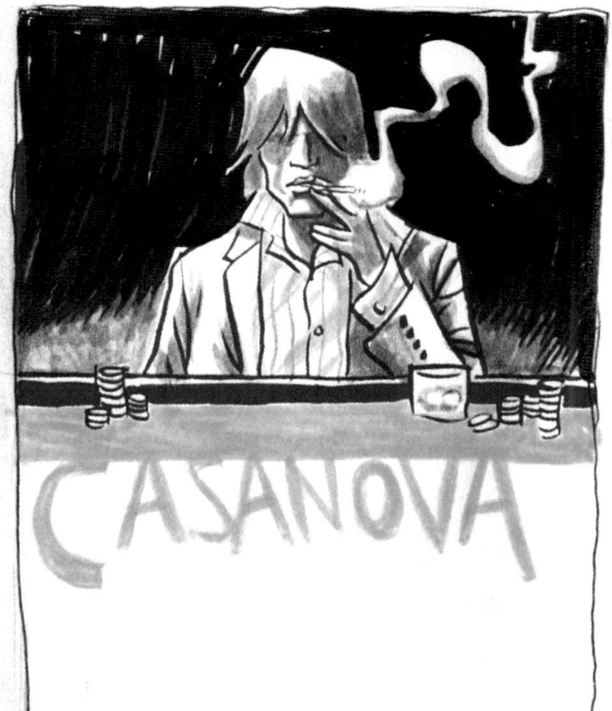
CASANOVA

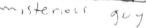

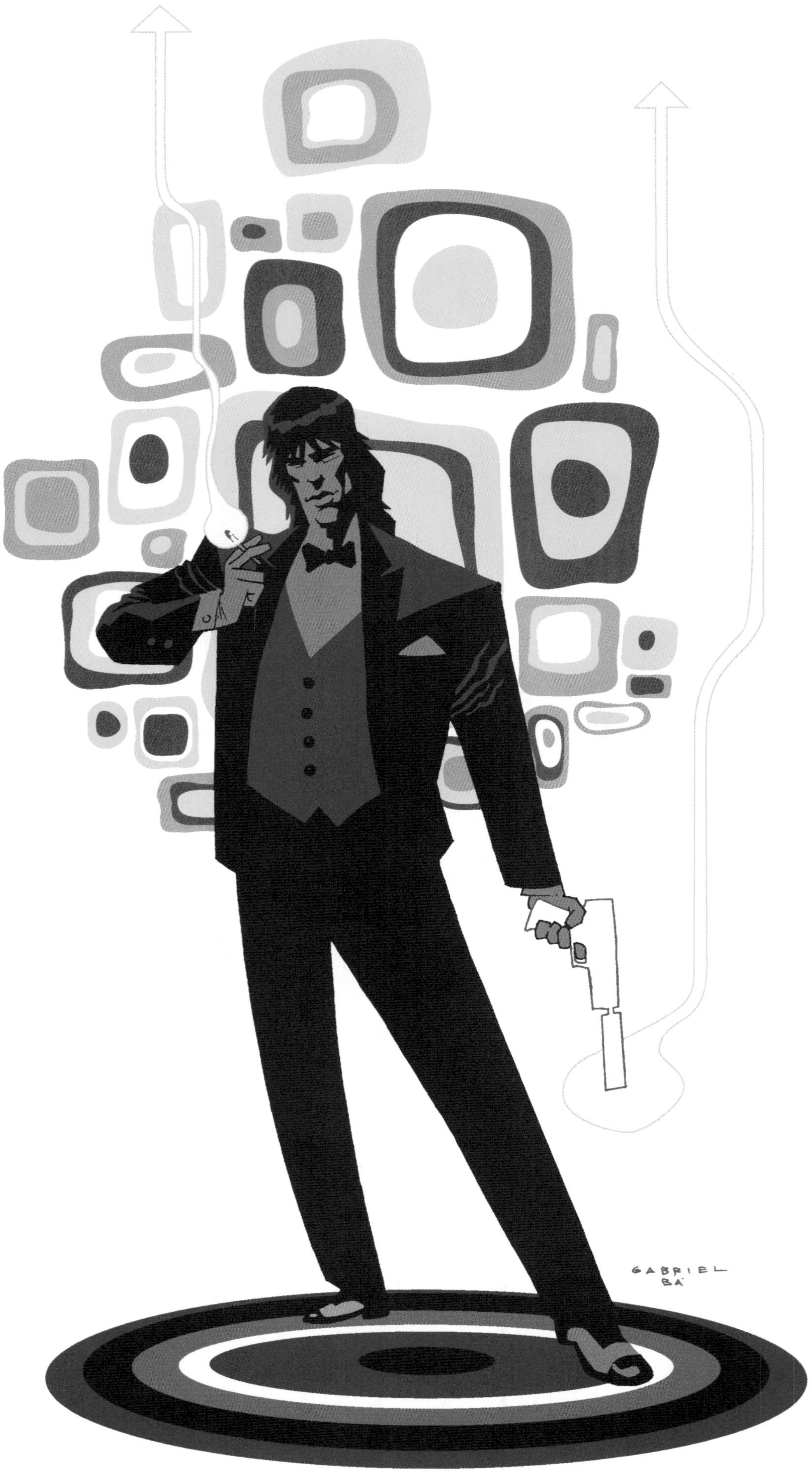
GABRIEL BÁ

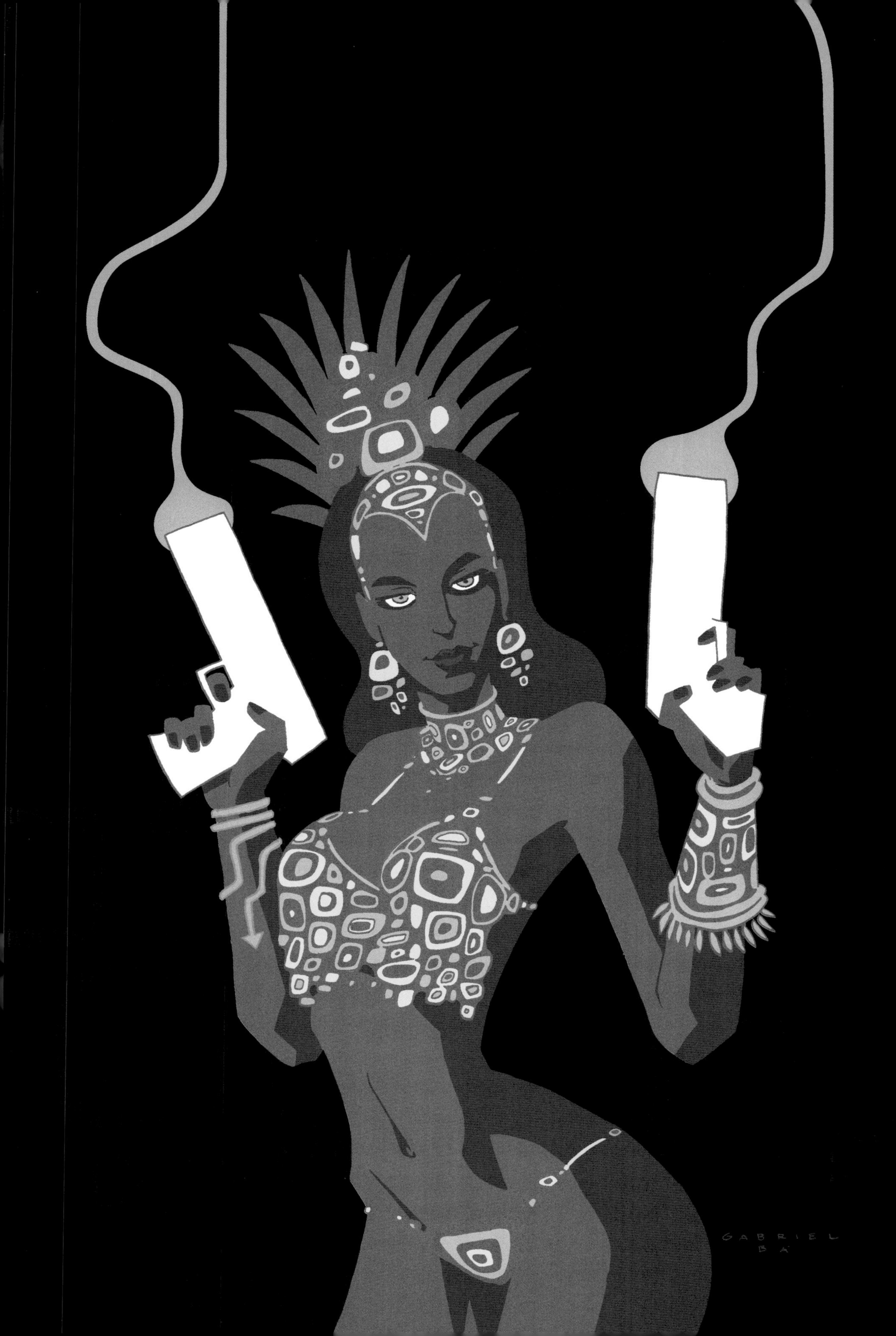
GABRIEL
BÁ

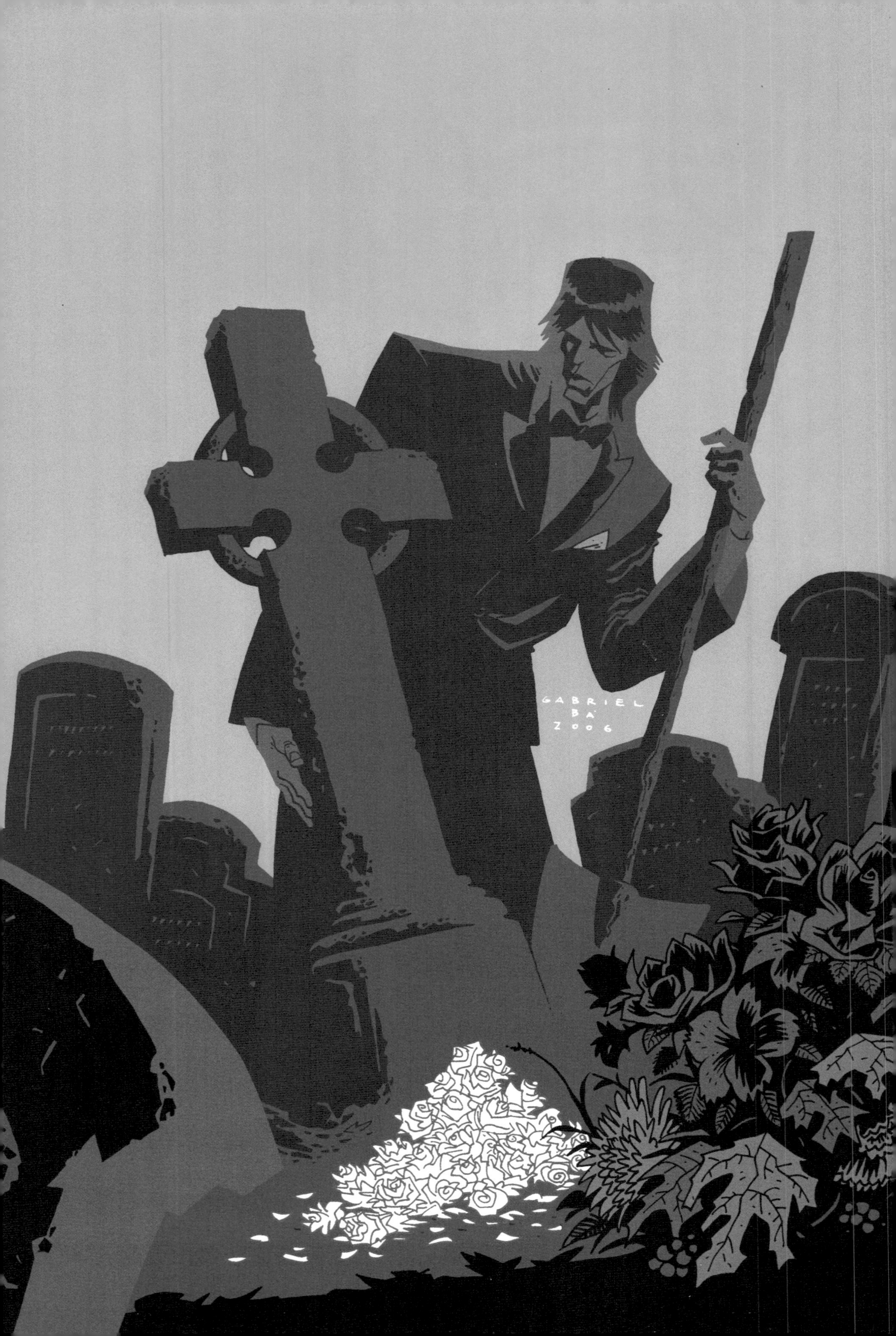
GABRIEL
BÁ
2006

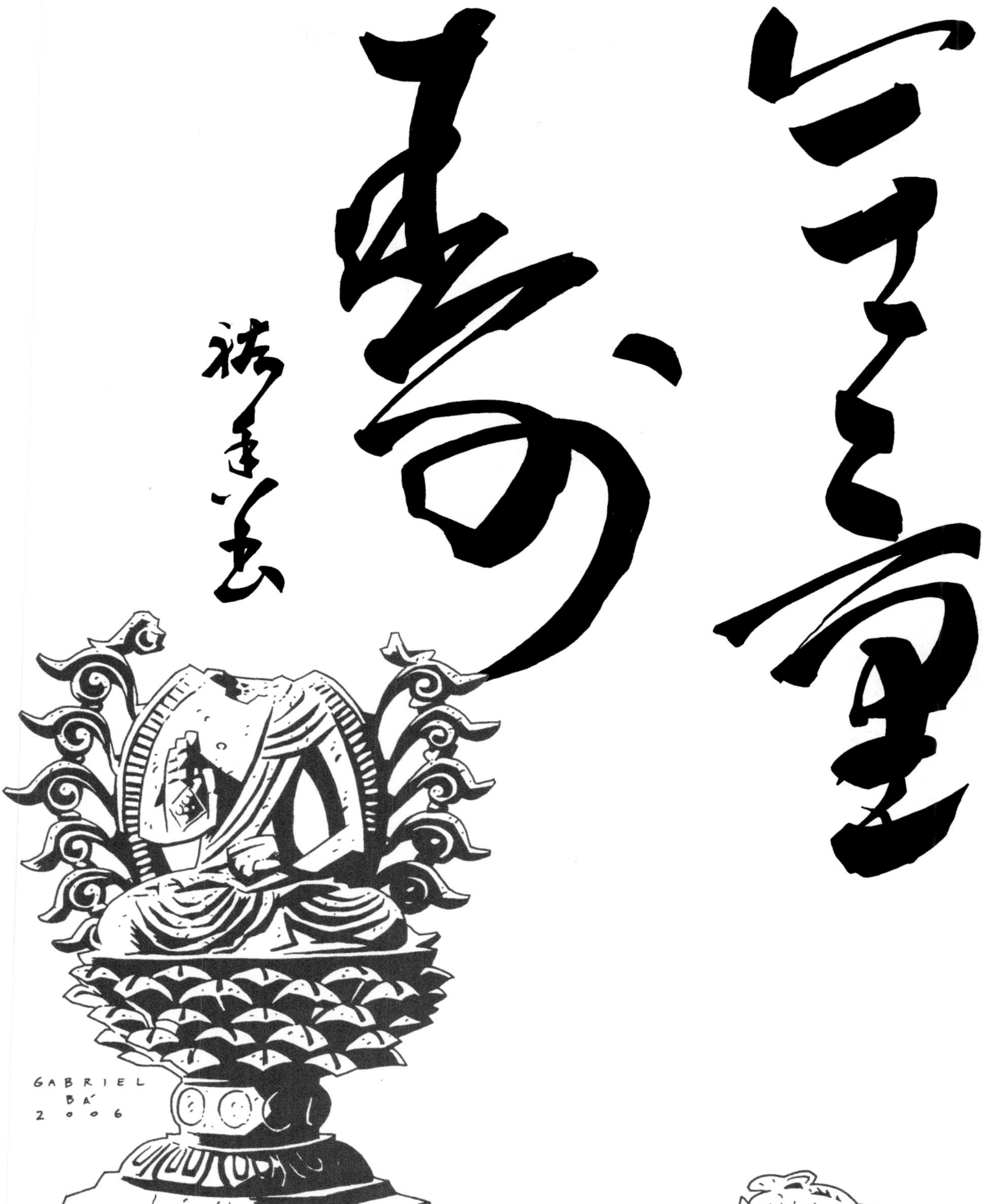
GABRIEL BÁ 2006

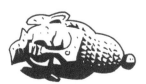

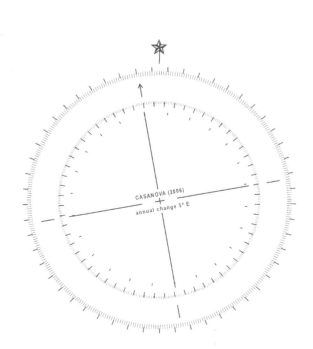

CASANOVA (2006)
annual change 5° E

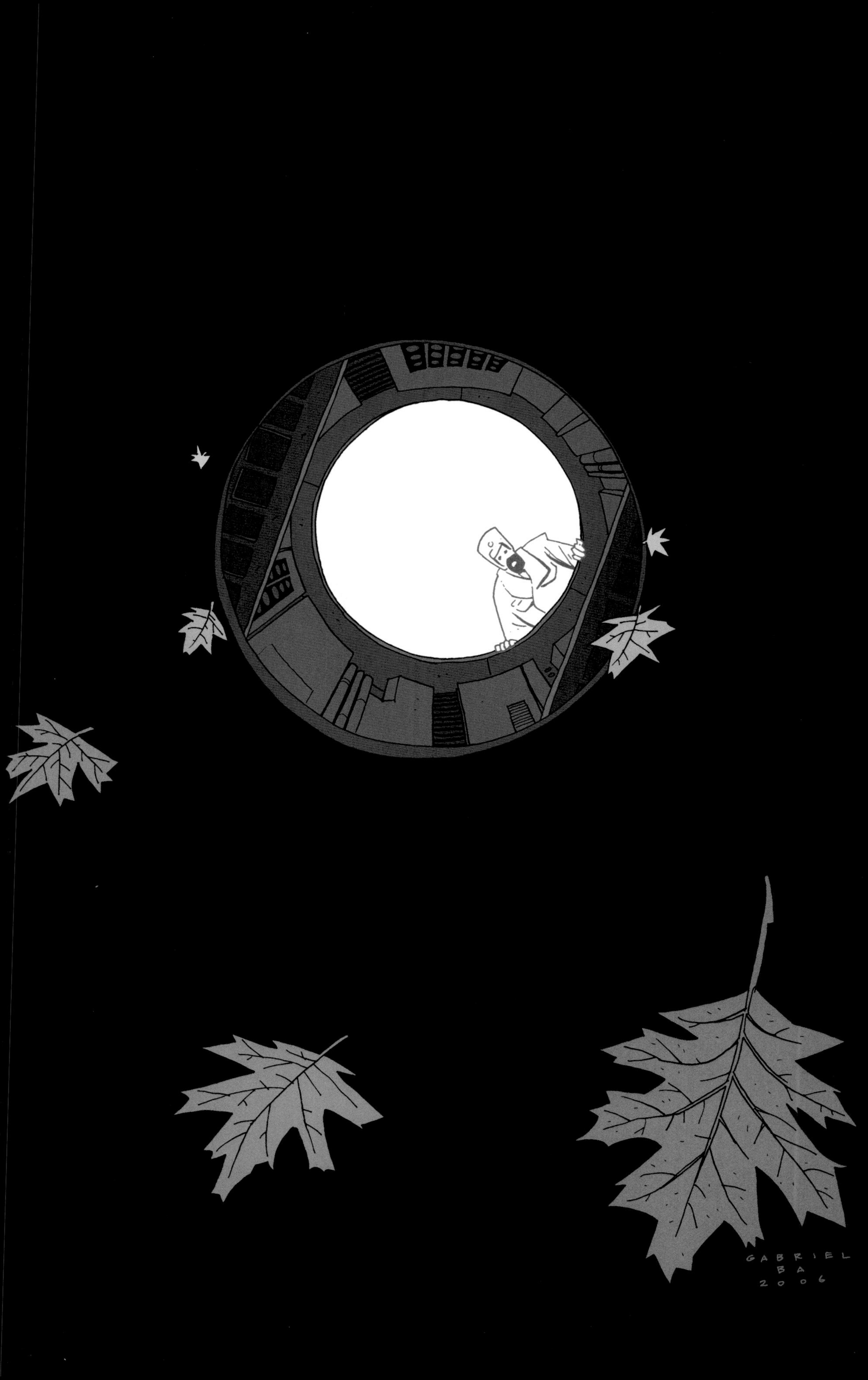
GABRIEL
BA
2006

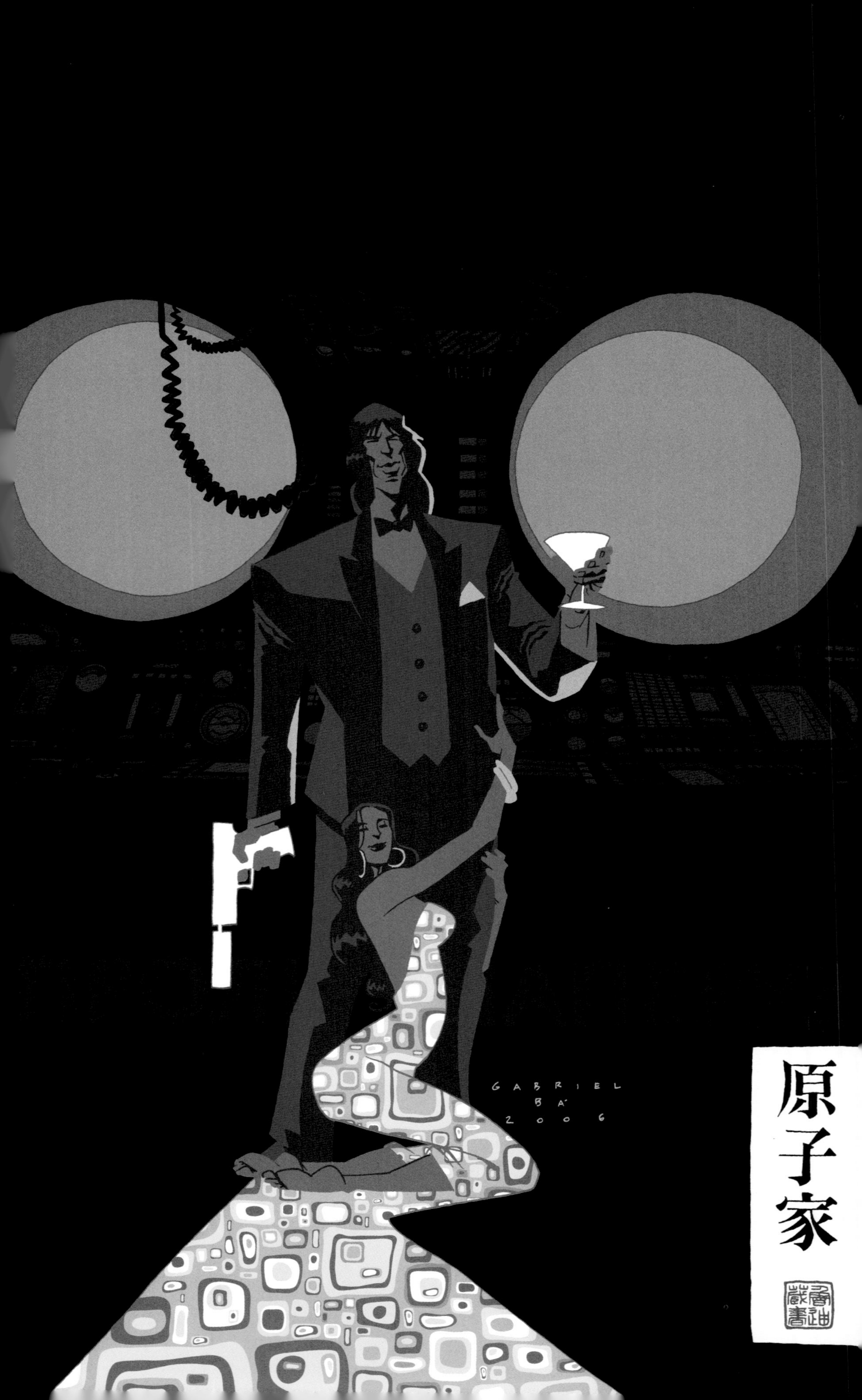
GABRIEL
BA´
2006

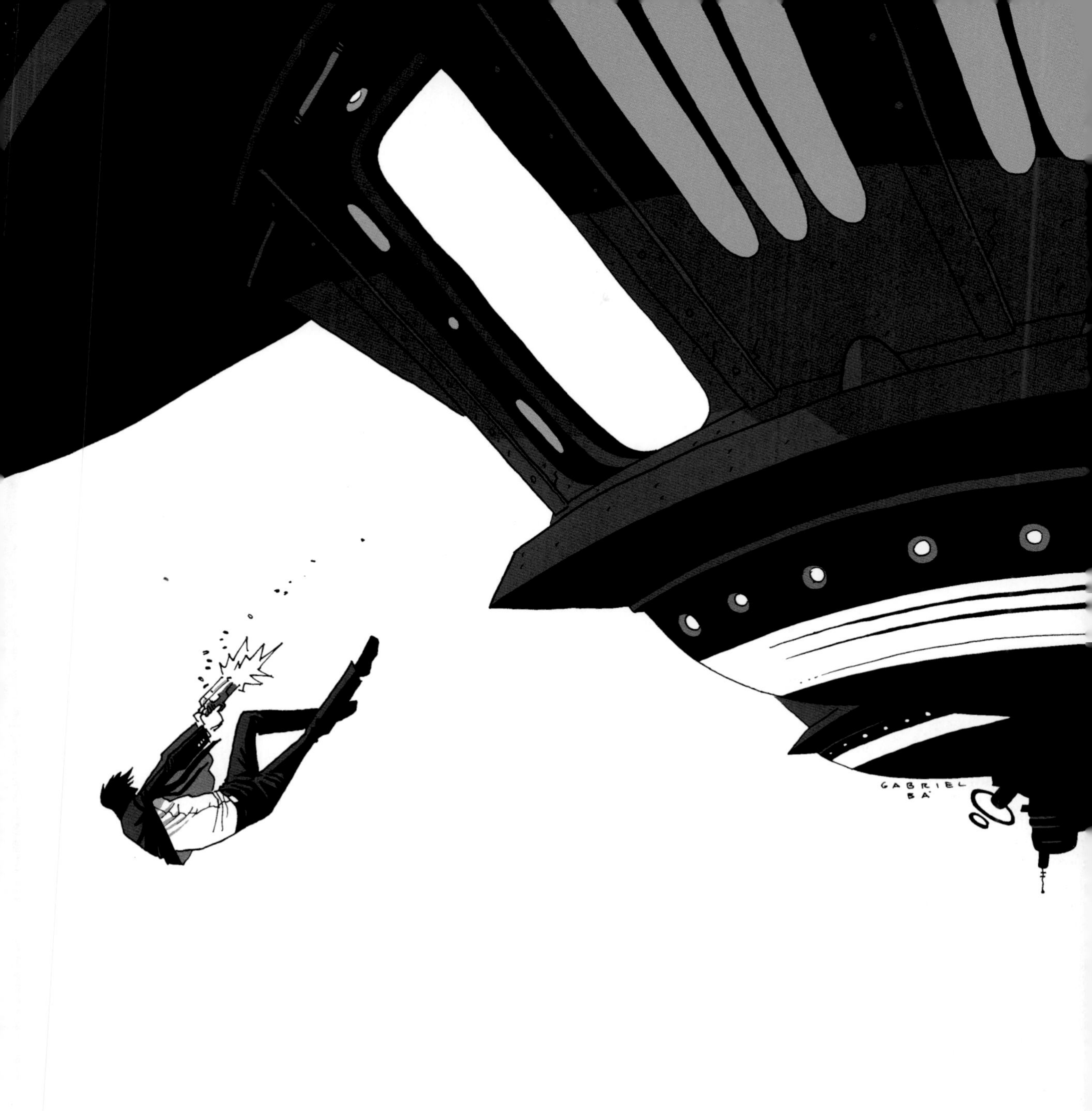
GABRIEL
BÁ

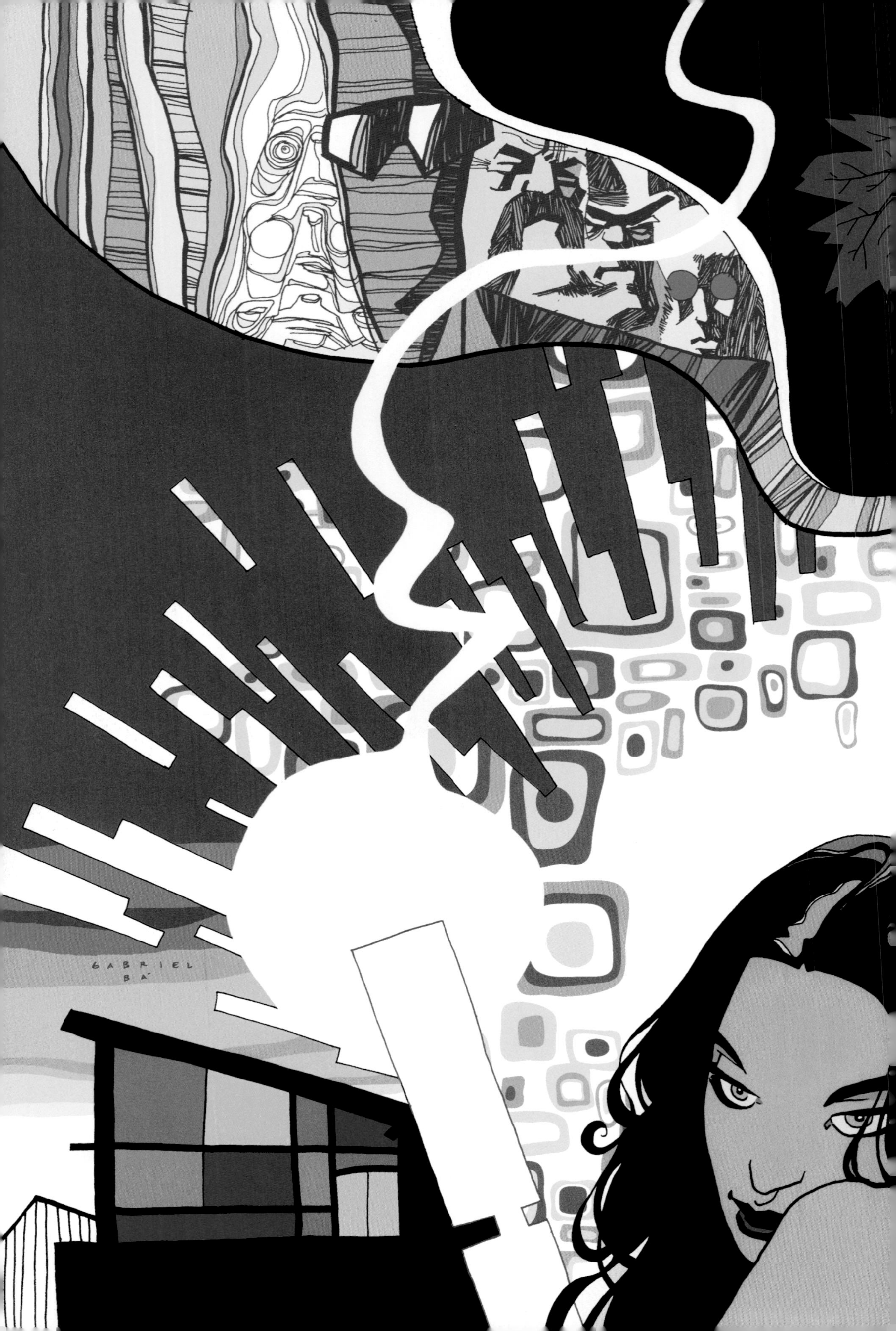
GABRIEL
BÁ

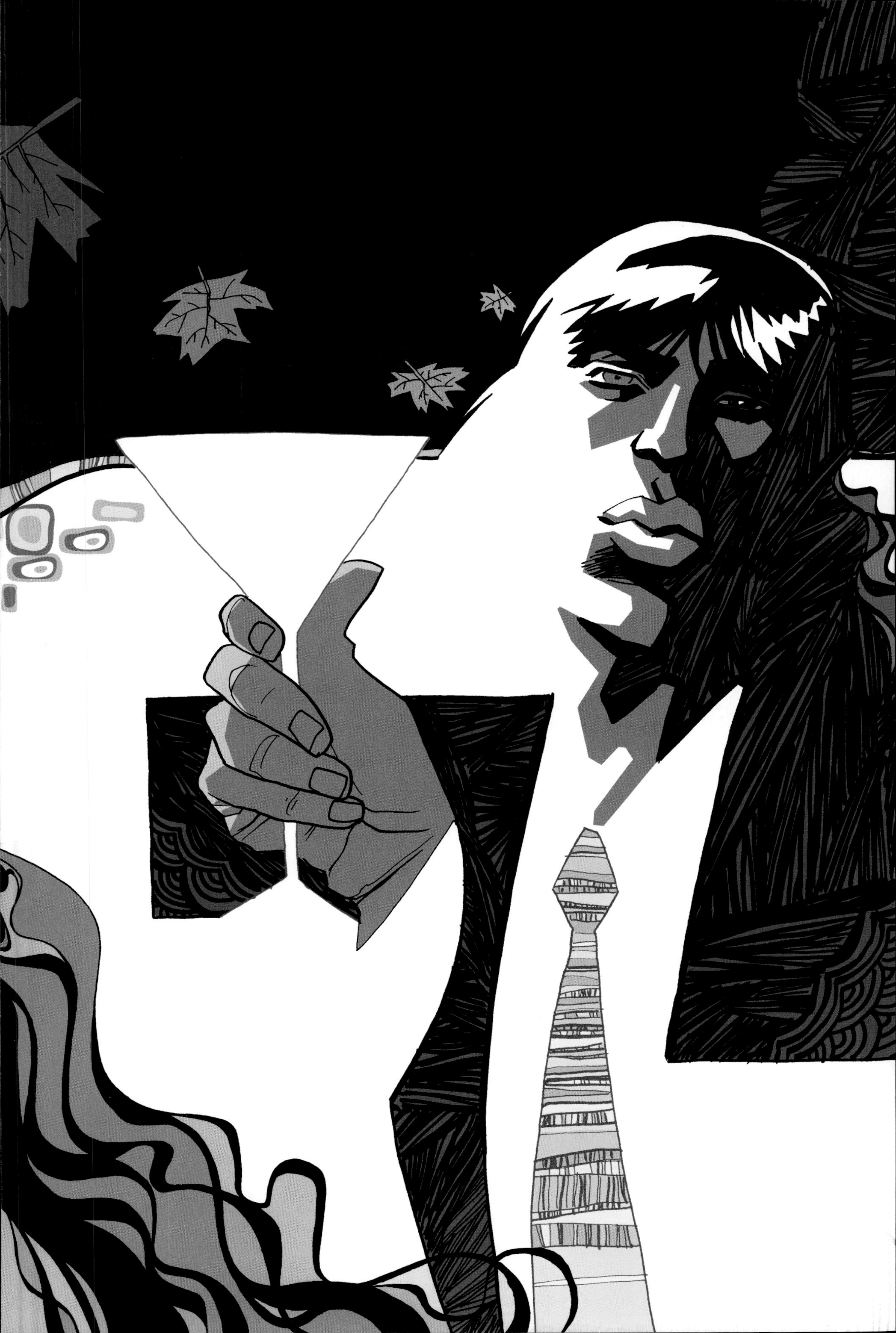

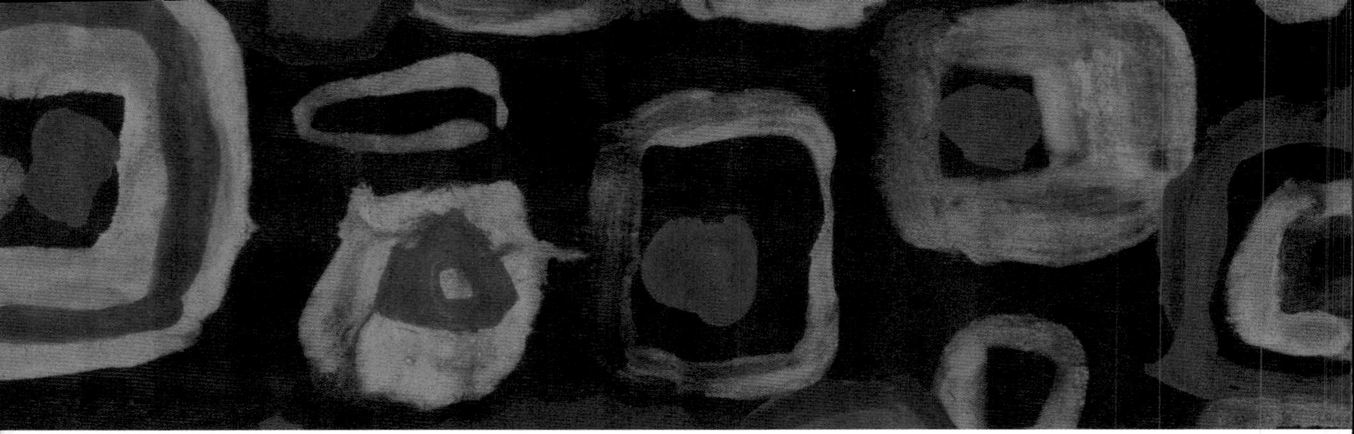

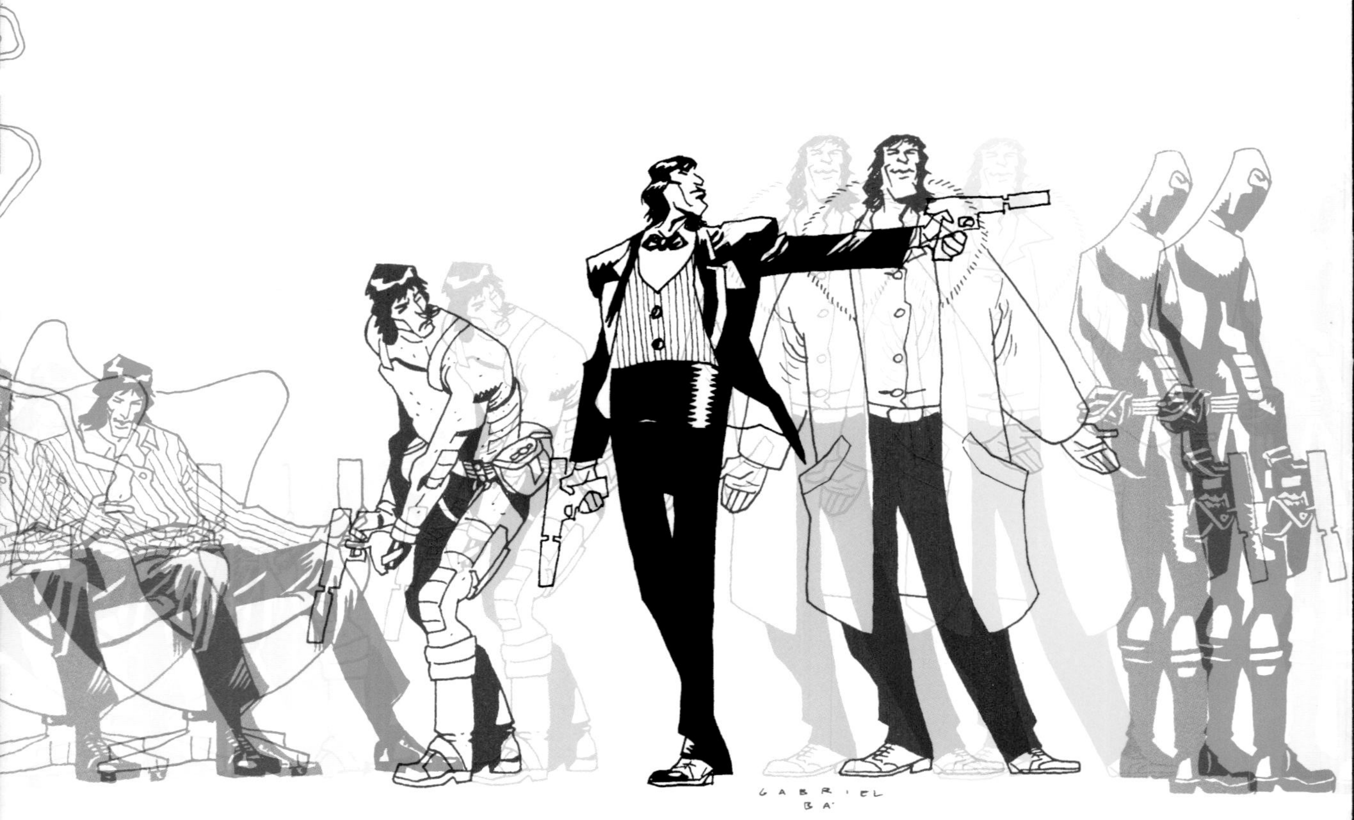
GABRIEL BÁ

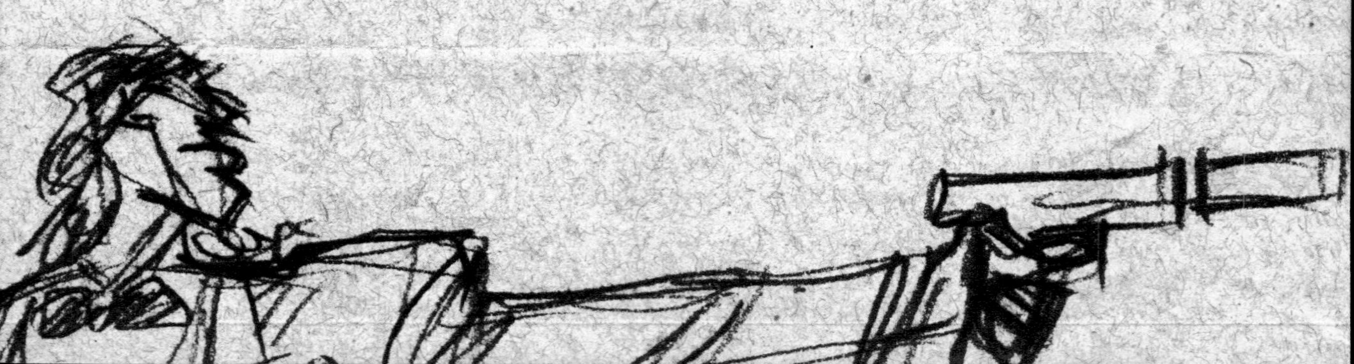

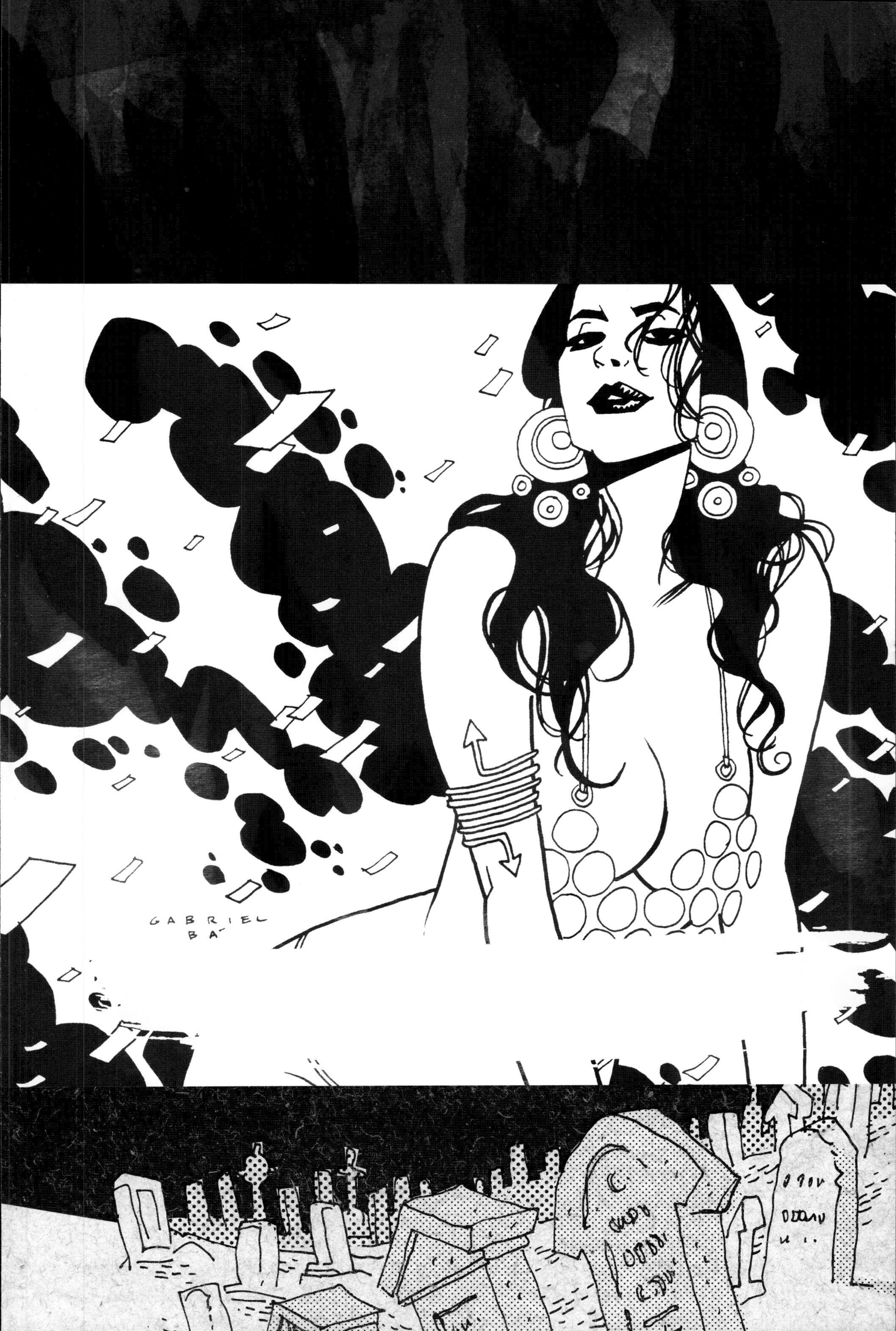
GABRIEL BA

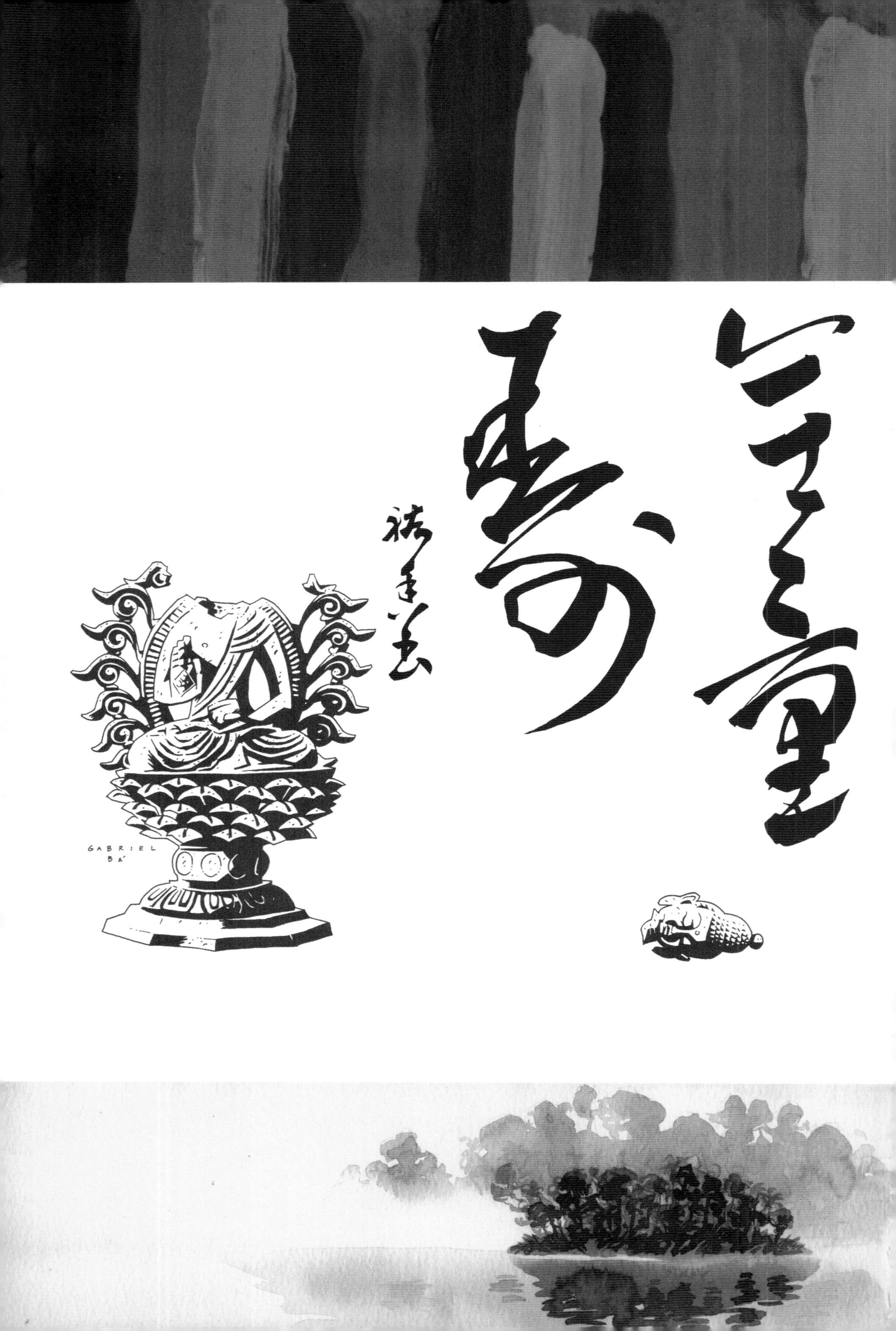
GABRIEL BÁ

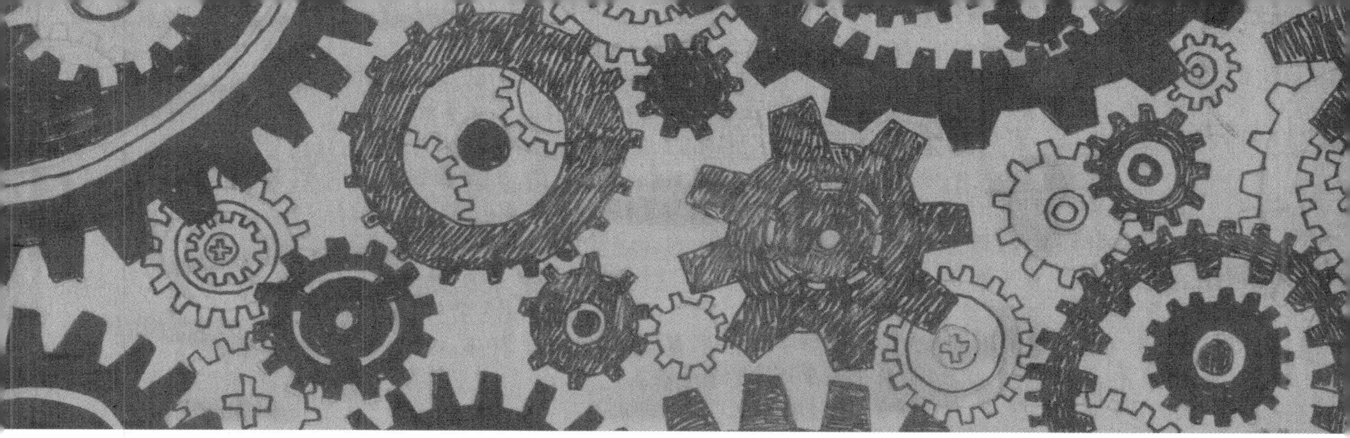

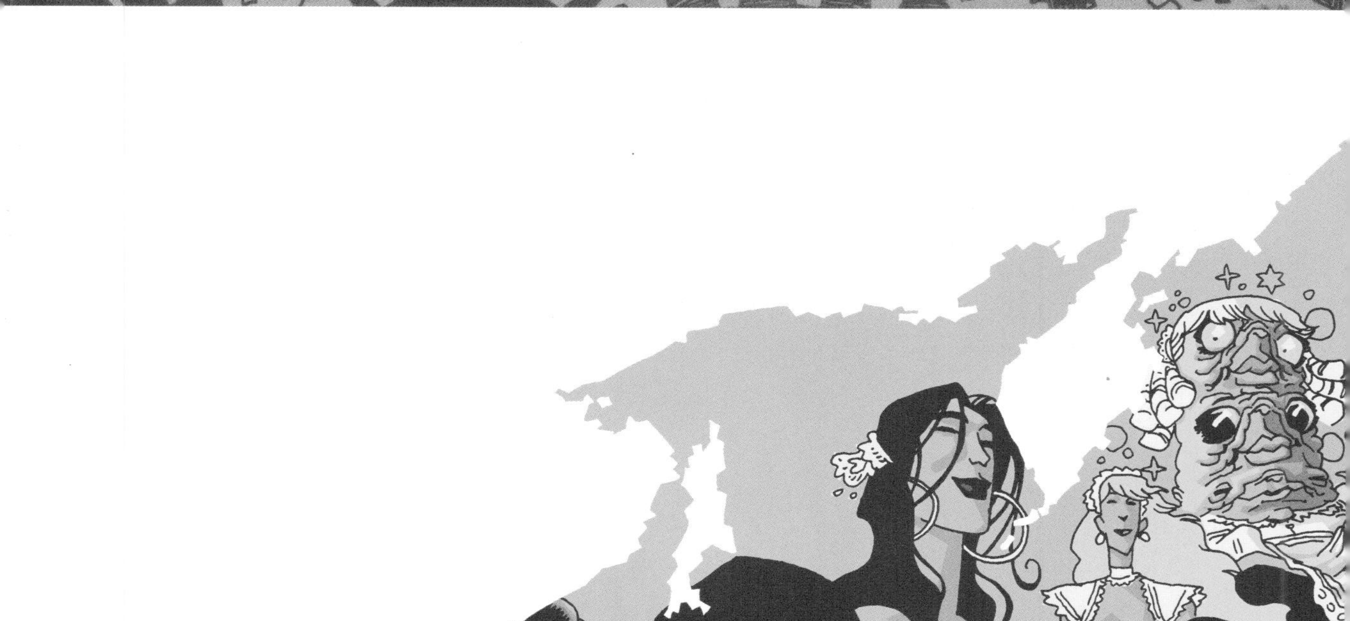
GABRIEL BÁ

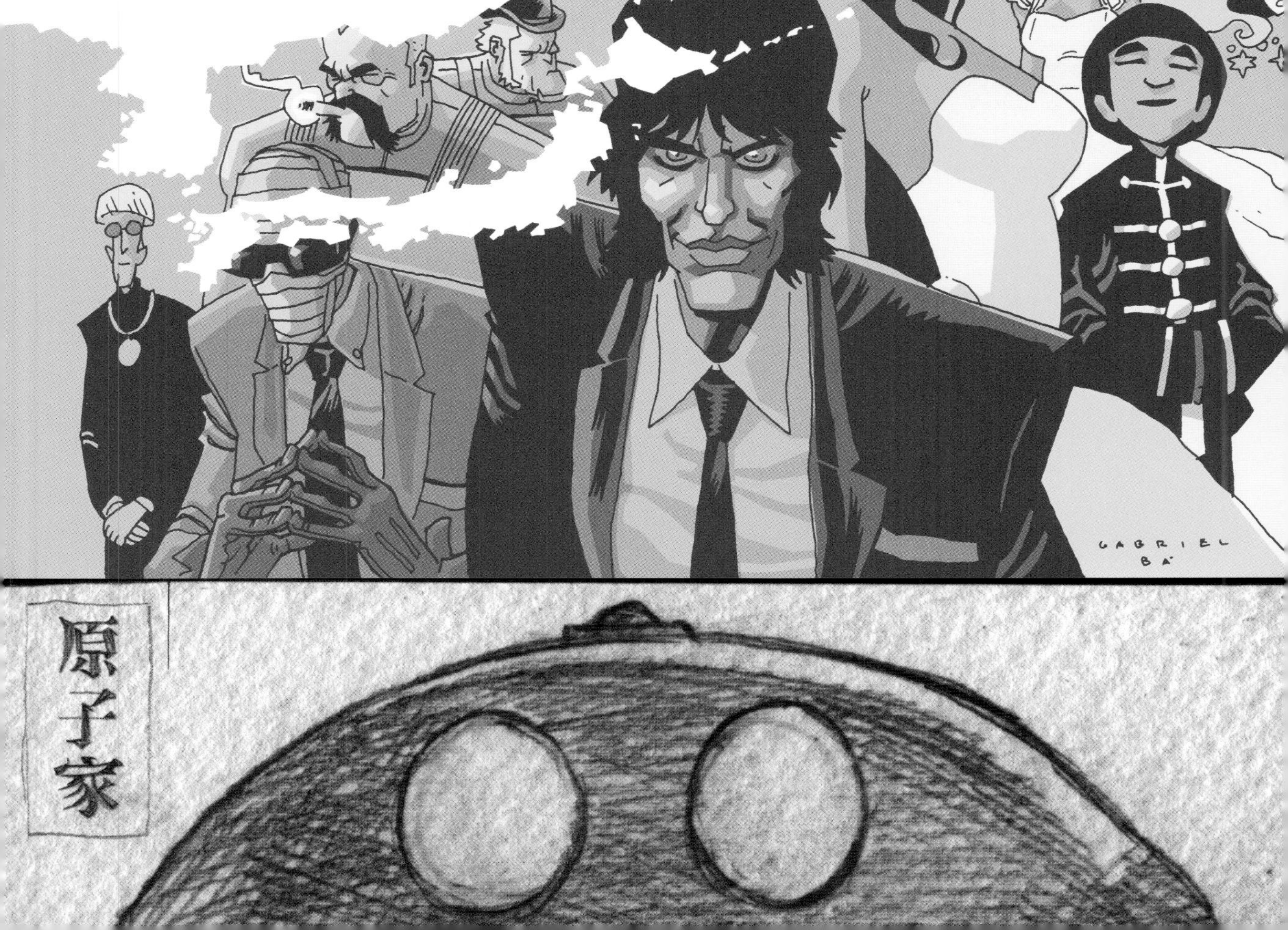
原子家

CASANOVA

MATT FRACTION
GABRIEL BÁ

LUXURIA

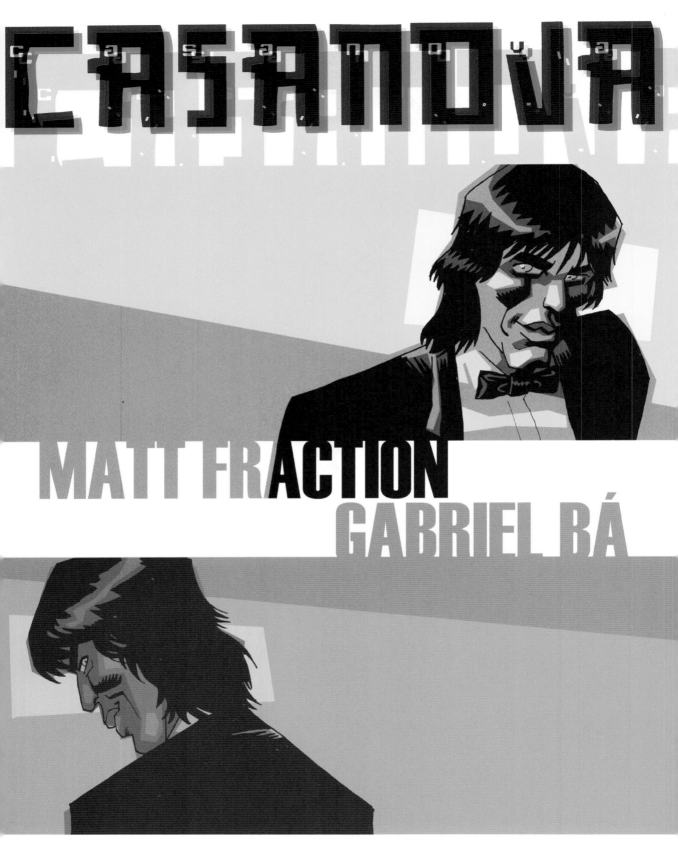

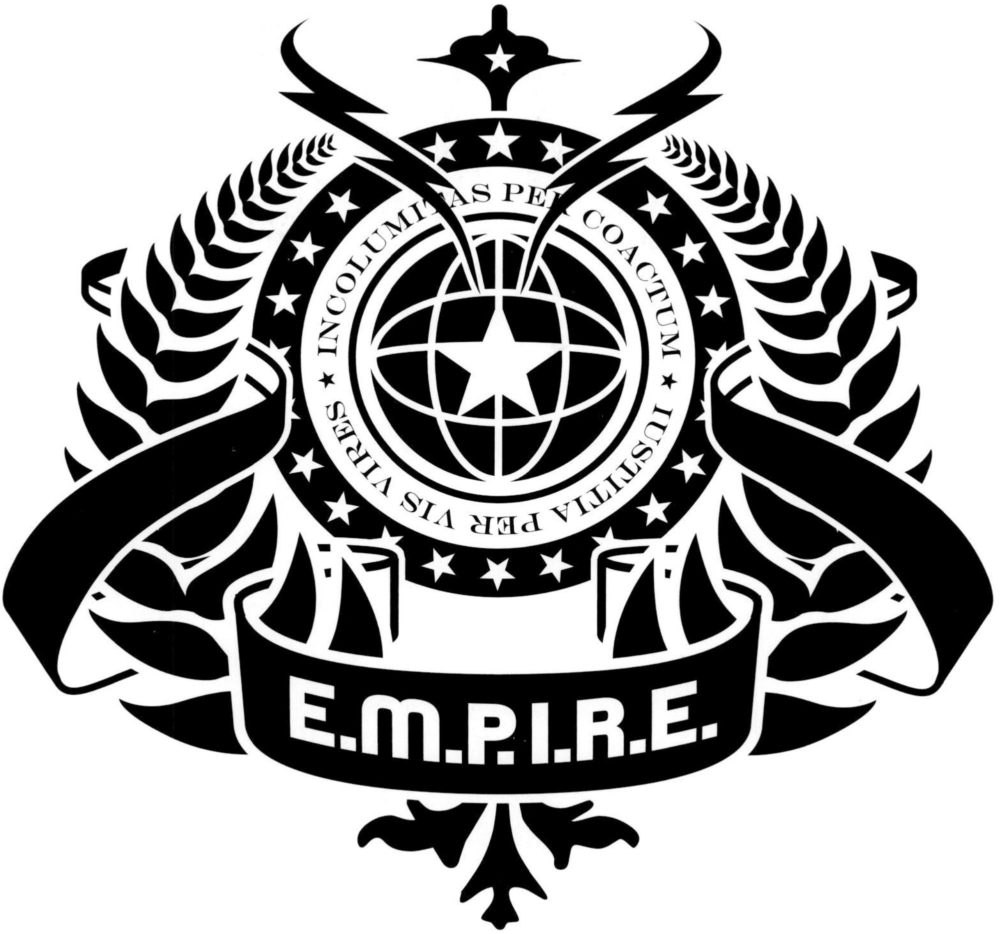
INCOLUMITAS PER COACTUM
IUSTITIA PER VIS VIRES
E.M.P.I.R.E.

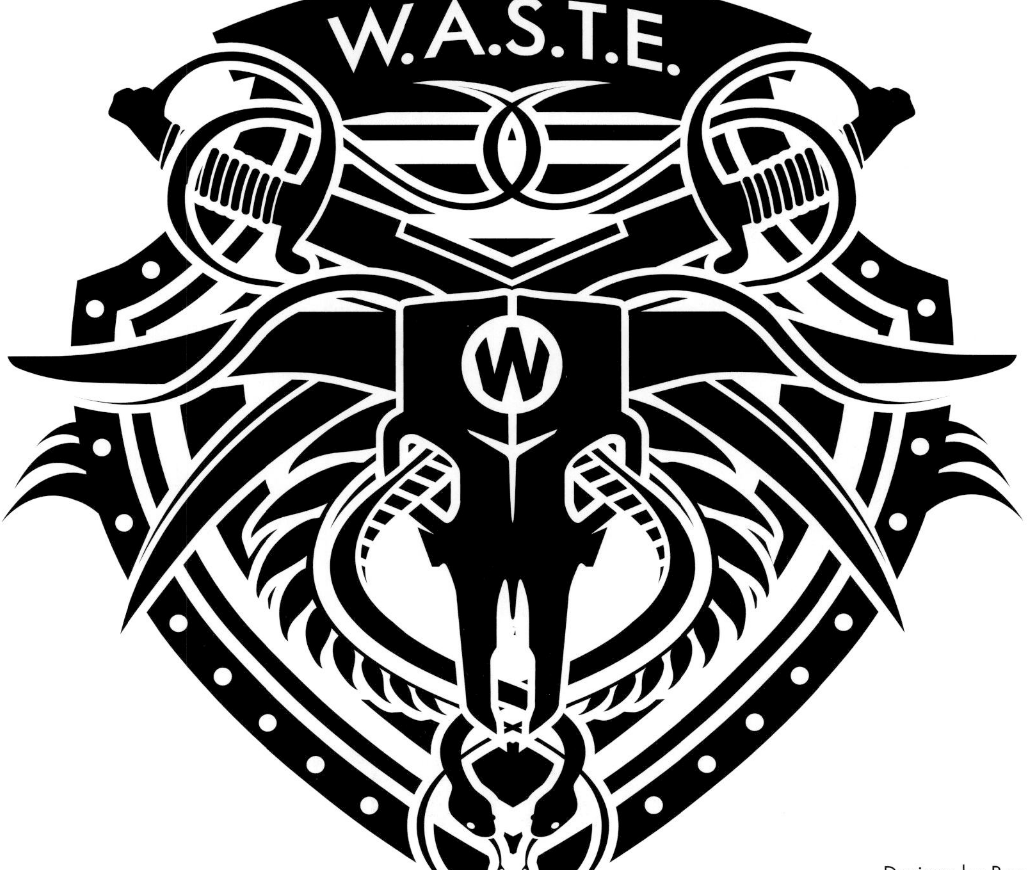
W.A.S.T.E.
W

Designs by Ben Radatz

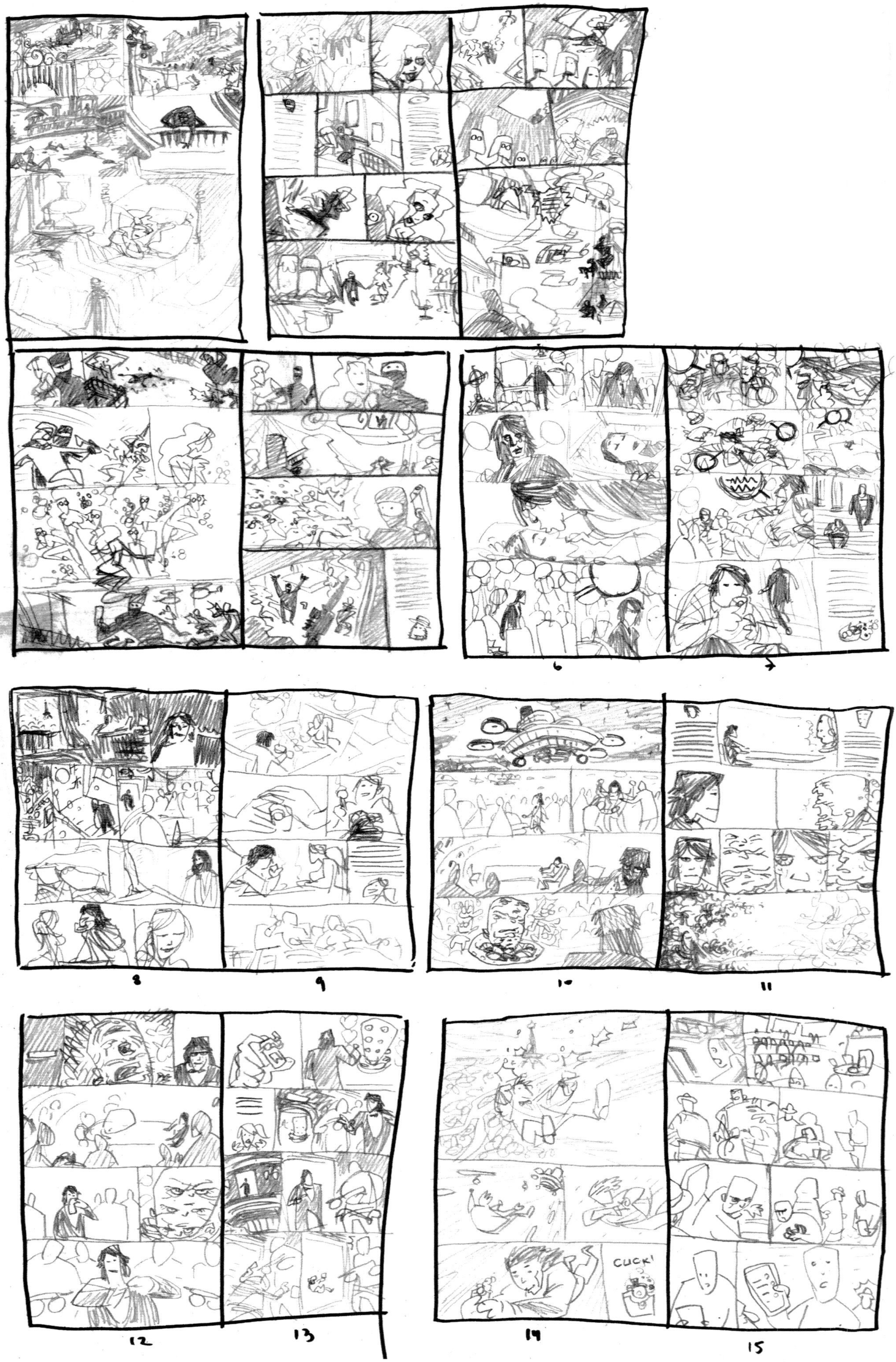
6
7
8
9
10
11
12
13
CLICK!
14
15

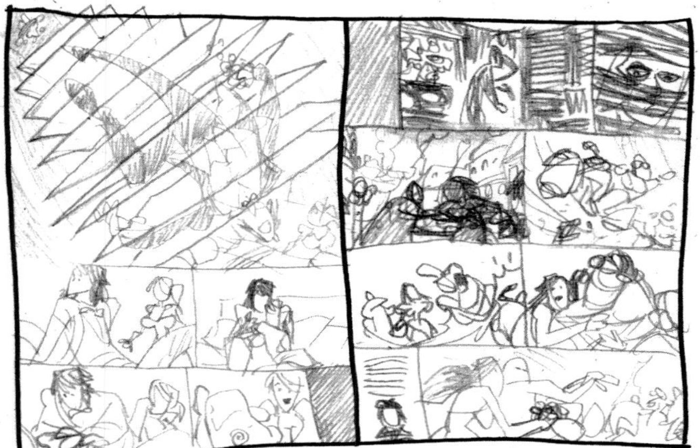

16 17

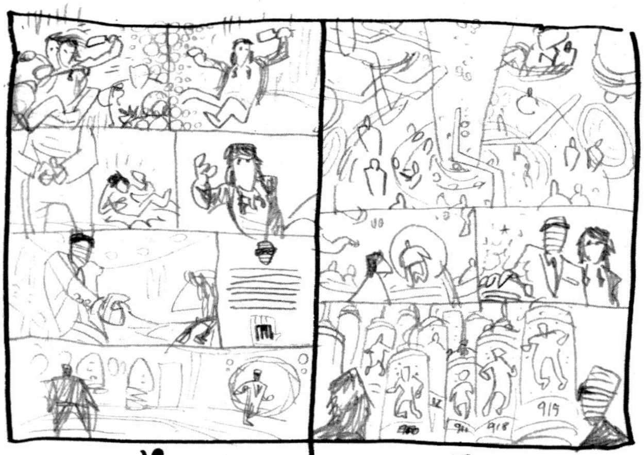

18 19

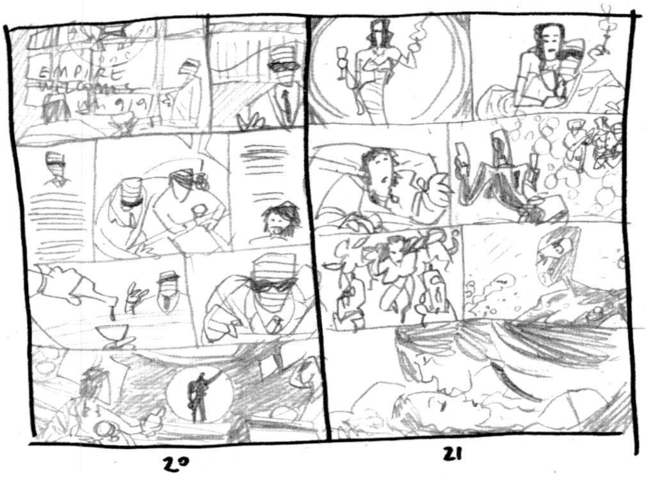
EMPIRE

20 21

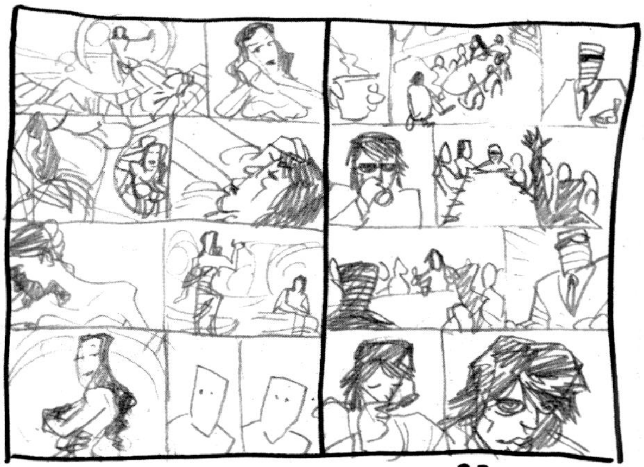

22 23

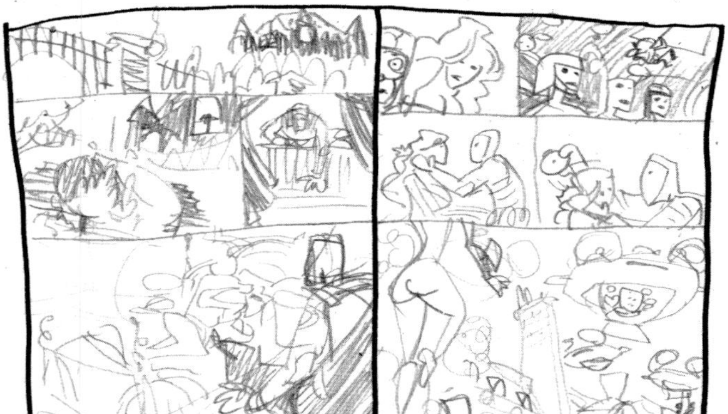

24 25

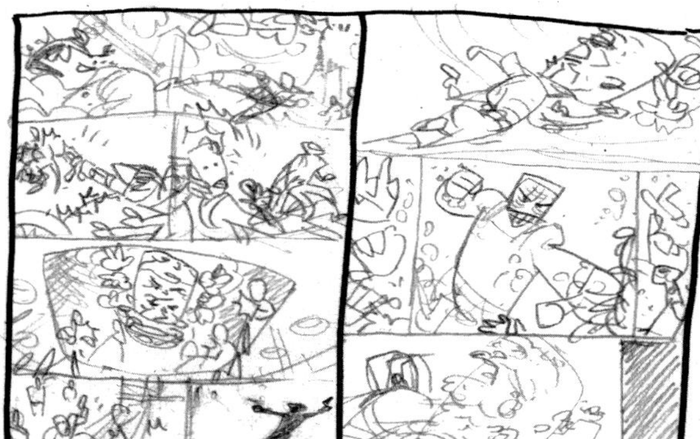

26 27

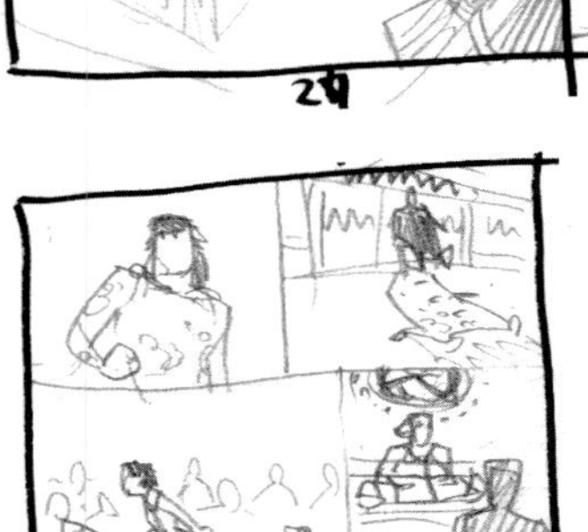
EXECUTION DAYS
MATT FR.
G. BA

28

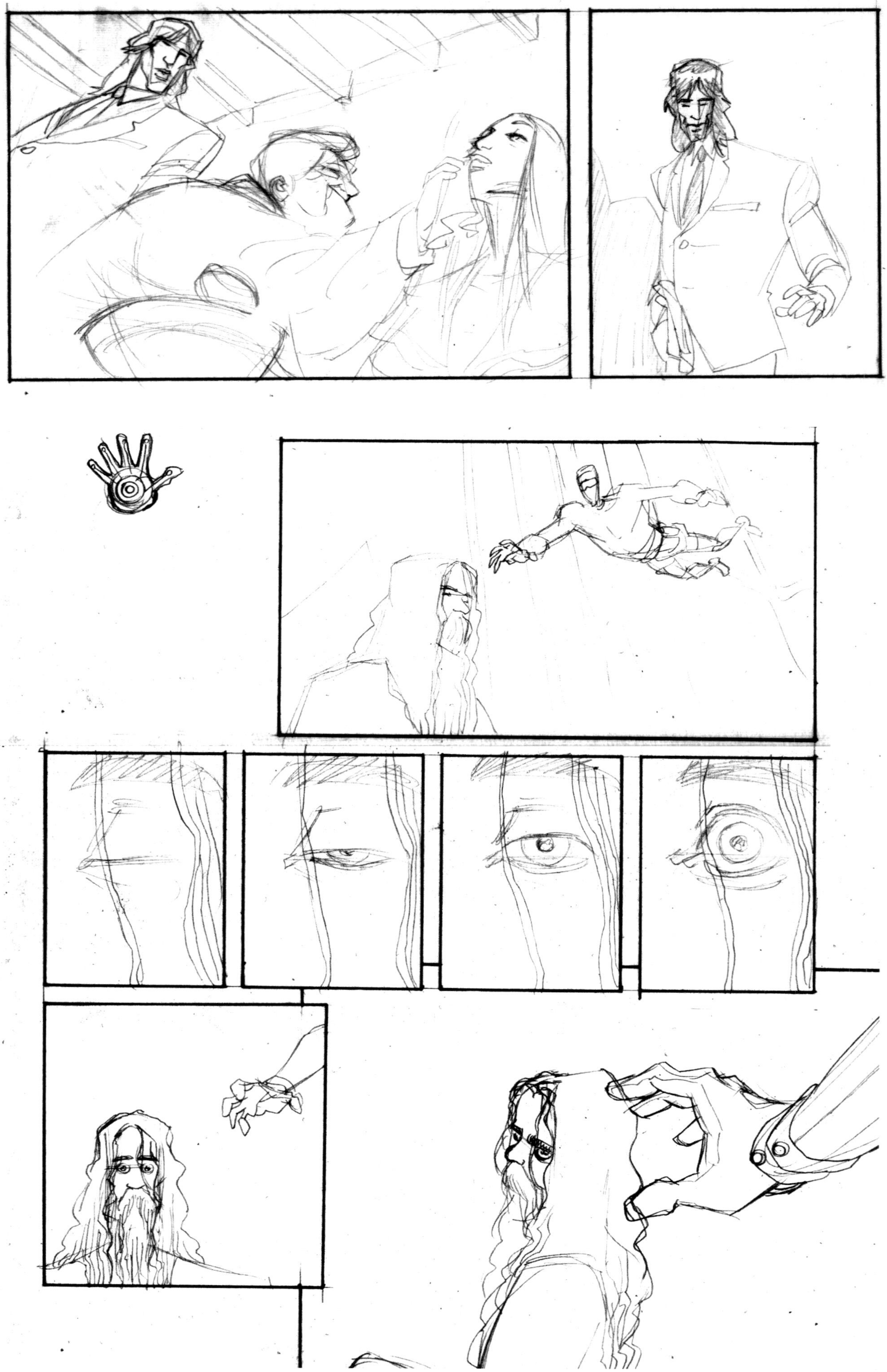

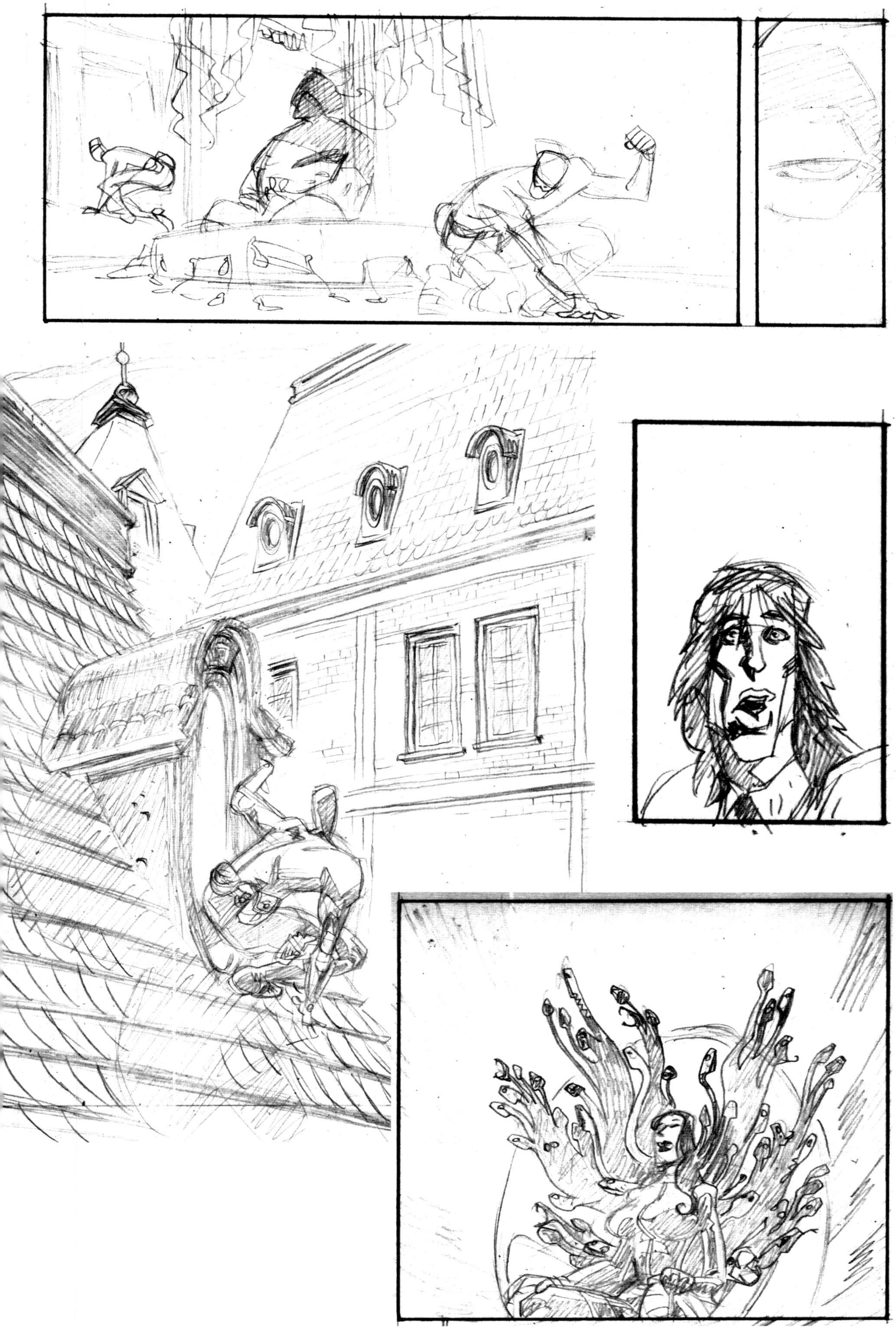

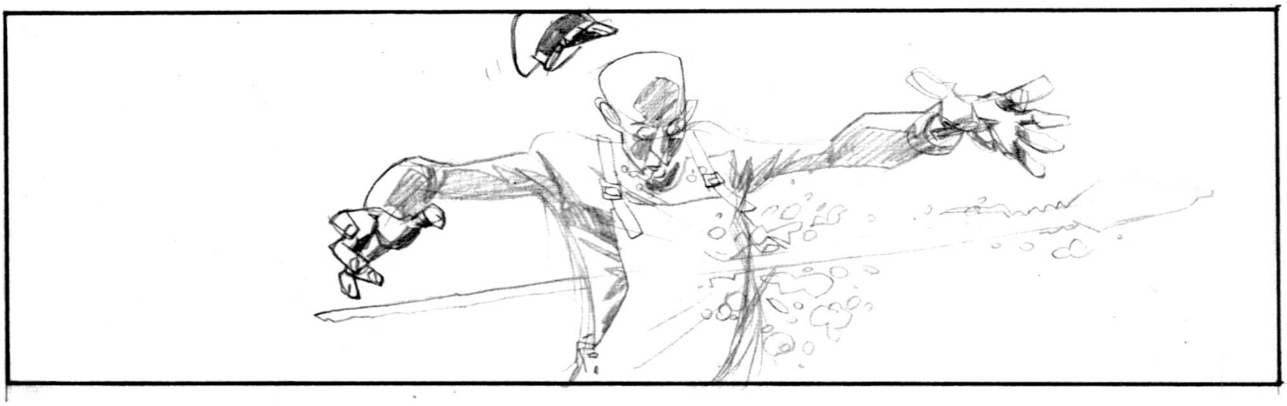

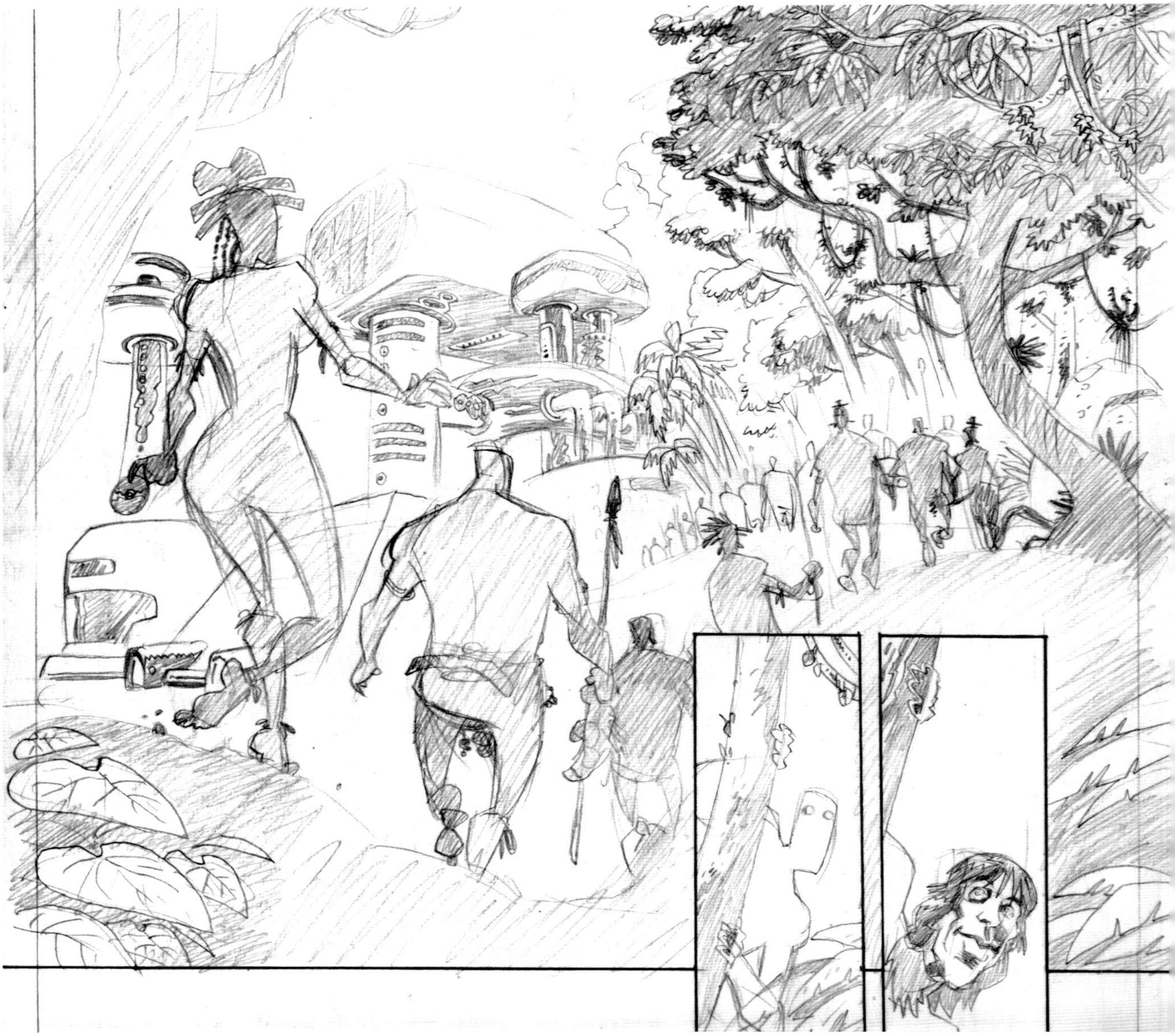

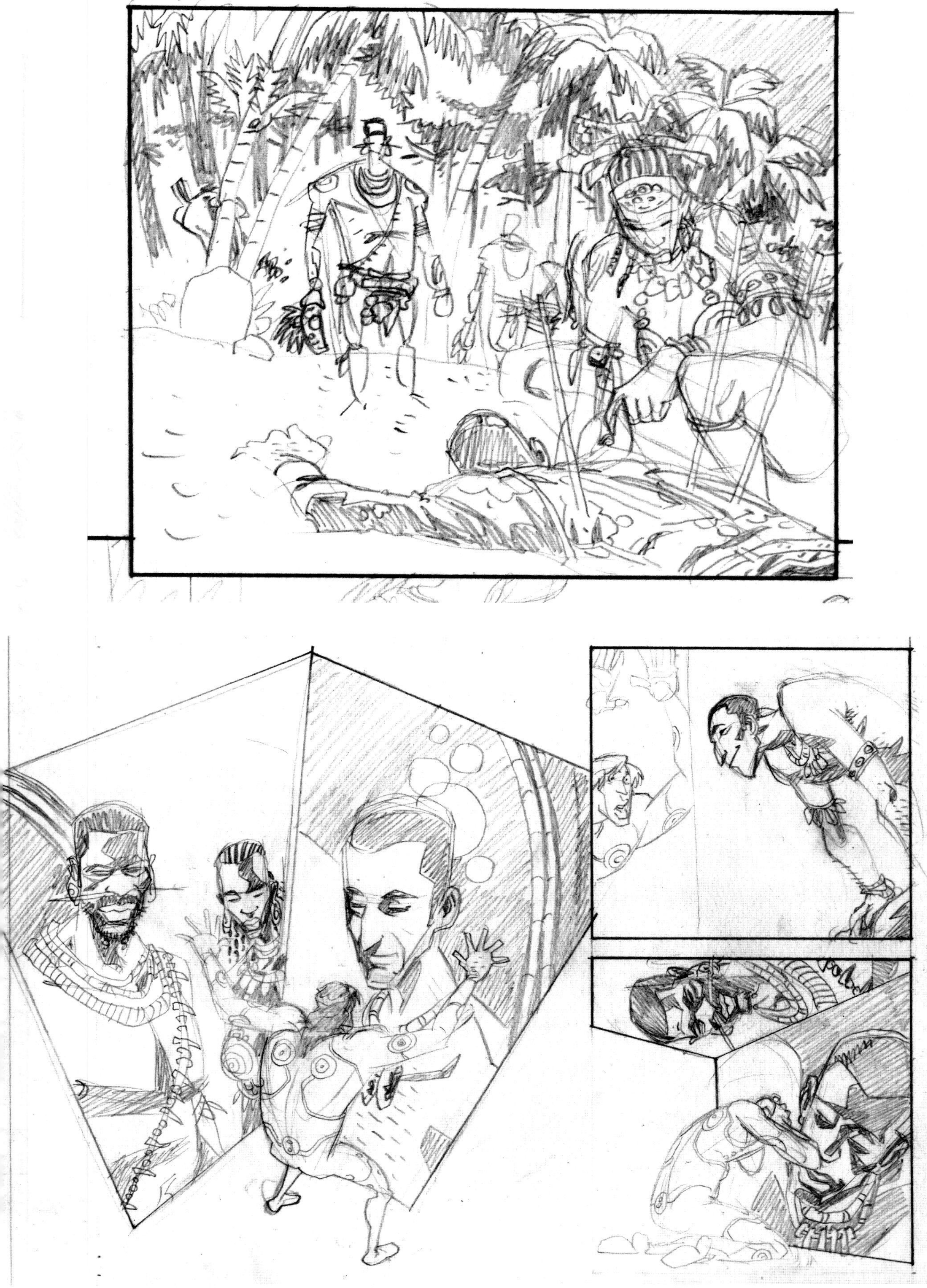

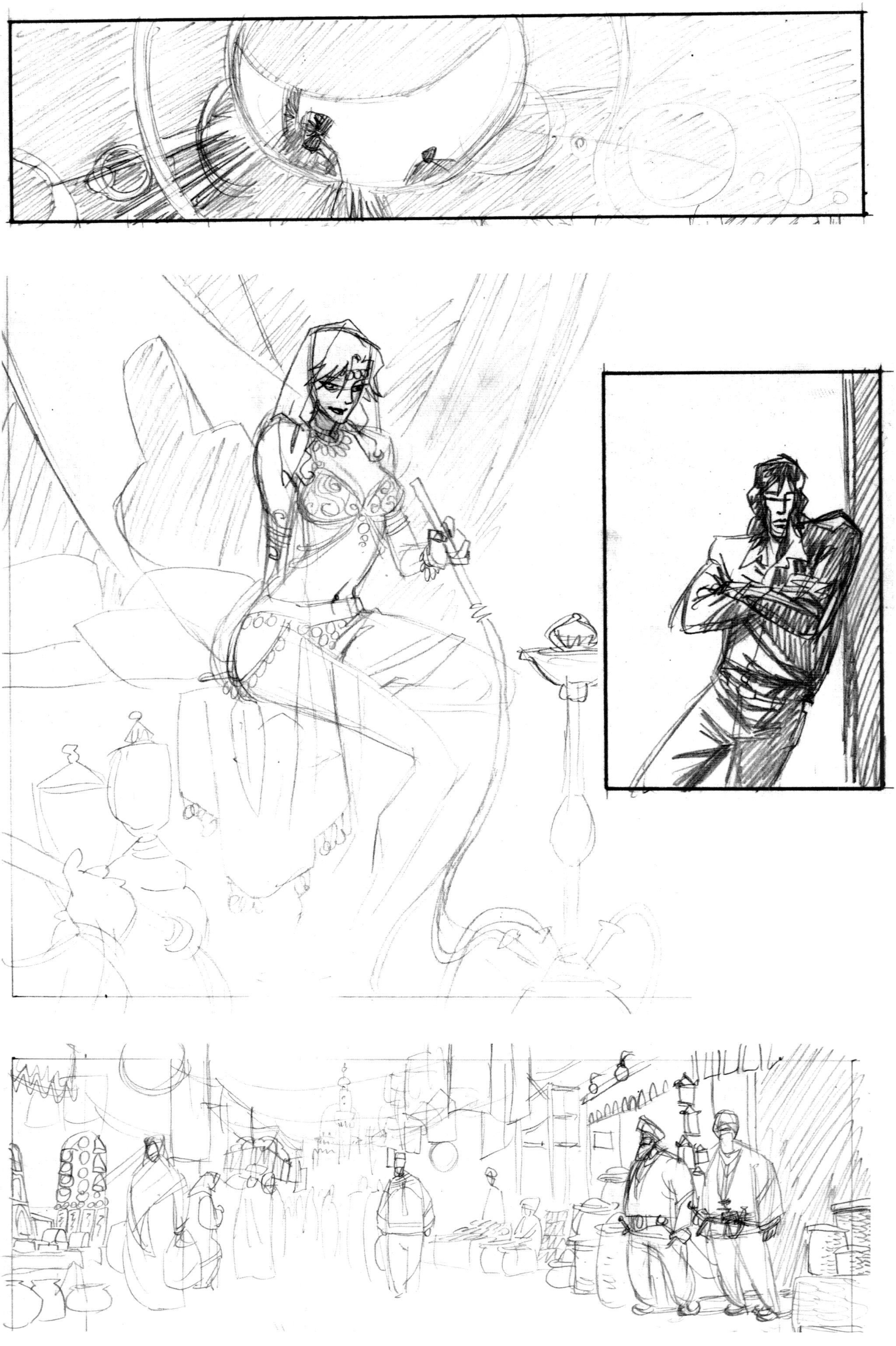

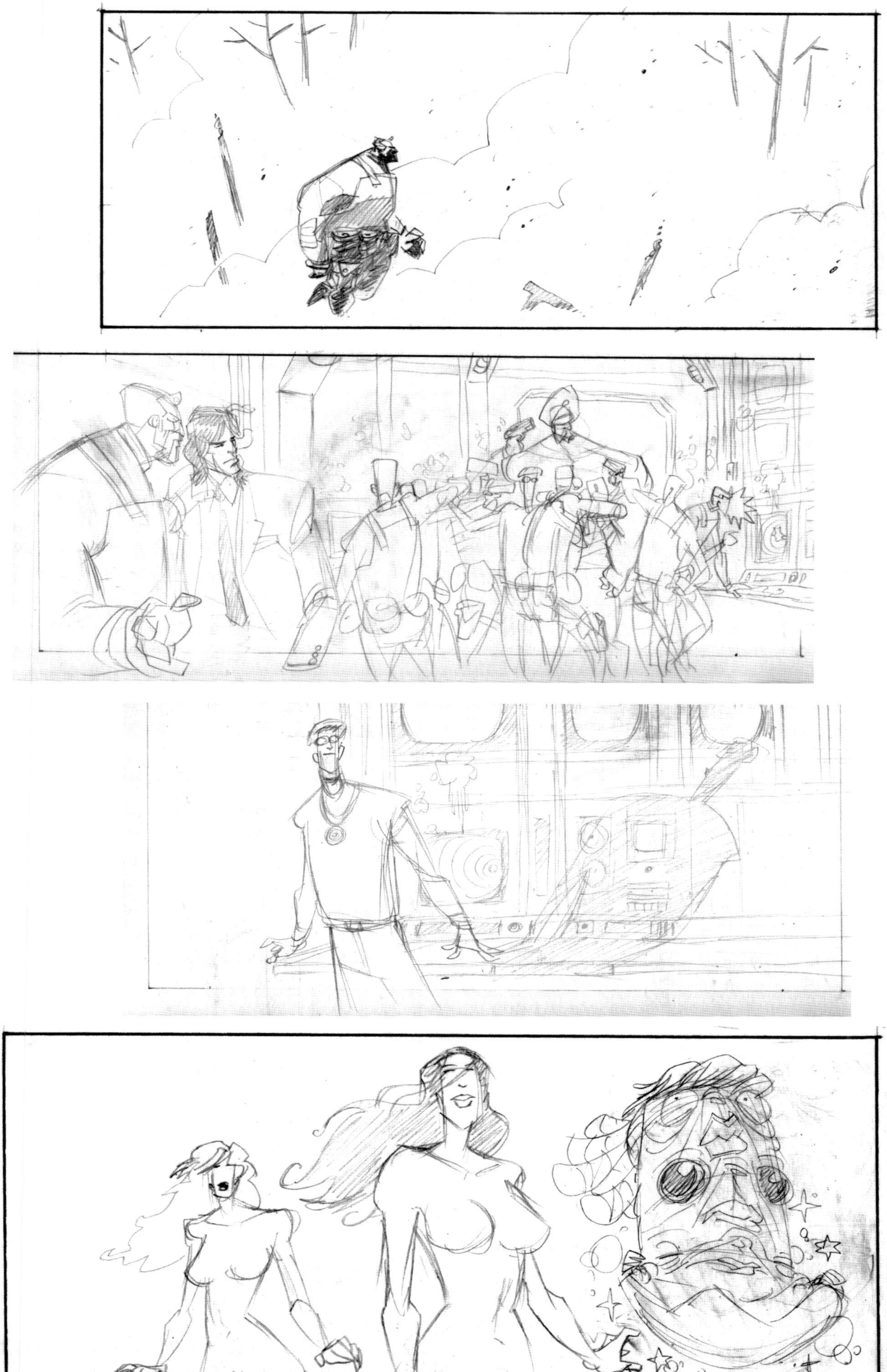

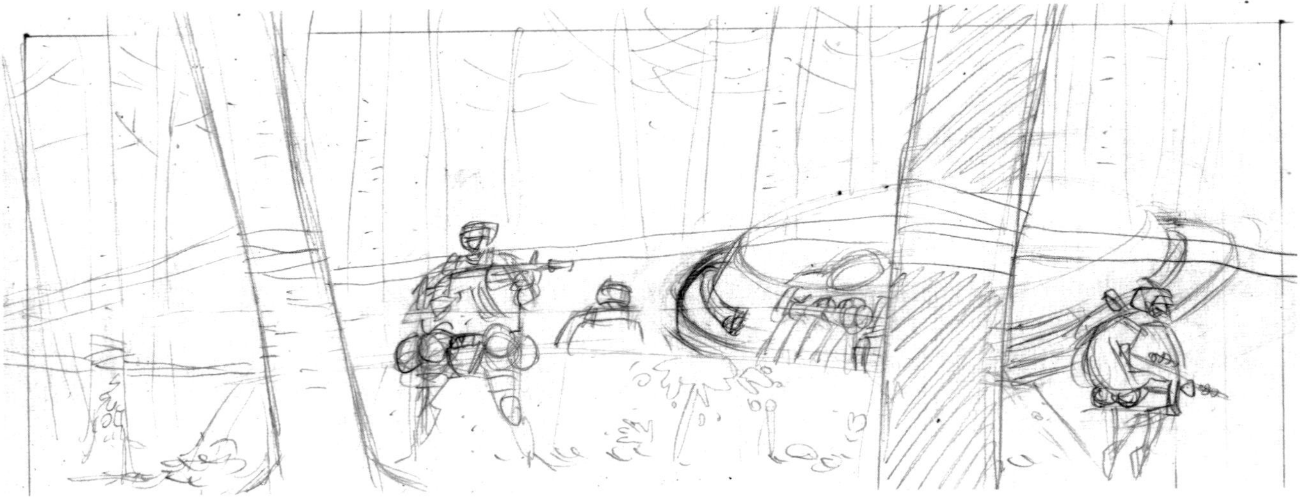

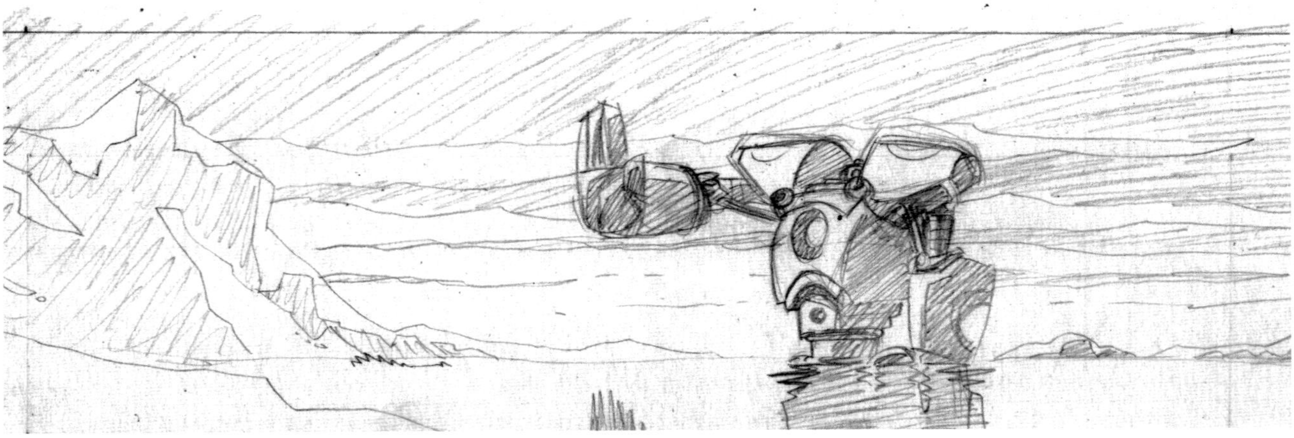

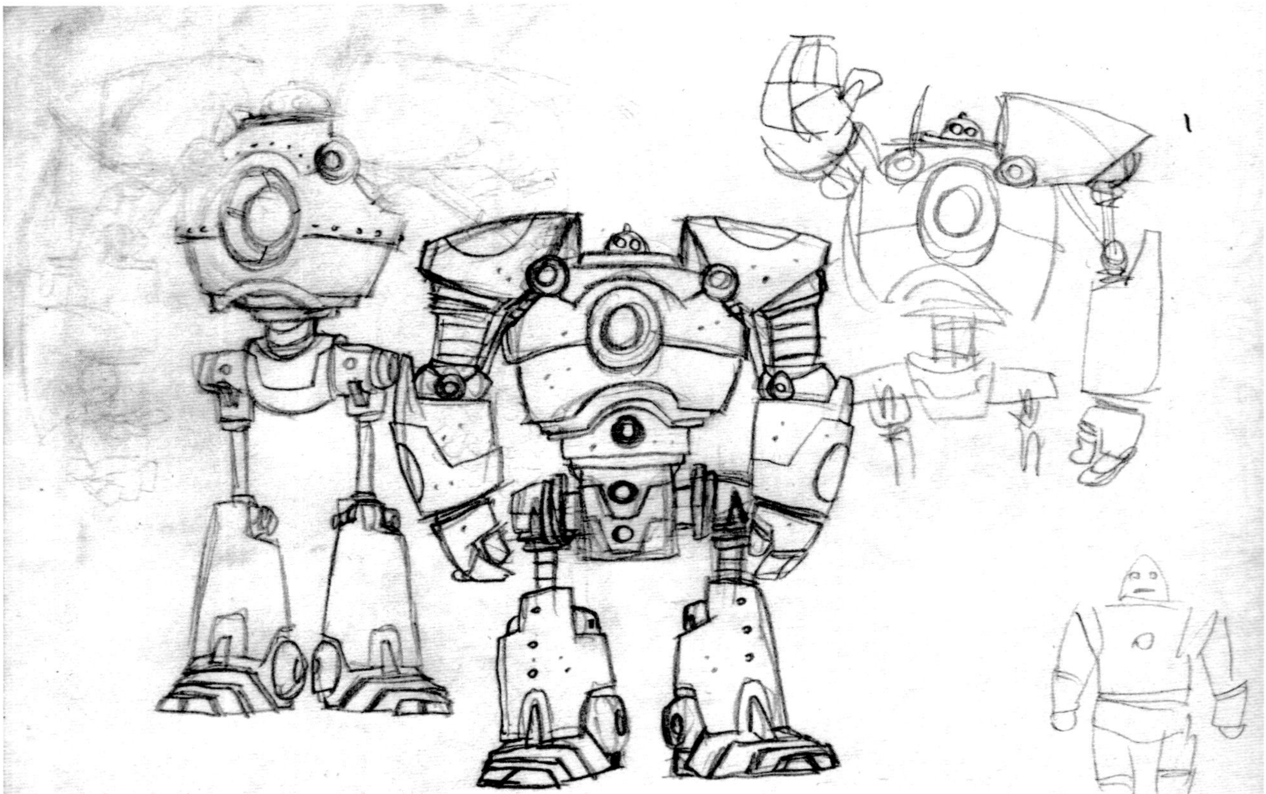

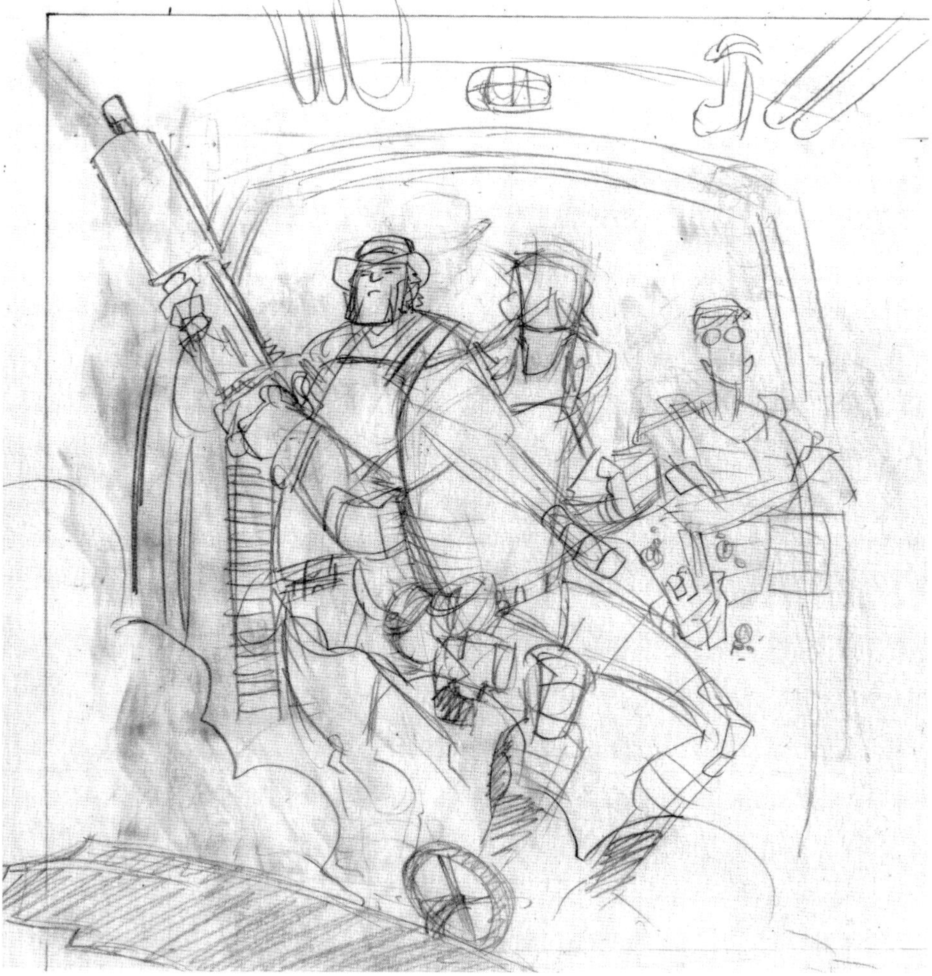

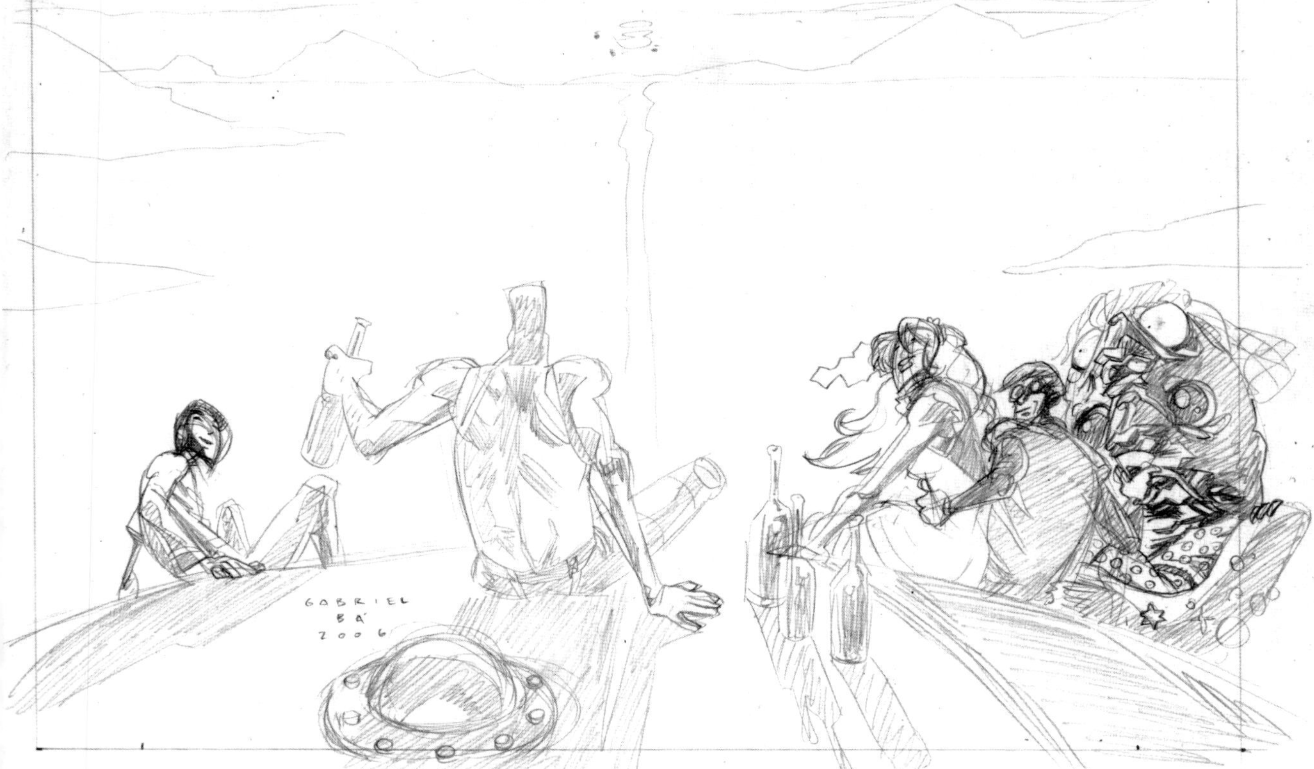
GABRIEL
BÁ
2006

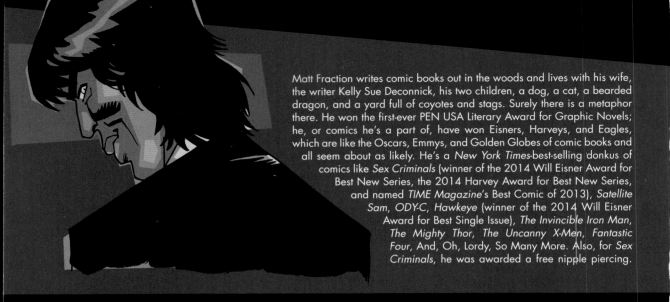

Matt Fraction writes comic books out in the woods and lives with his wife, the writer Kelly Sue Deconnick, his two children, a dog, a cat, a bearded dragon, and a yard full of coyotes and stags. Surely there is a metaphor there. He won the first-ever PEN USA Literary Award for Graphic Novels; he, or comics he's a part of, have won Eisners, Harveys, and Eagles, which are like the Oscars, Emmys, and Golden Globes of comic books and all seem about as likely. He's a *New York Times*-best-selling donkus of comics like *Sex Criminals* (winner of the 2014 Will Eisner Award for Best New Series, the 2014 Harvey Award for Best New Series, and named *TIME* Magazine's Best Comic of 2013), *Satellite Sam*, *ODY-C*, *Hawkeye* (winner of the 2014 Will Eisner Award for Best Single Issue), *The Invincible Iron Man*, *The Mighty Thor*, *The Uncanny X-Men*, *Fantastic Four*, And, Oh, Lordy, So Many More. Also, for *Sex Criminals*, he was awarded a free nipple piercing.

Gabriel Bá was born in a whole different dimension called São Paulo, Brazil, where he lives until this day. In fact, he has an evil twin brother, Fábio Moon, his partner in crime on most of his comics endeavours.

He's won awards for both his indie comics and mainstream projects and his work has been published in France, Italy, Spain, Greece, Japan and Germany, as well as in the U.S. and Brazil.

PA-ZOW!